U.S.S.R.

Heilongjiang

Jilin

Mongol

Liaoning

North
Korea

Peking

Tientsin

Hebei

Shanxi

Shandong

Henan

Jiangsu

Hubei

Shanghai

Auhui

Hunan

Jiangxi

Zhejiang

Fujian

Guangdong

ISLANDS IN THE
SOUTH CHINA SEA

Antiforeignism and Modernization in China: 1860-1980

Linkage between Domestic Politics and Foreign Policy

ANTIFOREIGNISM AND MODERNIZATION IN CHINA, 1860-1980

Linkage between Domestic Politics and Foreign Policy

By

Kuang-sheng Liao

Foreword by

Allen S. Whiting

The Chinese University Press
Hong Kong

St. Martin's Press
New York

Library of Congress Catalog Card Number 83-40629

ISBN 0-312-04374-0

For

Kay and Leslie

Contents

PART III: "ANTI-IMPERIALISM" AS
A POLITICAL FORCE

Tables and Figures

TABLES

FIGURES

Note on Romanization

Chinese names of persons, places, and terms are romanized in accordance with the *pinyin* system. There are some exceptions, as follows: (1) Prominent personal names: Sun Yat-sen, Yuan Shih-k'ai, and Chiang Kai-shek. (2) National capitals: Peking and Taipei. (3) Treaty ports: Amoy, Canton, and Tientsin. (4) Party: Kuomintang. These exceptions are made because the conventional spellings are more popularly used.

Foreword

Western analysis all too often resorts to hyperbole when characterizing Chinese attitudes and behavior, exaggerating either the good or the bad in a cyclical "love-hate" relationship. Harold Isaacs' classic formulation depicted these conflicting images as "scratches on our minds."[1] They might better be described as scars, so deeply do they seem to have penetrated. Thus when China is not painted in glowing colors as peaceful and pragmatic it is portrayed in dark hues of paranoia and political paroxysm.

One of the recurring phenomena supposedly characteristic of Chinese society is xenophobia. Its currency in the nineteenth century originated in anti-missionary riots. Then the Boxers' brutal behavior in 1900 which occasioned the siege and subsequent seizure of Peking by the troops of eight nations seemed positive proof of this malevolent force which allegedly lurked behind the smiling, deferential pose adopted toward the foreign presence. More recently, Communist attacks on "foreign imperialism" and "foreign spies" after the establishment of the People's Republic in 1949 revived the concept, climaxed by the Red Guard burning of the British chancery at the height of Cultural Revolution violence in 1967.

Yet despite the widespread attention given this presumed phenomenon, relatively little systematic empirical inquiry has tested its relevance except for monographic case-studies focused on specific, isolated instances.[2] Some written by foreigners have lacked a dispassionate understanding of Chinese behavior. Others written by Chinese have fit these outbursts into a preconceived political formula for explanation and justification. While these various works are valuable for detail and data, they rarely place the period and behavior under examination in a broader framework so as to test the generalized analysis which often accompanies their accounts.

Building on these case-studies and adding his own detailed research, Professor Liao has filled a major gap in our understanding of antiforeignism in China. He rejects the simplistic term, xenophobia, because it connotes a fear of foreigners which is not present in the overwhelming majority of such instances. He also does not try to force all antiforeign behavior into a single frame of explanation. Instead he analyzes antiforeignism as manifest in "hostile reactions to foreign countries," not foreigners *per se*. He carefully differentiates between behavior that aims at specific subgroups of the foreign community in China, for instance as between missionaries and businessmen in

[1] Harold R. Isaacs, *Scratches on Our Minds*. New York: John Day and Co., 1958.
[2] For a critical review of the literature, see Michael S. Hunt, *The Making of a Special Relationship*. New York: Columbia University Press, 1982.

the nineteenth century, and that which targets most, but not all, outsiders, as during the Cultural Revolution when even foreign communists fled China in fear for their lives.[3]

More important, Professor Liao traces the evolution of antiforeignism from its nineteenth century inception as anti-Christian violence, initially stimulated by the local gentry, to spontaneous mass action in response to the depredations of foreign governments seeking to carve China into spheres of influence "like a melon." From there the story moves to the role of antiforeignism in communist mobilization campaigns, culminating in its use by factions struggling for power in Peking.

This evolution in turn raises different explanatory variables. Externally, foreign aggression and incursions on Chinese sovereignty, manifest in the gunboat diplomacy of Great Britain, France, Germany, Japan, Russia, and the United States, during the so-called "century of shame and humiliation" triggered antiforeign resistance in various sectors of Chinese society. In the twentieth century "anti-imperialism" became the nationalistic banner against the "unequal treaties" for Nationalists (Kuomintang) and Communists alike.

Internally, antiforeignism served the post-1949 regime as a mobilization spur to unite "New China" behind the new leadership and to stimulate productivity in the absence of material incentives. Professor Liao's illuminating use of quantitative content analysis correlates antiforeignism and domestic politics, particularly under the combined impact of "leftist" ideological ascendancy and a struggle for power within the ruling elite. His own contribution to the case-study literature emerges here as he tests alternative hypotheses using Cultural Revolution materials.

Professor Liao ends on an optimistic note, "To sum up, the decline in Peking's antiforeignism is not a temporary phenomenon. Instead it is a new pattern of international behavior resulting from both internal and external developments," specifically citing the priority to modernize the Chinese economy and China's acceptance as a major actor on the world scene, especially by the United States.

To be sure, repeated rabid outbursts of attacks on foreign diplomatic personnel such as in 1967 is wholly unlikely given China's leadership and its overall orientation since 1976. However Professor Liao's use of the term "decline" prudently and properly implies that antiforeignism as a phenomenon has not been totally eliminated as an instrument of regime manipulation nor as an expression of regime discontent with particular foreign countries over given incidents.

[3]The author was Deputy Consul General at the American Consulate General, Hong Kong, 1966-68 where members of the Thai Communist Party and others were facilitated in leaving China for various destinations.

The continuing sensitivity of Chinese relations with other countries was suggested by the reemergence of nationalistic themes at the Twelfth Party Congress in September 1982. Secretary General Hu Yaobang declared, "Being patriots, we do not tolerate any encroachment on China's national dignity or interests. . . . Having suffered aggression and oppression for over a century, the Chinese people will never again allow themselves to be humiliated as they were before."[4] Vice Premier Deng Xiaoping put it in more pithy language:

> Independence and self-reliance have always been and will forever be our basic stand. We Chinese people value our friendship and cooperation with other countries and peoples. We value even more our hard-won independence and sovereign rights. No foreign country can expect China to be its vassal or expect it to swallow any bitter fruit detrimental to its own interests.[5]

These general admonitions received specific implementation during 1982-83 as China's domestic media reacted with an assertive nationalism to various external provocations.[6] Thus when Japanese textbook revisions softened the terminology describing Tokyo's aggression against China and its Pacific expansionism, weeks of newspaper and television coverage graphically recalled the sack of Nanjing and the grim years of war. *Renmin Ribao* headlines dramatically warned against an incipient revival of "Japanese militarism," although Tokyo's prompt apology, removal of the revisions, and continued limitation of defense expenditures to one percent of GNP argued to the contrary.

Similarly the defection of a Chinese tennis player to the United States where she was granted political asylum won nationwide coverage as a deliberate effort by "the United States Government to bring shame on China." *Renmin Ribao* justified the regime's suspension of official sports exchanges with the U. S. during 1983:

> Since the United States has taken this action, should the Chinese people swallow the insult and not react at all? . . . The Chinese people have continuously fought for several centuries and paid heavy sacrifices for the country's independence and territorial integrity. We cannot, nor will we, set relations with the United States above preserving our national dignity and state sovereignty.[7]

During the same period Prime Minister Margaret Thatcher provoked a parallel reaction to press conference remarks in Hong Kong after meeting in Peking on the colony's future. Her assertion that the related treaties were

---

[4]*Beijing Review*, September 13, 1962, pp. 29-33.

[5]*Ibid.*, September 6, 1982, p. 6.

[6]The following analysis and references draws on my article, "Assertive Nationalism in Chinese Foreign Policy," *Asian Survey*, August 1983.

[7]*Renmin Ribao*, April 9, 1983, in Foreign Broadcast Information Service (FBIS), April 11, 1983, p. B2.

"not invalid" and that "Britain keeps her treaties" prompted one comment:

> These three treaties . . . are the criminal records of Britain's brutal invasion of China and they are also evidence of the oppression and humiliation the Chinese people suffered in the past. . . . Now the time has passed forever when imperialism can ride roughshod and do as it pleases. The Chinese people have stood up.[8]

This recollection of past suffering echoes themes enunciated in October 1949 at the founding of the People's Republic. Their reiteration more than thirty years later is evidence of the continuity in Chinese articulation, and perhaps perception, where differences in foreign affairs arise. Moreover juxtaposing these points in time raises the possibility that antiforeignism, as expressed in assertive nationalism, may be utilized to strengthen ideological unity and legitimacy for a new leadership. In this regard, the dilution and reduction of Mao Zedong Thought after the Chairman's demise in 1976 led to problems similar to those faced in 1949.

Causation aside, the consequences of antiforeignism deserve attention abroad as well as within China. The recollection of past suffering can, of course, serve nationalistic purposes with little or no relevance for the outside world. It can establish a common denominator of bitter experience which bonds the group, providing "roots" of identity. It can also serve as a reminder of how much better is the present regime or social system compared with its predecessors. Neither of these two motivating factors concern present or future experience or expectation.

A third purpose, however, can be to caution against the possibility that history may repeat itself. Therefore one's guard should be raised against potential adversaries because of their past performance. Thus whereas an *affirmative* nationalism centers exclusively on "us" in positive terms, an *assertive* nationalism adds "them" with negative connotations. Antiforeignism thereby becomes express rather than implied.

This being the case two final observations are in order. First, to the extent that antiforeignism is a recurring phenomenon in Chinese statements about and analyses of foreign relations, it should be anticipated and not treated with alarm. It need not result in irrational or aggressive actions. Nor does it pose a serious threat to the well-being of foreigners in China under most circumstances.

Second, its public reiteration can constrain how the vast bureaucracy and relevant portions of Chinese society interact with the outisde world. Individual attitudes can be affected by assertive nationalism as can the

---

[8] *Zhongguo Xinwen She*, January 28, 1983, summary of Ding Genan article in *Jindai Shi Yanjiu* (Research of Modern History), No. 1, 1983, in FBIS, February 4, 1983, pp. B2-3.

individual calculus of personal and professional security. Where cues for authorized behavior are so centered in the media, as in China, the importance of rhetoric cannot be dismissed out of hand simply because it does not conform with reality as perceived abroad.

Given this perspective, Professor Liao's study is not only a valuable retrospective account of Chinese perceptions and behavior but is also valuable background for understanding how the world's largest society may interact with various countries and react to various situations where China's national interests are involved.

Allen S. Whiting
July 1, 1983   University of Arizona

Acknowledgements

As is so often the case, my research has benefitted directly or indirectly from the stimulation of my professional affiliation and the immediate environment in which the work was done. I have benefitted most directly from my teaching at The Chinese University of Hong Kong and research at Universities Service Centre. Both have provided an environment and facilities conducive to research and the completion of this book.

In particular, I am especially indebted to Allen S. Whiting, who not only stimulated my research interest but also constantly encouraged me to complete this study. I also want to note my appreciation to Wang Erh-min whose invaluable insights helped to complete this research. Michael Kao, James Hsiung, Ambrose King, Parris Chang, Byron Weng, Hsin-chi Kuan, Peter Lee, John Dolfin and Benjamin Ostrov kindly read the manuscript. Their criticisms and comments have greatly helped to sharpen the final analysis of this undertaking. I am indebted to Lau Yeefui and Moni Tai of the Universities Service Centre for their library assistance; Jean Xiong, Pollyanna So and Juanita Wong at the Centre for Contemporary Asian Studies; and Linda Mah and Angela Chan at the Department of Government and Public Administration of The Chinese University of Hong Kong for typing the drafts. I am further indebted to Dorothea Martin, Mary Ellis Gibson and Elaine Kurtenbach for their editing of the manuscript.

In addition, I am grateful for the financial assistance which helped support this research. In particular, I would like to thank the C. Y. Kwan Endowment Fund and the Institute of Social Studies (Institute of Social Studies and Humanities) of The Chinese University of Hong Kong and the Student Campus Work Scheme of United College, for supporting my field research in Hong Kong, the Academia Sinica in Taipei, and the Hoover Institution of Stanford University.

Last, but foremost, I would like to thank my wife, Kay for help, unusual patience, and encouragement. Needless to say, I am responsible for any mistakes in this book.

Introduction

Defense, the core of China's foreign policy during the last century, evolved in response to the encroachment of Western powers. The objectives of China's foreign policy have not changed from the Qing dynasty, through Kuomintang (KMT) China, to Communist China. Nor have they changed from the time of Mao Zedong to that of Deng Xiaoping. China's foreign policy is a matter of the Chinese nation dealing with the West. It has been more than one man's idea or the thoughts of a small group of politicians and intellectuals. Repeated invasion, or its threat, has proved that China has not found a sound foreign policy nor built up her capability to defend herself. If the history of modern China is a history of imperialist aggression against China, it is also a history of the Chinese people seeking to deter foreign invasion. Any study of Chinese politics or foreign policy would not be satisfactory if it left China's anti-foreignism unresearched.

Obviously, the prevention of foreign invasion requires two fundamental elements. First, it requires the internal strength necessary to resist foreign invasion. Such strength is achieved by the mobilization of internal resources for national defense, including the modernization of military, economic, social and political forces in China. In the 1980s China is still seeking such internal improvement. The Four Modernizations proposed by Zhou Enlai and continued by Deng Xiaoping show that China is still striving to achieve modernization, a goal pursued by their predecessors since the late nineteenth century.

The second requirement is seeking a foreign policy capable of mobilizing external support to check foreign aggression against China. This requires more than a written document or some fundamental principles. It demands a good understanding of Western culture, society and political processes. This presents a problem as difficult as mobilization and modernization. In the mid-nineteenth century, China was forced to look outside of its own boundaries and saw there a very different set of cultural and societal values. After a series of defeats, it is not surprising that the Chinese were increasingly hostile towards foreign countries. Without an understanding of the Western countries, the Chinese found it impossible to formulate a foreign policy, sound in both ideas and practice. The history of modern China proves that the Chinese were not able to successfully resolve this problem. Emotional resistance was too strong to accept new ideas from the West. This problem remained unchanged in the post-1949 period, and peaked in the Cultural Revolution. The emotional concerns manifested by the outbreak of mass antiforeign activities in the May

Fourth Movement and May Thirtieth incident led to the reinforcement of anti-imperialist sentiment, while the overheating of antiforeign sentiments kept the Chinese from handling foreign affairs rationally.

The impact of Western imperialism on China was immense. The threats to China from Westerners may be divided into three areas for the sake of analysis. These are military technology and ammunition, productive machines and merchandise, and culture and philosophy. Chinese responses to them were varied in different strata. Government and officials were first and foremost threatened by Western military technology and ammunition, which directly challenged the Chinese leaders' security and political leadership. The intellectuals and gentry class who were steeped in Confucianism and deeply rooted in Chinese tradition were challenged by Western political culture and philosophy. They supported the government and officials until the latter gave up their stand against the Westerners. The rest were businessmen, laborers and peasants who were the consumers. They constituted the great majority of Chinese society, but they did not rise to oppose foreign pressure until they felt the repressive effects of foreign capital and the superiority of foreign goods.

The government and its officials sought to deter the Western threat with armed force. Their solution was the introduction of Western military technology. The intellectuals in the beginning rejected Western ideas and utilized Chinese culture and tradition to defend their leadership in Chinese society. The consumers and the lower strata of people joined the business people in resisting foreign merchandise. The government and its officials succumbed to Western military threats after a series of defeats in war with Western states. This was followed by the intellectuals who became disillusioned with Chinese culture and tradition when they found the government had lost the capacity to defend China's interests. Later, they joined the consumers to form a mass movement to boycott Western merchandise.

From the mid-nineteenth century to the 1980s, two parallel forces emerged to defend China. One was the intellectuals and the government forces, the other was the masses which were not directly under the tight control of the government. The former were represented by prominent scholars and officials. They sought to understand the West and searched for an organized and institutional approach to deter "imperialism". Modernization by means of Westernization has been the key approach to building up the strength of China to resist foreign aggression. The failure of this approach gave rise to the second force: the antiforeign sentiments of the unorganized masses—the peasants, workers, students, and merchants. These people were mainly from the middle and lower strata of society. They did not have a close relationship with the governing class, nor with the government. They saw, however, that the government could no longer protect their lives and property, so they rose to form their own defense. This was the beginning of mass movements for the purpose of resisting foreign invasion.

The rise of resistance to foreign aggression started at the end of the nineteenth century, and continued into the twentieth century. During the warlord period, the anti-imperialist forces of the masses rallied to Sun Yat-sen's nationalist stand. After the death of Sun, the anti-imperialist forces supported Chiang Kai-shek in his Northern Expedition. During the Sino-Japanese war, these anti-imperialist forces supported Chiang's leadership but shifted allegiance to the Communist "anti-imperialist" front towards the latter part of the war. Since the Civil War, the Chinese Communist Party (CCP) has continued to utilize this movement by incorporating it into the Party ideology of anti-imperialism. Since 1949 anti-imperialism has been, to a great extent, guided and controlled by the political authorities. The growing strength of the masses' antiforeignism had the ironic effect of retarding modernization.

"Imperialism" is a foreign term brought to China, which owes its origin to Lenin. Prior to the publication of Lenin's "Imperialism, the Highest Stage of Capitalism" in 1916, Chinese intellectuals had developed a concept of *lieqiang* (Lieh-ch'iang) or the "Great Powers" to describe the aggressiveness and the superior military power of the Western countries. This term represented a strong and deep sentiment of national humiliation and frustration among the Chinese people. This national sentiment not only reflected the historical defeats suffered by the Chinese government at the hands of the Western Powers in a series of wars, but also reflected an imminent threat to the survival of China. The term reflected the loss of the Middle Kingdom's long-standing pride together with its traditional attitude of superiority toward foreigners, and marked the opening of a new era in China's relations with the West.

Lenin's concept of imperialism, which theorized that the development of capitalist countries and the aggressiveness and expansionism of the Western countires were related, provided Chinese intellectuals and revolutionaries with a theoretical foundation for their anti-Western sentiments. The term "imperialism" gradually replaced *lieqiang* among the anti-western intellectuals and revolutionaries, and anti-imperialism developed into one of the most popular political and social slogans of post-1949 Chinese politics. The concept of anti-imperialism has become an all-inclusive term which is used in ideology, domestic politics, and foreign policy.

This study will explore the development of antiforeignism in China since the mid-nineteenth century, and trace the origins of the concept and theory of "imperialism" and "anti-imperialism" among Chinese revolutionaries. It also examines the relationship between "anti-imperialism" and Peking's domestic politics since 1949. Chinese Communists have been strongly committed to making accusations against "U. S. imperialism". "Anti-U. S. imperialism" has become an integral part of their ideology and substantially affects Peking's internal politics as well as external relations. From the mid-sixties, Soviet revisionist social-imperialism also became a major target of mass denunciation. With the rise of leftism in the late 1950s, Peking became locked in a trap of leftism and antiforeignism which reinforced each other, and could not find its way out until the death of Mao Zedong followed by drastic changes in tactics if not in strategy. The goal here is to contribute to our understanding of the relationship between Peking's domestic politics and foreign relations, i.e., modernization and antiforeignism. The historical context of the topic under study is a rich weave of people and events. For the purpose at hand, however, only a broad outline is offered because to do more would unduly lengthen the book and diffuse the focus of attention.

This study consists of four parts. Part I is a brief history of the nineteenth-century Chinese search for strategies to deter foreign aggression and the rise of antiforeignism. As the Self-strengthening movement became the dominant approach to foreign encroachment in the last forty years of the nineteenth century, the government undertook a great number of defense projects, only for China's defeat to result in both antiforeignism and a crisis of authority. Chapter 3 explores the relationship between anti-Christian activities and the later development of antiforeignism. The two are closely related, but they are not the same. Most anti-Christian activities occurred at the local level and were supported by the local gentry class. In some cases, however, they were initiated by the gentry.

Part II deals with the rise of nationalism and the anti-imperialistic movement. Antiforeignism did not erupt as a national phenomenon until the early twentieth century, at which time national interests such as mining rights, railroad rights, and the threat of foreign investment in China became social and national issues. As a response to the threat to the survival of China posed by the major powers, antiforeignism became a national movement in domestic politics as well as foreign relations. Since the early 1900s antiforeignism has been expressed by the term anti-imperialism.

Chapter 5 discusses the significance of anti-imperialism in the development of the KMT. Sun Yat-sen, Chiang Kai-shek, and other major leaders all strongly supported the cause of anti-imperialism. It was the major plank in the KMT platform. The KMT vowed to achieve the goals of anti-imperialism, which included the abolition of unequal treaties and foreign concessions, fixed tariff rates, and control of foreign interests in China. To the KMT leaders the goal of anti-imperialism was realized when the Nationalist government in 1943 obtained the United States' and Great Britain's agreement to abolish their privileges obtained by unequal treaties in China. Following this achievement the KMT attempted to mobilize the masses by restoring traditional culture and virtue.

Part III includes five chapters and is the major focus of this study. The underlying theory in these five chapters is that anti-imperialism or "anti-U. S. imperialism" is an important mobilization ideology which constitutes a powerful political force for the CCP. Chapter 6 examines the development of the ideology of anti-imperialism and Mao Zedong's theory of the "paper tiger". It also investigates how "anti-U. S. imperialism" was conceptualized by the Chinese Communists. Some preliminary findings are drawn from the development of antiforeignism and its impact on domestic politics in the 1950s. These findings are particularly significant because they are relevant to current Chinese politics.

Chapters 7 and 8 examine how the Peking authorities manipulated anti-foreignism for domestic and external reasons in the period from 1960 to 1962. More specifically, Chapter 7 examines the relationships between "anti-U. S. imperialism" and mobilization for production, while Chapter 8 investi-gates the relationship between "anti-U. S. imperialism" and Peking's united front policy with the third world. In both chapters, important relationships are found. They support the hypothesis that antiforeignism rose when mobilization of the masses was at a high level.

Both Chapters 9 and 10 examine antiforeignism and its relationship with internal politics in the period of the Cultural Revolution, 1967-69. Chapter 9 confirms the hypothesis that antiforeignism rose when the impact of leftist movements was strong. Chapter 10 investigates how Maoists manipulated the denunciation of Soviet social revisionism and linked it with the condemnation of "China's Khrushchev," Liu Shaoqi, the former Chairman of State. The findings confirm the hypothesis that antiforeignism rose when the struggle for power was acute.

Chapter 11 of Part IV discusses the decline of antiforeignism since 1971. It finds that the decline of antiforeignism may be accounted for by changes in the Chinese Communist ideology and in society generally. Furthermore, the trend was encouraged by *rapprochement* between Washington and Peking, the admission of China into the United Nations, and most importantly, the change of American strategy in East Asia. A further decline in antiforeignism has been apparent since 1977 when China launched its full scale Four Modernizations program. These developments have forced Peking to restrict its ideology of anti-imperialism to the narrow sense of national equality and independence.

Chapter 12 generalizes from the findings in this study and suggests some theories on antiforeignism in China and on the relationship between antiforeignism and internal politics. Finally, it also establishes a theory of the relationship between modernization and revolution by examining the development of antiforeignism and the authority crisis.

CHAPTER 1
Conceptual Framework and General Theories

Modernization and Antiforeignism in China

Looking back over the last century, one can see the importance of moderniza-tion and antiforeignism in China's response to Western aggression. These were central issues in the political discussions from the beginning of the twentieth century. The process of modernization and the development of antiforeignism may be traced to the mid-nineteenth century when China was repeatedly defeated by the Western powers in a series of war. During a period of more than one hundred years, no one in the highest echelons of political power could afford to ignore these two concepts. The Self-strengthening Movement of the 1860s which aimed at modernization of the armed forces marks the initial response to Western pressure. At the time of the Tongzhi (Tung-chih) Restoration a number of modern institutions were established in order to promote western knowledge in China.[1] This Chinese response was based on the rational calculation that the superiority of the West was mainly in armaments, and that if China could learn from the West how to strengthen her defense, then she could deter any foreign aggression. The arch-designers of this policy of modernization were Zeng Guofan and Li Hongzhang. Unfortunately, this early modernization was proven a failure in the 1894 Sino-Japanese war.

Antiforeignism emerged among the Chinese people as a result of the failure of modernization, and in opposition to military aggression, economic exploita-tion and political repression by Western powers and Japan. Together with the development of nationalism in the early twentieth century, anti-imperialism became not only a popular slogan but also an important internal political force. In spite of strong urgings by liberals in the May Fourth Movement, Chinese governments were not able to commit themselves to modernization as long as they were confronted with internal fragmentation. In the period from the 1910s to the 1940s, the sentiment of anti-imperialism became so strong that both the KMT and the CCP had to accept it as part of their platforms.[2] After 1949, the Peking government converted the sentiment into a political ideology while replacing modernization with socialist construction. The ideology of

[1] See Mary C. Wright, *The Last Stand of Chinese Conservatism: The Tung-chih Restoration, 1862-1874*, Stanford, Calif.: Stanford University Press, 1957, pp. 196-221.

[2] See Donald A. Jordan, "China's Vulnerability to Japanese Imperialism: The Anti Japanese Boycott of 1931-1932," in F. Gilbert Chan (ed.), *China at the Crossroads: Nationalists and Communists, 1927-1949*, Boulder, Colorado: Westview Press, 1980, pp. 91-118.

anti-imperialism played a tremendous role in mobilization of the masses and became an integral part of the CCP ideology.

Modernization in China means the use of Western technology and weapons for the purpose of developing national power and wealth. "Chinese learning as the foundation and Western learning for practice" was the government policy toward modernization in imperial China. The Qing court did not intend to learn Western culture or values, not to speak of Western political systems.[3] The continuous Western impact on Chinese tradition and culture, however, inevitably involved changes in the value system of Chinese society. The introduction of popular education, newspapers, and Western culture gave tremendous impetus to social changes, and awakened the people to the dangers of foreign aggression. As these social changes led to changes in thinking and values, Western democratic ideas began to develop in China. Both reformers and revolutionaries believed that a drastic change in polity was a prerequisite for modernization. Foreign aggression threatened the survival of China and the imperial government had failed to protect the nation from foreign invasion. Under such circumstances, two developments occurred. First the people realized that the government could not protect them and that they must stand up to the foreigners by themselves. This awakening necessarily brought about strong antiforeignism. The first led inevitably to the second: an authority crisis. The imperial government was defeated by foreign countries in one war after another. Inevitably, the people lost their confidence in the government.[4] These two developments were aggravated when foreigners and foreign military forces were allowed to be stationed in China.

From 1860 to the early twentieth century, modernization helped to some extent the development of China through the improvement of education and communications. At the same time, it stimulated the rise of antiforeignism and brought about an authority crisis when the government was humiliated by foreign countries.[5] When "Self-strengthening" failed, antiforeignism rose and the authority crises were aggravated. The incessant foreign threat kept both antiforeignism and the authority crises at a high level. Failure to change the phenomenon was bound to lead to the collapse of the government or revolution (see Figure 1.1). The 1911, 1949 and 1967 revolutions in China all showed both strong antiforeignism and a high level of authority crisis.

Antiforeignism here is a generalized term indicating hostile reactions to foreign countries. In Chinese politics, antiforeignism has been expressed in

[3] Marius B. Jansen, *Japan and China: From War to Peace, 1894-1972*, Chicago: Rand McNally College Publishing Company, 1975, pp. 10-17.

[4] Theda Skocpol, *States and Social Revolutions*, New York: Cambridge University Press, 1979, pp. 74-79.

[5] *Ibid.*

Figure 1.1 Modernization Failure and Revolution

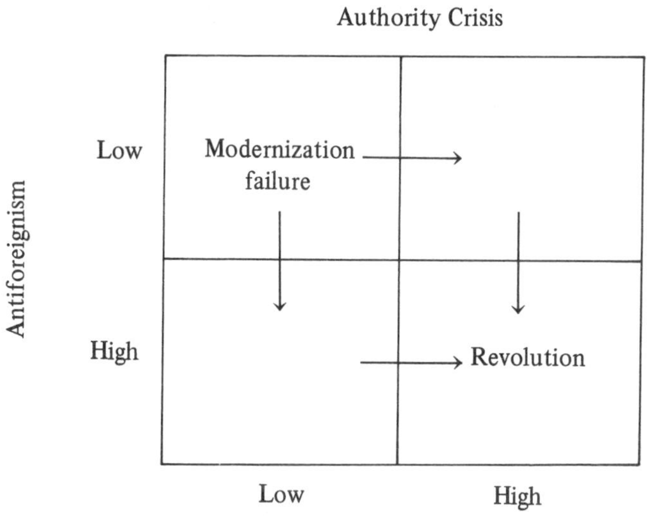

Authority Crisis

different phrases or slogans in different periods. The most frequently used term has been "anti-imperialism" which includes "anti-British imperialism," "anti-Japanese imperialism," "anti-U.S. imperialism," "anti-Soviet revisionism," etc. These slogans were created for specific targets in different periods. Antiforeignism in China has been expressed in articulated hostility by the media, rallies and demonstrations or boycotts.

China's antiforeignism in the 20th century has been an opposition to foreign oppression or aggression. It is different from xenophobia in that antiforeignism is a negative response to foreign countries while xenophobia is a fear of foreigners. Antiforeignism is a kind of collective sentiment toward foreign countries among the people. In other words, there is a clear relationship between foreign oppression and aggression, and antiforeign sentiments.

Antiforeignism in China during the period under study has three major characteristics. First, it includes injustices caused by foreign countries in China. These injustices include territorial concessions to foreign countries, tariff restrictions, unequal treaties, and all political and economic interests obtained by foreign countries through war or military threat. The Chinese strongly condemned these actions as foreign aggression, oppression, and exploitation. Second, antiforeignism includes a strong summons to struggle against foreign countries to eliminate these injustices which foreigners had imposed upon China. In other words, antiforeignism in China carries the meaning of changing the status quo by struggle with foreigners or foreign countries. Third, antiforeignism in China is utilitarian. It seeks to achieve national equality and independence. It is, therefore, a positive approach to the pursuit of national interest, and an active movement to get rid of foreign interference in China.

Antiforeignism is a mass sentiment caused by eocnomic, political, and military suppression by foreign countries. It is a defense of national interest rather than of culture or tradition. It originates from common attachment to the country. It is not a result of acculturation, which is a process that brings about modifications in a traditional culture as a result of contact with an advanced society. There is no dispute that cultural or racial conflicts took place after increasing contacts with the West in the mid-nineteenth century. Antiforeignism in China, however, is not a nativistic movement aimed at preserving Chinese tradition and culture. Antiforeignism is more political than purely cultural or religious. Cultural or religious conflicts can develop into vigorous nation-wide antiforeignism only when they are motivated by nationalism.

Antiforeignism in the 20th century is political and economic in nature. Since it closely relates to injustice and the attempt to change the status quo, antiforeignism may decline or rise for political or economic reasons. Antiforeignism usually cannot last too long if it is not constantly refueled by nationalism or ideology or manipulated by the government for other reasons. Unlike cultural conflict or religious conflicts, antiforeignism declines when political or economic conflicts are settled. Antiforeignism in China, however, lasted more than a century. This was due to incessant aggression and threat from the West and the manipulation of the issue by the Chinese leadership.

General Theories

A survey of some theories regarding internal politics and external relations will be helpful to the study of antiforeignism and modernization. For example, the traditional theory of placing blame explains the development of hostility in terms of frustration. The underlying argument of such a theory is that frustrations arising from obstacles to the achievement of a goal will develop into hostility toward others, if the reason for the frustration is buttressed by social norms. This frustration, then, will be redirected against others, the scapegoats, and will assume the form of hostility.[6]

Stagner also proposed a theory that the stronger the sentiment of nationalism, the more hostility will be generated by the experience of frustration, or by threats from another state.[7] Pruitt and Snyder suggest that hostility is positively correlated to the level of frustration or threat perceived.[8] They suggest that the reaction to a perceived provocation is a function of the general level of frustration experienced by an individual. In international politics, provocative behavior could identify another state as an appropriate target for the displacement of hostility. These theories owe their origins to the social-psychological concept that decision-makers are human, and behave no differently from other human beings. For the study of mass protest or mass hostility toward foreign countries, these theories provide some interesting ideas of the relations between international behavior and internal politics. In a country where external information is not tightly controlled by the government, the people may have a high degree of understanding of the development of international politics. Provocative actions of foreign aggression may stimulate mass protest due to patriotic feeling or nationalism. In this case, social-psychological theories may be important to the study of antiforeign mass protest. However, in a country like post-1949 China, where the mass media are controlled by the government and the Party, external information may not be released to the public unless the government approves. Under such circumstances, the government plays a much more important role in the development of public attitudes toward foreign countries than do governments in Western countries, where the flow of information is less controlled.

The linkage between internal politics and external behavior suggests a meeting place for the fields of international and comparative politics. The notion of linkage derives from the fundamental structure of the modern political system. Domestic institutions are pivotal in connecting internal politics with foreign policy. The government is simultaneously a participant in national and international politics. As James Rosenau pointed out, occupants of high office in national systems also occupy key roles in the international system. The way in which these dual responsibilities are balanced serves both to link the policy to its environment, and to delineate the

---

[6] See L. Berkowitz, "Aggression Cues in Aggressive Behavior and Hostility Catharsis," *Psychological Review*, no. 71, 1964, pp. 104-122. Also see L. Berkowitz, *Aggression: A Social Psychological Analysis*, New York: McGraw-Hill Book Co., 1962.

[7] R. Stagner, "Nationalism," in P. L. Harriman (ed.), *The Encyclopedia of Psychology*, New York: Philosophical Library, 1946.

[8] Dean G. Pruitt and Richard C. Snyder (ed.), *Theory and Research of the Causes of War*, N. J.: Prentice-Hall, Inc., 1969, p. 29.

boundaries between them.[9]

Scholars who adhere to a decision-making approach have called attention to a wide cluster of motivational, role, and organizational variables that operate within governments as determinants of foreign policy.[10] Others have emphasized the relationship between cultural, historical, societal, economic, and geographical characteristics and external behavior.[11] The basic theoretical linkage between internal politics and external behavior involves a recognition that both domestic and foreign policies are formulated by the same group of decision-makers. Consequently, external behavior is the result of domestic as well as external factors.

The current state of knowledge on the subject of linkage politics is far from satisfactory. As Rosenau has pointed out, the overwhelming weight of historical evidence supports the general proposition that domestic and international processes are inextricably intertwined. "Despite their abundance, however, the relevant data have never been organized and examined systematically, and there is a shortage of theory adequate to account for the dynamic linkages between the national and international system."[12] The same is true in the special case of links between internal politics and external behavior.

History suggests a mixed record on the relationship between internal politics and external behavior. For example, external conflict may stimulate as well as subdue internal dissension. Brooks (1969), in his study of protest movements against U. S. involvement in foreign wars, maintains that involvement in foreign wars has consistently resulted in heated internal controversy.[13] On the other hand, there are a number of historical cases that suggest just the opposite relationship. For example, the Japanese occupation of Manchuria in 1935-36 resulted in an anti-Japanese sentiment in China powerful enough to make negotiations between the Nationalists and Communists possible. In this case, war with a foreign power appears to have inhibited domestic conflict.[14]

[9] James N. Rosenau (ed.), *Linkage Politics*, New York: Free Press, 1969, p. 13.

[10] Richard Snyder, H. W. Bruck, and Burton Sapin, "The Decision-Making Approach to the Study of International Politics," in James N. Rosenau (ed.), *International Politics and Foreign Policy*, New York: Free Press, 1969, pp. 199-206. Also see David Braybrooke and Charles E. Lindblom, "Types of Decision-Making," in Rosenau, *op. cit.*, pp. 207-216.

[11] For example, Klaus Knorr, *The War Potential of Nations*, Princeton: Princeton University Press, 1956; and Bruce M. Russett, *International Regions and the International System: A Study in Political Ecology*, Chicago: Rand McNally, 1967

[12] *Linkage Politics, op. cit.*, pp. 4-5.

[13] Robin Brooks, "Domestic Violence and America's Wars: An Historical Interpretation," in H. D. Graham and T. B. Gurr (ed.), *Violence in America*, Washington: U. S. Government Printing Office, 1969, pp. 407-421.

[14] Franz Schurmann and Orville Schell, *Republic China*, New York: Vintage, 1967, pp. 148-149.

The impact of internal politics upon external behavior has been similarly ambiguous. A number of cases suggest that internal situations have been the source of external conflicts. For example, in his study of the Indonesia-Malaysia confrontation of 1962-65, Bernard K. Gordon has found a strong relationship between Indonesia's hostile attitude toward Malaysia and her own domestic dissension.[15] As another example, China's conflict with the Eight powers in 1900 has also been explained as the result of internal movements. It was the Qing government's support of these domestic antiforeign activities which triggered the Allied Army of Eight Nations to attack.[16]

Yet other historical cases demonstrate that internal factors may also inhibit external conflict. Examples are Russia's early withdrawal from World War I following the Revolution of 1917 and the United States' failure to intervene in the French takeover of Mexico during the period of the American Civil War.[17] In both these cases, domestic problems were of sufficient magnitude to suspend or inhibit external conflict.

Finally, there are a number of instances where external conflict has resulted exclusively from international interaction. The conflicts between Argentina and Chile in 1967-68 and the 1962 Cuban Crisis are examples.[18] Thus, arguments and evidence exist to support each of the following propositions: (1) foreign and domestic conflicts tend to foster one another, and are therefore positively correlated; (2) foreign and domestic conflicts tend to inhibit each other, and are therefore negatively correlated; (3) foreign and domestic conflicts do not influence each other and are uncorrelated. A brief examination of historical cases suggests that the relationship between internal politics and external behavior will vary according to the nature of internal and external conflicts. Such variations preclude any simplistic general theory of the relationship. The majority of cross-cultural quantitative research indicates little or no correlation between internal and external conflict. Sorokin in his time series analyses found only a slight relationship between internal politics

[15] Bernard K. Gordon, *The Dimensions of Conflict in Southeast Asia*, New Jersey: Prentice-Hall, 1966, pp. 86-96.

[16] Edmund O. Clubb, *The 20th-Century China*, 2nd edition, New York: Columbia University Press, 1972, pp. 24-33.

[17] Merle Fainsod, *How Russia is Ruled*, Cambridge: Harvard University Press, 1963, pp. 90-91; Thomas A. Bailey, *A Diplomatic History of the American People*, New York: Meredith Corporation, 1969, pp. 348-359.

[18] Robert N. Burr, "Argentina and Chile," in Steven L. Spiegel and Kenneth N. Waltz, (ed.), *Conflict in World Politics*, Cambridge: Winthrop, 1971, pp. 155-176; Ole R. Holstoi and *et. al.*, "Measuring Affect and Action in International Reaction Model: Empirical Materials from the 1962 Cuban Crisis," in *International Politics and Foreign Policy, op. cit.*, pp. 679-96.

and external conflict.[19] Rummel's cross-national correlational analyses suggest that internal conflict and external conflict are independent of each other.[20]

Raymond Tanter in his cross-national studies also finds little relationship between domestic and foreign conflict behavior. However, Tanter suggests that there may in fact be a causal relationship which is obscured by other phenomena, such as the personality characteristics of national decision-makers.[21]

In his *The Functions of Social Conflict* (1956), Coser hypothesized a stronger, more direct connection between domestic and foreign conflict in countries with rigid socio-political structures than in those with flexible systems, on grounds that the former generate greater needs for activities such as scapegoating, witch-hunts, and the search for external enemies.[22] Jonathan Wilkenfeld followed up Tanter's untested hypothesis that personality characteristics may intervene in the relationship between domestic and external conflict behavior. Wilkenfeld divides nations into three groups: Personalists, Centrists, and Polyarchs. The conclusion was that when one controls for type of political system, the more rigid types (centrist and personalist) exhibit higher correlations between domestic and foreign conflict than do the more flexible types (polyarchic).[23]

Wilkenfeld's findings confirmed the importance of political structure as an influence upon external behavior. In his research, China was classified in the centrist group of nations. His results thus indicate that China's internal conflict may be correlated with its external conflict behavior. However, the correlation between aggregate characteristics of nations does not elucidate the particular phenomena in which we are interested. In order to explore a more specific relationship between internal politics and external behavior, one must concentrate on the political system and environment factors.

Problems Under Investigation

In China's international behavior, two characteristics are worthy of special

[19] P. A. Sorokin, *Social and Cultural Dynamics*, vol. III. New York: American Book, 1937.

[20] R. J. Rummel, "Dimensions of Foreign and Domestic Conflict Behavior: A Review of Empirical Findings," in D. G. Pruitt and R. C. Snyder (ed.), *Theory and Research on the Causes of War*, New Jersey: Prentice-Hall, 1969, pp. 219-228.

[21] Raymond Tanter, "Dimensions of Conflict Within and Between Nations," 1958-60, *Journal of Conflict Resolution*, vol. 10, March 1966, pp. 48-64.

[22] Lewis Coser, *The Functions of Social Conflict*, New York: The Free Press, Fifth Printing, 1969, pp. 87-94.

[23] Jonathan Wilkenfeld, "Domestic and Foreign Conflict Behavior of Nations", in William D. Coplin (ed.) *A Multi-Method Introduction to International Politics*, Chicago: Markham, 1971, pp. 109-204.

attention. The first is China's verbal expressions of hostility. Since the early twentieth century, China has been vehement in denouncing those conceived of as enemies and rivals. Attacks on "British imperialism" and "Japanese imperialism" were frequent. Later in the 1940s, attacks on "U. S. imperialism" filled the pages of China's major newspapers. In the early 1960s, verbal hostilities were extended to India, as a reaction to the Sino-Indian border conflict, and China began to formulate the image of "Indian reactionaries." Meanwhile, the Japanese leadership was accused of being "reactionaries and collaborators" with "U. S. imperialism," because of Japan's pro-American foreign policy. By the middle of the 1960s, the Soviet Union was added to the list when China began to denounce it as "revisionist." During the Cultural Revolution, the Soviets were accused of "social imperialism", and Japan of "reactionary militarism." Attacks on foreign targets continued to occupy a remarkable portion of the coverage in daily newspapers and major Party magazines such as *Beijing Review, Hongqi* (Red Flag), and *Shi Jie Zhi Shi* (World Culture).

The second characteristic of China's international behavior which deserves attention is the antiforeign mass demonstration. Since the beginning of the twentieth century, a growing number of mass demonstrations and meetings have been organized to denounce foreign rivals. These movements sometimes were limited to several of the major cities. The number of demonstrations has increased spectacularly since 1949, however, and they are no longer restricted to major cities but have occurred over all of China. The movements have been organized or at least sanctioned by the central government. Conceptually, these antiforeign mass campaigns may be seen as the manifestation of China's ability to mobilize hostility toward external enemies. This is another important aspect of China's international behavior which should be further researched.

Various internal factors have been identified as major influences in the development of China's foreign policy: geography, historical heritage, xenophobia, ideological commitment, and national interest. Undoubtedly, such elements have shaped the fundamental principles of China's foreign behavior.[24] A close connection between domestic politics and foreign policy also has been noticed. As V. P. Dutt makes clear:

> An intimate relationship has always subsisted between domestic policy and foreign
> policy; the one can seldom be divorced from the other. In the case of Communist

---

[24] Allen S. Whiting, "Foreign Policy of Communist China," in Roy C. Macridis (ed.), *Foreign Policy in World Politics*, fourth edition, New Jersey: Prentice-Hall, 1972, pp. 291-306. Also see R. G. Boyd, *Communist China's Foreign Policy*, New York: Praeger, 1962, pp. 53-64.

China the interplay between the two has been so very close that changes in foreign policy can be directly related to those in the internal situation.[25]

The current stage of knowledge on the relationship between China's internal politics and external behavior is rudimentary at best. The subject has not received any rigorous examination to date. Lacking such an investigation, scholars and experts in the field find it difficult to explain and evaluate the real motivations of China's international behavior.

This study will examine how both internal and external factors lead to the development of antiforeignism from the late 19th century up to 1949. Furthermore, it will investigate the relationship between antiforeignism and mobilization for production in 1960-62, and the relationship between mobilization for power-seizure and China's international behavior in 1967-1969. Both these periods witnessed serious elite dissension in China. Natural disasters created an agricultural disaster of major proportions in the early 1960s. These economic difficulties stimulated a split among the top level leaders over proposed solutions. In order to overcome the problem, people at all levels were mobilized to assist in agricultural production. Workers, students, teachers, and soldiers were called on to participate. In the period from 1967 to February 1969, China was again preoccupied with internal political struggle. Maoists were engaged in a nation-wide mobilization of support to defeat their domestic opponents. As will be elaborated in later chapters, serious authority crises were occurring during both these periods.

Externally in 1960-62, China was engaged in the Taiwan Straits crisis and the Sino-Indian border conflict. Verbally, she expressed an extremely high degree of hostility toward the United States and Japanese governments. In 1967-February 1969, China was involved in unprecedented tensions with the Soviet Union which resulted in a bloody border clash. Despite preoccupation with domestic political turmoil, she also articulated strong hostility toward the United States' involvement in the Vietnam war.

The concurrence of external hostility and internal mobilization in Chinese history, leads us to hypothesize a relationship between these events. The exact nature of this relationship, however, is unclear. Does internal mobilization result in external hostility or vice versa? During both 1960-62 and 1967-69, the Chinese elite was deeply divided over questions of domestic policy. The significance of these internal struggles makes it appear more plausible that external issues were instrumental to domestic purposes rather than the other way around. As pointed out by Rosecrance:

[25] Vidya Prakash Dutt, *China and the World: An Analysis of Communist China's Foreign Policy*, New York: Praeger, 1966, p. 1.

> A society in the agonies of domestic transformation is not likely to regard international determinants as decisive. . . . In such circumstances, the government cannot usually afford independent preoccupation with external conditions. Most often, external policies are merely instrumental to internal purposes and rarely are internal programs fashioned in response to the international environment. Only after a measure of internal stability is attained can internal influences be expected to work.[26]

Thus, during periods of authority crisis, we would expect that the leadership might manipulate external issues for internal ends.

Ernst Haas and Allen S. Whiting, in their *Dynamics of International Relations* (1956), suggest that groups seeking self-preservation may be driven to a conflictual foreign policy in order to defend themselves against the onslaught of internal enemies. They explain:

> In times of extreme domestic tension among elites, a policy of uniting a badly divided nation against some real or alleged outside threat frequently seems useful to a ruling group. Elites, fearful of losing their position in the nation as a result of sharp ideological and group conflict, as in periods of rapid industrialization and large-scale social change, attempt to displace the attention of the disaffected portion of the nation away from its grievances and toward some outside target.[27]

In other words, the authors suggest external conflict or tension may be the result of a domestic authority crisis. At the same time, they do not propose that a struggle for elite self-preservation will necessarily result in war. Rather, they assert that once the elite feels more secure domestically, it is likely to cease its conflictual foreign policy. In light of the theoretical relationship between internal mobilization and external tension, as well as our preceding theoretical discussion it may be suggested that antiforeignism as expressed in China's media hostility and antiforeign mass campaigns may be explained by domestic considerations.

[26]Richard N. Rosecrance, *Action and Reaction in World Politics*, Boston: Little, Brown and Company, 1963, pp. 298-299.

[27]Ernst Haas and Allen S. Whiting, *Dynamics of International Relations*, New York: McGraw-Hill, 1956, p. 62.

PART I

THE FAILURE OF EARLY MODERNIZATION AND THE RISE OF ANTIFOREIGNISM

CHAPTER 2
In Search of Defense Against Foreign Aggression

Despite the lengthy history of Chinese cultural and political development of which Confucianists have been so proud, Chinese intellectuals and statesmen in the mid-nineteenth century were at a loss in handling foreign affairs. Chinese intellectuals and government officials were not well-informed about the rapid industrial development in Western Europe. The prevalence among intellectuals and officials of the Confucian concept of foreigners as barbarians prevented them from trying to understand Western culture and civilization. Following the Opium War of 1839-1842, the Chinese struggled to find an escape from increasing Western encroachment. The century subsequent to the Opium War was a history of struggle against Westerners. The devastating British firepower in the war forced the Chinese authorities to acknowledge British military superiority. It was the first time in modern Chinese history that the empire was compelled to sign an unequal treaty due to its incapacity to defend its boundaries against invaders. The Treaty of Nanjing constitutes a major turning point in the relationship between the Chinese empire and the West. By the middle of the nineteenth century, America, France, Belgium, Sweden, Norway and Russia had signed treaties with China on the same basis as Britain had, and were given the status of "most-favored nation" granted to England in the Nanjing Treaty. In the Treaty of Nanjing together with subsequent treaties concluded between China and Western countries, China formally allowed foreigners to conduct trade in the five treaty-ports: Canton, Amoy, Fuzhou, Ningbo, and Shanghai. Consular officers were allowed to reside in these cities. As a result, growing communities of foreigners were established in these treaty ports. Although the Opium War struck the Qing court as the greatest humiliation inflicted by the "Barbarians," the government, the gentry and the literati remained complacent about China's cultural and historical tradition. Between 1842 and 1859, no systematic approach was taken to defend China from the Westerners. Contacts between Chinese and foreigners were confined to treaty port areas and Western impact on Chinese society was not widespread.

The growth of the Chinese empire from the Qin (Ch'in) and Han dynasties to the Ming dynasty reflected the pride and superiority of the Chinese over the barbarians who surrounded China. In the Confucian world order the Chinese called their empire the Central Kingdom (*Zhong Guo*) and believed it represented a superior civilization occupying the highest rank in the world hierarchy. Such peoples as the Japanese, Koreans, Mongols, Turks, Tibetans and Vietnamese were thought to have inferior cultures and were therefore less civilized peoples.[1] Thus, the Chinese empire had little experience in handling international relations on a basis of equality and, to Chinese officials and literati, the tributary system expressed the natural world order.

Early Discussion of Strategy Toward Westerners

After the Opium War, some Chinese officers and literati were keenly aware of the superiority of military forces and technology in the West. The population in the coastal areas who had experienced the British and later French attacks and witnessed the Qing government's incompetent handling of Westerners, predictably feared further Western aggression. Naturally, discussion on how to handle the Westerners took place first among the officers and literati, for those who were in power in Peking, such as Emperor Dao Guang (Tao Kuang) and the Grand Councillor Wo Ren, faced a dilemma in the management of the "barbarians." Seeing the threat from the Westerners the Chinese government puzzled over an approach towards deterring them. It was not surprising that officials and literati trained in the Confucian classics and ignorant of science and technology had insufficient ability and knowledge to handle such a threatening problem. It was more than a debate between the hard line of the conservatives and a more flexible policy of the pragmatists. The core of the problem was how to deter increasing threats from the provocative Westerners.

Use Foreigners to Check Foreigners: Wei Yuan

Wei Yuan was one of the few officer literati who fully understood the imminent danger faced by the empire in the 1840s. His *Hai Guo Tu Zhi* (The Illustrated Gazetteer of the Maritime Countries) represented pioneer work in the search for a policy to deter "barbarian" aggression. His work was completed in 1842, soon after the Opium War. Wei clearly pointed out the importance of maritime defense in China's relations with the Westerners.[2] Like most of his contemporaries, Wei was confident of China's survival although the situation was undergoing drastic changes. His ideas appear to be more rational and pragmatic than emotional and idealistic. In contrast to most of the Confucians, Wei Yuan was surprisingly well-informed about world geography and the development of the West. He emphasized the necessity of

---

[1] John King Fairbank, *The United States and China*, third edition, Harvard University Press, 1971, pp. 137-138.

[2] Wang Jiajian (Wang Chia-chien), *Wei Yuan: His Concepts on the West and His Ideas of Maritime Defense*, History and Chinese Literature Series, no. 9, Taipei: National Taiwan University, 1964, pp. 59-90.

understanding the development and situation in the West and of studying Western technology particularly in ship-building and the manufacture of ammunition.[3] While Wei believed that understanding foreign countries and peoples was important for good diplomacy, he also believed that China's survival rested upon Chinese resistance to the "barbarians." Thus, the most important consideration was to enrich the state and strengthen the country, particularly its maritime defense. Wei suggested that the government should "use barbarians to check barbarians" as an active foreign policy to defend the interests of China.[4] For example, he suggested that China should be allied with Russia, France and the United States in opposing the United Kingdom. In the mid-nineteenth century, Wei Yuan's ideas on foreign policy represented a liberal view in contrast to the conservatives such as Wen Xian, who stubbornly refused to deal with the "barbarians" as equals.[5]

Use Trade to Deter Expansion of Barbarians' Influence

It was widely believed that the Westerners' initial advance to China in the mid-nineteenth century was mainly motivated by tremendous profit in trade with China. In the nineteenth century, Europe was undergoing an industrial revolution. Business and commercial activities were an integral part of national development. China, however, remained an agricultural economy. Chinese economic thought was still dominated by the Confucian physiocrats which ranked merchants the lowest in the Chinese social order. The clash during the Opium War proved that China had a completely different attitude toward economic matters from England and other European countries and that the Qing government was not fully aware of the coming threat from the European countries in the mid-nineteenth century.[6]

To change the Confucian concept of commerce and trade was not an easy task. During the two decades following the Opium War little fundamental progress was made toward learning Western technology for military purposes, much less for trade. From 1860 to 1880, however, Chinese gentry-scholars were concentrating on the Self-strengthening Movement to improve China's defense system. Together with this movement some early discussion on trade was taking place among the gentry-scholars. The improvement in the

[3] Hao Yenping and Wang Erhmin, "Changing Chinese Views of Western Relations, 1840-95" in *The Cambridge History of China*, edited by John K. Fairbank and Kwang-ching Liu, 1980, vol. 11 (Late Qing, 1800-1911, part 2), London, New York: Cambridge University Press, p. 148.

[4] Wolfgang Franke, *China and the West*, Translated by R. A. Wilson, New York: Harper Torchbooks, 1967, pp. 95-96.

[5] Wang Jiajian, *op. cit.*, pp. 42-46.

[6] Teng Ssu-yu and John K. Fairbank, *China's Response to the West*, Cambridge, Mass.: Cambridge University Press, 1961, p. 19.

understanding of the importance of trade could be seen from the increasing discussion of "trade war" in the 1880s.[7] Among others, Zheng Guanyin had a substantial understanding of the importance of promoting trade to deter Western aggression.

Zheng had worked for a Western corporation for twenty years and was later in charge of the Chinese government's Telegraph Bureau. In his close observation of a European business organization, he had been deeply impressed with the importance of trade for national development. His work entitled *"Shen Shi Wei Yan"* is one of the most important pioneer works on the topic written around the 1880s. In Zheng's analysis, Westerners treated trade as a war. The gentry, peasants, and artisans all helped the development of trade. Envoys were sent abroad because of trade, consulates were established to strengthen trade, and military forces were stationed in foreign fields because of trade.[8] The protection of trade by the state was beneficial not only for the livelihood of the people, but also for the development of the economy. Furthermore, Zheng pointed out that trade was the foundation of the state and the source of national strength. The development of trade was virtually an "invisible war." "The preparation for military war should be based on the development of such an invisible war." Thus, he urged the government to support the "trade war" by encouraging the development of technology in training and education.[9] Similar opinions were expressed in the 1890s by other Confucian officer-scholars such as Sheng Xuanhuai, Tan Sitong and Yan Fu. Later developments, however, indicated that it was too late for China to develop its trade to compete with the Western powers. The unequal treaties imposed by the West had become an important barrier to Chinese economic development.

The development of the concept of "trade war" had some important historical implications. First, it implied that the officer-scholar as well as the gentry class still had confidence that the Qing government could defend China from further Western aggression despite its defeats at the hands of the major powers. Second, it implied that the development of trade with foreign countries was not necessarily at variance with Chinese interests. If equal trade were developed with foreign countries, foreign trade could become an important method of enrichment for the country as well as for the people.[10]

[7] Hao Yenping and Wang Erhmin, *op. cit.*, p. 150.

[8] Wang Erhmin, *Zhong Guo Jin Dai Si Xiang Shi Lun* (History of Modern Chinese Thought), Taipei: Hua Shi Publishing Co., 1977, pp. 241-242.

[9] *Ibid.*, pp. 243-244.

[10] Key Ray Chong, "Cheng Kuan-ying (1840-1920)—A Source of Sun Yat-sen's Nationalist Ideology?", *Journal of Asian Studies*, vol. XXVIII, no. 2, February 1969, p. 250.

Third, it reflected the willingness of the Chinese people to compete with the Westerners peacefully up to the very end of the nineteenth century, despite the Western imposition of unequal treaties on China and some encroachment on Chinese territory. It represented the hope of the Chinese people that they could deal with the Westerners by means of a rational approach. Fourth, the concept of "trade war" indicated that the development of trade with foreign countries, would consolidate China's economy, strengthen it militarily, and recover its integrity. Thus, the "trade war" represented a rational foreign policy to deal with "imperialism". The objectives of trade were to enrich China and, finally to rid China of imperialists.

Use the People to Control "Barbarians"

Using the people to control "barbarians" was an important development in China's foreign relations in the nineteenth and twentieth centuries. After 1842, the hostility of the Chinese populace in the treaty ports rose unprecedentedly. In the mind of the people it was the Manchu government that was defeated, not the Chinese people. Antiforeignism was inflammatory and emotional. The people strongly believed that China was on the side of justice and that the English used opium to injure Chinese people, cheating them of their silver and cash.[11] The government used the demonstration of the people's hostility to strengthen itself in opposing the foreigners.

The fever of antiforeignism in the 1840s helped unite the people in the hope that the government could put a stop to foreign demands. For example, in 1848 Sir George Bonham, the governor of Hong Kong, asked for permission to enter the city of Canton. Permission had already been promised by Qi Ying, but Xu Guangqing, the governor of Guangdong, decided to heed anti-British public opinion expressed by a gentry-led militia of over a hundred thousand men which paraded in protest against Bonham's demands. The demonstration was so vigorous that the British yielded and postponed the issue of entry into the city indefinitely.[12] Xu Guangqing's approach was based on the manipulation of antiforeignism. It reflected two conditions: First, the officials believed that the people strongly supported the government at the time. The officials also believed that the government could use this support to confront the foreigners. The second condition was derived from Qi Ying and Xu Guangqing's mistaken assumption that foreigners feared the Chinese people.[13] Later, other officials who also urged using the feelings of the people to stop foreign pressure shared similar beliefs.

[11] Tong Tekang, *United States Diplomacy in China, 1844-60*, Seattle: University of Washington Press, 1964, p. 95.
[12] *Ibid.*
[13] Hao Yenping and Wang Erhmin, *op. cit.*, p. 151.

The use of popular sentiment to deal with foreign countries was new in Chinese society as well as in the government. It was a dangerous approach because it is always difficult to control the acts of the people when their passions become too strong. The use of people to control the "barbarians" could end up in disaster. There were incidents of killing missionaries which were attributable to the sentiment against foreigners. These incidents caused much diplomatic tension and lead to increased pressure from foreign governments.[14] In modern Chinese history, antiforeign activities were early types of mass movements which later developed into the "mass line" in Yanan and carried over into the post-1949 period. Government manipulation of popular antiforeignism culminated in the Boxer Uprising of 1900 which the Empress Dowager encouraged and in which she attempted to manipulate the angry population to control the "barbarians." The disastrous end of the Boxer Uprising forced the mass movement underground in the form of secret societies during the rest of the Qing dynasty.

It should be noted that antiforeign mass movements became a strong political force in China after the late Qing period. The later development of antiforeignism had significant impact on political development, e.g., the May Fourth movement, the rise of the KMT Nationalist force and the emergence of communist power. In the emergence of nationalism in China, antiforeignism and antiforeign mass movements played an important role, probably greater than has been realized.[15]

Management of Internal Rebellion and External Threat

The early improvement of relations between the Chinese imperial government and the British and French governments began after the conclusion of the 1860 Treaties of Peking, the result of the Anglo-French expedition to Peking. Peking was seized by the Anglo-French expeditionary forces without much of a fight. This shocked the imperial family and forced the emperor and his close relatives and associates to flee to Jehol in the north. The brutality of the Anglo-French forces exemplified in the burning of the Emperor's Summer Palace and the looting of the Emperor's wealth—as well as the demonstration of the West's destructive power—shook the ruling authority of the dynasty for the first time since its founding in the seventeenth century. Once again, as in the Opium War of 1839, the imperial government could not deter foreign invasion, and even failed to defend its capital. Following the fall of the capital, a peace treaty was concluded quickly by the commander of the Anglo-French forces and Prince Gong, the Treaties of Peking (1860).

[14] See chapter 3.
[15] See chapters 3 and 4.

Historically, the Treaties of Peking are the most significant documents between the Qing imperial government and the Western countries. They affected the subsequent development of the relationship between China and the West far more than anybody could have predicted at that time. Essentially, the Treaties of Peking, confirmed the 1858 Treaty of Tientsin. Eleven new ports were opened to foreign trade, including Tientsin and Shanghai and interior ports along the Yangtze River. Peking abandoned its previous insistance on tributary relations and for the first time in Chinese history Western ambassadors were permitted to reside in Peking.[16] Another important clause, later to be a source of trouble, was the right of Catholic missions to hold land, a stipulation secured by France. Later, most of the Western powers obtained this privilege through the most favored nation clause.

The Establishment of Zongli Yamen (Tsungli Yamen)

It was not until 1861, two decades after the Opium War, that the *Zongli Yamen* (Office in General Charge of Affairs Concerning All Foreign Nations) was established for the management of foreign affairs. The establishment of *Zongli Yamen* reflected the perception of an increasing need to institutionalize foreign affairs. During this period, the Qing court was under tremendous pressure from internal and external affairs. Because the Taiping and *Nian* rebellions grew rapidly and posed tremendous threats to the fate of the dynasty, the Qing government faced serious political turmoils. Military funds were exhausted. Under such circumstances Prince Gong, Gui Liang and Wen Xiang the three government officials most active in foreign affairs, proposed the establishment of *Zongli Yamen*. In their memorial, they made it clear that "the troubles at home were more serious at the moment than those coming from without, and so it was a matter of practical politics to get along with the foreign powers for the time being."[17] It is clear that the internal rebellion was an important consideration in the establishment of *Zongli Yamen*. A short-term foreign policy was drawn up by Prince Gong and his associates. "If we act in accordance with the treaties and do not allow the barbarians to exceed them by even an inch, if we give an appearance of sincerity and amity while we quietly try to keep them in line, then they will not suddenly cause us great harm for several years to come, even though they may make occasional demands."[18] This recommendation, in fact, clearly explained China's fundamental attitude toward foreign policy in the following decades. The

---

[16] Fu Qixue, *Zhong Guo Wai Jiao Shi* (History of Chinese Diplomacy), vol. 1, Taipei: Taiwan Shang Wu Printing Co., 1972, pp. 81-82.

[17] Masataka Banno, *China and the West, 1858-1861: The Origin of the Tsungli Yamen*, Cambridge, Mass.: Harvard University Press, 1964, p. 220.

[18] Masataka Banno, *op. cit.*, p. 221.

Zongli Yamen was a defensive measure in the management of foreign affairs.

Taiping Rebellion and the Western Powers

The new relationship between the Qing government and the Western powers after 1860 was further consolidated when the imperial government, after the death of Emperor Xianfeng (Hsien-feng), changed its foreign policy from stubborn resistance to co-operative appeasement. In the early 1860s the imperial government was desperately fighting to put down the Taiping rebellion. At Prince Gong's suggestion, the government welcomed the assistance provided by the Western powers to suppress the Taiping.[19] Clearly, the Taiping rebellion brought the imperial government and Western powers in China closer than ever before. Despite some dissension in the court over the acceptance of aid from the Western powers, more and more people gave their support to the use of Western ammunition and troops.

The congruence of interest between the imperial government and the Western powers became even more evident when the Taiping rebels launched a series of attacks against Shanghai in 1860 and 1862. These attacks led to the intervention of the Western powers for the protection of their own interests, and the intervention proved also a support to Peking's new conciliatory policy. Therefore some basic trust developed between the Chinese government and the Western powers in the period of fighting the Taiping rebels. This laid the groundwork for further co-operation between the two parties. In the face of internal political turmoils and external threats, the imperial government placed priority on suppression of the former. As stated in Prince Gong's memorial: "Under current circumstances, the Taiping and *Nian* rebellions are like a disease at the heart. The neighboring Russians, always with the ambition of encroachment, are like a disease on the back. And the British are interested in trade. However, they are ruthless and irrational. We cannot obtain independence if we do not restrict them. They are like a disease on the arms and legs. Thus, the Taiping and *Nian* should be eliminated first, the Russians next, then the British third."[20]

Following this calculation, the imperial court decided to seek westernization of its armaments for the immediate suppression of internal rebellion and for future resistance to foreign invasion.

[19] S. Y. Teng, *The Taiping Rebellion and the Western Powers*, Taipei: Rainbow-Bridge Book Co., 1968, pp. 284-316. Also see Richard J. Smith, *Mercenaries and Mandarins: The Ever-Victorious Army of Nineteenth Century China*, New York: The KTO Press, 1978, pp. 43-46.

[20] *Zhou Ban Yi Wu Shi Mo*, vol. 71, p. 18 in Jiang Tingfu (ed.), *Jin Dai Zhong Guo Wai Jiao Shi Zi Liao Ji Yao* (Compared Materials of Modern China's Diplomatic History), vol. I, Shanghai: Commercial Press, 1931, p. 324.

China's Early Modernization: The Self-strengthening Movement

Westernization of armament and industrialization was initiated in the Self-strengthening Movement which began in 1860 after the Second Opium War and ended in failure in the 1894 Sino-Japanese War. The movement represented China's determination to build up its military power through westernization. It became clear after the Second Opium War that Britain, France and other western countries would continue to push their trade interests in China. With the superior military power the western nations possessed, the Qing government had no chance to stop them. With this external threat and the pressure from domestic rebellions, the need for stronger military forces became unquestionable.

In a broad sense, the Self-strengthening Movement was a military reform which included the nationalization of the new regional armies, the revival of the militia system, a reduction in the size of the army, and modernization of armaments. These reforms were substantial parts of the Tongzhi (T'ung-chih) Restoration (1862-1874) and, with the exception of the modernization of armaments, were mainly concerned with domestic developments. The modernization of armaments represented the Westernization of Chinese military forces and involved not only Western technologies but also political involvement with the major powers. The Taiping rebellion and other political turmoils strengthened the conviction of Prince Gong and Wen Xiang that a comprehensive development of armaments was necessary for both the suppression of internal revolts and for resistance against external attack.[21] The Self-strengthening Movement was only a beginning and it remained one of the most important programs in the following century. The modernization of armaments began with the establishment of shipyards and arsenals. The movement is generally divided into three periods.

The First Period, 1861-1872

The first period (1861-1872) lasted from the beginning of the Tongzhi reign until 1872. The most remarkable development of this period was the establishment of the Jiangnan Arsenal in 1865. Zeng Guofan and Li Hongzhang were the major planners of this program. They convinced the imperial court that a first class arsenal was needed for the manufacture of modern arms and tools. The Arsenal represented the early determination of the government to learn Western skills for the modernization of Chinese technology. A translation office was attached to the Jiangnan project and engaged in a tremendous amount of translation work. Within a few years it had translated more

---

[21]S. Y. Teng, *op. cit.*, pp. 386-387.

than a hundred books in physics, chemistry and mathematics.[22]

Another development was the establishment of the Fuzhou Shipyard. Construction begin in 1866 under the direction of Zuo Zongtang. With a Frenchman, Prosper de Vaisseau Giquel as his chief consultant, Zuo imported steel, machinery and engines from France and timber and other material from Hong Kong and Burma. The shipyard was begun with 2,600 workers, including 75 Europeans. By 1874 the shipyard had assembled 15 ships. All were for military purposes. In addition to producing military hardware needed by the army and navy, the shipyard also introduced some training programs in engineering, the French and English languages, and navigation. Later, some courses in natural sciences such as chemistry, metallurgy, and mathematics were also introduced.[23]

The Jiangnan Arsenal and Fuzhou Shipyard were the two biggest projects in this period. Some other developments were the establishment of the Jinling Machine Factory in 1851, and the Tientsin Machine Factory in 1870, both proposed by Li Hongzhong. Also in 1871, the important port of Dagu was fortified with Western armaments. Some machine factories were established in such provinces as Yunnan, Fujian, Gansu, and Guangdong.[24] Clearly, some important preliminary progress was made in the introduction of Western scientific knowledge and the construction of Western armaments.

The Second Period, 1872-1884: The Development of Military-Related Enterprises

By 1872, the deterioration of the financial situation made it difficult to continue the development of the military industry. During this period, the Qing government exhausted its financial resources on the internal rebellions, the war indemnity and the expenses of the military industry. In addition, income resources from taxes such as land and salt were being curtailed due to the devastation caused by wars and rebellions. This made it clear the Self-strengthening Movement must be accompanied by a development of the economy. Without strong economic support, the Self-strengthening Movement would soon collapse. Emphasis was placed on those industries and enterprises relating to military industry established in the first period. The development

[22]Guo Tinyi, *Jin Dai Zhong Guo Shi Gang* (An Outline History of Modern China), Hong Kong: The Chinese University Press, 1974, pp. 210-212.

[23]Zhang Kuohui, *Yang Wu Yun Dong Yu Zhong Guo Jin Dai Qi Ye* (Westernization Movement and the Enterprise in Modern China), Peking: China Social Science Publishing Co., December, 1979, pp. 184-216.

[24]Wang Erhmin, *Qing Ji Bin Gong Ye De Xing Chi* (The Rise of Military Industries in the Qing Dynasty), Taipei: Institute of Modern History, Academic Sinica, 1963, pp. 106-112.

of these industries required planning, specific knowledge, technology, and capital. Since these skills were lacking, the government sent groups of students to be trained in America.[25] To fill the immediate need, however, technicians, engineers and advisers were recruited from the West. Unlike the previous military industries, the enterprises during this period were joint enterprises between government officials and merchants. More specifically, they were managed by the government officials and financed by the merchants.

In 1872, Li Hongzhang requested that the China Merchants Steamship Company be established. According to Li, the development of marine transportation would facilitate the Chinese merchants' competition with Western steamships, which dominated the coastal trade in China. In times of peace, steamships would promote trade. In times of war they would help transport troops and ammunition. Thus, marine transport would be beneficial to both trade and defense.[26] Li's ideas for the development of marine transportation, in fact, implied a trade war with the Western countries, as suggested by Zheng Guanyin. The China Merchants Steamship Company expanded rapidly. The company started with three steamships in 1872, and by 1877 it owned 30 ships.[27]

Mining was another important enterprise developed in this period. Li Hongzhang sought to reduce materials requested by the military industry and sought wealth to support the economy.[28] At Li's suggestion, the Kaiping Mining Factory was established in 1877. The production of coal increased steadily. It became one of the more important enterprises in the period of the Self-Strengthening Movement. In the 1870s and 1880s a great number of mining enterprises were undertaken in Yunnan, Guangxi, Anhui, Guizhou, Hebei, Hubei, Jehe, Jiangxi, Jiangsu, Taiwan, and Northeast China.[29] Li Hongzhang's initial support was essential to the mining industries which were developed with the utilization of Western machinery, technology, and some foreign engineers and advisers. Like marine transportation, mines were organized with private financing but managed by government officials.

Telegraphic communication was also considered an important part of the modern defense industry. In the 1870s, communication in China was mainly

[25] Y. C. Wang, *Chinese Intellectuals and the West, 1872-1949*, Chapel Hill: The University of North Carolina Press, 1966, pp. 42-43.

[26] Mo Anshih, *Yang Wu Yun Dong*, Shanghai: Remin Publishing Co., 1956, pp. 91-92.

[27] See Albert Feuerwerker, *China's Early Industrialization*, Cambridge, Mass.: Harvard University Press, 1958, pp. 96-98.

[28] Liu Kwangching, "Li Hongzhang in Chihli: The Emergence of a Policy, 1870-1875," in *Approaches to Modern Chinese History*, edited by Albert Feuerwerker, Rhoads Murphay, Mary C. Wright, Berkeley, Calif.: University of California Press, 1967, pp. 97-98.

[29] Zhang Kuohui, *op. cit.*, p. 42.

restricted to mail delivered on horseback. The delivery of mail between Shanghai and Peking took six days. The first telegraphic bureau was established at Tientsin in 1880, again, at the suggestion of Li Hongzhang. According to Li, the most important reason to develop telegraphic communication was for the mobilization of military forces in case of war.[30] Therefore telegraph lines were initially established between Tientsin, Dagu, Jiling, Zheng Jiang, Suzhou and Shanghai, the strategic cities near Peking. In 1882, a cable link between Nanjing and Shanghai was completed. Two years later, it was extended to Hankou. By 1883, lines connected Shanghai, Fuzhou, and Hong Kong and connected Canton and Kowloon. All of the telegraphic equipment was purchased abroad. Thus, by the early 1880s most of the important coastal cities were linked by cable. Communication in trade was improved, and government communication was much more efficient than ever before.

Another important development of military-related enterprises was the construction of railroads. Railroads were not widely known in China until the 1870s. The introduction of railroads was closely related to the British trade companies. In order to reduce the cost of land transportation British merchants were anxious to see the construction of railroads. In the 1860s and 1870s, they constructed two short railroads near Peking and Shanghai. Chinese residents strongly objected to both lines and, subsequently tore them down.[31] Li Hongzhang, however, still advocated the construction of railroads in 1880. Li's ideas were based mainly on military and economic considerations. According to Li, railroads would effectively shorten the distance between one place and another. In case of disorder, distant points could be reached by troops and officials.[32] Economically, railroads could facilitate better distribution of food and materials nationwide. On the one hand, they could cut the prices of food and improve the supply; on the other, they could help develop domestic trade and mining enterprises.[33] Despite his urgings, Li's railroad ideas won little support from the imperial court. The first railroad was completed to the Kaiping Mines in 1881 for the transportation of coal. It connected Tangshan and Xugezhuang, a span of 11 kilometers. However, the lack of court support forced the suspension of rail construction.

These enterprises begun in the second period of the Self-strengthening Movement were originally designed to support military industries and to develop the economy. A common problem faced by Li Hongzhang and those who supported Self-strengthening was the lack of competent entreprenuers

[30]Mo Anshih, *op. cit.*, p. 101.
[31]H. B. Morse, *The International Relations of the Chinese Empire*, vol. 3, Reprint, Taipei: Book World Co., 1960, p. 76.
[32]Mo Anshih, *op. cit.*, p. 108.
[33]*Ibid.*

who could be placed in charge of these enterprises. As mentioned above, intellectuals in China were trained in the Confucian classics; few had modern industrial knowledge. Thus, a great number of Western engineers and technicians had to be appointed to these newly-established enterprises.[34] However, the top management was appointed by the government. These officials played an important role in the development of these enterprises leading to further understanding and co-operation developing between the officials and the Westerners.

The joint enterprise between government officials and merchants was not an ideal form of business. Due to a shortage of government capital, the projects were financed by the merchants. To them, these enterprises were investments. The management, however, was controlled by officials who were not profit-oriented. In addition, these enterprises were formed for the purpose of supporting military industries. Markets were confined to government-owned industries. Furthermore, the materials, equipment and machinery were purchased abroad at high cost. All these factors made these enterprises unprofitable from the beginning.[35] It is not surprising, therefore, that they did not develop very satisfactorily.

The Third Period, 1885-1894

This period began immediately after the Sino-French War. Although it had been 25 years since the beginning of the Self-strengthening Movement China again lost a war this time to the French. More than half of the military vessels assembled by Fuzhou Shipyard were sunk by the French navy in Chinese harbours. On land, Chinese troops could not match the superiority of French forces. Vietnam became a colony of the French. The Chinese imperial court was once again frustrated and humiliated. More skepticism was voiced about the Self-strengthening Movement. More people urged the government to pay more attention to internal affairs. In spite of the increasing pressure, the imperial government felt that national defense, particularly the modernization of armaments, remained the most important problem. Wei Yuan maintained that maritime defense was the key to national defense. After the Sino-French war, it became even clearer that without a strong navy, China could not resist external enemies. Thus, the establishment of a competent navy became the top priority in this period.[36]

[34] Mo Anshih, *op. cit.*, p. 115.

[35] Chuan Hansheng, *Hanyehping Gong Si Shi Lui* (A Brief History of the Hanyehping Coal Mining and Smelting Company, 1890-1926), Hong Kong: The Chinese University Press, 1972, pp. 237-245.

[36] See John L. Rawlinson, *China's Struggle for Naval Development, 1839-1895*, Cambridge, Mass.: Harvard University Press, 1967, pp. 129-153.

The Sino-French war proved that weapons and ammunition manufactured by the Chinese were inferior to those used by the French. And the naval vessels made in China were already obsolete. Consequently, Li Hongzhang decided to purchase strong defense forces, both land-based and naval, from the West. The most remarkable manifestation of this policy was the formation of the Northern Fleet in 1888. Almost all the vessels were purchased abroad. Twelve were purchased in England, five in Germany, and only five were made in China.[37] It was the most expensive project among all the Self-strengthening undertakings. At the time, this fleet was the strongest naval force in Asia.

In addition to naval expansion, railroad construction became better accepted during this period. The Tientsin Railroad Company was formed as a result of Li Hongzhang's proposal in 1887. It was designed as a joint official-merchants corporation. However, not as much capital was raised as had been originally planned. This led to borrowing from foreign corporations.[38] The railroad company during this period completed important railroads such as the Peking-Tientsin railroad, the Tangshan-Shanhaiguan railroad, and the Jilong-Taipei-Xingzhu railroad (in Taiwan). Despite tremendous political efforts made by Li Hongzhang and Zhang Zhidong in their disputes with conservatives such as Yu Lianyuan and Hong Liangpin, and despite financial efforts expended in raising funds from merchants and foreign corporations, total railroad construction during this period was only about 400 kilometers.

The steel industry also benefited from development during this period. In 1890, Zhang Zhidong, governor-general of Hubei and Guangdong, initiated the establishment of the Daye Mining Corporation and the Hanyang Arsenal. Steel, obviously, was the foundation industry for military and railroad construction. The development of iron mining and the arsenal in Hubei were conceived by Zhang as good measures to cut down the import of steel from the West, and to insure the supply of steel to military industries. This was a giant project: it cost 5 million taels per year from its beginning.[39] It was the first steel complex in China. Due to financial pressure it was re-organized to become merchant-owned though it began as a government-owned corporation. Although the development of the steel industry was financially exhausting, it undoubtedly contributed to the development of many other industries.

Clearly, during the third period of the Self-strengthening Movement projects were developed on a much larger scale than during the second period. The Northern Fleet, the Daye Mining Corporation and the Hanyang Arsenal

[37] Ibid.

[38] See Lee Enhan, "China's Struggle for a Native Financed Railway System," in Bulletin of The Institute of Modern History, vol. V, Taipei: Academia Sinica, 1976, pp. 447-531.

[39] Chuan Hansheng, op. cit., pp. 15-20.

represented the Self-strengtheners' indefatigable efforts to modernize China's defense system and the determination of the imperial government to proceed with the Self-strengthening Movement. This period also proved that the bureaucracy of the imperial government still had some power to mobilize and to allocate its resources.

The Failure of the Self-strengthening Movement

Before the Sino-Japanese War, it appeared that China had most of the important modern industries needed for national defense. In thirty-five years, the imperial government had changed most of its fundamental concepts and attitudes towards technology and science. The strategy toward the West was clearly shown in the Self-strengthening Movement. Unequivocally, the Self-strengtheners wanted to learn Western technology in order to resist the Westerners. However, Li Hongzhang and Zhang Zhidong's understanding of modernization was only superficial. It is arguable that imperialism and internal rebellions left them little time to devote to these new undertakings, so that they were compelled to take shortcuts. This argument could be supported by looking at difficulties in policy-making in the court, the rebellions of the 1860s, and the increasing demands made by the Western powers and the Japanese. However, after the middle of the 1860s domestic rebellions were suppressed, but Chinese officials still treated Western learning and technology as appendages that could be grafted on to the foundation of Chinese knowledge.[40] Japan also started its modernization program in the middle of the 1860s and proved to be more successful. This comparison makes it necessary to examine the problems in the Self-strengthening Movement.

Looking at the development of the whole movement, it becomes clear that the movement relied too much upon Western equipment and technology. Despite the fact that the imperial government had sent a number of students to Europe and America throughout these 35 years, the projects undertaken in the second and third periods remained heavily dependent on the purchase of Western weapons and ammunition as well as on the employment of foreign advisers. This is seen in the purchase of the ships for the formation of the Northern Fleet and the establishment of the Daye Mining project and the Hanyang Arsenal as well as in the construction of railroads. All of these proved that China was not yet independent. Her modernization was at the mercy of the Western powers. Under such circumstances, China was in no position to repel external invasion.

[40] Joseph R. Levenson, "The Intellectual Revolution in China," in Albert Feuerwerber (ed.), *Modern China*, N. J.: Prentice-Hall, Inc., 1964, pp. 154-162.

Secondly, the whole Self-strengthening Movement was too much dominated by the government itself. As indicated above, military industries were owned by the government. Military-related industries were financed by merchants and managed by government officials. In addition, industries such as textiles and machine tool factories were either owned by the government or jointly by the government and merchants. Weaknesses became clear when most of these industries ran up deficits due either to poor management or to lack of capital. It is questionable whether the officials in management were capable of running the factories and corporations.[41] The government virtually became an obstacle to development. This left the people at a loss to find a direction in which to proceed.

Thirdly, as a result of this institutional approach, progress was restricted. Culturally speaking, the whole society remained based on Confucianism. Most of the population had not been introduced to modern knowledge. The most capable people were not trained in the fields of natural science and engineering, or commerce. People were not encouraged to take part in these activities unless it was necessary. Thus, from the beginning, traders in China could not compete with foreigners. There were increasing discussions of trade and a "trade war", as mentioned above, in the 1870s and 1880s. However, short of capital, organization and proper government support, Chinese businessmen and corporations went bankrupt, one after another.[42] Before the Sino-Japanese War in 1894, China had a serious shortage of competent people with modern education. The government's efforts to modernize were restricted to the defense system and left social and political institutions untouched. These problems were too serious to be solved by the imperial government before its collapse in 1911.

Summary

The ruthless defeat of China by the Japanese in the Sino-Japanese War showed that the modernization of her defences was not good enough to deter external enemies who were more advanced militarily and economically than China. Tens of millions of yuan had been spent in military industries, military-related enterprises, and the formation of a naval force. For a while, Asian peoples and the Chinese themselves believed that China had strengthened herself already. This dream vanished in 1894. China again was defeated by an imperialistic country, Japan, which had historically been despised by the Chinese. Among the people, confidence in the Self-strengthening Movement

---

[41] See Albert Feuerwerker, *op. cit.*, pp. 145-150, 242-250.
[42] See Zhang Kuohui, *op. cit.*, pp. 339-366.

collapsed. Officials in the government continued to push forward with purchases of arms and weapons from the West. However, time was running out. People were seeking an alternative method of deterrence against imperialism—a political reform or revolution.

CHAPTER 3
The Anti-missionary Movements and Antiforeignism, 1860-1900

Large-scale antiforeignism in China did not develop until the latter part of the nineteenth century. The traditional Chinese attitude of contempt for inferior cultures had been formed long before the rise of Manchu power in China. The cultural superiority which the Chinese assumed could not easily be destroyed by Western guns and ships. The Opium War and the Anglo-French invasion inflicted defeats upon the imperial government and forced it to admit the superiority of Western armament. These defeats were restricted to Canton, Shanghai, and other coastal areas and had little impact on Chinese culture and society. Before 1860, Westerners in China were restricted to treaty ports and had little contact with the rest of the Chinese populace. Few cultural conflicts were seen during this period. There is little evidence supporting the idea that the Chinese were hostile to foreigners immediately after the Anglo-French expedition.

Before 1860, the number of missionaries in China was too small to have created many conflicts with the Chinese populace. Missionaries engaged in preaching were restricted to treaty ports only.[1] As a result of the Anglo-French expedition, the imperial government gave in to all the demands for access to Chinese territory and to the Chinese population. In the treaty with France, China legally permitted Christianity in China. The treaty guaranteed Chinese subjects the right to practice Christianity and abrogated all previous documents that had been directed against the Christian religion. The imperial government gave French missionaries the right to preach and practice their religion freely anywhere in China.[2] French missionaries were also allowed to purchase and own houses and land in China. Through the most-favored-nation clauses in the earlier treaties, these privileges were also applicable to all other missionaries. The 1860 Treaties opened up the Chinese interior to foreigners and led to spectacular development in the Christian crusade. For example, in 1870, ten years after the Treaties of Peking was ratified, the estimated number of Chinese Catholics increased to 400,000.[3] But Christianity in China proved to be a controversial issue, fueling sentiments of antiforeignism.

---

[1] Jerome Ch'en, *China and the West*, London: Hutchison & Co., 1979, p. 92.

[2] Guo Tingyi, *Jin Dai Zhong Guo Shi Gang, op. cit.*, pp. 147-148.

[3] Paul A. Cohen, *China and Christianity*, Cambridge, Mass.: Harvard University Press, 1963, p. 70.

Christianity and Confucianism

Chinese culture and tradition in the late Qing period were deeply rooted in Confucianism. After competition with Taoism and Legalism in the Han dynasty and later struggles with Buddhism in the Sui-Tang period (A.D. 581-906), Confucianism was established as orthodoxy in the Sung period (A.D. 960-1279). Despite the fact that Confucianism dominated most of the important areas of culture and ethics, Buddhism was also widespread and generally well accepted by the people. The development of Buddhism was gradual and took place over many centuries. Most important of all, it did not arouse serious mass resistance.[4] In contrast to the development of Buddhism, Christianity, as introduced into China after the Anglo-French invasion, was inseparable from imperialist aggression against China. Missionaries were protected by foreign forces, and most important of all, Christianity developed under a system of unequal treaties. Thus, from its very beginning, it represented the notion of Western political and cultural superiority. As a result, the conflict between Christianity and Chinese culture was inevitable.

Before any discussion of conflict between Christianity and Confucianism, it should be noted that Christianity is a religion, and Confucianism a school of thought. Confucianism focuses on human society and its moral tenets. Like other religions, Christianity focuses on the after-life and the saving of the soul. In this respect, Confucianism had no concrete counter-doctrine of faith.[5] It is true that Confucianism had some anti-religious traditions. Confucianists, from Confucius on, discouraged the discussion of spiritual, mysterious and supernatural things. This was also a fundamental source of conflict between Confucianism and Buddhism in the Tang Dynasty.[6] The differences between Confucianism and Christianity were many. Hostility, however, between Christianity and Confucianism derived mainly from cultural, social and political conflicts, not merely religious questions.

In the first place, Confucianists held Christianity in contempt. The traditional Confucian attitude was to treat foreign customs and cultures as heresy (*Yi-duan*). The distinction between China (*hua*) and "barbarians" (*yi*) led to the demarcation between civilized and uncivilized worlds or between orthodoxy and heterodoxy. Confucianists for thousands of years defended their orthodoxy in China. Not surprisingly, most Confucianists in the late Qing, seeing the increasing expansion of Christianity in China and the growing

---

[4] See Arthur Wright, *Buddhism in Chinese History*, New York: Atheneum, 1965.

[5] Julia Ching, *Confucianism and Christianity*, Tokyo: Kodansha International, 1977, pp. 7-10.

[6] Arthur Wright, *op. cit.*, pp. 86-107.

number of converts, felt it was their sacred responsibility to refute heresy. A great number of the writings and activities of Confucian scholars and officials were designed to impede the development of Christianity.[7]

Secondly, conflict between Confucianism and Christianity also derived from competition for leadership in cultural activities. For over a thousand years Confucianism had represented the main stream of Chinese cultural and intellectual development and occupied a leading position in Chinese society. In spite of the fact that the Christian missionaries were mainly devoted to preaching Christianity, they could, at the same time, exert tremendous influence upon Chinese life through their contacts with the Chinese people. Thus, inevitably Christian missionaries played a similar role, in socializing and educating people, to that of the Confucianists. This naturally met with jealousy and an unfriendly response from the Confucian intellectuals.[8]

Thirdly, social practice was another source of conflict between Confucianism and Christianity. For example, Christianity prohibitde the worship of ancestors, and this met with frequent denunciation from many Confucianists. Worship of ancestors had been practiced by most Chinese Confucianists, and by those who were not exactly 'Confucianists', as an extremely important part of social custom for thousands of years. It was considered the most fundamental part of social practice in Chinese culture and tradition and a manifestation of the "three bonds and five relationships." Another important source of opposition from the Confucianists was centered on the issue of Christian belief in the equality of all people before God. In the Confucian social hierarchy, each person was given a place in accordance with his social role e.g. prince, minister, father, son, husband and wife.[9] This social order was the basis of social relationships and could in no way be changed. Confucianists in late Qing believed that they defended not only the culture and tradition but also the very society of China.[10]

These sources of conflict existed not only between Confucianism and Christianity, but also between Confucianism and Buddhism and other religions. Any new religion or culture that came to China inevitably met with strong resistance from Confucianism. Christianity however, aroused strong

---

[7]Lu Shiqiang (Lu Shih-chiang), *Zhong Guo Guan Shen Fan Jiao Yuan Yin* (Anti-Christian Movement, 1860-1874), Taipei: Institute of Modern History, Academia Sinica, 1966, pp. 195-200.

[8]Paul A. Cohen, *op. cit.*, pp. 77-107.

[9]Lu Shiqiang, "Wan Qing Zhong Guo Zhi Shi Fen Zi Dui Ji Du Jiao Yi Li De Pi Chi" (Critique Against Christianity by Intellectuals in the Late Qing Period), *Li Shi Xue Bao* (Bulletin of Historical Studies), Taipei: National Normal University, vol. 2, 1974, pp. 149-150.

[10]Paul A. Cohen, *op. cit.*, p. 103-n. 24.

antiforeignism in Chinese society in the latter part of the 19th century.[11] In order to explore the origin of antiforeignism, it is necessary to examine the development of Christianity and the response from the Chinese populace, particularly, the gentry.

The Gentry and Anti-Christian Activities

The term 'gentry' or *shen-shi*, broadly speaking, refers to social groups who played political and administrative roles in Chinese society. A great proportion of them had connections with landholdings. The gentry was a stratum of families who closely identified with the Confucian traditions and values.[12] Like Confucian scholars, they also championed the cultural legacy of the society. Some of the gentry obtained degrees by passing government examinations, or titles through giving donations. In this sense they represented cultural leadership at the local level. Most important of all, they were educated in Confucianism. Many of them were engaged in public works and cultural activities, and were persons of considerable influence in society.[13]

In addition to the conflicts which originated from the competition between Confucianism and Christianity stated above, the gentry's position in society was considerably threatened by the missionaries' activities of preaching, teaching and counselling. Before the arrival of the missionaries, education and cultural affairs had been part of the gentry's prerogatives. To preach to the people was to insult the gentry, for they were custodians of Chinese traditions and values. To teach the people was to offend the gentry, for education was their domain and a demonstration of their cultural leadership. To give counselling to the people was to compete with the gentry, for it offended the pride of Confucianism. To help the people in any way was also to threaten the gentry, for they were the social elite.[14] All of this shows the inevitability of conflict between the role played by the gentry and the missionaries' efforts. With their close connection with the government, the gentry could influence local and provincial officials, and with strong roots in society, they could mobilize the people to oppose the missionaries.[15]

The coming of missionaries to the interior of China, protected by humiliatingly unequal treaties that were a result of imperialist invasion, was

[11] See Jiang Tingfu, *Jin Dai Zhong Guo Wai Jiao Shi Zi Liao Ji Yao*, *op. cit.*, vol. 2, pp. 70-104.

[12] Chang Chung-li, *The Chinese Gentry*, Seattle: University of Washington Press, 1955, pp. 6-8.

[13] *Ibid.*, pp. 51-70.

[14] Lu Shiqiang, *Zhong Guo Guan Shen Fan Jiao De Yuan Yin*, *op. cit.*, pp. 151-173.

[15] Fei Hsiao-tung, *China's Gentry*, First Phoenix Edition, Chicago: The University of Chicago Press, 1968, pp. 17-32.

insulting to the gentry, although they could do nothing about it. Great aversion to foreigners developed among the gentry when they saw China again and again defeated by Western powers.[16] Motivated by a Christian crusade, missionaries moved into the inner regions establishing chapels, churches and monasteries. To the Chinese populace, the activities of the missionaries represented the advance of Westerners in China, and their feelings were mixed. Missionaries built large nurseries to help raise children, schools to aid education, hospitals to improve the health of the people.[17] Unquestionably, the Chinese people who received help from missionaries were grateful to them, and were the people most likely to be converted to Christianity. However, in the eyes of the gentry, all of these social missions represented challenges to the gentry's own cultural and social status, and threatened to disrupt their cultural legacy.

Anti-Christian literature was circulated in Jiangxi, Hunan, Guizhou and many other provinces in the 1860s.[18] Anti-missionary incidents were usually instigated by the circulation of inflammatory anti-Christian literature. Anti-Christian actions were many and often ended in the killing of both missionaries and Chinese rioters, and were frequently accompanied by the destruction of church property.[19] With the threat of foreign military power to back them up, missionaries sought protection from the Chinese government. Local authorities were compelled to handle these incidents and mete out punishment to the rioters or murderers with no regard for the sympathies of the gentry. This naturally further antagonized the gentry.

The case of Zhou Han is a good example. Zhou Han was an official in Changsha, the capital of Hunan. Between 1890 and 1899 he undertook the publication of thirty-three pieces of anti-Christian literature. They were widely circulated in Hunan, Hubei, and the Changjiang basin.[20] Following the increase of anti-Christian incidents in 1891 in these areas, Zhou's writings aroused the attention of foreign consuls. After much investigation, H. W. Andrews, American Consul; N. Shoorsky, Russian Consul; J. Dautremer, Vice Consul of France; and M. Niclassen, Vice Consul of Belgium lodged a joint protest with Zhang Zhidong, the governor of Hunan. Zhou Han, however, was strongly supported by the gentry in Hunan. According to Zhang's estimate,

---

[16]Sasaki Masaya, *Shinmatsu no Haigai Undo* (Antiforeign Movement during the Late Qing Period), Tokyo: Gen Nan Do Book Store, 1968, pp. 125-127.

[17]Jerome Ch'en, *op. cit.*, pp. 122-137.

[18]Paul Cohen, *op. cit.*, p. 303, n. 24.

[19]Guo Tingyi, *op. cit.*, p. 215. Also see Time Table in *Jiao Wu Dang*, vol. 3, Taipei: Institute of Modern China, Academic Sinica, 1974.

[20]Lu Shiqiang, "Zhuo Han Fan Jiao An" (Zhou Han's Anti-missionary Incident), *Bulletin of Institute of Modern China*, Taipei: Academia Sinica, vol. 2, 1971, pp. 418-419.

Zhou was supported by 9 out of 10 persons in Hunan and Hubei.[21]

Local officials were hesitant to take action against Zhou. However, the British envoy, John Walsham, and the German ambassador, M. von Brandt, categorically demanded that the *Zongli Yamen* arrest Zhou Han. Under pressure from the Western powers, Zhang Zhidong could not help but execute the order from the *Zongli Yamen*.[22] Zhou was dismissed from his official post in 1892. A great number of the gentry were antagonized by this government action.[23] By contrast, the missionaries felt that Zhou should have been given a stiffer penalty. In fact, Zhou's publication of anti-Christian literature was not terminated with his dismissal. His activities resumed after the Sino-Japanese War.

Characteristic of antiforeignism from 1860 to 1884 was the fact that most of the incidents were independent of each other and directly caused by local responses to Christianity. This was particularly true in the Hunan-Jiangxi incidents of the 1860s and was also true of the Tientsin and Nanjing incidents of 1870. There was little evidence to connect them directly with any political objectives.[24] These conflicts and hard feelings cooled down as anti-missionary incidents became less frequent and less serious in the early 1880.[25] With the increasing advances of the interests of the Western powers and Japan, however, the anti-missionary movement expanded again in 1884 after the Sino-French War.

In the early 1890s, an important change began to occur. Antiforeign agitation began to spread and was no longer a matter of independent incidents such as the case of Zhou Han. The increasing circulation of antiforeign literature evidently had an important impact on the outbreak of related incidents. In the 1890s, hostility to Christianity gradually developed into a widespread phenomenon which could be sparked off by a single incident. For example, in the Changjiang area in 1891, there were a great number of anti-missionary incidents in 9 *xian* (county), resulting in damage to, and destruction of, churches and the beating and killing of missionaries.[26] A great number of anti-missionary publications were circulating in this area, denouncing Christianity as an absurdity and a fallacy and urging the people to

---

[21] *Ibid.*

[22] Lu Shiqiang, "Zhou Han's Anti-missionary Incident," *op. cit.*, p. 427.

[23] Sasaki Masaya, *Shinmatsu no Haigai Undo*, *op. cit.*, pp. 146-147.

[24] See H. B. Morse, *The International Relations of the Chinese Empire, op. cit.*, Vol. 2 (1861-1893), pp. 124-137.

[25] Li Chien-nung, *The Political History of China, 1840-1928*, trans. and ed. by S. Y. Teng and Jeremy Ingalls, Stanford, Calif.: Stanford University Press, paperback edition, 1967, pp. 174-176.

[26] See H. B. Morse, *op. cit.*, vol. 2 (1861-1893), pp. 220-260.

expel all foreigners from China.[27] A great number of antiforeign incidents resulted from this development. Consequently, more than twenty military vessels were brought up the Changjiang river by the major Western powers to protect the Westerners in this area. Thus, there was a large-scale development of an anti-foreign movement resulting from anti-Christian sentiment as early as the 1890s.[28]

The attitude of the imperial government was a key to the development of antiforeignism. It is unlikely that the development of anti-Christian activities would have been allowed to persist from the 1860s to the 1890s if the government had not been in sympathy with them. From the early period, after the Treaties of Peking, the imperial government was ambiguous about the clause that provided Christian missionaries the right to preach and practice their religion in China. This ambiguous attitude was partly due to the fact that the right was provided by an unequal treaty which represented an insult to the imperial government.[29] Officials at the provincial level occasionally had to show the missionaries courtesy and provide them with protection due to their formal obligations, but, by giving accommodation to missionaries, the officials could antagonize their superiors, their colleagues, and even their followers inside the bureaucracy of the government. In the countryside, the officials, having lost the trust of the people, could be confronted by the gentry. Therefore, officials found themselves in a dilemma over protecting missionaries and suppressing anti-Christian incidents. This difficulty was seen throughout the period from the 1860s to the 1890s. The case of the Nanchang incident of 1862 is an example that shows the dilemma of an official's implementation of the treaty obligations to protect missionaries.[30] In this case, when some members of the gentry class inflamed the people's feelings Governor Shen Bao-zhen did not stop the circulation of the inflammatory handbills. As public order was severely jeopardized and the situation worsened, he had to take two lines of action. First, he warned the gentry and populace not to cause disturbances, then he tried to reach an understanding with the more influential members of the gentry. Following the outbreak of incidents, Shen punished nobody. No arrest was ever made.[31]

The ambiguity continued in the 1890s as illustrated in the case of Zhou

[27] See Chronology in H. B. Morse, *op. cit.*, vol. 2, pp. XXIII–XXXV.

[28] *Ibid.*, pp. 124–137.

[29] Lu Shiqiang, "Yi He Tuan Bian Luan Qian Xi Si Chuang Sheng De Yi Ge Fan Jiao Yun Dong" (The Anti-missionary Movement in Sichuan before the Boxer Uprising), *Bulletin of Institute of Modern History*, Taipei: Academia Sinica, 1969, pp. 118–123.

[30] Paul A. Cohen, *op. cit.*, pp. 93–94.

[31] *Ibid.*

Han mentioned above.[32] Thus, antiforeignism, which originated mainly from anti-missionary movements, continued over forty years with the imperial government and local officials trying to appease the antiforeign sentiments. It was no surprise that the Dowager decided to use the antiforeign Boxers to expel the foreigners in 1900.

The Impact of the Anti-Christian Movement on Chinese Politics

Politics in the late Qing period, as we have already seen, overwhelmingly emphasized the defense of the country from external conquest. Defeats in the Opium War and by the Anglo-French expedition caused gentry and officials to oppose Westerners. Militarily, the officials undertook the modernization of armaments to defend the country. Culturally, the gentry developed anti-Christian sentiment in defense of Confucian culture and tradition. Consequently, a defensive attitude against Western culture and knowledge developed. Ironically, these two responses were contradictory to each other. As was proved in the Sino-Japanese War, simply modernizing armaments was not sufficient to repel an external enemy. China needed to modernize its culture, society and political system. Traditionalism was the opposition force which hindered the development of these modernizations. From this point of view, the sentiment of antiforeignism delayed the modernization of China and weakened the deterrent force that China could offer against external aggression.[33] The emergence and development of antiforeignism did, however, have a significant impact on subsequent political development.

In the first place, the anti-Christian sentiment provided a common ground for the gentry and people to cooperate in opposing missionaries. In anti-Christian activities, gentry gained political support from the people and in many riots against missionaries' secret societies played a role.[34] From 1860 to 1900, the gentry and the people gained experience in organizing antiforeign activities. Thus, in the Boxer Uprising, antiforeign support could be mobilized within a short period of time and this support proved to be a source of tremendous political power. Antiforeignism emerged as a mobilization force, introduced as an essential means to oppose imperialism.

[32] "Zhou Han's Anti-missionary Incident," *op. cit.*, pp. 426-429.

[33] Liao Kuang-sheng, "China's Modernization and the development of Antiforeignism," Hong Kong: *Dousou bi-monthly*, no. 39, July, 1980, pp. 1-5.

[34] Paul A. Varg, *Missionaries, Chinese and Diplomats*, New Jersey: Princeton University Press, 1958, p. 33.

Secondly, the development of antiforeignism led to the gentry's acceptance of violence in their opposition to foreign countries in spite of the traditional Confucian emphasis on peace. Confucianism urged humanitarianism and harmony towards other peoples. Since the 1860s, however, the gentry's agitation spawned a great number of anti-Christian incidents, which resulted in bloodshed and destruction. In other words, the gentry revised Confucian principles in their relations with foreigners. This introduced a violent approach to repelling imperialism. Furthermore, acceptance of violence as a political solution eliminated for the gentry any barriers against supporting Sun Yat-sen's revolutionary movement.

Thirdly, the anti-missionary movement as discussed above, was based on the preservation of Chinese tradition and culture from foreign influence. In the development of the anti-Christian movement, the consciousness of a nation gradually emerged. The embryo of nationalism was conceived in the anti-Christian movement. Early nationalism was based on the defense of tradition and culture and on antiforeignism. It grew while the pressure from Western powers increased. The advance of foreign interests in the first decade of the 20th century by the major powers contributed to the later growth of nationalism in China. The anti-missionary movement provided a catalyst for the development of nationalism.[35]

Expansion of Antiforeignism: Anti-Christian Sentiment After the Sino-Japanese War

In the eyes of the Chinese, Japan's stance was that of a recipient of Chinese culture; its status was inferior to that of China. In 1853, Japan was compelled to conclude the American-Japanese Treaty as a result of Commodore M. C. Perry's visit. However, in the 1860s and the 1870s, following the Meiji Restoration, Japan undertook a modernization program under which she became a centralized state for the first time. She began to concentrate on adopting Western culture and to seek the scientific and technical knowledge of the West. An expansion policy was adopted in the early 1870s. In 1874, Japanese troops attacked Taiwan. One year later, Japan started to expand her influence to Korea, then a tributary state of China. In the 1880s, Japan and China engaged in a struggle to control Korea, and in 1894, the Sino-Japanese

[35] Yip Ka-che, "Religion and China's Nationalism," *Zhong Guo Xian Dai Shi Chuan Ti Yan Jiu Bao Gao* (Research Report on Special Topic in Contemporary China), Taipei: Zhong Guo Guo Min Dang Dang Shi Wei Yuan Hui, 1972, vol. II, pp. 293-294.

War broke out over this issue.[36] In a few months, Li Hongzhang's Northern Fleet was destroyed, and the Liaodong peninsula was occupied by Japanese forces. China was defeated in March 1895.

The impact of China's defeat by Japan in 1895 was immense. Politically, it proved that China's tremendous efforts in the modernization of armaments had failed to repel an external enemy. The Self-strengthening Movement from 1860-1894 had been in vain. Furthermore, the defeat in the war of 1894 demonstrated that the Qing government was incompetent and powerless to assume responsibility for the defense of the nation. This made the people aware that they could no longer rely upon the Qing government to save the nation from conquest. They had lost their trust in the government. Intellectuals particularly were shocked by the fact that China could not even defend herself against a small and historically inferior country like Japan. As a result they formed various movements trying to save the country. For example, Kang Youwei and Liang Qichao pressed for reform.[37] However, their attempt failed when the "Hundred Days Reforms" were toppled by a coup d'etat initiated by the Empress Dowager. Another response was the revolutionary movement led by Sun Yat-sen which later overwhelmed the reformist movement. The revolutionary movement, however, had little success inside China before 1911.

A striking development soon after the Sino-Japanese War was the increase in anti-Christian incidents in 1895 and 1896. The worst riots were at Chengdu in Sichuan in May and at Gutien in Fujian in August 1895. The former were directed against French, English and American missionaries, the latter against English and American missionaries. The incidents at Chengdu were most remarkable.[38] It was reported that the populace in Chengdu was discontented with the English, French and Americans due to the fact that they did not help China during the Sino-Japanese War. These incidents touched off further incidents in ten counties. Consequently, within a few months, more than thirty Protestant churches and some forty Catholic churches were damaged or burnt.[39]

As foreign pressure grew, the number of anti-Christian incidents greatly

[36] Guo Tingyi, *op. cit.*, pp. 224-227.

[37] *Ibid.*, pp. 374-383.

[38] Lu Shiqiang, "Wan Qing Shi Qi Ji Du Jiao Zai Si Chuang Sheng De Chuang Jiao Huo Dong Ji Chuang Ren De Fan Ying" (MIssionary Activities and the Anti-Christian Movement in Sichuan During the Late Qing Period), in *Li Shi Xue Bao* (Journal of Historical Studies), Taipei: National Normal University, no. 4, 1976, pp. 265-302.

[39] *Ibid.*

increased. In 1897-98, Russians occupied Port Arthur and Dairen and the Germans occupied Qingdao. Later, the British controlled Weihaiwei, and the French occupied Canton.[40] China was in a crisis of partition. For example, in Sichuan massive anti-Christian incidents broke out in thirty-seven counties These incidents were initiated by Yu Dongchen, a coal miner. Yu had about ten thousand followers. They moved like an army and confronted government officials. They burnt or damaged churches from May 1898 to March 1899. In September of 1898, the local government of Eastern Sichuan tried to reorganize and equip Yu's followers in order to turn them into local guards. During negotiations between Yu's representative and the deputy commander of the Eastern Sichuan District, Yu's forces kidnapped the deputy commander. Consequently the negotiations fell through and the commander decided to fight Yu. War broke out between government forces and Yu's followers and raged from mid-October to mid-December. Yu was arrested after being defeated. The government made a settlement with the French bishop, paying an indemnity of around 1.2 million taels for repairs to and reconstruction of churches.[41] This was the largest incident up to this time of anti-Christian activities. Yu had not only the support of the gentry but also of the masses. His uprising represented an unprecedented case in anti-Christian activities.

Clearly, anti-Christian incidents expanded substantially after the 1895 Sino-Japanese War. Antiforeign mobs attacked churches not simply because of religious conflicts, but because they believed that their revenge against the foreigners would bring a restoration of national pride. For example, in his resistance against government forces, Yu Dongchen published a proclamation declaring that his followers were righteous soldiers fighting for the people and the nation, that the cause of his opposition to Christianity was to eliminate heresy in order to preserve sacred customs, and that he wanted revenge for the country in order to erase the humiliation of the people.[42] Anti-Christian incidents were an emotional response of the people to foreign pressure.

Meanwhile, Zhou Han's anti-Christian literature was again circulated after the Sino-Japanese War. According to a report written by a British consul, Zhou's book was reprinted in five provinces and widely circulated in seven

---

[40] Guo Tingyi, *op. cit.*, pp. 287-298.

[41] Lu Shiqiang, "The Anti-missionary Movement in Sichuan Before the Boxer Uprising," *op. cit.*

[42] See Guy Puyraimond, "The Kolao Hui and the Antiforeign Incidents of 1891," in Jean Chesneaux (ed.), *Popular Movement & Secret Societies in China, 1840-1950*, Stanford, Calif.: Stanford University Press, 1972, pp. 113-124.

provinces.[43] After seeing Germany's occupation of Jiaozhou, and the Russian takeover of Port Arthur, and increasing attempts by Western powers to impose their will on China, Zhou publicly wrote a proclamation that strongly urged the people to rise to expel foreigners and destroy heresy. He demanded that loyal subjects and righteous people should be prepared to exterminate foreigners.[44] This indicated that he was no longer simply fighting against Christian missionaries but against all foreigners. Since he claimed his cause was to save the nation as well as its culture and tradition, he became a great hero among the people fighting against foreigners in the days before the Boxer Uprising. Although Zhou was arrested by the authorities, millions of copies of his writings were circulated among the populace.

The "carving of the Chinese melon" resulted in the imperial government loosing much of its control over its own territories. By 1899, most of the important harbours along the Chinese coast were under the control of Western powers. Outer and Inner Mongolia and Xinjiang were the Russians' sphere of influence. Shandong was Germany's; the provinces in the Changjiang region and Tibet were England's. Fujian was Japan's, while Yunnan, Guangxi, Guangdong, and Sichuan were France's sphere of influence. Under such circumstances, the imperial government was paralyzed.[45] Its land and populace were open to foreign countries. And there was no successful effort from the government to defend the country. The whole project of the modernization of armaments had failed. The only alternative defense was to use the poeple. Using the people to control the "barbarians" became the final resort.

The Boxer Uprising and Use of the People to Control "Barbarians", 1900

By 1900, it was abundantly clear that an antiforeign fervor was on the upsurge. The people, whether peasants, workers, gentry, or intellectuals, increasingly feared further foreign aggression against China. Unrest became prevalent in many areas, so much so that the reform movement was definitely doomed. The imperial government was crippled due to foreign control of many parts of China. Despite the fact that anti-Christian incidents continued to take place in China more often than before, the hostility had clearly shifted to opposing foreign aggression rather than Christianity.[46] Of immediate

[43] Great Britain, Foreign Office, China, Embassy and Consular Archives, Correspondence, F. O. 228:1096.

[44] *Ibid.*

[45] Fu Zixue, *Zhong Guo Wai Jiao Shi* (Diplomatic History of Modern China), Taipei: Taiwan Commercial Publishing Co., 1972, vol. 1, pp. 151-158.

[46] In this analysis, the author does not agree with the theory of cultural imperialism which claims that Christianity played an important role in the development of Chinese

concern was the destiny of the nation, whether or not it could survive partition by foreign powers. As history had proved, rational responses to foreign aggression, i.e. the modernization of armaments and the reform movement, were not effective in deterring external aggression.

Among nation-wide antiforeign activities, the *Yi He Tuan* (Boxers) emerged as the most remarkable movement. This group developed from the Big Knives Society (the *Da Dao Hui*), one of the many secret societies. At the end of the nineteenth century the Big Knives Society was flourishing. Its members claimed that they could be possessed by spirits and that they were impervious to bullets. As a result those who were hostile to the Christian churches joined the Society in increasing numbers. Considering that the survival of the nation was at stake, the Society coined the slogan "Support the Qing and Destroy the Aliens" and renamed itself *Yi He Tuan* (Righteous Harmony Group). The Boxers burnt down churches and killed missionaries in Shandong province, causing protests from various foreign countries. As a result of these incidents the anti-Christian activities were stopped by Yuan Shih-k'ai, then governor of Shandong.[47]

At the suggestion of her associates, however, the Empress Dowager decided to use the Boxers to fight the foreigners. She believed that this was the opportunity to wipe out national shame.[48] Regardless of some dissenting opinions, the court declared war against all nations who had relations with China. Consequently, violence broke out, a great number of churches were burnt down and missionaries and church members were killed. The legation areas were attacked. Foreign embassies in the capital were harrassed.[49] Consequently, the Allied Army of the Eight Nations was formed and marched on Tientsin and Peking. The several hundred thousand Boxers dispersed. Peking and Tientsin were occupied by foreigners. The use of the people to control the "barbarians" was an illusion. The manipulation of the people to deter foreigners turned out to be a foolish game.

Summary

The rise of Chinese antiforeignism in late nineteenth century was stimulated not so much by missionary movements as by the awakening of the

---

nationalism. See Arthur Schlesinger, Jr. "The Missionary Enterprise and Theories of Imperialism," in John K. Fairbank (ed.), *The Missionary Enterprise in China and America*, Cambridge, Mass.: Harvard University Press, 1974, pp. 365-366.

[47] Fu Qixue, *Zhong Guo Wai Jiao Shi*, vol. 1, *op. cit.*, p. 166.

[48] *Ibid.*, p. 167.

[49] See Paul A. Varg, *op. cit.*, pp. 47-48.

Chinese people against foreign threat.[50] The people, seeing that the defense efforts of the government during the last forty years had failed, rose to oppose foreigners in China. Christian missionaries were a vulnerable target for their attacks. It is evident that anti-missionary sentiment was not the major focus of antiforeignism during the period following the Sino-Japanese War. Instead, foreign aggression was the source of hostility among the people. Anti-missionary incidents and antiforeign riots became inseparable. Anti-missionary sentiment gradually gave way to economic, political and military conflicts with the West.[51] Antiforeign activities represented not so much a cultural and social movement as a political movement motivated by patriotism and nationalism. The movement evolved from a few scattered incidents into a mass movement of thousands of people, from a contest of cultures to an important political force.

[50]This opinion is in contrast with Paul Cohen's contention that foreign missionaries were a decisive factor in the rise of Chinese antiforeignism in the nineteenth century. See *China and Christianity*, *op. cit.*

[51]John E. Schrecker, *Imperialism and Chinese Nationalism*, Cambridge Mass.: Harvard University Press, 1971, p. 92. According to the author, the reformers opposed the West primarily for nationalistic reasons while the militant conservatives were particularly hostile to missionaries and Christianity for cultural reasons.

PART II

ANTI-IMPERIALISM FOR NATIONAL EQUALITY AND INDEPENDENCE

CHAPTER 4
Antiforeignism and Nationalism
in the Early 20th Century

The Boxer Uprising represented the last attempt made by the imperial government to control the "barbarians." After the war, the imperial government had no more courage to confront the foreigners and gave in to external pressure. From this time, the Western Powers were more often than before called *"Lieqiang"* (the Powers) instead of "barbarians," in recognition of their superiority. The people, however, continued to oppose foreign interference and the sentiment of antiforeignism persisted in spite of the great chaos following the defeat by the Allied Eight Nations.

Anti-missionary incidents continued to occur in some parts of China although missionaries were better received in many major cities and provinces. A great number of them were heavily engaged in educational work. Many hundreds of schools were opened for teaching Chinese youths. In 1905, the total number of schools under Protestant mission control in China was 2,585. The number of pupils was 572,683.[1] Western knowledge was widely introduced to the youth of Peking, Shanghai and other important cities. The missionary role in education seemed now to meet with less opposition that in the latter part of the 19th century. The appeal of Western education was undoubtedly related to the abolition in 1905 of the Imperial Examination System which had fostered the study of the Confucian classics.

During this period, the Chinese people initiated movements to demand their rights from imperialists. Previously, antiforeignism sought to deny foreigners power in China. Up to the Boxer Uprising, anti-missionary incidents aimed only at destroying or eliminating foreign things; no constructive ideas were put forth. After the Boxer Uprising, due to an increased understanding of the West and an awakening to the immediate danger faced by China, the Chinese people sought protection for national interests and the restoration of national rights. They urged the restoration of control over railroads and mines and demanded the abolition of the supervision of customs by Western powers. Most important of all, they demanded an end to unequal treaties and extraterritoriality. The significance of this period is clearly that antiforeignism now developed into nationalism. And nationalism in China was represented unambiguously by strong and explicit articulation of ideas for national reconstruction.

[1] H. B. Morse, *The International Relations of The Chinese Empire, op. cit.*, vol. 3, 1894-1911, p. 413.

Early Nationalism and the "Movement Resisting Russia", 1900-1905

Nationalism was first developed in Europe. The concept of a nation emerges when people have a common language, culture, and history. Nationalism is essentially an attachment of the individual to the people, place and society. It develops when the nation-state becomes the most important form of political organization. For example, before 1870, German-speaking people were separated into the states of Austria and Prussia. Nationalism served to unify the disunited people. In the early twentieth century, nationalism gradually changed its meaning. It became closely related to self-determination. For example, Norway separated from Sweden in 1905, Czechoslovakia, Hungary and Austria emerged as independent nation-states from the Austro-Hungarian empire.[2] During this period, most parts of Southeast Asia remained colonies of European states, China was still under the domination of the Western Powers but the Chinese people had begun to oppose them.

There is little dispute about the fact that China had ethnocentric nationalism long before the coming of the Westerners. Ethnocentrism was based on cultural and historical development. In the early Qing period, some Chinese scholars such as Huang Zongxi (Huang Tsung-hsi, 1610-1695) and Gu Yanwu (Ku Yen-wu, 1613-1682) opposed alien rule by the Manchus. Huang and Gu both reacted against the political oppression of the early Qing period and stimulated the growth of Chinese national feeling against alien conquest.[3] Anti-Manchu sentiment, which was, of course, strongly repressed, died down in the late eighteenth century. Nationalism in China in the early twentieth century, like nationalism in European countries and in developing countries after World War Two, was stimulated by tremendous pressure from the outside.

In the early twentieth century, Liang Qichao, a leading Chinese intellectual, maintained that the Chinese had strong culturalism but had no equivalent concept of nationalism, as the Europeans had. He argued that the Chinese took China as a world (*tianxia*) rather than as a nation (*guojia*). He further pointed out that because the Chinese tended to think of China as a world rather than as a nation it prevented the development of patriotism in China.[4] Joseph Levenson clearly illustrated Liang's viewpoints on nationalism, when he said:

[2]John G. Stoessinger, *The Might of Nations*, New York: Random House, Fifth edition, 1975, pp. 80-82.

[3]S. Y. Teng and John K. Fairbank, *China's Response to the West: A Documentary Survey, 1839-1923*, Cambridge, Mass.: Harvard University Press, 1961, pp. 7-11.

[4]Liang Qichao, "Xinmin Shuo" (Doctrine of New People) in *Yin Bing Shi Quan Ji*, Hong Kong: Tian Xing Chu Ban She, 1974, pp. 1-7.

In 1900, he (Liang) wrote that Europe and Japan stigmatized China as a nation without patriotism. The sickly state of Chinese patriotism, Liang maintained, was the root cause of the nation's accumulated weaknesses. Nationalism was lacking because the court, not the nation, was the traditional focal point of allegiance and because the Chinese had been unaware that significant peoples other than themselves existed in the world.[5]

Liang Shumin, another leading Chinese scholar, held a similar opinion on nationalism. He perceived traditional China as a society with a strong sense of ethics and culture rather than a sense of nation-state. According to him, the government in traditional China served to rule but not to govern; it simply did not carry out the function of a modern state.[6] Evidently, modern nationalism did not develop in China until the people recognized the reality and formidableness of foreign peoples. The presence of foreign military forces and incessant conflict with the Western powers and Japan in the late nineteenth and early twentieth century, in fact, helped the Chinese develop nationalism. Thus, a sense of challenge was essential to China's nationalism. This was fully illustrated in the Movement Resisting Russia, the Anti-America Boycott, and the Movement for Recovery of National Rights.

The development of nationalism in China is clearly seen in the movement of "Resisting Russia" in the wake of interference by Allied forces during the Boxer Uprising. During the uprising, Russia poured troops into Manchuria and afterwards virtually controlled most of Manchuria. China's territorial integrity over Manchuria was severely challenged by Russia. In February 1901, the Russians demanded a treaty with China in order to place Manchuria, Mongolia and Xinjiang under their sphere of influence.[7] This greedy demand shocked the Chinese as much as the other Allies.[8] In response to the Russian advance, Chinese gentry and businessmen in Shanghai first organized meetings and passed out circulars protesting against Russian aggression and her demands.[9] The movement called on the Chinese government to refuse Russian demands for further interest in China and to resist Russian domination in Manchuria. Organizations for "Resisting Russia" (*Ju E Hui*) were formed in major cities such as Peking, Shanghai, Tientsin, Hangzhou, Suzhou, and spread over many provinces in the Central and Eastern parts of China in addition to

[5] Joseph R. Levenson, *Liang Ch'i ch'ao and the Mind of Modern China*, Berkeley: University of California Press, 1970, p. 111.

[6] Liang Shu-min, *Zhong Guo Wen Hua Yao Yi* (Outline of Chinese Culture), Taipei: Zheng Zhong Shu Ju, 1975, Eighth printing, pp. 163-168.

[7] Fu Qixue, *Zhong Guo Wai Jiao She, op. cit.*, pp. 186-188.

[8] A. Whitney Criswold, *The Far Eastern Policy of the United States*, New Haven: Yale University Press, 1964, Fourth printing, p. 83.

[9] *Ju E Yung Dong, 1901-1905* (Movement Resisting Russia), Peking: Zhong Guo She Hui Ke Xue Chu Ban She, 1979, p. 3.

Manchuria, Mongolia, and Xinjiang.[10] Many overseas organizations were also formed in Tokyo, San Francisco, Hong Kong and Singapore to support this movement.

The movement weakened after mid-1901 but became a hot national issue again in April 1903 when the Russian government attempted to delay its withdrawal of troops from Manchuria.[11] Student movements were launched to protest against Russian aggression. *Ai Guo Hui* (Patriotic Associations) were formed in Shanghai, Peking and provinces in the Central and eastern parts of China.[12] Chinese authorities curbed the movement on the grounds that it might merge with revolutionary activities. Nevertheless, protests against Russia continued off and on until early 1905. The awakening of the Chinese people to the fact that national survival was at stake apparently stimulated the spirit of nationalism. Therefore, it is clear that budding nationalism in China was closely associated with antiforeignism. It was this movement protesting against Russia that mobilized businessmen and students to take part in national mass movements. This marked a new phase in antiforeign movements in China, which now rose to defend China's national interests.

Anti-American Boycott of 1905

Another manifestation of the new sense of nationalism was the boycott of American trade in 1905. The boycott was completely political and had nothing to do with opposition to Christianity. It was adopted by the Chinese people as a means of strengthening the position of their government on the request for unrestricted immigration of Chinese into the United States.

Restrictions on Chinese immigration were started in the Immigration Treaty of 1880 which gave the United States the right to regulate Chinese labor. In 1882, the U. S. Congress passed the Restriction Act of 1882 which excluded Chinese laborers for ten years. Further restrictions were imposed by the Scott Act of 1888 and the Geary Act of 1892. The 1888 legislation limited the return of Chinese who had temporarily left the United States with the intention of returning later, while the 1892 bill required the registration of all Chinese living in the United States.[13] This legislation was clearly discriminatory against the Chinese and caused definite discontent among the Chinese people. However, little public protest was voiced in China in the 1880s and the 1890s.

[10]*Ibid.*, pp. 4-57.
[11]*Wu Yuzhang Hui Yi Lu* (Memoirs of Wu Yuzhang), Zhong Guo Qing Nian Chu Ban She, 1978, pp. 18-21.
[12]*Ibid.*, pp. 280-310.
[13]C. F. Remer, *A Study of Chinese Boycotts*, Baltimore: John Hopkins Press, 1933, pp. 29-30.

Another treaty was signed between the United States and China in 1894. This provided for the exclusion of all Chinese laborers for a period of ten years. In 1904, this treaty expired and the Chinese government refused to renew it and asked for a revision. This was the direct cause of the boycott of 1905.[14]

The Anti-American Boycott of 1905 represented the rising concern of the Chinese people over China's relationships with the major powers. It was an initiative of the people in pursuit of their interests. It was also an indication of an awakening national consciousness and an increase in confidence among the people, particularly the merchants.[15] After the Sino-Japanese war, the Chinese government encouraged the growth of private enterprise. In 1896, a Commercial Bureau was established in Peking to take charge of various business regulations such as registration, corporation law, bankruptcy law, and the establishment of chambers of commerce in important commercial and industrial areas responsible for developing business.[16]

National industries rapidly expanded. For example, while in 1890 only 7 new factories were established, the number increased to 17 in 1895 and 23 in 1904.[17] Together with the development of national industry, merchants and industrialists were seen as increasingly important in society. They had capital, status, and social prestige as a result of the development of their enterprises. The Anti-American boycott of 1905 was a demonstration of the power of this newly-developed class of merchants and industrialists.[18] The boycott was called by the General Chamber of Commerce in Shanghai on May 10. It spread to Canton, Tientsin, Hankou, Chongqing and Hong Kong through local chambers of commerce.[19]

While commercial people were the initiators of the boycott, the intellectuals and students were enthusiastic followers. They held meetings in support of the decision made by the Chamber of Commerce in Shanghai. The press also played an important role in mobilizing support. Chinese newspapers in Shanghai gave wide coverage to the event. *Shen Bao* (*Shen Pao*) and *Shi Bao* (*Shih Pao*) were the two most active papers reporting the news of the boycott.[20] The boycott was vigorously carried on for about one month. Although

---

[14] *Ibid.*

[15] H. B. Morse, *op. cit.*, vol. 3, pp. 434-435.

[16] Guo Tingyi, *Jin Dai Zhong Guo Shi Gang* (An Outline History of Modern China), Hong Kong: The Chinese University Press, 1979, p. 370.

[17] Hou Chi-ming, *Foreign Investment and Economic Development in China*, Cambridge, Mass.: Harvard University Press, 1965, p. 135.

[18] Zhang Chunwu, *Zhong Mei Gong Yue Feng Chao*, Taipei: Taiwan Commercial Printing Co., 1965, pp. 51-53.

[19] *Ibid.*

[20] *Ibid.*

the economic effect was not substantial enough to disrupt Sino-American trade nation-wide, American trade was severely hurt in Shanghai and Canton. Large stocks of American goods could not be moved in the two cities.[21]

The Anti-American boycott of 1905 was an important mass response to an international issue in China. The boycott was peaceful and legally acceptable in the international community, unlike the Boxer Uprising. Despite the fact that the boycott was neither successful in disrupting Sino-American trade nor in changing the U. S. policy toward the exclusion of Chinese labor, the mobilization of merchants, intellectuals, students, and other people in the boycott was a great step forward in Chinese foreign relations. After 1905 there were continuous nation-wide movements undertaken by the Chinese people, particularly by the newly rising merchant class and the local gentry class. Their efforts in the struggle against foreign domination and pressure were seen in the push for the restoration of mining and railroad rights and in the antiforeign boycotts of the 1910s and 1920s.

Movement for Recovery of National Rights

Another development of Chinese nationalism in the early 20th century was the movement for recovery of national rights in mines and railroads. The victory of Japan in the Russo-Japanese War of 1904-1905 had a significant psychological impact on the Chinese people. For the Chinese it laid to rest the fiction that the white race was superior to the yellow race and showed that an Asian country after modernization could defeat a European country. This greatly boosted the confidence of the Chinese people; they were convinced they too could develop into a strong country as Japan had done. The new direction in which the Chinese turned was to imitate the Japanese. Politically, they wanted to establish a constitutional polity. Economically, they wished to get rid of interference by foreign countries in their economic development. This gave a boost to Chinese nationalism.

Before the 1894 Sino-Japanese war, foreign investment for mining enterprises was refused. This policy was changed, however, due to financial difficulties and the increased pressure of foreign aggression in China. In 1898, Zhang Zhidong, the governor of Hunan and Guangdong, advocated using foreigners to develop railroads and mining in order to maintain a balance among powers, changing his earlier view that mining was a source of profit and should not be open to foreigners.[22] The new policy suggested by Zhang was supported by Li Hongzhang and was soon approved by the *Zongli Yamen.*

[21] C. F. Rember, *A Study of Chinese Boycott, op. cit.*, pp. 36-38.

[22] Li En-han, *Wan Qing De Shou Hui Kuang Quan Yun Dong* (Restoration of Mining Rights Movement During the Late Qing Period), Taipei: Academia Sinica, 1963, p. 11.

Encouragement of foreign investment became a new policy in China in 1898. The new policy was based on the belief that the investment of foreign capital in China could help develop mining industries and railroad construction and could be beneficial to the national economy and the livelihood of the people. With this understanding, the 1898 Public Regulation on Mining and Railroads was approved by the imperial government.[23] This was the first time that foreign merchants were allowed to take part as partners in the corporate contracting for mining and railroad construction. According to the Public Regulation, foreign shares should be less than half of the corporate stock, and the corporation should be managed by Chinese. These provisions were intended to keep foreigners from controlling Chinese corporations.[24]

The control over foreign investment by the government, however, was weakened following the Boxer Uprising. On the one hand, the financial strength of the imperial government deteriorated due to the burden of indemnity imposed by the Eight Powers. On the other, the increasing partition of China into spheres of influence by the major powers reduced the control of the Chinese government over mining and railroads. As a result, in 1902 the restriction of management to Chinese and the requirement that the majority of shares be owned by Chinese were both abolished.[25] With these restrictions removed, investment became one of the approaches to the seizing of control of mining and railroad construction by the major powers.

In the early twentieth century, France, the United Kingdom, Germany, Russia, and the United States had gained important mining rights in China.[26] In fact, most of the important mining rights controlled by the major powers were gained through political intrigue rather than investment. For example, Russian control of mining rights in Manchuria, German rights in Shandong, and French and British rights in Yunnan, were obtained through diplomatic and political approaches together with the expansion of their spheres of influence in China.[27] Most of the important mining industries were to fall under the control of the major powers. For example, the Kaiping coal mine fell under British control in 1901. The Fushun coal mine, the largest coal mine in China, was seized by the Japanese in 1905. The Hanyeping Iron and Coal Mining Corporation, the most important industrial complex in China, was

---

[23] *Ibid.*

[24] *Ibid.*, pp. 16-17.

[25] *Ibid.*, p. 18.

[26] See Yen Zhongping, *Zhong Guo Jing Dai Jing Ji Shi Tung Ji Zi Liao Xuan Ji* (Compiled Statistical Materials of the Modern Chinese Economy), Peking: Kuo Xue Chu Ban She, 1955, p. 126.

[27] Zhang Chunwu, *op. cit.*, pp. 52-53.

seized by the Japanese in 1913.[28] Despite attempts made by the Chinese government and people to recover mining rights, by 1930 more than ninety important mines remained under foreign control; 18 by the U. K., 12 by the French, 9 by the Germans, 8 by the Russians, 3 by the Americans, and 42 by the Japanese.[29] Since these mining rights controlled by major powers represented Western aggression against China in the eyes of the Chinese, the issue was no longer whether foreign investment was beneficial, but whether China could resist the foreign powers. Mining rights became a hot issue in the development of national consciousness in the early twentieth century and in the rising fervor against imperialism in the 1910s and 1920s.

The political implications of these foreign controlled mining enterprises were many. First of all, they represented the continuous expansion of Western interests in China through the manipulation of political pressure and unequal power. In the development of the unequal treaties between China and the West, the concession of extraterritorial rights to foreigners caused a serious loss of some Chinese governmental functions and resulted in strong hostility against foreigners among the people. Since the Treaty of Nanjing in 1842, the Chinese government had accepted the demands for extraterritoriality imposed by Western powers. After the Boxer Uprising, Japan, the United States, Britain, France, Germany, Russian and some other European countries exercised extraterritorial rights in China.[30] As a number of scholars have observed the Chinese government did not fully appreciate the seriousness of the concession she was making in granting such "rights."[31] In accordance with extraterritoriality, the Chinese government had no jurisdiction over nationals or commercial companies belonging to the major powers. Foreigners throughout China were subject to arrest by Chinese officials, but, after arrest, had to be taken at once to their respective consuls for trial. Foreign corporations based in treaty ports were entitled to enjoy extraterritorial rights, and thus were free from any control by the Chinese government.[32] By 1918, there were fifteen countries claiming extraterritoriality in China. Foreign mining corporations were registered under the corporation law of the treaty powers, and did not have to meet the requirements of Chinese law. Consequently, they jeopardized the integrity of China's sovereignty.

---

[28] *Ibid.*

[29] Wu Chengming, *Di Guo Zhu Yi Zai Jiu Zhong Guo De Tou Zi* (Investments by Imperialists in Old China), Peking: Zhong Guo Shi Xue She, 1956, p. 38.

[30] Charles Denby, "Extraterritoriality in China," in *American Journal of International Law*, October 1924.

[31] *Ibid.*

[32] Westel W. Willoughby, *Foreign Rights and Interests in China*, Baltimore: The John Hopkins Press, 1927, pp. 569-577.

After the 1905 Russo-Japanese war, rising national consciousness stimulated the co-operation of the local government and local gentry in an effort to reclaim the mining rights lost to foreigners. From 1905 to 1911 the movement for the reversal of concessions was intended to recover the right of railroad construction and the mining rights seized by foreign countries, through peaceful means. The earliest efforts were made by the officials and gentry of Hunan, Hubei, and Guangdong in 1905 when they attempted to purchase the construction rights to the Canton-Hankou Railroad from the American-China Development Co. In the several years following, the movement to recover railroad rights affected most railroads, such as the Peking-Hankou Railroad and Shanghai-Ningbo Railroad.[33] Some of the railroads were fully recovered by revision of the original contracts, some were partially recovered. In both cases, the Chinese government and gentry made tremendous efforts to meet financial demands for compensation to foreign investors.[34]

During the same period, the movement for recovery of mining rights was taking place in Hebei, Shandong, Shanxi, Henan, Anhui, Zhejiang, Sichuan, Yunnan and Fujian. All foreign mining rights in China became the focus of the movement and the expansion of foreign rights in mining was checked. Remarkably, China did recover some mining rights, particularly in undeveloped mines. These were recovered through the cancellation of contracts when the foreigners failed to start the mining operation before the deadline stated in the agreement. Four mines in Zhejiang, three in Fujian, and several in Sichuan were recovered in this way. Some other mines were recovered due to the strong insistence of the government officials and local gentry for the revision of original contracts with foreign businessmen.[35] In these cases, negotiation of new terms required the Chinese side to make compensation in order to recover mining rights. The amount of compensation was always higher than the capital invested by foreigners. One mine in Anhui, four in Shanxi, seven in Yunnan, and five in Shandong were recovered through this approach.[36] The third kind of recovery of mining rights was repossession of those concessions voluntarily given up by foreigners due to a lack of investment value. The mines recovered in Shandong from Germany were in this category and again compensation had to be paid.[37] To the Chinese the restoration of mining rights, whether valuable or not, provided satisfaction to national pride and independence.

---

[33] *Di Guo Zhu Yi Yu Zhong Guo Tie Lu* (Imperialism and the Chinese Railroads), Shanghai Renmin Chu Ban She, 1980, pp. 203-220.

[34] Li En-han, *Wan Qing De Shou Hui Kuang Quan Yun Dong, op. cit.*, p. 69.

[35] *Ibid.*, p. 266.

[36] *Ibid.*, p. 267.

[37] *Ibid.*

It is clear that the local gentry class played an important role in the claiming of mining rights. In contrast to anti-missionary incidents prior to 1900, however, the movement to reclaim mineral rights from foreign concessionaries was based on rightful and rational claims. It was not an attempt to expel all foreign mining interests from China or to abolish all unequal treaties. Instead, it was merely seeking to reclaim some mining rights based on original contracts which were concluded between foreign enterprises and Chinese companies. The development of this mineral-rights recovery movement was largely based on the principles of international law, and bargaining and peaceful means were used to achieve the goal. The nationalist-minded Chinese, whether government officials or local gentry, appeared to have given up the antiforeign emotional outbursts of the late nineteenth century. Antiforeignism was no longer disruptive of Sino-foreign relations, nor violent in pursuit of national interests. The gentry class in the provinces often got into direct negotiations with the foreign concessionaries on behalf of local interests. It would appear that the rise of the gentry class in the Chinese political scene helped check the Western powers' expansion in China at a time when the government was unable to stop them.

Following the Republican Revolution in 1911, the political situation became worse. Local warlords emerged, wielding military power, while the republicans failed to re-establish a central government in China. Growing foreign domination attracted a nation-wide response to foreign interests in China. Opposition from the people to foreign economic, political, and military interference became a movement against imperialism and a manifestation of the momentum of nationalism which grew in response to the major powers' efforts to bring China under their dominance.

Foreign Investment in China

In spite of the initial success of the rights recovery movement, an important development in China's foreign relations in the early twentieth century was the drastic increase of foreign investments by the major powers. Before the 1895 Sino-Japanese War, there was only a small amount of foreign capital in China and limited impact of foreign enterprises on the Chinese economy. But in 1895, foreigners secured the right to build and own industrial plants in the treaty ports. In 1897 the Russians began the construction of the Chinese Eastern Railroad. In 1907 Dairen was opened to trade and Japanese investments increased rapidly. Foreign investments—a symbol of foreign economic invasion—fueled the spirit of Chinese nationalism and added to the momentum of antiforeignism. For the purpose of understanding the impact of the major powers on the rise of anti-imperialism in China, it is necessary to briefly examine early twentieth-century foreign investment in China, the period in which nationalism and anti-imperialism developed.

Foreign investments in China may be examined in accordance with the estimated value of foreign properties, business investments, and foreign loans. In this brief discussion, a general picture of foreign investment will first be presented, followed by a discussion of foreign loans and foreign business investments. There are a number of works that estimate the foreign investments in China for the first three decades of the twentieth century. The most comprehensive and authoritative estimates on foreign investments in China before 1931 are those by C. R. Remer. Remer defined foreign investments as a source of income owned by a foreigner who lived in China or outside of China. A foreigner could be an individual, a firm, or a government. By this definition, his estimates were mainly based on the total assets of foreign enterprises and government obligations.[38] These estimates have been widely used by researchers both inside and outside of China.

Remer's estimates are shown in Tables 4.1 and 4.2. In 1902 Great Britain held 33% of the total foreign investments, Russia 31.3% and Germany 20.9%. In 1914, Great Britain retained her leading position. However, Germany, Russia, Japan and France were by now of approximately equal importance. The most remarkable change was the position of Japan, whose investments in China had increased to 13.6% in 1914 from 1% in 1902. In 1931, Japanese investment was about equal to that of Great Britain, and Japan became one of the leading creditor countries. Russia, the United States, and France were about equal. American and Japanese investments had grown vigorously, Japanese investments having increased over 500% and American about 400% (see Table 4.2).

Foreign Loans

Foreign loans and direct business investments are also two important items in foreign investments. After the 1895 Sino-Japanese War, the Chinese government faced serious financial straits due to war indemnities to major powers and increasing domestic expenses. Between 1895 and 1910, before the downfall of the Qing government, US$270 million in foreign loans were solicited from the major powers.[39] As a result of these loans, customs, salt taxes, and some inland taxes fell under the control of the major powers, customs revenue being totally forfeited to foreigners. Financial problems continued in the following period. It is estimated that foreign loans amounted

[38] C. F. Remer, *Foreign Investment in China*, New York: Howard Fertig, 1968, pp. 62-69. Also see Wu Chengming, *op. cit.*, pp. 152-153.
[39] Wu Chengming, *op. cit.*, p. 36.

Table 4.1

FOREIGN INVESTMENTS IN CHINA, 1902, 1914, 1931

By Creditor Countries—Percentage Distribution

	1902		1914		1931	
	Millions of U. S. Dollars	*Percentage of Total*	*Millions of U. S. Dollars*	*Percentage of Total*	*Millions of U. S. Dollars*	*Percentage of Total*
Great Britain	260.3	33.0	607.5	37.7	1,189.2	36.7
Japan	1.0	0.1	219.6	13.6	1,136.9	35.1
Russia	246.5	31.3	269.3	16.7	273.2	8.4
United States	19.7	2.5	49.3	3.1	196.8	6.1
France	91.1	11.6	171.4	10.7	192.4	5.9
Germany	164.3	20.9	263.6	16.4	87.0	2.7
Belgium	4.4	0.6	22.9	1.4	89.0	2.7
Netherlands					28.7	0.9
Italy					46.4	1.4
Scandinavian countries					2.9	0.1
Others	0.6	0.0	6.7	0.4		
	787.9	100.0	1,610.3	100.0	3,242.5	100.0

Source: C. F. Remer, *Foreign Investments in China*, New York, 1968 (First published in 1933), p. 76.

Table 4.2

FOREIGN INVESTMENTS IN CHINA, 1902, 1914, 1931

Relatives for the Chief Countries

Investments for 1914 = 100

	1902	1914	1931
Great Britain	42.8	100	195.8
Japan	0.5	100	517.7
Russia	91.5	100	101.4
United States	40.0	100	399.0
France	53.2	100	112.3
Germany	62.3	100	33.0
Total (all countries)	48.9	100	201.4

Source: *Foreign Investments in China, op. cit.*, p. 77.

to US$520 million between 1911 and 1926.[40] These loans were made by major powers to individual warlords. Thus foreign loans became important political weapons used by the major powers to interfere in Chinese finance and politics. It has been noted by Wu Chengming, a Marxist economist in China, that the prolonged civil wars among warlords between 1912-1927 could be attributed to financial and military assistance from the major powers.[41]

Two types of loans, as shown in Table 4.3, were made by foreign powers. One was military and financial loans, the other was railroad loans. The former were borrowed by Chinese governments for the purpose of paying domestic expenses, and the maintenance and improvement of the armed forces. Before its 1911 downfall, the Qing government relied heavily upon loans from Great Britain, France, and Germany. In return, these countries obtained Chinese customs revenue and salt taxes as collateral. In the negotiation for a financial or military loan from these countries, the Qing government and later the warlords as well had to make some political concessions to them. Thus, in addition to tax mortgages and heavy interest, the major powers obtained political promises from the Chinese government. After 1911, it became a clearly recognized phenomenon that warlords needed the financial support of major powers due to financial difficulties. This problem became acute when fighting broke out between warlords.[42] Therefore, each warlord had his foreign ally. For example, Wu Peifu (Wu P'ei-fu) was supported by Great Britain, Duan Qirui (Tuan Ch'i-jui) by Japan, and Feng Yuxiang (Feng Yu-hsiang) by Russia. In this way, spheres of warlord influence, propped up by major powers, developed in the 1910s and 1920s.

Table 4.3
FOREIGN LOANS IN CHINA, 1902-1936
New Balance of Each Year (In million U. S. dollars)

	Military and Financial Loans	Railroad Loans	Total
1902	246.8	37.6	284.4
1911	220.0	167.9	387.9
1914	383.5	192.5	576.9
1925	486.9	311.3	798.2
1930	540.5	356.6	897.1
1936	468.0	346.1	814.1

Source: Wu Chengming, *Di Guo Zhu Yi Zai Jiu Zhong Guo De Tou Zi*, Peking: Zhong Guo Shi Yue She, 1956, p. 75.

[40]*Ibid.*

[41]*Ibid.*

[42]Hu Sheng, *Di Guo Zhu Yi Yu Zhong Guo Zhen Zhi* (Imperialism and Chinese Politics), Peking: Renmin Chu Ban She, 1978, 8th edition, pp. 147-152.

Railroad loans from major powers were normally smaller than financial and military loans. These, however, grew tremendously in the 1910s and 1920s. The creditors were guaranteed interest and capital payments by the profit from the railroads. Such loans were generally used for the construction of railroads. However, it is likely that some railroad loans were spent for financial and military purposes. The major powers, however, often used railroad loans for the expansion of their spheres of influence.[43] They could control material supplies, engineering design, and even interfere in the management of the railroad.

Table 4.4
FOREIGN LOANS IN CHINA, 1902-1936
Balance of Country Each Year (In million U. S. dollars)

	1902	1914	1930	1936
Britain	109.4	195.7	162.9	150.1
U.S.A.	4.5	7.3	50.8	64.4
France	61.0	119.9	102.7	90.9
Germany	78.3	127.1	93.6	89.4
Japan	–	37.4	373.3	258.2
Russia	26.1	45.1	–	–
Others	5.1	43.5	113.8	161.1
Total	284.3	576.0	897.1	814.1

Source: Wu Chengming, *op. cit.*, p. 77

As shown in Table 4.4, in 1902, Great Britain, France, and Germany were China's three major creditors. In 1914 loans from France and Germany were increased substantially although Great Britain remained the leading creditor. In the 1910s competition for giving loans to China was keen. Japan and the United States increasingly became involved in the competition. This situation can be seen clearly in 1930 when Japan emerged as the leading creditor with a total loan of US$373.3 million, about ten times that of 1914. The United States had US$50.8 million, about seven times that of 1914. In contrast, the loans from Great Britain, France, Germany decreased. This reflected the competition among major powers in the expansion of their economic and political interests in China.

[43]Wu Chengming, *op. cit.*, p. 76.

Foreign Direct Business Investments

Foreign direct business investments were investments of foreign capital in various enterprises. The capital was brought in by foreigners who were themselves in China or who represented persons or corporations outside of China. Before the 1895 Sino-Japanese war, there was a small number of foreign firms conducting shipping, shipbuilding and trade business in China. Most of them were located in treaty ports. After the war, there was a drastic increase of foreign manufacturing and factories due to government permission for foreigners to establish factories in China. As a result, foreign capital for manufacturing industries was drawn to China.

Direct investments by the major powers in China between 1910-1930 included various enterprises such as banking, trading, transportation, utilities, railroads, manufacturing, etc. For a general understanding of the development of foreign direct investments in China, we may look into the distribution of capital in direct investment among six major powers. As shown in Table 4.5, in 1902 Great Britain and Russia were the two major investors in China. Great Britain rose to the leading position in 1914, showing a sharp increase in invested capital. Another remarkable development was the increase of Japanese investment in 1914 which was recorded at 210 million dollars, about 20% of the total investments. Between 1914 and 1931, Great Britain maintained its leading position. Japan and the United States showed significant increases in their percentages of the total investments among the six countries. Japan's investment increased to 36.9% in 1931 from 19.4% in 1914 while the United States went up to 6.3% from 3.9%. Russia, France, and Germany decreased their percentages of investment.

Table 4.5
BUSINESS INVESTMENTS IN CHINA BY COUNTRIES,
SHOWING PERCENTAGE DISTRIBUTION

	1902		1914		1931	
	Millions of U. S. dollars	*Per Cent of Total*	*Millions of U. S. dollars*	*Per Cent of Total*	*Millions of U. S. dollars*	*Per Cent of Total*
Great Britain	150.0	29.8	400.0	36.9	963.4	38.9
Japan	1.0	0.2	210.0	19.4	912.8	36.9
Russia	220.1	43.7	236.5	21.8	273.2	11.1
United States	17.5	3.5	42.0	3.9	155.1	6.3
France	29.6	5.9	60.0	5.5	95.0	3.8
Germany	85.0	16.9	136.0	12.5	75.0	3.0
	503.2	100.0	1,084.5	100.0	2,474.5	100.0

Source: *Foreign Investments in China, op. cit.*, p. 99.

In Remer's analysis, foreign investments contributed to the growth of the Chinese economy by providing capital and technological know-how to early industrial development. The Chinese economy entered a new era of industrial development with the introduction of modern types of organization and management, Remer argued that capital for Chinese was of fundamental importance and that capital had to come in large part from outside the country due to the poverty of the Chinese people.[44] Hou Chi-ming (1964) believed that foreign investment encouraged economic modernization. Among others, Hou states that the most obvious link between foreign investments and China's economic modernization was that investment not only performed the pioneering entrepeneurial function of introducing modern technology into a number of fields but actually financed a large share of the modern sector of the economy.[45] In his opinion, railroads, coal mining and pig iron were dependent upon foreign finance, even up to 1937. In manufacturing industries such as shipbuilding, sawmills, and electric works, foreign-owned factories accounted for more than 50 per cent of the total output in 1933. Of course, the growth of the modern sector of the Chinese economy was not the product of foreign capital alone. The role of foreign capital, however, in financing industries and business and in introducing modern management of business organizations, as well as fundamental technology, undeniably was constructive in the development of the Chinese economy.

It was well-known that during this period foreign enterprises as a whole were stronger financially than their Chinese counterparts. This may have been because of larger amounts of capital or because of their ability to borrow from foreign sources at lower rates or because they had better management. In addition, foreign enterprises enjoyed extraterritorial rights which exempted them from Chinese taxes and levies. With these advantages and privileges, foreign enterprises invariably threatened the very existence of their Chinese counterparts. The Chinese gentry class and merchants increasingly perceived these foreign enterprises and investments as a serious threat to Chinese enterprises.

Together with the rise of nationalism in the 1920s, hostility towards foreign enterprises emerged first among the merchant and gentry classes and later among the workers.[46] This development of antagonism against foreign investments aggravated already prevailing antiforeignism and reflected the economic aspect of anti-imperialism. Thus, the sentiment of anti-imperialism in the decade from 1920-1930 was an expression of the nationalistic fervor of the gentry and merchant classes opposing foreign investments.

[44] C. F. Remer, *Foreign Investment in China, op. cit.*, pp. 685-689.
[45] Hou Chi-ming, *op. cit.*, p. 127.
[46] Hu Sheng, *op. cit.*, pp. 163-170.

The impact of foreign investments on China's economy has been a complicated issue. It was one of the major issues under attack in the period of the May Fourth Movement. Like nationalists elsewhere who condemned colonialism in Africa and Asia, nationalistic politicians such as Sun Yat-sen and Chiang Kai-shek denounced these foreign investments in the 1910s and 1920s as exploitative and repressive. They claimed these investments severely damaged the Chinese economy.[47] The Communists attacked these direct investments from a different angle. For example, Mao Zedong declared that foreign factories repressed China's native industries and led to their decline. In 1939 in his "The Chinese Revolution and the CCP," Mao pointed out:

> The imperialist powers have gained control of all the important trading ports in China by these unequal treaties . . . They have also gained control of China's customs, foreign trade and communication. They have been able to dump their goods in China, turn her into a market for their industrial products, and at the same time subordinate her agriculture to their imperialist needs.
>
> The imperialist powers operate many enterprises in both light and heavy industry in China in order to utilize her raw materials and cheap labor on the spot, and they thereby directly exert economic pressure on China's national industry and obstruct the development of her productive force.[48]

Communist scholars also attributed the stagnant economy and the decline of the national economy in the late 1920s and early 1930s to foreign enterprises in China (see Table 4.6). Furthermore, Wang Jinyu pointed out that, after World War I, the imperialist powers resumed their aggressive activities in China and expanded their enterprises. This again exerted tremendous pressure on Chinese national industries. As a result, Chinese national industries declined substantially.[49]

The divergent views among scholars on the impact of foreign investments on the Chinese economy will probably never be reconciled. Remer's and Hou's arguments were based on their evaluation of the early developments in the Chinese economy. The importance of foreign capital and technology to modernization could not easily be denied. The question, however, raised by the Chinese was whether the Westerners brought more benefit than harm. The Chinese emphasized the destructive effects of foreign investment based on the interest gained by foreign countries. To a certain extent, it is true that foreign investments had some repressive effect upon the Chinese economy. This repressive relationship was inherent in the Sino-foreign economic relationship,

[47]See Sun Yat-sen, The Second Lecture of Nationalism in *San Min Zhuyi*, Taipei: Zheng Zhong Shuju, 1974, pp. 15-27.

[48]Mao Zedong, *Selected Works of Mao Zedong*, Peking: People's Publishing Co., 1967, p. 6311.

[49]Wang Jinyu, "China's National Industries during the Second Revolutionary War," Peking: *Xin Jian She*, 1953, December. Also see Wu Chengming, *op. cit.*, p. 113.

Table 4.6
DECLINE OF CHINESE NATIONAL INDUSTRIES

	Factories Established	Index	Registered Capital (in 1,000)
1928	250	100	117,843
1929	180	72	64.023
1930	119	47.6	44,947
1931	113	45.2	27,691
1932	87	34.8	14,585

Source: See Wu Chengming, op. cit., p. 75.

owing to the superior financial resources of the West. The most important factor, however, was that these relationships were protected by unequal treaties. Therefore, the condemnation of foreign investments went hand-in-hand with strong sentiments against unequal treaties. The fervor of anti-imperialism indicated the antagonism that resulted from the combination of both. Thus, the anti-imperialism movement included both political and economic aspects of antiforeignism which had not existed before the twentieth century.

Attacks on foreign investments in China were vehement in the 1920s and 1930s. They came from all levels of society. During the period of the May Fourth Movement, the voices of protest were mainly those of students and intellectuals, and these were joined by workers in Peking and Shanghai. Denunciation of foreign investment became a manifestation of nationalistic spirit.[50] In the 1920s both the KMT and the CCP championed nationalistic opposition to foreign investments. Their attitudes were strongly tinged with nationalist fervor. Both parties denounced the dominance of foreign investment in the Chinese economy, the control of maritime customs, and the protection of foreign enterprises under foreign laws and unequal treaties. These attacks were basically an extention of anti-imperialist fervor in the May Fourth Movement. In the 1920s and 1930s, however, foreign investment again became a nation-wide issue around which the KMT and the CCP struggled for leadership.[51]

[50] Chan Duanzhi, Wu Si Yung Dong Zhi Shi de Ping Jia (Assessment on the History of the May Fourth Movement), Shanghai: Shen He Shu Dien, 1935, pp. 225-243.
[51] Chow Tse-tsung, The May Fourth Movement, Stanford University Press, paperback edition, 1967, pp. 356-357.

Antiforeign Boycotts, 1908-1926

The period under study is generally considered a chaotic period during which China lacked an efficient central government. Politics in China were characterized by wars among warlords after 1911. None of the warlords had sufficient strength to set limits to the increasing foreign investments and political interference by foreign powers. This period was also characterized by the advance of Japanese political interest in China going hand in hand with its economic investments. Under such circumstances and together with the rise of nationalism, a political force emerged among people opposing injustice or "aggression" toward China committed by foreign powers. Because no government could protect them, the Chinese people began to search for methods to deal with the foreign powers themselves. If the period of 1908-1926 was the period in which the Chinese people learned to challenge "imperialism," it was also the period when they learned to mobilize themselves to resist foreign pressure.[52] Antiforeign boycotts were the most concrete demonstration of anti-imperialist sentiment in China during this period.

As seen in the preceding section, the Chinese gentry and merchants were able to organize a movement resisting Russia in 1901, and boycotts to protect American discrimination against Chinese immigrants in immigration laws in 1905. As the Japanese pushed further into China, boycotts against Japanese commodities increased in China. In the 1910s and 1920s there were a few large scale boycotts in protest against the Japanese. In response to Japan's pursuit of her interests in China, the Chinese masses became increasingly hostile.

The Boycott Against Japan, 1908

The first boycott against the Japanese took place in March, 1908. The cause for this boycott was the discontent of the people of Southern China over the arrogant Japanese manner in dealing with the "Tatsu Maru" incident. The "Tatsu Maru" was a Japanese ship seized by Chinese officials on the ground that contraband arms and munitions had been found aboard. The Japanese government immediately denounced the seizure as illegal and demanded the release of the "Tatsu Maru," the payment of an indemnity, and an apology by the Chinese government for its treatment of the Japanese flag. The Chinese government gave in to the Japanese demands.[53] This resulted in a tremendous outburst of resentment in Canton, and the guilds and merchants of that city declared a boycott of Japanese products in retaliation for the Japanese

[52] Ding Shouhe and Yin Xuyi, *Cun Wusi Qimen Yungdong Dao Makesi Zhuji de Chuangbo* (From May Fourth Movement to the Spread of Marxism), Peking: Sanlian Shudian, 1979, pp. 88-129.
[53] C. F. Remer, *A Study of Chinese Boycott, op. cit.*, p. 41.

demands. Some merchants burned Japanese merchandise which they had on hand. Shipments of Japanese products were delayed in Canton and Hong Kong.[54] In May, Chinese newspapers were full of news about the boycott, which spread in the South. The boycott continued in force. As late as November, even, a riot broke out in Hong Kong over a dispute arising from the boycott.

The importance of this boycott lies in the increasing concern of the people with foreign relations. Antagonistic sentiments rose when the people saw their incompetent government give in to foreign pressure. At the time, the imperial government was paralyzed by the political and economic interests of the major powers. Financially, it was heavily in debt to foreign powers. Under such circumstances, the central government was reluctant to back up local governments in negotiating with foreign countries in defense of local interests. The boycott of 1908, like the boycott against American goods in 1905, showed that merchants were very concerned with Sino-foreign relations.

The Boycott Against Japan, 1915:

If the period from 1900 to 1911 saw the early development of Chinese nationalism, then the period of the 1910s and 1920s can be seen as the high-tide of nationalism. Soon after the fall of the Qing dynasty, China was divided by warlords. It is noteworthy that Chinese nationalism continued to expand and to awaken the consciousness of the people in spite of the weak central core of national leadership. One important factor in this development was the increasing activity by foreign powers, particularly Japan. The threat from outisde stimulated the people to sustain their nationalism and, as a result, stirred up fervid anti-imperialism. This was the case in the 1915 boycott against Japan. In early 1915, as soon as the Japanese government presented the Twenty-one Demands to Yuan Shih-k'ai, various movements to resist the demands originated in Shanghai and other major cities.

The Twenty-one Demands were directed at putting Manchuria and the lower Yangtze Valley under Japanese control. Yuan Shih-k'ai was under tremendous pressure from Japan. When a Japanese ultimatum forced Yuan to accede, a vigorous nation-wide boycott soon developed. The boycotts spread from Andong and Dalian in Manchuria to Fuzhou and Canton in the south, from Chongqing in Sichuan to the eastern cities of Hangzhou and Ningbo, to say nothing of the major cities such as Peking, Shanghai, and Tientsin. Together with the boycott, a movement 'to buy Chinese goods' also developed. The boycott lasted from April to August of that year.

The 1915 boycott manifested the concern of Chinese people over attempted

---

[54] Far Eastern Review, "The History of Boycott and the Economic Impact of Boycott on Japanese Products," trans. in *Dong Fang Za Zhi*, Shanghai, 1929, vol. 26, no. 3, p. 53.

Japanese aggression. It fully reflected the intensity of nationalism in China during the period. Unlike the 1905 boycott against America, the 1915 boycott spread to most of the important areas of China. Various patriotic organizations such as the 'Citizen's Patriotic Society' and the 'Society to Propagate the Use of National Goods' were formed by various elements in Shanghai.[55] Thus, a greater mobilization of mass opposition grew and expanded along with the full development of nationalism.

Anti-Japanese Boycotts in the 1920s:

Although the boycott of 1915 appeared to die out in the fall, antiforeignism did not decline with it. The period was followed by the so-called 'May Fourth Movement Period'. This New Culture Movement was triggered by prestigious scholars such as Li Dazhao (Li Ta-chao), Chen Duxiu (Chen Tu-hsiu), Hu Shi and Cai Yuanpei (Tsai Yuan-p'ei), and a great number of students in Peking and Shanghai. During this period Chinese culture and tradition were reassessed. Voices of intellectuals and students were widely raised calling for an end to foreign influence and interference. A series of student movements was launched.[56] It is not surprising that students played a leading role in boycotts during this period. In fact, boycotts against Japanese commodities continued throughout the 1920s and further expanded in the 1930s.

Boycotts in the 1920s may be examined according to their immediate causes. There were at least five boycotts directed against Japan and one of them was also against Britain. The first boycott was directly caused by the May Fourth incident of 1919 which opposed the transfer of German rights in Shandong to the Japanese as decided by the Peace Conference in Versailles. Students in Peking launched a strike and organized mass meetings on May 4. A boycott against Japanese goods was announced on the same day. It was soon followed by student-organized boycotts in Shanghai, Tientsin, Nanjing, Canton, and other large cities. A few days later, the Chamber of Commerce of Peking and chambers of commerce throughout the country declared an anti-Japanese boycott to remain in effect until Jiaozhou was returned.[57] These boycotts were much larger in scale than previous ones. There was little pause in anti-Japanese agitation in 1920. The boycott extended from cities to towns and villages in Central and Southern China. During the Washington Conference in which the Shandong issue was negotiated, many demonstrations by students took place in Shanghai, Peking, Tientsin and

---

[55] *Ibid.*, p. 57.
[56] Chow Tse-tsung, *The May Fourth Movement, op. cit.*, pp. 117-144.
[57] "Merchants Strike in Shanghai," *The North-China Herald*, CXXXI, 2704, (Shanghai, June 7, 1919), p. 650.

Hankou.[58] When the Japanese handed over their rights in Shangdong to the Chinese administration, the boycott gradually lost its original impetus and declined in the middle of 1921.

The boycott of 1919-1921 provides an important clue towards understanding the Chinese nationalist movement during the period. Its remarkable developments characterize the Chinese antiforeign movement. In the first place, the participation of students helped mobilize people in support of the boycott. Earlier boycotts, although supported by some student organizations, were mainly backed up by chambers of commerce and similar organizations. This illustrates the progression from merchant-initiated antiforeignism to student-led antiforeignism. In the second place, the boycott of 1919-1921 carried the boycott deeper into society, and was extended to areas outside large cities. As a result, it received much more effective support from consumers. This was apparently due to the widely-propagated anti-Japanese sentiment aroused by the students. Another characteristic was the great enthusiasm demonstrated by the propaganda against the Japanese.[59] It lasted nearly three years until the withdrawal of the Japanese from Shandong. The people awakened to the dangers of foreign aggression, spontaneously mobilized themselves to oppose foreign domination of China when the government had failed to do so.

The second boycott took place in March of 1923 in a revival of the controversy over the Liaodong Peninsula. A note asking the Japanese government for the return of Dalian and Lushun (Port Arthur) to China was rejected. In support of the demand made by the Peking government, more than 50,000 students assembled in Shanghai to protest against Japan's decision not to return the leased territory. The meeting also declared a boycott of Japanese goods. The boycott first spread to major cities such as Hankou and Wuchang and later to other large cities particularly those in the Yangtze Valley and in the North. The boycott was intensified by the Humiliation Day Commemoration on May 7 and May 9. Japanese shipments were halted on the Yangtze River as anti-Japanese agitation spread throughout the area. The protest lasted through July and declined in August. The boycott, like the boycott of 1919-1921, was led by students and was supported by chambers of commerce.[60] It was organized to support the demand made by the Chinese government.

The Boycott of 1925 and 1926:

The year 1925 saw changes in the leadership and methods of boycotts. In

[58]*Wu Si Yun Dong Hui Yi Lu* (Memoirs of the May Fourth Movement), Peking: Zhong Guo She Hui Ke Xue Chu Ban She, 1979, pp. 70-85; 243-248; 255-261; 265-273.
[59]Chow Tse-chung, *The May Fourth Movement, op. cit.*, pp. 99-116.
[60]Hou Chi-min, *op. cit.*, p. 151.

1925 and 1926, there were three interrelated boycotts. The first boycott directed against the Japanese, was in support of a labor dispute in Shanghai. A strike was launched by 70,000 workers. The boycott began at the end of May and continued until the end of September. The second boycott, against British goods, was caused by the shooting of several Chinese in Hankou on June 12, 1925, when they attacked the British armory, and by the Shameen incident in Canton where British guards fired on Chinese demonstrators and killed forty Chinese in late June. The third boycott started at the end of June and was directed against the British in Hong Kong. It continued through a large part of 1926 and did not come to an end until mid-October.[61]

The important feature of the boycotts during 1925 was the alignment of the students with laborers in Shanghai. It was the first time workers were involved in the struggle with foreigners. In both the anti-Japanese boycott and the anti-British boycott the workers refused to work in Japanese and British cotton mills, to man their ships, or to unload their cargo. The strike became a powerful weapon and made the boycott effective. This new relation between students and laborers reflected the continuous development of antiforeign boycotts and the influence of the KMT and the Communists. Another important development in the boycotts of 1925 and 1926 was the involvement of the KMT. This was particularly clear in the boycott against the British in Hong Kong. Although it initially had the support of merchants and students, it was later dominated by the KMT. The boycott did not end until the KMT decided to end it.[62] This indicates that the KMT had created the organizations in control of this mass movement as well as the labor organization, and had also planned to play a leading role in the boycott. The anti-Japanese and anti-British sentiments extended into 1927. In fact, antiforeignism grew even stronger in 1927 due to the Northern Expedition and the KMT's campaign for an anti-imperialist movement. A number of riots, strikes, and boycotts occurred as a result of conflicts between Chinese and foreigners and, more importantly, as a result of clashes of KMT troops with British and Japanese troops. The clash between British and KMT troops in Shanghai led to an anti-British boycott in April. [63] The most serious boycott, however, was the anti-Japanese boycott caused by the landing of Japanese marines at Hankou in April.[64] In Shanghai and Canton there were strikes against Japanese goods. Railroad workers refused to transport Japanese goods in June. Later, the strike spread to Manchuria where a large anti-Japanese movement was taking place.

[61] "The History of Boycott and the Economic Impact of Boycott on Japanese Products," *Dong Fang Za Zhi*, Shanghai, vol. 26, no. 3, *op. cit.*, pp. 64-65.
[62] C. F. Remer, *A Study of Chinese Boycott, op. cit.*, pp. 106-107; 109-110.
[63] *Ibid.*, pp. 128-132.
[64] *Ibid.*, p. 132.

It is noteworthy that antiforeign boycotts were first organized by merchants or chambers of commerce in large cities and only later became a major approach of the people towards opposing foreigners. Granted the strong sense of nationalism in the 1920s, almost any conflict between Chinese and foreigners which resulted in casualties would lead to a boycott. These boycotts, as well as strikes, dealt a serious blow to foreign trade, as can be clearly seen in Table 4.7. Although many factors influenced Sino-Japanese trade throughout this period, the boycotts had negative effects upon Japanese exports in 1908, 1909, 1915 and 1921-1924.

Table 4.7
ANTI-JAPANESE MOVEMENT AND JAPAN-CHINA TRADE
1907-1926
(in 1,000 Japanese Yuan)

Year	Japanese Export to China	Japanese Import from China	Total
1907	85,619	59,182	144,801
*1908	60,505	50,966	111,472
*1909	73,087	46,886	119,973
1910	90,037	68,569	158,606
1911	88,152	61,999	150,151
1912	114,823	54,807	169,630
1913	154,660	61,223	215,883
1914	162,370	58,305	220,675
*1915	141,122	85,847	226,969
1916	192,712	108,638	301,350
1917	318,380	133,271	451,651
1918	359,150	281,707	640,857
1919	447,049	322,100	769,149
1920	410,270	218,090	628,360
*1921	287,227	191,678	478,905
*1922	333,520	186,344	519,864
*1923	272,190	204,678	476,868
*1924	348,398	237,543	585,941
1925	468,438	214,657	683,095
1926	421,861	239,410	661,271

*shows serious effects by boycott.
Sources: *Dongfang Za Zhi*, vol. 26, no. 3 (February 10, 1929), p. 65.

Politically, the most important development was the increasing participation of the laborers and students. Students had been activists in the May Fourth Movement and afterwards they continued to play an important role in antiforeign movements, whether in boycotts or strikes. The participation of the workers, however, was not seen until 1925. This was due to the late development of antiforeign sentiment among workers and the indirect impact on their lives of intermittent boycotts. The late participation of workers calls into question the credit given by Mao and leftist authors to workers in the antiforeign movement.[65] The explanation for the early involvement of the merchants is that the boycotts could eliminate foreign goods from the market place. This reduced the pressure of foreign goods and improved the competitive position of local goods in the market. Thus, merchants were keener in opposing foreign investment than workers.

Summary

Chinese nationalism emerged in the early twentieth century from antiforeignism. This antiforeignism took two forms: one was the boycott against foreign goods; the other was the movement for the recovery of national rights. Both of these actions, in turn, continuously reintensified nationalsim.

This antiforeignism differed from that of the late nineteenth century in the following ways: twentieth-century antiforeignism interacted with nationalism whereas late nineteenth-century antiforeignism was fueled by ethnic and cultural conflicts. Second, antiforeignism in the early twentieth century involved a greater number and variety of people and became a nation-wide movement whereas nineteenth century antiforeignism was scattered and related to local or regional incidents. Third, antiforeignism in the early twentieth century was constructive in the pursuit of national interests and was no longer oriented towards the expulsion of foreigners from China; instead it was part of the struggle for national equality and independence.

In spite of the Chinese struggle for national equality and independence, foreign influence on Chinese politics and the economy was not reduced. On the contrary, foreign investment and loans to China increased rapidly and political dominance by foreign governments remained in force. The Chinese people fought against such foreign political and economic dominance and continued to organize boycotts to oppose it. Merchants, workers, students and intellectuals were involved in the boycotts. These antiforeign boycotts were an important form of resistance, on the part of the people, to foreign dominance at a time when the Chinese authorities, because they were divided, were unable to control it.

---

[65] *Selected Works of Mao Tse-tung*, vol. II, 1967, Peking: Foreign Languages Press, p. 325.

CHAPTER 5

Kuomintang and Anti-imperialism, 1927-45

The KMT emerged as an important political party in the early twentieth century and led the revolutionaries in the overthrow of the Manchu government in 1911. Sun Yat-sen, the founder of the KMT, vowed to unify China and to build a 'new China' based on his *San Min Zhuyi* (*San Min Chu I*). Up to his death in 1925, Sun was perennially frustrated with the political situation of China which was divided and controlled by warlords. During his last two years Sun vehemently attacked imperialists and their interference in China's politics. Specifically, he advocated that unequal treaties, tariff restrictions, and foreign concessions should be relinquished in order to recover China's national independence and sovereignty.

This chapter will first deal with the unequal treaties, the KMT leaders' concepts and theories toward imperialism, antiforeign mass movements, and the policy which evolved regarding the Japanese invasion. Finally, there will be a discussion of the concrete efforts to regain national independence and sovereignty through the relinquishing of tariff restrictions, unequal treaties and foreign concessions.

Tariff Restriction and Unequal Treaties in China

China had suffered tariff restrictions since the Anglo-Chinese wars in the middle of the 19th century. Tariff restrictions limited Chinese customs duties to five per cent and allowed changes in the rate conditional upon the consent of all the treaty powers. Under the Treaty of Tientsin in 1901, China pledged her customs revenue as security for the Boxer Indemnity. The Treaty also forced China to accept foreign management of her customs collections. Tariff rates were fixed by unequal treaties and revenue went into the hands of foreign governments. This situation was hotly protested against by public opinion in China as "economic aggression by the imperialists."

Tariff autonomy could not only increase the revenues of the Chinese government but also protect local products from foreign dumping. The autonomy issue was raised in vain by China's delegation at the Paris Conference of 1919 and again at the Washington Disarmament Conference of 1921-22. The Washington Conference appointed a commission for the further study of this problem. The commission did not meet until 1925 and failed to agree upon a report.

Extraterritoriality was a symbol of imperialist aggression. Before the downfall of the Manchu government in 1911, a great number of foreign governments obtained concessions and extraterritoriality in China. From the late 1910s, there was increasing condemnation of unequal treaties and extra-territoriality. The Chinese officials and people attributed extraterritoriality to the "Imperialistic oppression" of the foreign powers, as perpetuated in the unequal treaties. It was described as a "legacy of the old dynasty" that "has not only ceased to be adaptable to present day conditions, but has become detrimental to the smooth working of the judicial and administrative system of China." It was denounced as an unwarranted limitation of China's sovereignty, which should be relinquished in order to readjust China's inter-national relations "on a basis of friendly equality in matters of jurisdiction."[1]

The growing domestic pressure against the unequal treaties and extra-territoriality had no effect on the international scene. This issue was also raised at the Peace Conference at Versailles in 1919, but failed to obtain support from the major powers. Due to a growing attitude which attributed all the evils existing in China to the effects of extraterritoriality, the case was sub-mitted again to the Washington Conference on the Limitation of Armaments in 1921. No solution was worked out.

Sun Yat-sen's attitude toward unequal treaties and extraterritorial rights was strengthened after his contact with Adolf A. Joffe, a Soviet envoy, in January, 1923. Joffe told Sun that the Russian Government was ready and willing to enter into negotiations with China on the basis of renunciation by Russia of all the treaties which the Tsarist government imposed on China, including the treaty and agreements relating to the Chinese Eastern Railway.[2] Sun's firm attitude was also shown in the Manifesto of the First National Congress of the KMT, January, 1924. In the Manifesto, the KMT championed a strong external policy relating to unequal treaties as follows:

(1) All unequal treaties such as those providing for leased territories, extraterritorial privileges, foreign control of the customs tariff, and exercise of political authority on Chinese territories which impair the sovereignty of the Chinese nation, should be abolished, and new treaties should be concluded on the basis of absolute equality and mutual respect for sovereign rights.

(2) All countries that are willing to abandon their special privileges in China and to abolish their treaties which impair Chinese sovereignty

---

[1] H.G.W. Woodhead, *Extraterritoriality in China*, Tientsin: Tientsin Press, Ltd., 1929, p. 2. For treaty provisions relating to extraterritoriality in China, see Thomas F. Millard, *The End of Extraterritoriality in China*, Shanghai: The A.B.C. Press, 1931, pp. 247-249 (Appendix H).

[2] Milton J. T. Shieh, *The Kuomintang: Selected Historical Documents*, 1894-1969, New York: St. John's University Press, 1970, p. 72.

should be accorded most-favored-nation treatment.

(3) All other treaties between China and the foreign powers which are in any way prejudicial to the interests of China should be revised according to the principle of non-infringement of each other's sovereignty.

(4) The payments due on the refunding of the Boxer indemnity should be entirely devoted to educational purposes.

(5) As long as they do not impair China's political interest, the foreign loans made by China should be properly secured and repaid.

(6) Foreign loans contracted by irresponsible governments in China, such as the Peking regime founded on bribery and usurpation, were used, not to promote the welfare of the people, but to maintain the existence of the militarists or to further their policy of bribery and stealing. The people of China should not hold themselves responsible for the repayment of such debts.

(7) A conference consisting of delegates from social and commercial organizations, such as banks, chambers of commerce, and educational institutions, should be called to devise ways and means for the repayment of foreign loans, in order to free China from the semi-colonial status arising from economic bondage.[3]

The KMT's attitude toward unequal treaties showed impatience as the Northern Expedition started. In the Manifesto on the Northern Expedition, September, 1924, the KMT stated:

> We have entered the present civil war as fighters against militarism. After the battle is won our first duty will be to use the power of the Revolutionary Government to clean out all sinister influences of counter-revolution in order to prepare a clear road toward freedom and self-government. We shall then demand the revision of unequal treaties and the abolition of all special privileges in order to protect our national interests in foreign relations and to eradicate imperialist influence in China. New treaties will be concluded in accordance with the principles of international equality and mutual respect of sovereignty. After China has achieved her political equality, we may expect the following developments:
>
> 1. National freedom from external restrictions will enable China to develop her national economy and to increase her productivity . . .
> 2. After the abolition of unequal treaties, China's new laws will be applied throughout her territories, including the existing leased settlements; and in this way, nowhere will the counter-revolutionary influences find a stronghold for their sinister activities.[4]

---

[3] This translated text appears in Tyau Min-chien, (ed.), *Two Years of Nationalist China*, Shanghai: Kelly and Walsh, 1930, pp. 443-449 and pp. 29-33.

[4] This translated text appears in Leonard Hsu's book, *Sun Yat-sen*, Los Angeles: University of Southern California, 1933, pp. 142-145.

Foreign concessions and settlements were also objects of the Chinese protest. Their continued existence was opposed on the ground that they limited Chinese sovereignty. The Chinese authorities could not levy taxes within these areas without the consent of the municipal authorities. And Chinese citizens could be arrested there only after a warrant was countersigned by a foreign consular official. It was widely and ardently believed that the existence of foreign-controlled municipalities on Chinese soil was an encroachment upon Chinese sovereignty.

When Wang Chonghui presented his arguments to the Washington Conference (1921-22), he pointed out:

> It is a further disadvantage to the Chinese that foreigners in China, under cover of extraterritoriality, claim immunity from local taxes and excise which the Chinese themselves are required to pay.[5]

The existence of these foreign concessions was based on unequal treaties and particularly on extraterritoriality. It would have been impossible for these foreign concessions to exist after the restoration of the territorial rights to Chinese control. Thus, abolition of extraterritorial rights would have substantially affected foreign properties and the security of foreigners. These considerations were the core of the issue. It was not surprising that governments which enjoyed extraterritorial rights resisted the Chinese demands.

Sun Yat-sen's Theory of Revolution and Anti-imperialism

Unlike most of his contemporaries, such as Kang Youwei and Liang Qichao, who advocated a reform of China under a constitutional monarchy, Sun represented a radical revolutionary stand which advocated the overthrow of the imperial system and the establishment of a republic in China. Despite the widespread antiforeign sentiment in the early twentieth century, there was no comprehensive investigation of the impact of the 'great powers' on China. In his 'Principles of Nationalism', which was adopted in 1894, emphasis was given to the overthrow of the Manchus rather than to the expulsion of Western dominance.[6] Thus, in 1912, after the abdication of the Manchu emperor, Sun Yat-sen declared that the principles of nationalism had been achieved. It is clear that during this period Sun's nationalism did not link imperialism and revolution. In the Manifesto on the Organization of the KMT, August, 1912, Sun pledged to maintain international peace through good

[5]Wesley R. Fishel, *The End of Extraterritoriality in China*, New York: Octagon Books, 1974, pp. 57-58. Also see H.G.W. Woodhead, *op. cit.*, p. 41.

[6]Zou Lu, *Zhong Guo Guo Min Dang Shi Lue* (The Brief History of Kuomintang), Chungking: Shangwu Publishing Co., 1944, p. 25.

faith in diplomacy and respect for the status quo and to devote the KMT exclusively to domestic reconstruction.[7] In the Manifesto of the KMT Platform, August, 1913, diplomacy was emphasized. The Manifesto stated:

> As a weak country, we should be adept in diplomacy in order to survive as a nation. In so doing, it is necessary to come to grips with the world situation. China has suffered many set-backs in her foreign relations simply because of ignorance in international affairs. Concessions have been made as a result of the intimidation of foreign powers. The subtlety of diplomatic practice is difficult to describe. However, the basic principles are: Establishing closer ties with friendly nations. In the present circumstances, China is not yet in a position to cope with the foreign powers effectively. So it is desirable to have them maintain their established policies without upsetting the status quo. Thus, we will be able to concentrate on our domestic reform. This plan on foreign policy represents the tenth stand of our Party political platform.[8]

Nationalist fervor was widespread in China during the May Fourth Movement. China awakened to a vigorous nationalistic sentiment and a new spirit. Generally, the May Fourth Movement has been defined as a nationalistic movement and intellectual revolution including a literary revolution, a new tide of thought, the student movement, the merchants and workers' strikes, and boycotts against Japan.[9] It reflected cultural, social, economic, and political problems in China during the period. It revealed internal confusion and external supression by the great powers. The movement was directly ignited by the May Fourth incident mentioned in the previous chapter which occurred in protest against the Shandong resolution of the Versailles Peace Conference in 1919. The anti-Japanese campaign was the underlying political force for this incident and the stimulus for nation-wide nationalistic fervor. Interpretations of the significance of the May Fourth Movement vary greatly because of different emphases. For the intellectual liberals such as Hu Shi and Jiang Menglin the May Fourth Movement was a "cultural movement." They emphasized the cultural aspects of language reform and the rise of humanism.[10] Jiang Menglin was also aware of the national sentiment aginst the aggression of the great powers. Jiang questioned, however, the value of the so-called New Cultural Movement. He also criticized those who did not pay due respect to traditional Chinese civilization. His attitude became the ideological mainstream of the KMT. However, Communist leaders such as Chen Duxiu and Li Dazhao regarded the May Fourth Movement as a movement "against aggression." They thought of it not merely as a patriotic

[7] Milton J. T. Shieh, *op. cit.*, p. 38.

[8] *Ibid.*, p. 51.

[9] Chow Tse-tsung, *The May Fourth Movement*, Stanford, Calif.: Stanford University Press, 1967 (paperback edition), pp. 2-6.

[10] *Ibid.*, p. 339.

movement but also as an aspiration towards human liberation.

Discussions of imperialism are also to be found among the writings of other KMT leaders such as Dai Jitao, Zhu Zhixin and Hu Hanmin. In the May Fourth Movement period, Dai stressed economic disorganization. According to Dai the invasion of Chinese markets by foreign goods and the intervention of foreign powers in the Chinese economy had led to the economic stagnation of China. However, in the later period he shifted his position closer to Chiang Kai-shek's and stressed Chinese tradition and adopted a rightist interpretation of the *San Min Zhuyi*.[11]

Zhu Zhixin, a revolutionary hero of the KMT, was an outspoken opponent of imperialism. In 1919 he held that imperialism aimed at extending one nation's power over other nations. According to Zhu, imperialism violated the principle of coexistence and necessarily involved aggression. He attributed the development of imperialism to militarism. When a state was threatened by a foreign aggressor it would mobilize its national resources to build up its military power in the name of self-defense. Since it would seem a great waste if the military power that had been built up were not utilized, imperialist conquests offered an outlet for military energy. Imperialism, therefore, was the ultimate development of militarism rather than, as Lenin maintained, the last phase of capitalism. Zhu maintained that nationalism, militarism and imperialism were related and that the antidote to imperialism was socialism. Socialism, according to Zhu, would promote national spirit without leading to later national conflicts.[12]

During the period of the May Fourth Movement from 1919 to 1921, none of Sun's writings directly accused the great powers of imperialism. Obviously, Sun's attitude toward the great powers was very cautious in this period.[13] On January 1, 1923, the Manifesto of the KMT modestly pointed out that the KMT would employ every effort to accomplish the revision of the treaties. It stressed that the KMT must enforce universal education as a means of improving the cultural level of the whole nation in order to get equal status recognition with the other peoples of the world. The text of the Manifesto reads:

> In accordance with the Principle of Nationalism our Party will continue to work for the removal of all inequalities of status between our nation and foreign powers and we shall continue to work also for the integration of all the people of our country as a single Chinese nation. With respect to the principle of the

---

[11] Chester C. Tan, *Chinese Political Thought in the Twentieth Century*, New York: Doubleday & Company, Inc., 1971, p. 177.

[12] *Ibid.*, p. 186.

[13] Lyon Sharman, *Sun Yat-sen, His Life and Its Meaning*, Stanford, Calif.: Stanford University Press, 1968 edition, pp. 216-219.

self-determination of peoples which has received increasing acceptance since the conclusion of the European War, we accept this principle as favorable to the development of all the peoples within the nation and we shall also work for recognized equality of status among the other peoples of the world. To achieve this goal we must enforce universal education as a means to improvement of the cultural level of the whole nation. We must also employ every effort to accomplish revision of the treaties in order to restore our nation to a position of freedom and equality with the international family.[14]

Sun and Adolf A. Joffe, an agent of the Comintern, met in mid-January, and on January 26, 1923, they issued a joint manifesto. Sun increased his attack on imperialism when he began cooperation with the Communists in 1924. Before this period Sun looked at the Chinese revolution only in its relation to China's internal problems. His attack on imperialism is seen in the Manifesto of the First Congress of the KMT in January 1924. He declared that unequal treaties which provided leased territories, extraterritoriality, and foreign control of the Chinese customs, should be abrogated. For the first time, Sun openly condemned collaboration between warlords and imperialists, and he attributed China's recurrent civil wars to conflicts of interest between the foreign powers. He regarded imperialist economic exploitation and foreign capital as the curses of Chinese industrialization. Along this line, he claimed that imperialism had reduced China to the status of a semi-colony and any struggle for national liberation had to be directed against these extraneous forces. However, unlike Lenin's theory that imperialism is the highest stage of capitalism, Sun saw it as a "policy of aggression upon other countries by means of political force." He attributed the First World War to the rivalry between Britain and Germany for control of the sea, and to the great powers' ambition to secure more territory.

Sun asserted that the chaos in China was accounted for by militarism and foreign imperialism and that, while the constant combination of the two had kept China in subjection, it had raised national sentiment against the foreign powers. More concretely, Sun considered imperialism as political expansion based upon military power. In the 1924 manifesto before the Northern Expedition, he further attacked foreign imperialists and their support to warlords. He stated:

> The counter-revolutionaries have been able to survive because of the support of foreign imperialists; there is abundant evidence to prove the truth of this statement. In 1913 when Yuan Shih-k'ai decided to suppress the revolutionary movement by force in order to make himself the emperor of China, the Consortium Loan of two hundred and fifty million pounds was put through; and so Yuan was given a huge sum for military expenditure.

---

[14]Milton J. T. Shieh, *op. cit.*, p. 69.

Afterward, throughout the regimes of Feng Guozhang and Xu Shichang, each period of civil war was preceded by a hugh foreign loan. Recently, just as Cao Kun and Wu Peifu decided to send a punitive expedition to the southeastern provinces, the Gold Franc Case, which had been pending for a long time, was suddenly settled. All these facts serve to show without the least doubt that the direct cause of our civil wars during the last thirteen years has been militarism, and the indirect cause has been imperialism . . .

Moreover, this war is not only directed against militarism, but also against imperialism, whose support has made the existence of militarism possible. Not until then will the root of the counter-revolution be permanently eradicated and China elevated from the position of a sub-colony to that of a free, independent nation.[15]

Thus during this later years Sun's nationalism was directed against foreign aggressors. He thought that to obtain independence and equality, China had to free herself from the imperialist yoke, to recover her lost territory and sovereignty, and to unify the separate elements and create a sense of solidarity among her people. The blame placed on "foreign imperialism" for China's republican failure made Sun a symbol of anti-imperialism and a national hero.[16] This new standpoint clearly departed from his previous claim that world peace and friendly relations should be maintained between nations.

Sun linked the recurrent wars to the fact that all the peoples of Europe were imbued with the policy of imperialism. War was a conflict of imperialism between states. "So the effect of the war was merely the overthrow of one imperialism by another imperialism; what survives is still imperialism."[17] He saw that the only approach to fighting imperialism was to revive China's lost nationalism and "to use the strength of our four hundred millions to fight for mankind against injustice; this is our divine mission."[18] Thus Sun's approach to counter imperialism was to revive nationalism in China. This is clearly stated in Lecture Five delivered on February 24, 1924. Sun pointed out: "If we do not find some means to recover our lost nationalism, then China will not only perish as a nation but also perhaps as a race."

Sun proposed two methods to revive nationalism in China, the first would be to awaken the four hundred million people to see where they stood. They must be made to understand China's danger in the face of political and economic oppression by the great powers and the rapid growth of population among the powers. "These three disasters," according to Sun, "are already

[15]*Ibid.*, p. 88.

[16]C. Martin Wilbur, *Sun Yat-sen: Frustrated Patriot*, New York: Columbia University Press, 1976, pp. 199-204.

[17]*San Min Chu I*, Taipei: China Publishing Co., 1974, p. 43.

[18]Harold Z. Schiffrin, *Sun Yat-sen and the Origins of the Chinese Revolution*, Berkeley, Los Angeles: University of California Press, 1968, pp. 287-288. Also see *San Min Chu I, op. cit.*, p. 24.

upon our heads, and our people are in a most dangerous situation." He quoted the Chinese sayings, "A nation without foreign foes and outside dangers will always be ruined," and "many adversities will revive a state."[19] He believed that if a nation thinks that it has no outside dangers, that it is perfectly secure, that it is the strongest country in the world and foreigners would not dare to invade it, and that defense is therefore unnecessary, such a nation will crumble. As a Chinese proverb says, "The desperate beast can yet fight." He said: "When we are driven to no place of escape, then we have to raise our energies to a life and death struggle with our enemies."

The second method to revive nationalism, according to Sun, was unity. He said that the Chinese people had never had national unity but rather the unity of family and clan groups. "If we want to recover our lost nationalism," he declared, "we must have some kind of group unity, large group unity." Therefore, he suggested bringing about the unity of a large group on the foundation of small united groups, i.e., the clan groups and the family groups. If the Chinese could cooperate to achieve unity, according to Sun, it should be easy for them to revive their nationalism. "If the whole body of citizens can realize a great national unity upon the basis of our clan groups, no matter what pressure foreign nations bring upon us, we will not fear." So the fundamental way to save China from her imminent destruction would be to attain unity.

Sun's theory is one of the earliest suggestions of an approach to countering imperialism. His major concern was to build a strong, unified China to stand up against foreign powers. In sum, he believed that imperialist policies aimed against China by the great powers could be diverted once the Chinese were awakened to the danger of foreign oppression and threats, and nationalism had emerged. He was optimistic about future unity among Chinese. His anti-imperialist sentiments were aimed at the unification of China. He did not, however, suggest how the imperialists might be expelled from China. Neither did he suggest how to cope with imperialism after China had achieved its independence.

The KMT's Anti-imperialism after Sun Yat-sen

Sun Yat-sen's death left his Party with a legacy of determination to eliminate warlords and foreign intervention. At the second National Congress of the KMT, in January, 1926, a manifesto was announced setting forth three official policies of the KMT after Sun's death. First of all, the policy of anti-imperialism was strongly maintained. The manifesto stated that China had lost its liberty and equality due to the bondage of the unequal treaties. "What

[19] *San Min Chu I, op. cit.*, p. 29.

imposed the bondage of unequal treaties on China? It was imperialism." Therefore, the overthrow of imperialism should be the first task of the national revolution.[20] Secondly, the KMT clearly followed a pro-Soviet Union policy. Following Sun's view: "We must bring about a thorough awakening of our own people and ally ourselves in a common struggle with those people of the world who treat us on the basis of equality." The Manifesto pointed out that "among the nations which have treated us as equals and have defeated imperialism through their own efforts, thus, achieving a position of equality, is Soviet Russia." It further indicated that "our Party has cooperated sincerely with Soviet Russia." Despite the smears and provocations of imperialists and their tools, such as warlords, bureaucrats, and local despots, this collaboration has been continued." Thirdly, it declared that the foundations of imperialism had been shaken since the European war and that they have been beset by conflicts of interest, jealousies, and other frictions.[21]

Hu Hanmin was an important KMT leader competing for top leadership when Sun Yat-sen died. In his "The Interrelationships of the Three Principles of the People" (1928) he also discussed the development of imperialism. Hu saw militarism, capitalism, and bureaucracy as the three forces of imperialism and the desire of individuals for domination as the basic factor in each. Territorial expansion benefits both the economic interests of the capitalists and gratifies the vainglory of the militarists.[22] As Hu saw it, Sun's Three Principles were the best weapon against imperialism, because they took the nation as their basis and hit directly against individualism. According to Hu, modern history proves that whenever the individual is the basis of the state, nationalism degenerates into militarism, democracy into class politics, and the welfare state into capitalism. He felt that Communism and *San Min Zhuyi* shared a common goal—the establishment of a society in which all property belongs to the people and is used by the people for the people. But, he held, communism defeats its own end. It is based on class struggle and aims at establishing class rule—the dictatorship of the proletariat.[23]

Chiang Kai-shek was another leader competing for top leadership of the KMT. He was a graduate of Baoting Military Academy and spent four years at a military college in Tokyo. He took part in Republican revolutionary activities from 1911 to 1913, but his political career began when Sun appointed him President of the Whampoa Military Academy. After the victory of the Northern Expedition in 1928 he became one among a few important leaders in the KMT. In the early 1930s he shared power with Wang

[20] Milton, J. T. Shieh, *op. cit.*, p. 112.

[21] *Ibid.*, pp. 112-113.

[22] Chester C. Tan, *op. cit.*, p. 197.

[23] *Ibid.*, p. 198.

Jingwei. Due to his military power, Chiang eventually emerged as the top leader in the mid-1930s. Japan's increasing aggression made him the indispensable leader of China. After becoming the "supreme national leader" Chiang accepted Sun Yat-sen's *San Min Zhuyi* as the fundamental guideline for governing China. In the face of increasing threats from Japan his most urgent task was to unify China through a strong government. He saw that an effective resistance against Japanese aggression would require the mobilization of all national resources under a centralized, powerful leadership. The war of resistance against Japan was a war of the *San Min Zhuyi* against belligerent imperialism.[24] As a national leader in China, Chiang's immediate concern in the period of resistance against Japan was to save China from Japanese occupation.

Chiang attributed the weakness and problems of China to unequal treaties which seriously affected her politics, law, economics, ethics, and psychology. Politically, Chiang believed, like Sun, that secret activities conducted by the imperialists had led to the wars among the warlords. Extraterritoriality and foreign leases provided the imperialists with places for espionage activities. Supplies of ammunition and privileges on railroads given to the imperialists encouraged and promoted the struggles among the warlords. Meanwhile, unequal treaties damaged China's national defence and law. For example, the Boxer Protocol gave foreign military vessels the right to enter some ports in China. Extraterritoriality gave the foreign consulates powers of judicial adjudication in the areas of foreign leases. As a result the Chinese government lost its power to maintain law and order in these areas.[25]

Economically, Chiang asserted that unequal treaties damaged China's economy. The unequal treaties provided the foreign powers with the right to navigate inland areas, to construct railroads, to exploit mines, to issue currency, and to trade and build factories in coastal areas. These rights hampered economic production in China and assured the control of the national economy by foreign powers.[26]

Moreover, Chiang also pointed out the serious effects wrought by unequal

[24] Chiang Kai-shek, "Yao Di Kang Ri Ben Di Guo Zhu Yi Bi Xian Yao Di Kang Ri Ben Wu Shi Dao De Jing Shen" (Resisting Japanese Imperialism One Must First Resist the Japanese Samurai Spirit), in Bei Hua (ed.), *Kan Zhan Yu Ge Ming* (War of Resistance and Revolution), Shanghai: Meishang Yuan Dong Hua Bao She, 1939, pp. 48-64.

[25] Chiang Kai-shek, *Zhong Guo Zhi Ming Yung* China's Destiny), Taipei: Chen Chung Books Co., 1975, reprint, pp. 49-55. For discussion of foreign lease in China see a case study in John E. Schrecker, *Imperialism and Chinese Nationalism: Germany in Stantung*, Cambridge, Mass.: Harvard University Press, 1971.

[26] *China's Destiny, op. cit.*, pp. 56-60. For mass responses to imperialism in 1920s. See Harold R. Isaacs, *The Tragedy of the Chinese Revolution*, second revised edition, New York: Atheneum, 1966, pp. 64-73.

treaties upon society, morality, and psychology. Due to unequal treaties, according to Chiang, rural life had declined while urban life had become over-developed. Clan and rural organizations had fallen apart. As a result, self-interest took the place of traditional self-respect and led to the decline of the virtue of mutual aid. A psychological effect of the unequal treaties was loss of confidence and respect among the Chinese people toward Chinese culture and tradition. Consequently, they welcomed Western culture and despised their own.[27] This was, according to Chiang, the crisis of cultural aggression and the most serious problem confronting the national spirit. Accordingly, he repeatedly urged the abrogation of the unequal treaties.

In order to cope with these problems caused by the unequal treaties, Chiang also urged reform in society and the revival of traditional virtues and the national spirit. He believed that the prerequisite for nation building was to revive Chinese traditional virtues and social norms in order to rebuild self-confidence and the social order. Thus, while urging revolution, social reform and movements to revive traditional virtues were the main work of his program.[28] In 1932, in his speech to the Central Political Academy, he stated that the most important condition for national survival was to develop self-confidence and that revitalizing the new Chinese nation and accomplishing the Chinese revolution should be preceded by a restoration of traditional morality.[29] In response to this belief, in 1934, he called for a "New Life Movement" urging the revival of the national 'soul' and the reestablishment of traditional virtues such as the Four Social Bonds and the Eight Virtues.[30] He tried to develop a new social consciousness and martial spirit through a revival of China's old moral virtues.

After the abrogation of the unequal treaties in 1943, Chiang reiterated the importance of internal unity. As he said, "China's destiny depended upon whether or not unequal treaties could be abrogated. Now they are abrogated, and China's destiny will depend upon whether we can unify ourselves in internal politics and the concentration of national power."[31]

[27] Ho Mingzhong, *Zhong Guo Chih Min Yung Te Zongho Yen Jiu* (A Comprehensive Research on China's Destiny), Suzhou, 1946, pp. 30-31.

[28] See Mary C. Wright, "From Revolution to Restoration," in Joseph R. Levenson, ed., *Modern China*, London: The MacMillan Co., pp. 99-113.

[29] Chiang Kai-shek, *Kang Zhan Yu Ge Ming* (War of Resistance and Revolution), 1938, Shanghai: Wenhua Bianyi Guan, vol. III, p. 4.

[30] Samuel C. Chu, "The New Life Movement before the Sino-Japanese Conflict: A Reflection of Kuomintang Limitation in Thought and Action," in *China at the Crossroads: Nationalists and Communists, 1927-1949*, (ed.) Gilbert Chan, Colorado: Westview Press, 1980, pp. 37-67.

[31] *China's Destiny, op. cit.*, p. 200. For Chiang's attitude toward the Communists and Japan, see Theodore White and Annalee Jocoby, *Thunder out of China*, New York: William Sloane Associates, 1946, pp. 33-47.

In foreign relations he asserted that national freedom and national equality should be applied in a post-war international organization and in the development for restoration of the culture and the economy. He stated that political, economic, or military aggression between nations and the subsequent relationships and institutions were the causes of war and that these causes of war constituted imperialism.[32] Thus, he urged that China should oppose any kind of imperialism in any part of the world. Like most people during this period, however, Chiang concentrated more on opposition to the Japanese than to imperialism in general. Both his anti-war sentiments and anti-imperialism derived from war devastation in China and the Chinese desire for peace.

KMT and Antiforeign Mass Movement

The period from 1927 to 1945 in China may be divided into two stages. The first stage from 1927 to 1937 was a decade characterized by the rise of Chiang Kai-shek after the Northern Expedition and by the increasing attacks by Japanese militarism. During this period, China remained divided by the warlords. The second stage was the war era; it was a period of full-scale war during which the Chinese were fighting against Japanese aggression. It is not in dispute that the great majority of the Chinese population suffered greatly during the war. Furthermore, politics in China were extremely complicated during the whole period from 1927 to 1945. Chiang Kai-shek faced both internal opponents and external enemies. Internally, Chiang was constantly struggling with the warlords and the Communists.[33] Externally, the KMT government vowed to restore China's sovereignty and to resist Japanese invaders.

Despite Chiang Kai-shek's victory in the Northern Expedition, China did not develop into a unified country in the late 1920s. The old warlords such as Yan Xishan, Feng Yuxiang, and Li Zongren still maintained their regional power bases. In addition, the KMT was plagued with factional struggles. Chiang Kai-shek, holding military power, struggled to establish leadership in the Party. He faced challenges, however, from senior leaders such as Hu Hanmin and Wang Jingwei. In other words, there was no single person capable of unifying different factions inside the KMT in the 1920s. Seeing this weakness in the Chinese political scene, Japanese militarists were encouraged to expand their forces in China.

---

[32] *China's Destiny, op. cit.*, p. 215.
[33] James S. Sheridan, *China In Disintegration*, New York: The Free Press, 1975, pp. 183-206.

Antiforeign mass activities continued to increase in China during the period from 1927 to 1937. As in the past, the Chinese people used boycotts to protest against foreign countries. In the late 1920s, the Nationalist government was not yet able to control all local activities protesting against foreign countries in spite of its growing power in central China. Nevertheless, KMT branches in major cities such as Peking, Shanghai, Tientsin, and Canton, always attempted to exercise leadership in antiforeign movements either openly or covertly. For example, in early 1927, strong anti-British feeling prevailed in Hankou and as a result a riot broke out between British marines and anti-British elements. Anti-British sentiment soon expanded to neighbouring areas in the Yangtze Valley where demonstrations were held in Jiujiang, Yichang, and Changsha. Pressure was so high that the British decided to evacuate these major cities. Boycotts were organized in Canton and Fuzhou in January. Laborers and students in Canton joined in these boycotts against the British. In March, a renewal of anti-British sentiment erupted in Shanghai, Canton and Fuzhou, when the British refused to recognize the Nationalist government in Canton.[34] At the end of March, 1927, the Nationalist troops entered Nanjing, and a flare-up of antiforeignism soon developed there. Meanwhile, a boycott against British goods was declared when a clash took place between the British troops and Shandong troops who attempted to enter Shanghai by force. Anti-British agitation was the main target for antiforeign activities in early 1927. The KMT, however, was not directly involved in the organization and leadership of these anti-British activities.

While Chinese nationalism continued to develop, the Japanese government was following a tough and expansionist policy in China. An accompanying shift of target in mass protest from the British to the Japanese took place in April, 1927 as a result of the landing of Japanese marines at Hankou. There was a series of demonstrations held there and in other cities such as Suzhou and Changsha. Boycotts against Japanese goods were organized again in Shanghai, Canton, Wuhu, and Amoy.[35] These boycotts resulted in a decrease of Japanese exports to China in the summer of 1927. In response to the increase of Japanese troops stationed along the Shanghai and the Shandong railroad from Jinan to Qingdao and to Japanese demands for the recognition of special interests in Manchuria, anti-Japanese sentiment rose rapidly. Japan became the major target of protest in the summer of 1927.

Anti-Japanese sentiment was renewed in 1928-29 as a result of a clash between Japanese troops and the Nationalist army at Jinan on May 3, 1928.

[34] C. F. Remer, *A Study of Chinese Boycotts*, Baltimore: The Johns Hopkins Press, 1933, p. 128.
[35] *Ibid.*, p. 130.

This incident led to a great number of casualties on both sides and, more significantly, a nation-wide denunciation of "Japanese imperialism" resulted. Boycotts were soon underway in major cities such as Shanghai, Canton, Nanjing and Shantou. In addition to boycotts, many seizures of Japanese goods were carried out. Anti-Japanese Societies in major cities played an active role in organizing these activities. The local KMT branch in Canton and Tientsin also organized boycott committees and led major anti-Japanese activities.[36] In early 1929, the strongest anti-Japanese sentiment came from Hankou where a Chinese laborer was killed by a Japanese marine in a traffic accident. A vigorous boycott was accompanied by a strike of Chinese workers employed by Japanese in Hankou. This movement soon spread to Tientsin and Shanghai, in February and March; some funds were collected to support strikes by the workers in Hankou.[37] The movement gradually quietened down in April and anti-Japanese sentiment was relaxed in the latter part of the year. The Japanese military advance in China, however, kept the sentiment alive throughout the 1930s.

In the period from 1931 to 1932, China was characterized by unprecedented anti-Japanese fervor and by increasing Japanese aggression. After 1931, a series of conflicts took place. The Wanbaoshan incident in 1931 created new tension between China and Japan. It resulted from a dispute in June between Chinese farmers and Korean immigrants at Wanbaoshan in Manchuria.[38] In July, a clash between the Chinese farmers and Japanese police took place and led to public resentment in China. In mid-July, a boycott was called by the Chinese Chamber of Commerce in Shanghai. With support from the Jiangsu Provincial KMT headquarters, the Shanghai KMT District, the labor unions and other organizations, the boycott soon became an effective movement in Shanghai. Similar developments took place in Tientsin, Hankou and Canton. Local KMT branches in these major cities played an active role in boycotts and demonstrated their leadership in the anti-Japanese movement.[39]

The Mukden incident, in September 1931, was a clear indication of Japan's aggressive policy towards China. On September 18, the Japanese launched a massive military attack at Mukden (Shenyang) and in the following days Japanese military forces occupied Southern Manchuria. The whole of Manchuria fell under the control of the Japanese forces. The Nanjing government and the Chinese authority in Manchuria under the warlord, Chang Xue-liang, were unable to take any effective action to stop the Japanese offensive.

[36] *Ibid.*, p. 137-138.
[37] *Ibid.*, p. 140.
[38] Fu Qixue, *Zhong Guo Wai Jiao Shi*, Taipei: Taiwan Commercial Press, 1972, vol. 2, p. 472.
[39] C. F. Remer, *op. cit.*, pp. 157-159.

In the face of increasing Japanese aggression in Manchuria, a nation-wide boycott was soon organized. Practically all of the major cities joined the anti-Japanese boycott within a few days of the Mukden incident. In late September, representatives of students, workers and guilds jointly launched a giant demonstration in Shanghai with the support of KMT branches.[40]

The Mukden incident caused wide-spread resentment against Japanese aggression in China. Antiforeign sentiment alone, however, did not serve the KMT as well as before. Many people became more determined to fight against the Japanese rather than against the communists. Soon after the Mukden incident, public opinion increasingly attacked the defensive policy of the KMT government (See next section). Students in Shanghai, Nanjing, and Peking petitioned the Nanjing government, demanding a war with Japan.[41] In December, 1931, students attacked KMT branch offices in Shanghai, Hangzhou and Wuhan. They posted slogans such as "down with the KMT" and "unite against imperialism." In early 1932, students in Peking refused to attend classes in protest against the Nanjing government. In April, students in Xian organized an Association for United Resistance against the Japanese and attacked the KMT branch office there.[42] These activities by the students clearly showed that the KMT could no longer control mass activities as it had before the Mukden incident.

The development of a mass movement against the KMT naturally pleased the Communists. The Chinese communists were confronted by the KMT's superior military forces when the Mukden incident took place. In February 1931, the Communists publicly urged the workers, soldiers, students and the armed masses to fight against the Japanese imperialists and the KMT.[43] After the Mukden incident, the CCP declared itself a patriotic force in resisting the "Japanese imperialists".[44] The CCP lost no opportunity to strengthen its penetration of various mass organizations. By 1935, the Communists were able to organize a number of student movements and workers' strikes in major cities. For example, in November and December, 1935, student organizations were formed with the support of the Communists in most of the major cities. These student organizations petitioned Chiang Kai-shek for a cessation of civil war between the KMT and the Communist forces and urged a joint resistance

---

[40] See Donald A. Jordan, "China's Vulnerability to Japanese Imperialism: The Anti-Japanese Boycott of 1931-1932," in Gilbert Chan (ed.), *op. cit.*, pp. 91-123.

[41] John Israel, *Student Nationalism in China, 1927-1937*, Stanford: Stanford University Press, 1966, pp. 47-86.

[42] Guo Tingyi, *Jin Dai Zhong Guo Shi Gang* (An Outline History of Modern China), Hong Kong: The Chinese University Press, 1979, p. 661.

[43] *Ibid.*, p. 640.

[44] *Ibid.*

against the Japanese invasion. A nation-wide student movement emerged. Students from Canton, Shanghai, Nanjing, Tientsin, Changsha, Wuhan, and Xian were involved in this movement.[45] The student movement became an important opinion group requesting a 'united front' in fighting against the Japanese. In May, 1936, students in Shanghai formed the National Salvation Association which urged the formation of a 'united force' against "Japanese imperialism."[46] The anti-Japanese mass sentiment finally drove the KMT and the CCP together in the wake of the Xian incident, of December, 1936. The Chinese Communists utilized anti-Japanese mass organizations to attract support from society. The antiforeign mass movement helped them expand tremendously. Throughout the Sino-Japanese war from 1937 to 1945, both the KMT and the CCP continuously competed for leadership in the mass organizations. Both parties had penetrated the masses before the second civil war broke out in 1947.

Kuomintang Policy Towards Japanese Invasion

The Mukden incident marked a new large-scale invasion by Japanese forces. Within a week, the whole of Manchuria was in the hands of the Japanese militarists. The Nationalist government protested against the bloody Japanese aggression and appealed to the League of Nations. No sign of Japanese withdrawal was shown in spite of these diplomatic efforts. During this same period, the Nationalist government was confronted by the expanding Communist forces. Between 1930 and 1934 Chiang launched five campaigns to exterminate the Communists but the Communists successfully escaped to Yanan and established a self-sufficient base there in December 1936. Although the Nationalist government decided to eliminate its domestic enemies before engaging itself in an external war, the Xian incident of December 1936 forced Chiang Kai-shek to form a "United Front" with the Communists in order to fight against the Japanese.

In order to reach an agreement with the KMT, the Communists offered four concessions in February, 1937:

1. To abandon the policy of armed insurrection to overthrow the National Government.
2. To reorganize the Soviet regime in Shanxi as the government of a 'Special Region' of the Republic of China, and to reorganize the Red Army as a unit of the national army, under the direction of the Nanjing Government and its military Council respectively.
3. To establish in the 'Special Region' a democratic system based on universal suffrage.
4. To stop the confiscation of landlords' land.[47]

---

[45] Guo Tingyi, *op. cit.*, p. 662.
[46] John Israel, *op. cit.*, pp. 131-132.
[47] Stuart Schram, *Mao Zedong*, Baltimore: Penguin Books, 1966, p. 200.

The Japanese militarists initiated the Marco Polo Bridge Incident in July 1937, taking massive military action to occupy northern China. In response to this increasing aggression, the KMT and the Communists reached an agreement on terms similar to those set out by the Communists. The second "United Front" between the KMT and the Communists was, in fact, expedited by Japanese aggression.

The incident at the Marco Polo Bridge in 1937 gave the Japanese militarists an excuse to occupy strategic areas outside Peking. The Nationalist government, however, had already determined to fight Japanese aggression following the United Front agreement with the Communists. On July 17, 1937, Chiang Kai-shek at a summer meeting at Lushan resolutely announced that China faced "a struggle for national survival," and ordered Chinese forces to resist Japanese aggression resolutely. He declared, "China will not give up hopes of peace until all hope is gone, China will not allow itself to be sacrificed and will fight to the last. . . . We will sacrifice ourselves and resist, because this is now inevitable." He announced; "Our attitude is to deal with war, but not initiate a war. . . . Once we get into war we will have no opportunity to negotiate because we are a weak country. . . . Then we will fight on for the final victory. . . ."[48]

The Communists under the leadership of Mao Zedong, supported Chiang's strong attitude towards Japanese aggression. They, however, showed impatience with Chiang's efforts in seeking negotiation. An announcement by the Politburo of the CCP, entitled "For the Mobilization of All the Nation's Forces for Victory in the War of Resistance," stated:

> The initial changes in the KMT's policy with the Xian Incident and the Third Plenary Session of its Central Executive Committee as their starting point, Mr. Chiang Kai-shek's Lushan statement of July 17 on the question of resistance to Japan, and many of his measures of national defence, all deserve commendation. The troops at the front, whether the land and air forces or the local armed units, have all fought courageously and demonstrated the heroic spirit of the Chinese nation. In the name of the national revolution, the CCP ardently salutes our patriotic troops and fellow-countrymen throughout China.
>
> But on the other hand, even after the Lugouqiao Incident of July 7 the KMT authorities are continuing to pursue the wrong policy they have pursued even since the September 18th Incident, making compromises and concessions, suppressing the zeal of the patriotic troops and clamping down on the patriotic people's national salvation movement.[49]

Chiang Kai-shek sought military withdrawal by the Japanese government through a peaceful approch in order to avoid a great war between the

---

[48] Fu Qixue, *op. cit.*, vol. 2, p. 580.

[49] *Selected Works of Mao Zedong*, vol. 2, Peking: Foreign Language Press, 1967, pp. 23-24.

two countries. His efforts were in vain. The Japanese opened a second front in Shanghai in August, and attacked Nanjing, the capital of the Nationalist government, in December. Nanjing fell in mid-December, 1937, with a notorious massacre of approximately 100,000 Chinese civilians. The Japanese government proposed to negotiate with China, but this offer was rejected by the Nationalist government. Then, the Japanese forces moved south where an important confrontation took place in the Wuhan area. On October 25, 1938, after several hundred encounters and clashes, the Nationalist forces were ordered to relinquish their bases after over four and a half months of resistance. At approximately the same time, the Japanese also occupied Canton. In occupying these major cities, the Japanese forces were compelled to divide themselves over widespread areas inside Chinese territory. The occupation took more than one year to achieve and made the original Japanese strategy for a quick victory impossible.

In December, the Japanese government proclaimed a "New Order in East Asia." The Japanese premier, Prince Konoe, attempted to end the war with the Nationalist government and offered three principles for negotiation. They were: friendship and amity; mutual defense against communism; and economic cooperation. Under the circumstances, the Nationalist government under the leadership of Chiang Kai-shek resolutely refused to negotiate with the Japanese government while the Japanese occupied a large area of Chinese territory.

Wang Jingwei, however, maintained that China should end the long war with Japan in order to avoid devastation. He urged the Nationalist government at Chongqing to accept the Japanese offer.[50] Chiang Kai-shek and his supporters refused any negotiation and expelled Wang from the Party. As a result, Wang fled from Chongqing and organized his own government at Nanjing and signed an agreement with Japan in March 1940.

The war continued and in July 1940, the Japanese again attempted to negotiate with the Nationalist government. The Japanese offered to withdraw from North China, but this was rejected by Chiang Kai-shek. One year later, in July, 1941, the Japanese government proposed the so-called "Lenient and Peaceful" terms as follows:

(1) No indemnity and territorial concessions.
(2) Withdrawal of Japanese forces from south of the Great Wall, recovery to the pre-1937 situation.
(3) Collaboration between the Nationalist government and Wang Jingwei's Nanjing government.
(4) Recognition of Manchuguo by the Nationalist government.[51]

[50]Fu Qixue, *op. cit.*, vol. 2, p. 596.
[51]*Ibid.*, vol. 2, pp. 602-605.

Chiang resolutely rejected these terms for the following reasons. First, the Japanese government's attitude was not consistent. The militarists did not share the opinion of the civilians for peaceful negotiations. There was no guarantee that the Japanese government was sincere in making peace. Secondly, Wang Jingwei was a traitor; his government was illegal. It was impossible for the Nationalist government to collaborate with Wang's Nanjing government. Thirdly, Manchuria was part of China. The Nationalist government would never recognize its independent status. Therefore, for the Nationalist government, it was not desirable to negotiate with the Japanese when large areas of Chinese territory were occupied by them. In addition to the reasons explained by Chiang Kai-shek, the Nationalist government had also improved its relations with the U. S. and Britain. In December 1940, the U. S. government approved a loan of 100 million dollars to China and the British government also provided ten million pounds in loans, so that China was no longer alone. These developments further discouraged Chiang Kai-shek from negotiating with the Japanese.

The Japanese attack on Pearl Harbour marked a new beginning for Chinese resistance to Japanese aggression. China formally announced war with Japan on December 9, 1941, two days after the Pearl Harbour attack. This ended China's long ordeal in isolation. After that China played an important role in the Pacific War. Chiang Kai-shek was appointed Supreme Commander of the Allied Powers in the China Region. In addition to providing loans and war materials to China, the Allies increasingly recognized China as a major power in the world. China's international status reached its climax when the Japanese surrendered in 1945.

Struggle for Independence and Sovereignty, 1927-1945

Sun Yat-sen and his successors had vowed to achieve national independence and equality by relinquishing unequal treaties. In July, 1927, the Nanjing Government declared that customs autonomy would be instituted by China on September 1, 1927. This was rejected by the foreign powers led by Japan. Due to the failure of this attempt, a different approach was taken in 1928. There was no more talk about a unilaterial action by China. Instead, C. T. Wang, the Foreign Minister, invited the powers to negotiate new treaties on the basis of complete equality and mutual respect for each other's sovereignty.[52]

The development of negotiations with the powers was very successful despite initial Japanese refusal to negotiate. The first favorable response came from Washington. In July, 1928 the U. S. government agreed to negotiate with China's delegate, T. V. Sung, then Finance Minister, and accepted the

[52] Hollington K. Tong, *Chiang Kai-shek*, Taipei: China Publishing Co., 1953, p. 168.

annulment of provisions concerning tariff rates in existing trade treaties and conceded China's tariff autonomy. Following American support to China's tariff autonomy, Great Britain, France, Germany, Italy, Norway, Denmark, Spain, Belgium, and Portugal also agreed to negotiate with China based on equal interest in the same year. Under such great pressure, Japan finally accepted China's demands and signed a new trade treaty with China, recognizing China's tariff autonomy. In March, 1929, China achieved a great success in the establishing of tariff autonomy. The Nationalist government and Chiang Kai-shek considered it a great victory in China's diplomatic history and in the struggle with imperialist foreign powers.[53]

In the eyes of the Chinese in 1927, foreign governments could be classified into four groups according to their positions in regard to extraterritoriality. The first group included governments which did not have extraterritorial rights in China. These countries were those which did not have any interest in China such as Turkey, Bulgaria, Romania, Albania and the South American states. The second group consisted of governments which previously enjoyed extraterritorial rights but had lost them after the First World War. These countries were Austria-Hungary, Germany and Russia. The third group of countries included those whose treaties with China had expired, and who had conditionally agreed to renounce their extraterritorial rights from January, 1930. These countries were Belgium, Italy, Portugal and Spain. None of them had substantial interests in China. In the fourth group were the so-called Powers. These countries refused to recognize China's right of unilateral abrogation; they were the United States, Brazil, France, Great Britain, Japan, Norway, the Netherlands, Sweden and Switzerland. C. T. Wang, the Minister for Foreign Affairs of the Nationalist Government, requested the British, American, Dutch, Norwegian and Brazilian envoys in China to relinquish extraterritorial rights in China in April, 1929. The British rejected the request on the grounds that the British government did not consider that conditions for the abolition of extraterritorial rights in China had been met.[54] The American reply also disappointed the Nationalist government in its refusal to relinquish extraterritoriality on the ground that there did not exist in China a system of independent Chinese courts, free from extraneous influence, which were capable of adequately doing justice between Chinese and foreign litigants.[55]

The issue of extraterritoriality was widely discussed in public and among Nationalist officials. For example, when Mr. Y. L. Tang, Vice Minister for Foreign Affairs, outlined the program of the Nationalist Government for

[53] Fu Qixue, *op. cit.*, vol. 2, pp. 393-397.
[54] H.G.W. Woodhead, *op. cit.*, p. 62.
[55] *Ibid.*, p. 65.

1929 he said that the year 1929 was to see the abolition of extraterritoriality, the abrogation of foreign coastal shipping privileges, the return of the foreign settlements and concessions, and the withdrawal of the foreign garrisons.[56] Many efforts were made to abolish foreign privileges in China, but little was achieved by the Nationalist Government. In fact, the abolition of these foreign privileges was completed only in 1941 and 1942 after the Nanjing government declared war against Japan after the Pearl Harbour incident. At least two reasons accounted for such disappointing developments between 1927 and 1940. The first reason was that China remained disunited, and it took some time for the Nanjing government to consolidate its power. As a matter of fact, a number of internal problems remained to be solved, such as the establishment of the authority of the Central Government over local areas and the development of the economy. China remained a weak country. The powers intended to delay the equality issue as long as these weaknesses of the Chinese government lasted. Secondly, the increasing aggression by the Japanese militarists distracted Chinese determination to negotiate with the other powers. Resistance to the Japanese military advance became the highest priority in China. Thus, the Nationalist government did not force other powers to relinquish their extraterritorial rights in China.

While the Sino-Japanse war brought great destruction to the country it did help the Nationalist government to abolish extraterritorial rights in China. After 1941 and Pearl Harbour, China became an important ally to the United States and Great Britain in the Pacific war against Japan. China's determined spirit in fighting Japanese militarism was highly respected in the West.[57] The American government approved an additional loan of US$500 million to the Nationalist government and the British government also provided a new loan of 50 million British pounds to China. These loans helped the Nationalist government to stabilize its economy. In addition, a great amount of materials and aid were brought to China. China's international status was raised to that of a major world power.[58] Consequently, a notice from the U. S. and British governments in October, 1942 informed the Nationalist government that both the U. S. and British governments had decided to give up all privileges and to conclude equal and reciprocal treaties with China.[59] The relinquishment of unequal treaties, foreign concessions, and other privileges was undoubtedly a great success for KMT war-time diplomacy. On the conclusion of new equal treaties with the United States and Great Britain in January 1943, Chiang Kai-shek broadcast to the country a message declaring the

[56] Ibid., p. 8.
[57] The China White Paper, Vol. I, Stanford University Press, 1967, p. 37.
[58] Ibid., pp. 28-33.
[59] Ibid., pp. 34-36.

significance of the victory which China had achieved. He said:

> "After fifty years of bloody revolution and five and a half years of a war of resistance, we have at last transformed the painful history of one hundred years of the unequal treaties into the glorious record of their abolition. . . . By doing so, the United Nations, who are our comrades-in-arms, have shown beyond peradventure that their object in this war is to fight for humanity and justice. . . . With our past humiliations wiped out and our independence and freedom regained, we can have the chance to make our country strong."[60]

Obviously, Chiang believed that the major aims of the Principle of Nationalism would be achieved when the Sino-Japanese War was over.

Summary

There is no dispute that the KMT was originally a revolutionary party that led the anti-imperialistic movements in the early twentieth century. Anti-imperialism was clearly defined in its platform as the goal of foreign policy. This goal was continuously pursued by Chiang Kai-shek after the death of Sun Yat-sen. From the very beginning, the objectives of anti-imperialism were defined as the abolition of the unequal treaties, foreign concessions, extra-territoriality, and fixed tariffs, and opposition to foreign aggression. These objectives were achieved by the KMT government under the leadership of Chiang Kai-shek in 1945. Since then, the sentiment of antiforeignism has been discouraged and a diplomacy based on equality, freedom, and independence has been championed by the KMT government.

The war of resistance forced Chiang Kai-shek and the KMT government to mobilize the people to defend China. Nevertheless, the Chinese Communists penetrated into various mass organizations in the name of fighting Japanese imperialists. The war with Japan provided the Chinese Communists with an excellent opportunity to expand their influence. Japan's aggression forced the Chinese to support Chiang's mobilization and unification but it also provided a destructive force which prevented the KMT from fully achieving its goal. Japan, therefore, created and destroyed KMT China.

---

[60] Hollington K. Tong, *op. cit.*, p. 299.

PART III

"ANTI-U.S. IMPERIALISM" AS POLITICAL FORCE

CHAPTER 6
"Anti-U.S. Imperialism" and Leftism in China, 1950s

The CCP was founded in 1921, during the turbulent period of the May Fourth Movement. During this period, a new cultural movement was triggered and various types of activities were developed. On the one hand, the movement opposed imperialism and feudalism; on the other, it opposed the old morality and aimed at promoting new culture. It was not until the late 1920s that the CCP emerged as an important political force and became a serious threat to KMT leadership. The purpose of this chapter is to explain how anti-imperialism became an important part of Communist ideology in China and how "anti-imperialism" developed into "anti-U.S. imperialism." The first question requires a close investigation of CCP's ideological development from its early years. The second question calls for an examination of Peking's perception of threat from "U.S. imperialism" and Mao Zedong's theory of the "paper tiger."

Both the ideology of anti-imperialism and Peking's perception of the U. S. contributed to Peking's antiforeignism in the 1950s, which led to the isolation of China from the West, and to incessant purges of the "rightists." As long as political purges and a power struggle continued, more people were driven into being "leftist." Leftism became a powerful weapon to defeat opponents, and raised antiforeignism to a higher level than before.

Early Ideological Development of Anti-imperialism

From its formation, the CCP championed struggles for working class liberation and for the proletarian revolution, and vowed to eliminate foreign privileges in China imposed by unequal treaties. In the manifesto of the Second National Congress of July 1922, the CCP declared that the policy of a united front was not equivalent to surrendering to the capitalists. It pursued the immediate aim of quelling internal disorders by overthrowing the military cliques, of ending oppression by international imperialism, and of achieving the complete independence of the Chinese nation.[1] The CCP put forth such slogans as "down with the warlords" and "down with international imperialism." The CCP criticized Sun Yat-sen's KMT for often falling into erroneous notions, e.g. relying on foreign powers for help in the Chinese national revolution. The CCP asserted that such requests for help from the

---

[1] Conrad Brandt, Benjamin Schwartz, and John K. Fairbank, *A Documentary History of Chinese Communism* (hereafter cited as *A Documentary History*), New York: Atheneum, 1966, p. 64.

enemy not only cost the KMT the loss of leadership of the national revolution but also made the people dependent on a foreign power, thus destroying their confidence and spirit of national independence.[2]

After the breakdown of the first united front in 1927, the CCP asserted that Chiang Kai-shek, who represented the bourgeoisie, had openly discarded the anti-imperialist struggle and declared war against the proletariat, and that Chiang had concluded a counter-revolutionary alliance with feudal reactionaries, the warlords, and the imperialists.[3] This is the earliest accusation against Chiang of collaboration with imperialists and feudal reactionaries. From then on, the CCP identified Chiang and imperialists together as a clique and therefore the enemy of the Chinese people. In the 1928 Political Resolution of the Sixth National Congress of the CCP, the Party urged the overthrow of the rule of imperialism and the warlord-KMT regime.[4] The Party urged inducing the working class masses and the petty-bourgeoisie to participate in these struggles against the imperialists, the warlords, and the KMT government.[5] Under the leadership of Li Li-san, the CCP continued to utilize the propaganda of the anti-imperialist struggle in urban areas. It set August 1 as Anti-imperialist-war Day in 1929.[6] It urged that the anti-imperialist struggle should be strengthened through co-ordination with the anti-world-war movement and the "support-the-Soviet Union" movement, and that the anti-imperialist movement must be closely co-ordinated with the workers' movement, the anti-KMT movement, and the anti-militarist struggle.[7]

In Mao's Report to the Second All-China Soviet Congress (1934), he advocated that the soviets must strengthen their leadership of the anti-imperialist struggle throughout the whole country as well as the revolutionary struggle of the workers and peasants in KMT territory. He asserted that by utilizing the concrete facts of the KMT's surrender to imperialism, the soviets might arouse the national consciousness and class consciousness of the masses in the KMT regions to a sharp struggle against imperialism and its lackey, the KMT. Thus, he called for the masses to organize and arm themselves, to fight for the independence of China, and to drive imperialists out of China in the

[2]*Ibid.*, p. 71.

[3]*Ibid.*, p. 93.

[4]*Ibid.*, p. 143. For the nature of this congress, see Benjamin Schwartz, *Chinese Communism and the Rise of Mao*, Cambridge: Harvard University Press, 1966, pp. 115-116.

[5]*A Documentary History*, p. 152.

[6]*Ibid.*, p. 167.

[7]*A Documentary History*, p. 171. The communists in this period were divided in their attitude toward revolutionary strategy and the role of imperialism in the Chinese Revolution. See Arif Dirlik, "National Development and Social Revolution in Early Chinese Marxist Thought," *The China Quarterly*, no. 58, April-June 1974, pp. 286-307.

regions under Japanese occupation.[8] This was an early example of hatred against imperialism applied to mass mobilization.

In the Yanan period, evidence of opposition to imperialism was even clearer. In the name of fighting Japanese imperialism a new united front was adopted by the CCP after the Xian incident of December 1936. From then on, the CCP saw itself as the major force in the war of resistance. Emphasis was placed on the overthrow of Japanese imperialism.[9] In following the policy of the united front, the CCP publicly declared that it had abandoned all of its policies of overthrowing the KMT by force. The CCP officially became one of the important political forces in the war of resistance. Massive propaganda and nation-wide movements were conducted in order to awaken the masses and to mobilize all possible forces in the war effort. Opposition to Japanese imperialism became an important political force during this period.

Mao's Theory of Revolution and Imperialism

Mao's early view of imperialism is seen in his "The Chinese Revolution and the CCP (1939)." Like Sun Yat-sen and Chiang Kai-shek, Mao saw that the imperialist powers used and continued to use military, political, economic and cultural means of oppression, and that China had became a semicolony or colony. In "The Chinese Revolution and the CCP", Mao said:

> Through wars and unequal treaties the imperialist powers have controlled all the important trading ports, have acquired extraterritoriality, have operated industries, and have monopolized China's banking and finance. The imperialist powers have supplied the warlords with large quantities of munitions and a host of military advisers to keep them fighting among themselves. Through missionary work and the establishment of hospitals, schools, and the publication of newspapers, the imperialists have conducted a policy of cultural aggression.

In other words, Mao, Sun and Chiang shared similar fundamental attitudes toward the imperialist policies aimed against China.[10]

Departing from this basic understanding of imperialism, Mao analyzed imperialism from the point of view of class struggle. The imperialist powers, according to Mao, had established a network of comprador and merchant-usurer exploitation rights across China and had created a comprador and merchant-usurer class in their service, so as to facilitate their exploitation of

---

[8] *A Documentary History, op. cit.*, p. 238.

[9] See Chalmers A. Johnson, *Peasant Nationalism and Communist Power*, Stanford: Stanford University Press, Reprint 1967, pp. 31-70.

[10] For discussion of the KMT, the CCP, and student movements against imperialism in 1930s, see John Israel, *Student Nationalism in China, 1927-1937*, Stanford: Hoover Institution, Stanford University Press, 1966, pp. 305-331.

the masses of the Chinese peasantry and other sections of the people. Following the Comintern's line, Mao pointed out that imperialism first allies itself with the ruling strata of the previous social structure, with feudal lords and the trading and moneylending bourgeoisie, against the majority of the people. He adopted Stalin's idea that imperialism is the force that supports and preserves the feudal remnants and their entire bureaucratic-militarist superstructure. In Mao's analysis, the imperialist powers, on the one hand, hastened the disintegration of feudal society and the growth of elements of capitalism, thereby transforming a feudal society into a semi-feudal one while, on the other hand, they imposed their ruthless rule on China, reducing an independent country to a semicolonial or colonial country. Mao maintained that the large-scale invasion by Japanese imperialism in 1931 had turned a large chunk of China into a Japanese colony and that the purpose of the imperialist powers in invading China was not to transform a feudal China into a capitalist China. On the contrary, their purpose was to transform China into their own semicolony or colony.[11]

In the same article, Mao said: "Under the twofold oppression of imperialism and feudalism, and especially as a result of the large-scale invasion of Japanese imperialism, the Chinese people, and particularly the peasants, have become more and more impoverished, living in hunger and cold and without any political rights." Therefore he concluded that the contradiction between imperialism and the Chinese nation and the contradiction between feudalism and the great masses of the people were the basic contradictions in modern Chinese society. But he stated that the contradiction between imperialism and the Chinese nation was the principal one. According to Mao, these contradictions and their intensification must inevitably result in the incessant growth of revolutionary movements. He said: "The great revolutions in modern and contemporary China have emerged and grown on this basis of their basic contradictions." Thus, Mao developed his theory of revolution based on his analysis of imperialism and feudalism.

In Mao's doctrine of revolution, the chief targets or enemies at the first stage of the Chinese revolution were imperialism and feudalism, i.e., the bourgeoisie of the imperialist countries and the landlord class in China.[12] As he saw it, the upper stratum of the Chinese bourgeoisie, represented by the reactionary clique within the KMT, had collaborated with imperialism and betrayed the Communist Party, the proletariat, the peasantry, and the Chinese revolution.[13]

[11] Mao Zedong, "Chinese Revolution and the Chinese Communist Party," *Selected Works of Mao Zedong*, Peking: Foreign Languages Press, 1967, pp. 305-331.
[12] *Ibid.*
[13] *Ibid.*

Mao advocated two tasks for the revolution. A national revolution to over-throw foreign imperialist oppression and a democratic revolution to overthrow feudal landlord oppression were required. He said: "These two tasks are inter-related. Unless imperialist rule is overthrown, the rule of the feudal landlord class cannot be terminated, because imperialism is its main support.... Conversely, unless the feudal landlord class is overthrown, it is impossible to overthrow the imperialist rule, because the feudal class is the main social base of imperialist rule in China." Thus, Mao urged the carrying out of these two tasks together.

In short, the concept of imperialism has been one of the most important elements in Mao's theory of revolution. Mao not only developed a theory of imperialism based on class struggle but also linked imperialism with Chinese revolution. This provided an ideological foundation for Peking's anti-imperialism movements in the post-1949 period.

Anti-Imperialism as an Ideology

Mao's ideas of imperialism have become an important part of Chinese communist ideology. Ideology is a systematic set of ideas with consequences for action. Generally, Chinese communist ideology may be divided into pure ideology which is a set of ideas designed to give the individual a unified and conscious world view and practical ideology which is a set of ideas designed to give the individual rational instruments for action. Marxism is regarded as the major part of pure ideology, while Leninism and the thought of Mao Zedong are regarded as the principal components of practical ideology. In fact, practical ideology includes revolutionary experience gained in the process of the Chinese revolution. The Chinese communists adopted the concept of imperialism from Lenin. The practical applications of anti-imperialism, how-ever, are based on revolutionary experience and the needs of the Party. Thus, anti-imperialism is practical ideology. Like other parts of practical ideology, the concept of anti-imperialism developed in line with political development.

From Lenin's point of view, imperialism is the highest stage of capitalism. Imperialism is the stage of monopolistic, declining and dying capitalism. By means of exporting capital, imperialists suppress and exploit the peoples of other states. Politically, imperialism is reactionary and will ally itself with all reactionary forces to suppress the revolutions of other states. For ideological purposes, Peking openly accepted this Leninist theory of imperialism.[14]

Lenin's theory of imperialism was an attempt to explain the fact that

---

[14]*Liening Lun Di Guo Zhu Yi* (Lenin's Discussion on Imperialism), Peking: People's Publishing Co., 1974, pp. 2-9.

revolution had not yet taken place in the most highly developed capitalist countries. His explanation was that capitalism had found a way out of the contradictions which Marx had described in the Communist Manifesto. The way out was expansion over the whole world in search of cheap raw materials, ready markets for commodities, excess capital, and most important, cheap labor which could be exploited in unprecedented measure. Lenin maintained that imperialism is not a policy that can be adopted or abandoned at will, but an inevitability of rotting and moribund capitalism.[15] Imperialism was seen as the only way by which the proletarian movement in the developed countries could be neutralized or robbed of its most dangerous weapon. The bourgeoisie could succeed in averting an increase in the misery of the masses by distributing the profits which the capitalist system had obtained through exploitation of its colonies. Lenin, like Marx, however, asserted that capitalism cannot function without leading to crises and revolutionary situations.

These Leninist ideas are rarely seen in the Chinese media. On the contrary, millions of copies of works propagandize Mao's theory of revolution and imperialism and his theory of the "paper tiger". For mobilization purposes, these became much more important than Lenin's theory of imperialism. Through a powerful propaganda machine, the Chinese masses were indoctrinated with Mao's theory of revolution and imperialism. To oppose imperialism became an article of faith for the masses.

Peking's denunciation of imperialism has three important characteristics. First, despite the fact that Peking openly accepts Marxism and Leninism as its guiding thought and foundation of ideology, Peking's sentiments opposing imperialism seem to be based more on historical experience and nationalistic sentiments than on Marxism-Leninism. Lenin's theory of imperialism only serves as a theoretical justification for China to oppose imperialistic aggression. In December 1956, Mao said: "Imperialism is to be seen in those countries, i.e., Britain, the United States, France, Holland, which took part in the Allied Armies of the Eight Nations, those which burned our Yuanming Garden, seized Hong Kong and Taiwan. . . ."[16] In this definition, Mao clearly used the historical record as a criterion for imperialism. Thus, it is quite clear that Mao's concept of imperialism was based on historical interpretation. In mentioning the Allied Armies of the Eight Nations, he was thinking of the atrocities perpetrated by those powerful foreign countries.

Secondly, anti-imperialism has served important functions in internal

[15] Alfred G. Meyer, *Leninism*, New York: Praeger University Series, 1956, p. 241, footnote.

[16] *Mao Zedong Si Xiang Wan Sui* (Long Live Mao Zedong's Thought: hereafter cited as *Wan Sui*), p. 63. In fact, Mao made a mistake here, the eight countries involved were Britain, the U. S., Italy, Germany, France, Japan, Austria, and Russia, and did not include Holland.

politics. From Peking's point of view, imperialism has threatened China since the Opium War of the 1840s. As Mao said in "the Chinese Revolution and the CCP": "After the Opium War, China, step by step, fell into the state of a semi-colonial and semi-feudal society. Since the 1931 Japanese invasion, China has become a colonial, semi-colonial, and semi-feudal society."[17] Mao further maintained that when imperialism launches a war of aggression against a country, all the various classes of such a country, except for a few traitors, can temporarily unite in a national war against imperialism. At this point, the principal contradiction is between the imperialists and the country concerned, while all the contradictions among the various classes within the country are temporarily relegated to a secondary and subordinate position. He again used examples in Chinese history such as the Opium War of 1840, the Sino-Japanese War of 1894, the Boxer Rebellion of 1900, and the Sino-Japanese War of 1937-45 to support his theory.[18]

Thirdly, conceptually, Mao believed in the inter-relationship between internal politics and external causes. Mao also pointed out that, in the era of capitalism, and especially in the era of imperialism and proletarian revolution, the interaction and mutual impact of different countries in the political, economic and cultural spheres are extreme. Mao used the example of the October revolution in Russia to support his argument: "The October Socialist Revolution ushered in a new epoch in world history as well as in Russian history. It exerted influence on internal change in the other countries of the world and, similarly in a number of particularly profound ways, on internal change in China."[19] Mao stated that, "the fundamental cause of the development of a thing is not external but internal; it lies in the contradiction within the thing."[20] At the level of society he said, "Changes in society are due chiefly to the development of the internal contradictions in society, that is, the contradiction between the productive forces and the relations of production, the contradiction between classes and the contradiction between the old and the new." However, he also believed that external causes are important to internal changes. He said that "external causes are the condition of change and internal causes are the basis of change, and that external causes become operative through internal causes."[21]

[17]"Chinese Revolution and Chinese Communist Party," *op. cit.*
[18]*Selected Readings from the Works of Mao Zedong (Selected Readings)*. Peking: Foreign Languages Press, 1971, p. 110.
[19]*Ibid.*, p. 88.
[20]*Ibid.*, p. 87.
[21]*Ibid.*, p. 88.

Peking's Perception of Threats from "U.S. Imperialism"

The Chinese Communists had no official contact with the United States until the 1941 Pearl Harbor incident made the Americans join the Nationalist government in fighting the Japanese on the Asian continent. The United States and the Nationalist government were soon drawn into a close alliance and Americans and military equipment flowed into China. While the U.S. gave strong support to Chiang Kai-shek's Nationalist government, some American diplomats feared that American support for Chiang could antagonize the Communists and force them onto the side of the Soviet Union. A team of two dozen Americans, the so-called "Dixie Mission," visited Yanan in the summer of 1944 with the permission of the American government.[22] Frank conversations and friendly attitudes between the Communists and the Americans in Yanan led both to believe that cooperation between the two parties could be beneficial to both sides. In September, 1944, General Stilwell was even thinking of sending U.S. military aid to the Communists. The idea was soon given up when Chiang Kai-shek and Patrick J. Hurley, President Roosevelt's special envoy to China, put pressure on Roosevelt. Hurley proposed that the Communists should negotiate with Chiang. But the negotiations failed. During this period, the Communists were cut off from any foreign aid and blockaded by the Nationalist forces; they were eager to cooperate with the Americans. In order to obtain some support from the Americans, Mao and Zhou sent a cable to Washington expressing their interest in a trip to America. No response was received from Washington. Roosevelt was convinced by Hurley that he should not deal with the Communists.[23]

As soon as the Japanese surrendered, the keen competition between the Nationalists and Communists for expansion of controlled areas was unleashed. The Communists had military bases in 19 provinces controlling a population of around 100 million. This represented a large expansion of its power since 1937 when the second United Front was formed in order to fight Japanese aggression. Both the Communists and the Nationalists were eager to seize Wang Jingwei's Japanese occupied areas and the weapons and ammunition stored there. In view of this situation, President Truman ordered that all Japanese and Wang's forces in China should immediately surrender their positions and arms only to the Nationalist government. This gave a substantial headstart to the Nationalists in the competition with the Communists. Washington's policy, however, was to mediate in the conflicts and to avoid American involvement in a civil war. In keeping with this policy, General

[22] See Michael Schaller, *The United States and China in the Twentieth Century*, New York: Oxford University Press, 1979, pp. 95-103.
[23] *Ibid.*

George C. Marshall was, in December 1945, appointed to lead a peace-making mission to China to help form a coalition government. Due to keen interest on both sides in seizing leadership, by early 1947, it was clear that the formation of a coalition government was impossible. In January of that year a large-scale civil war flared across the country. Consequently, the Marshall Mission was recalled by President Truman. China was left to its fate.

Profound hostility developed during the Civil War when the Communists attacked the U.S. for her support to Chiang Kai-shek in the fight against them. In 1949 when the Chinese Communists swept into power, Peking followed the so-called "leaning to one side" policy and aligned itself with the Soviet Union. Peking perceived the U.S. as the principal enemy. It repeatedly protested against the U.S. "armed invasion" of Taiwan. The United States was considered the most important threat to China. Domestically, Peking still faced a period of consolidation of power. Its national defense forces were still in an early stage of construction. Under such circumstances, Peking naturally sought any possible ally to deter a possible U.S. invasion. Preventing a possible invasion by "U.S. imperialism" had the highest priority in Peking's policy. Peking's hostility toward Washington further intensified during the period of the Korean War. Under the Treaty of Mutual Alliance of 1950, the Soviet Union provided military security and economic assistance to the Chinese Communists. During these early years Peking regarded the Sino-Soviet Alliance as the main opposing force to the "imperialist camp headed by the United States."

With the stationing of the U.S. Seventh Fleet in the Taiwan Strait in 1950 and the resumption of U.S. military shipments to Taiwan in 1951,Peking feared a U.S. invasion. The campaign of "Resist-America, Aid-Korea" was a nation-wide movement to resist possible U.S. invasion. Millions of people participated in demonstrations in support of this campaign. The perception that the U.S. was the arch enemy did not change markedly during the next few years. For example in 1955, an editorial in the *RR* said that "in the current international situation, in order to strengthen our national defense, liberate Taiwan, strike down the aggression of imperialism, and maintain the independence of sovereignty and territorial integrity, we ought to develop industry."[24] The pressure of the U.S. military force clearly served as an ideological motivation for Peking to mobilize its people. The editorial continued: "The imperialist power still surrounds us, we must prepare to cope with any sudden incident. . . . This requires every Communist to give up individual interests and rely upon the knowledge and strength of the masses and the knowledge and the strength of the Party to overcome any difficulty,

---

[24]*Renmin Ribao (RR)*, April 5, 1955.

and struggle for the great victory of the socialist undertaking."[25]

The importance of the policy of deterrence may also be understood in terms of Peking's domestic political mobilization. In 1955, Peking used slogans of anti-imperialism to mobilize its people in various kinds of movements. In his article entitled "Raise Alertness, Oppose Numbness," Luo Ruiqing, then Minister for Public Security, said:

> As long as classes and class struggle still exist in the world, our enemy will not forget us for a moment. Thus they will not desist from their sabotage against us for a moment. Evidence proves that whenever we make one progressive step in the revolution, it inevitably leads to ruthless antagonism and senseless sabotage from enemies, both internal and external. They will create any possible plot and use poisonous means to stop our socialist revolution.[26]

Despite the fact that the threat of U.S. invasion was perceived as imminent and dangerous, Peking's policy of alliance with the Soviet Union was questioned. In 1956, Mao reiterated that the policy of alliance with the Soviet Union was correct. He repudiated those who suspected this policy and favored a middle of the road policy between the Soviet Union and the U.S. in order to obtain money from both sides. Mao pointed out three reasons why China could not follow this path. First, the U.S. was a strong imperialist force which had oppressed China for a considerable period of time. Second, if China stood between them, it would look as if China was independent, while in fact, China would not be independent because she was a weak country. Third, the U.S. was not reliable. She would not provide sufficient aid to China.[27] Implicit in this reasoning was the fact that Mao believed that the Soviet Union was not an imperialist power and did not and would not oppress China. China could be independent after allying itself with the Soviet Union, because the Soviet Union was reliable, and would provide China with sufficient assistance. Of course history has shown that Mao's assumption in 1956 was overly optimistic.

Mao's Theory of "U.S. Imperialism": The Paper Tiger

In his talk with the American correspondent Anna Louise Strong in 1946 Mao first put forth the theory of the paper tiger. He said that Chiang Kai-shek and his supporters, "the U.S. reactionaries," were all paper tigers. He pointed out: "Speaking of U.S. imperialism, people seem to feel that it is terribly strong. Chinese reactionaries are using the 'strength' of the United States to frighten the Chinese people. But it will be proved that the U.S. reactionaries,

[25] *Ibid.*
[26] *RR*, June 30, 1955.
[27] *Wan Sui, op. cit.*, p. 63.

like all reactionaries in history, do not have much strength. . . . All reactionaries are paper tigers. In appearance, the reactionaries are terrifying, but in reality they are not so powerful."[28] This theory was based on Mao's analysis that the Soviet Union was the defender of world peace and that the U.S. was the enemy of China with its policy of continuing to support Chiang Kai-shek in the civil war. Peking did not claim this theory was created by Mao, but declared, "This thesis is derived from Lenin's scientific proposition that imperialism is moribund and decaying capitalism."

In 1957 Mao spoke of the concept of "the people" varying in content in different countries and in different periods of history in the same country, as does the concept of "the enemy":

> During the War of Resistance Against Japan, all those classes, strata and social groups opposing Japanese aggression came within the category of the people, while the Japanese imperialist, the Chinese traitors and the pro-Japanese elements were all enemies of the people. During the War of Liberation, the U.S. imperialists and their running dogs . . . were the enemies of the people, while the other classes . . . which opposed these enemies, all came within the category of the people. At the present stage, the period of building socialism, the classes . . . which support and work for the causes of socialist construction all come within the category of the people, while the social forces and groups which resist the socialist revolution and are hostile to, or sabotage, socialist construction are all enemies of the people.[29]

Based on this analysis, Mao did not use ideology as a criteria for the division of "the people" from "the enemy", instead, he used their attitude toward national causes such as opposing Japanese aggression, the war of liberation, and building socialism. In short, those who favored these causes are "the people" and those opposed are "the enemy". Thus, it is evident that imperialists are not necessarily the enemies of China; only those who oppose China's national causes are "the enemy".

There have always been different opinions over policy toward "U.S. imperialism" in China. As reported by the *RR* in 1958, a great number of people still held superstitions and illusions about U.S. imperialism, and respected and feared it.[30]

> Some other people still overestimate the force of 'imperialist reactionaries' and see only its strong points, so that they believe that the West is advanced and the East is far behind and that the real strength of the West should not be underestimated. Another group of people believe the best way to deal with imperialism

---

[28] "Talk with the American Correspondent Anna Louise Strong," *Selected Reading*, vol. IV. Peking: Foreign Languages Press, 1969, pp. 97-101.

[29] "On the Correct Handling of Contradictions Among the People," February, 1957, see *Selected Works of Mao Zedong*, vol. V. Peking: Foreign Languages Press, 1977, p. 385.

[30] *RR*, editorial, October 27, 1958.

is not to provoke it: the more provocation against it, the less advantage for world to peace.[31]

It was because these people still overestimated, feared, and respected imperialism that Mao reiterated his theory of the paper tiger.

Mao's theory of the paper tiger, like Sun Yat-sen's opinion, was optimistic about the future of China and believed that the imperialist power was declining and the power of the Chinese people was rising. Even the atom bomb, Mao said, is a paper tiger which the U.S. reactionaries use to scare people. He said, "It (atom bomb) looks terrible, but in fact is not, because the outcome of a war is decided by the people, not by one or two new types of weapon."[32] In his talk with A. L. Strong, Mao said, "The Chinese of Taiwan, the people of Lebanon, and all U.S. military bases in foreign territories are like nooses tied around the neck of 'U.S. Imperialism'. The Americans themselves, and nobody else, made these nooses, and they themselves put them round their necks and handed the other ends to the Chinese people, the Arab countries and all the people throughout the world who love peace and oppose aggression."[33] According to Mao the longer the U.S. remains in these places, the tighter the nooses round its neck will become. Thus, Mao claimed it is imperialism which fears the people, not the people who fear imperialism. Mao's attitude remained the same in 1970. In a statement to foreign guests he said:

"U.S. imperialism, which looks like a huge monster, is in essence a paper tiger, now in the throes of its death-bed struggle. In the world today, who actually fears whom? It is not the Vietnamese people . . . who fear U.S. imperialism: it is U.S. imperialism which fears the people of the world."[34]

The theory of the paper tiger serves the purpose of reducing the people's fear of superior U.S. forces. The core of Mao's argument is that imperialism is not as strong as it looks. Mao's was a defensive rather than an offensive attitude toward imperialism. It attempted to eliminate the pessimism brought about by the strength of U.S. armed forces and nuclear weapons. Obviously, Mao understood that this pessimism was a serious stumbling block to the Party's mobilization of the people in the face of a strong enemy. Thus, the theory of the paper tiger was used to strengthen morale for the fight against imperialism. Since Mao believed that it is the people who decide the result of war, and not weapons, he believed that morale was an essential ingredient in fighting imperialism.

[31] RR, editorial, November 12, 1958.
[32] "Talk with the American Correspondent Anna Louise Strong," op. cit.
[33] RR, September 9, 1958.
[34] New China News Agency, Peking, May 20, 1970.

This theory not only served to strengthen the confidence of the people in China but also that of people in similar situations throughout the world who face a superior enemy. Without eliminating psychological pessimism, Peking would find it impossible to urge the people of the world to form a united front to fight imperialism. By the same token, it would be very difficult to carry out a policy of deterrence of U.S. invasion. Thus, it is evident that the theory of the paper tiger was an important psychological device for mobilization in internal politics and for propaganda in foreign relations.

In 1958 Mao republicized his theories of the 'intermediate zone' and the 'paper tiger.' These two theories, in fact, strengthened the theoretical basis of Peking's "anti-imperialism." The theory of the "Intermediate zone" characterizes the Afro-Asian states as oppressed and exploited countries, and the people in these states as eventually rising to oppose imperialism. The theory of the "Paper Tiger," as discussed above, stressed the weakness of imperialist countries beset by serious internal and external problems. Despite the superior military strength of these imperialist countries, they would be confronted with the overwhelming power of the people. Thus, according to Mao, the people were becoming united by the strength of their anti-imperialist sentiment, and imperialism would eventually be defeated by the people of the world.

Peking's Foreign Policy of "Leaning to One Side" and Isolation From the West

One of the most important consequences of Peking's ideology of "anti-U.S. imperialism" was its foreign policy of "leaning to one side." Peking aligned itself with the Soviet Union politically and militarily. In 1950, Mao Zedong signed with Stalin the Treaty of Mutual Alliance. This alliance with the Soviet Union provided the Peking government with military security and economic assistance. Indisputably, Soviet aid was both indispensable and invaluable at a time when Peking badly needed financial assistance and technical know-how for its industrial development. By the end of 1957, the Soviet Union supplied China with complete sets of equipment and technical aid for 211 major industrial enterprises. Moscow also sent a total of 10,800 specialists to China to assist in industrial development and in the training of Chinese workers and technicians.[35] Soviet aid also led to significant changes in the Chinese educational system and cultural policies which brought China closer to the Soviet Union but isolated China from the West for twenty-five years. In its early period, Peking adopted an irreconcilably hostile attitude towards the West. Mao Zedong explained Peking's pro-Soviet policy to the Chinese

[35] "Sino-Soviet Cooperation," *Beijing Review*, No. 29, April 29, 1958, p. 20.

People's Political Consultative Conference in 1950, he said:

> In the two years since the founding of the People's Republic of China, we have
> won great victories in all fields of work. We have won these victories by relying on
> all the forces that can be united . . . . Internationally, we have relied on the firm
> unity of the camp of peace and democracy headed by the Soviet Union . . .[36]

In 1950, Zhou Enlai delivered a Political Report to the Third Session of the
first Chinese People's Political Consultative Conference in which he called
on the Chinese government to completely wipe out the cultural aggression
of the American imperialists, and to gradually eliminate pro-American,
worship-American, fear-American ideas during the "Anti-U.S. Aid Korea
Movement".[37]

Peking's hostility towards the U.S. was eased after the Korean War cease-
fire agreement in 1953. In 1954, however, the anti-U.S. drive was again in full
swing in China during the movement for the liberation of Taiwan. For more
than two decades Peking continued to attack "U.S. imperialism."

In spite of the deterioration in Peking's relations with the Soviet Union
since the early 1960s, China's relations with the West were not improved.
From 1954 to 1957, China endeavoured to improve diplomatic relations with
the newly independent countries and with neighbouring countries in Asia.
Her relations with Japan, however, remained tense. In fact, in 1959 after the
U.S.-Japan Security Treaty was agreed upon by both governments, Peking
started to perceive Japan as a collaborator with the U.S. After the Treaty
was signed in May, 1960, Peking's hostility towards Japan reached a new post-
World War II high, with violent anti-Japanese mass demonstrations on a
nation-wide scale.[38]

In addition to the U.S. and Japan, Britain, France and West Germany also
had problems with China. Britain established diplomatic relations with Peking
early in January 1950. But the Chinese accorded no privileges to the British
government. British firms and consulates were gradually forced to close
down. In 1956-57 Peking attacked Britain as "imperialist and colonialist"
when British troops moved into Egypt. Throughout the 1950s, relations
between the two countries were not normalized. In the 1950s, France and
West Germany were also perceived by Peking as members of the "capitalist

[36] Opening address delivered by Mao Zedong at the China People's Political Consultative Conference. See "Great Victory in three mass movement" (October 23, 1951) in
Selected Works of Mao Tsetung, vol. V, p. 61.

[37] Zhou Enlai's Political Report to the Third Session of the first Chinese People's
Political Consultative Conference, 1950 in *Zhou Enlai Xuan Ji* (Selected Work of Zhou
Enlai), Hong Kong: Yishan Publishing Co., 1976, pp. 37-42.

[38] Harold C. Hinton, *Communist China in World Politics*, Boston: Houghton Mifflin
Company, 1966, pp. 376-384.

camp" and "collaborators of the U.S. imperialists." Except for a small amount of trade, there was little cultural contact between Peking and these Western countries. "Leaning to one side" meant that China had practically cut herself off from the West.

In the first decade after the establishment of the Peking government, the Chinese communists set themselves to learn from the Soviets in every respect. Culturally, the government accepted Soviet practice in the distinction of proletarian art and literature from that of the capitalists, and they shared a similar contemptuous attitude toward Western culture. This attitude resulted in Peking's policy of prohibiting the importation and circulation of American and Western European books and publications in China. Consequently, little knowledge of Western development was available to the people of China. They were instead introduced to those Soviet writings and publications which the government considered the best. Similarly, the CCP accepted most Soviet industrial equipment and set up plants on the Russian model. Because they read only Soviet books and publications, the Chinese engineers and intellectuals learned only about Soviet developments.[39]

Furthermore, in most of the educational institutions the authorities introduced the Russian language as the second language in place of English. The change made it very difficult for the younger generation to learn anything from the West, and further isolated the Chinese people from Westerners.[40] A decade of isolation from the West clearly was an obstacle to the development of science and technology. This isolation undoubtedly strengthened Peking's anti-U.S. policy and created many serious problems for China's future modernization.

Antiforeignism and Political Purges in 1950s

Another serious consequence of Peking's ideology of "anti-U.S. imperialism" was recurrent political purges. As illustrated above, in the post-1949 period, imperialism remained a target of mass denunciation. Like capitalism, imperialism—Leninist style—is the ideological enemy of the Party and the People, so the Chinese communists denounced imperialism from the perspective of class struggle. The CCP launched a series of political movements purging rightists and capitalists in China in order to consolidate its power. Since capitalism was the enemy of the socialist revolution and since imperialism was politically reactionary because it attempted to suppress the

[39] *Wo Men Kan Sixiang Gai Zao Yu Gao Deng Jiao Yu Gong Zuo* (Our Observation of Thought Reform and High Education Work), in *Wenhui Bao*, Shanghai, May 20, 1959.

[40] "Jiao Yu Jie De Jiao Tiao Zhu Yi" (Dogmatism in Educational Society), *Jiao Shio Bao*, Peking, May 28, 1957.

socialist revolution, both capitalists and imperialists were considered enemies of the Chinese socialist revolution. In the class struggle, capitalists in China were the target of political rectification. Those who were linked with imperialism or foreign capitalists were believed to be the supporters of internal capitalists. Thus, in each movement of class struggle, internal capitalists and reactionaries, together with imperialism, became the target of purges.

In the first decade, the Peking government's policy of antiforeignism was reflected in both external and internal movements. Large-scale campaigns such as the "Resist America and Aid Korea" campaign clearly were mass activities against U.S. imperialism. The "Resist America and Aid Korea" campaign was carried on until 1953. Most of the important domestic campaigns such as the "Three Antis and Five Antis," the "Suppression of Counter-revolutionaries," and the "Anti-Rightist" movements were launched to liquidate people who had relations with foreigners and who had foreign capitalist ideas, particularly those persons "opposing Party policies." In fact, these campaigns were strengthened by antiforeign sentiment or "anti-imperialism."

In the 1951 First Campaign of Suppression of Counter-Revolutionary Elements, churches were closed down and foreign missionaries were expelled from China. A great number of people who were related to foreigners in one way or another were treated as foreign spies. During the 1952 "Three-Antis and Five Antis" campaign, industrialists and businessmen were requested to submit a detailed report on their past background and their thoughts were reviewed. Those who were related to foreigners were either investigated or arrested. The "Suppression of Counter-Revolutionary Elements" in 1955 was a most bitter ideological struggle, in which a great number of intellectuals who were educated in the West were purged and many who were sympathetic to Western ideas were also arrested. A strict categorization of class affiliation was undertaken. It dealt a serious blow to the intellectuals. (See Table 6.1)

In 1956, a Campaign to Suppress Counter-Revolutionaries and a Rectification Campaign were launched in which a great number of accused counter-revolutionaries were purged. A great deal of propaganda was aimed at the public. The campaign lasted about two months and was suspended when some party members feared things might get out of hand as they had in Hungary and Poland. The year 1957 was a difficult year for those who worked in art and literature. As a result of the "Let a hundred flowers bloom, a hundred schools of thought contend" movement, an "anti-rightist" campaign was initiated to purge those who did not support party policies in the arts. China's cultural development suffered a severe blow owing to the merciless

Table 6.1
POLITICAL CAMPAIGNS, 1950-1959

Year	Name of Campaigns	Main Activities	Time Consumed	Remarks
1951	Resist-America and Aid-Korea Movement	(1) aroused anti-American feelings; (2) encouraged students to join the army; (3) forced donations for purchase of airplanes and artillery.	About half a year	These campaigns were carried on until 1953
	First Campaign of Suppression of Counter-Revolutionary Elements	(1) urged remnant Nationalist military and political personnel to register with the Communist government; (2) accused hidden counter-revolutionaries.	About one month	
1952	Three-Antis and Five-Antis Campaigns	(1) submit a detailed report on one's own background; and review one's own thought; (2) urged businessmen to pay evaded taxes; (3) urged popular support to battlefronts.	About three months	Targets of these campaigns were industrialists, businessmen and cadres
1955	Second Campaign of Suppression of Counter-Revolutionary Elements	(1) review of thought; (2) ideological struggles; (3) strict classification of class affiliations.	About two months	The most bitter ideological struggle
1956	Suppression of Counter-Revolutionaries; and Rectification Campaign	(1) propaganda; (2) accusations of counter-revolutionaries.	About two months	Campaigns suspended due to anti-Communist revolutions in East Europe
1957	Rectification Campaign; (Blooming and Contending Campaign); Anti-Rightists Campaign	(1) self-criticism among students and teachers with Party membership; (2) participation of non-party-member students and teachers in the rectification campaign; (3) Retaliation against non-party-member students and teachers by those with party membership.	About eight months	Three campaigns closely related to one another
1959	Campaign against Rightist Tendencies	Study of documents issued by 8th Plenary Session of the Central Committee of the Chinese Communist Party	About two months	Campaigns carried out on a local basis in response to the Central Committee of the Communist Party

repression of many well-known artists and intellectuals.[41]

At the Fourth Session of the First National People's Congress in July, 1957, Lu Dingyi said:

> Our socialist revolution has been basically completed but not completely achieved, the victory of our socialist revolution has been basically consolidated, but not completely consolidated. Domestically, Taiwan remains to be liberated, there are still some anti-revolutionaries and some remnants of the landlord, bureaucrat, and capitalist classes. Externally, there is a group of aggressors led by U.S. imperialism. They plot to overthrow the people's government every minute and every second. ... A small group of rightists oppose socialism. They will not give up their exploitation. They dream of taking the capitalist road and will resort to a last struggle. These rightists ... have close connections with internal and external reactionaries and have ample experience of political struggle and armed struggle. Thus, we still have a long period of class struggle. Furthermore, this struggle will sometimes be very sharp and intense. This is certain.[42]

Liu Shaoqi, then Chief of State, in the second session of the Eighth Central Committee of the CCP, 1958, stated that the rightist clique of the capitalist class was the agent of imperialists, remnants of feudalists, and Chiang Kai-shek's KMT. He thus linked the internal enemy with external enemies.[43] This also clearly reflected the opinion of Chinese leaders that the threats from the internal opposition and external enemy were linked with each other. And the struggle against internal enemies must be accompanied by opposition to imperialism.

Following the "Great Leap Forward" in 1958, an Anti-Rightist Campaign was carried out again in literary and art circles. These "anti-rightist thinking" and "anti-revisionism" struggles lasted more than two years. Any criticism of Party policy was branded as "rightist." Fu Feng, the most famous living Chinese author, was purged because of his "capitalist thinking." After the failure of the "Great Leap Forward," China was soon engulfed in a serious power struggle among the top echelon of leaders. In the early 1960s, a strong force of "Leftists" led by Mao Zedong was rising.[44] This stream of "Leftism" reached its climax in the 1966-69 Cultural Revolution.

In addition, there were various mass meetings such as meetings in support

[41] *Zhao* Cong (Chao Ts'ung), "Art and Literature in Communist China," *Communist China 1949-1959*, Vol. III, Communist China Problem Research Series, Hong Kong: Union Research Institute, 1961, pp. 158-159.

[42] *RR*, July 12, 1957.

[43] See "Political Report of the Central Committee of the Chinese Communist Party to the Eighth National People's Congress," *Xin Hua Ban Yue Kan*, no. 11, Peking, May 5, 1958.

[44] See "On Questions of Party History," *Beijing Review*, no. 27, July 6, 1981; also see Frederick C. Teiwes, *Politics and Purges in China*, New York: M. E. Sharpe, Inc., 1979, pp. 493-527.

of African riots, meetings in protest at U.S. military bases in Japan, meetings in sympathy with political coups in the Middle East, meetings in celebration of the October Revolution, Red Army Day, Labor Day and so forth. In these campaigns and mass gatherings all students, workers and soldiers were required to take part without exception. In these meetings, protests or condemnations of "U.S. Imperialism" were frequently given prime importance.

Power Struggle, Leftism, and Antiforeignism

Chinese political developments in the 1950s showed that when power struggles increased, leftism and antiforeignism rose as well. As a result of continuous purges against "rightists" and "pro-rightist elements," as well as "counter-revolutionaries," leftism became the popular norm in society. The term "rightist" became a political weapon in the battle against internal opponents. This was clearly reflected in the power struggle between Mao Zedong and his opponents in 1959-62.

For example, signs of opposition to Mao Zedong's leadership surfaced in the criticism and comments of upper-level Party leaders in 1959. Dissatisfied with the results of the "Great Leap Forward" (GLF) and the People's communes, some party leaders voiced their personal opposition to Mao's support of the communes. These leaders blamed the "GLF" for the fact that many areas were suffering an unprecedented shortage of food. In addition to natural disasters, they pointed to human factors responsible for the economic decline. These debates over the "GLP" and the People's communes culminated in the 8th Plenary Session of the 8th Central Committee of the CCP in Lushan in September, 1959. During this meeting Peng Dehuai, Minister for National Defense, and Huang Kezheng, Chief of Staff for National Defense, heatedly attacked Mao's assertion of the great success of the "Great Leap" and the People's communes. Mao denounced Peng, Huang and Zhang Wentian at the meeting as 'rightist opportunists' of an anti-Party clique.[45] As a result, they were condemned in an article entitled "The Great Call" published by *Hongqi* on September 1, 1959:

> If we allow such rightist opportunist ideas to spread among us, they will seriously endanger our undertakings; after this point was clearly made at the 8th Plenary Session of the 8th CCP Central Committee, there is no doubt that the entire Party and the people throughout the country will, under the leadership of the CCP Central Committee headed by Comrade Mao Zedong, resolutely struggle against such rightist opportunist ideas.[46]

---

[45] "Resolution of the 8th Plenary Session of the 8th Central Committee of the C.P.C. concerning the Anti-Party Clique headed by Peng Teh-huai," *Beijing Review*, no. 34 August 1967, pp. 19-20.

[46] *Ibid.*, p. 12.

The Lushan meeting was a clear example of how Mao defeated his opponents by denouncing them as "rightists".

Political struggle continued in 1960 and 1961. Another group of Mao's opponents emerged during this period. These leaders included Liu Shaoqi, then Chief of State, and vice-premiers, including Deng Xiaoping, Chen Yun, Tan Zhenlin, and Bo Yibo, and the then mayor of Peking, Peng Zhen. Serious divergences between Mao's group and his opponents developed in 1961. These differences, unlike those of 1959, extended beyond agricultural policy to include political, industrial, cultural, and educational matters. Liu and Deng developed a group which formed a more pragmatic and ideologically moderate faction within the Party. A confrontation took place at the Enlarged Central Working Conference in January, 1962. During this meeting Mao's supporters and the Liu-Deng group openly disputed their points of view. Liu Shaoqi took a strong stand against Mao and his "Three Red Banners." Liu claimed that the economic disaster was mainly due to human factors, which had brought the economy to a state of near-collapse, and that it probably would take seven or eight years to recover.[47] Lin Biao made the point that some mistakes were inevitable. Zhou Enlai defended Mao by emphasizing that there had been more gain than loss.[48] Because of Lin's and Zhou's support, Mao still was in a stronger position than the Liu-Deng group.

Mao's leftism was greatly intensified as a result of the increasing challenge by the Liu-Deng group. Mao presided at a Work Conference of the Central Committee held at Beidaihe at the end of August and early September to fight back against his critics.[49] At this conference, Mao strongly emphasized his leftist faith in class struggle. He pointed out: "The elimination of the system of ownership by the exploiting class through socialist transformation is not equal to the disappearance of struggle in the political and ideological spheres. . . . The capitalist ideology has been in existence for decades and hundreds of years. The bourgeoisie can be born again, and we must be on the alert against this."[50] Several top economic officials, Chen Yun, Li Fuchun, Li Xiannian, Bo Yibo and Deng Zihui, were criticized by Mao. Serious disputes developed among CCP leaders over the future course of economic

[47]"The Crimes of Liu Shaoqi," *Shoudu Hongweibin*, Peking, February 22, 1967, pp. 1-2.
[48]"Background of Anti-revolutionary Incident of Chang Guan Lou," *Zhong-gong Wenhua Dageming Ziliao Huibian* (Collection of Materials on the Great Cultural Revolution), ed. Ding Wang, vol. II, Hong Kong: Mingbao Yuekan, 1967, pp. 561-62.
[49]"How To Be a Good Communist, Is a Revisionist Program Opposed to the Thought of Mao Zedong," *Guangming Ribao*, April 8, 1967, trans. in *Current Background*, no. 827, pp. 1-50.
[50]*Ibid.*

development. Mao finally called a halt to further retreat from the Party line.[51] It is clear that in this conference Mao launched a counter-attack against the Liu-Deng group. He criticized Liu and others for promoting the rightist line of capitalism and indulging in criminal activities antagonistic to the proletarian headquarters.[52] Mao openly reiterated his leftism and used hostile and harsh criticism against his opponents.

Signs are clear that a strong leftist trend, led by Mao, developed as a result of political struggle. In late September 1962, Mao convened and presided over the 10th Plenum of the 8th Central Committee. The atmosphere at this meeting was still as tense as it had been at the August-September Working Conference. Mao issued a call: "Never forget the class struggle!" He emphatically pointed out that "the utilization of novels to carry out anti-Party activities is a great invention to overthrow political power, it is always necessary first of all to create public opinion, to work in the ideological sphere. This is true for the revolutionary class as well as for the counter-revolutionary class." Explicitly, he attacked dissenters as capitalist roaders who attempted to overthrow socialist China by using novels to influence public opinion. The Communique of the 10th Plenum of the 8th CCP Central Committee called on "the people of the whole country to hold higher the illustrious banners of the General Line of building socialism, the "GLP", the People's communes, and the leadership of the Chairman, and fight to win new victories for China's socialist cause."[53] It was becoming apparent that this was no longer a policy debate, but rather a power struggle between Mao and the dissenters.

In sum, from 1960 to 1962, the Chinese leadership developed a serious split between Mao's leftist faction and his opponents. What had begun as a dispute over economic policy rapidly developed into political conflict and power struggle. Strong leftist campaigns, such as the 'Four Cleans', the 'learn from the PLA', and the Socialist Education Movement, led by Mao, were used to struggle against his opponents. These political conflicts continued in the period 1963-66, finally culminating in the Cultural Revolution of 1967-69.

In the development of the Mao-Liu political struggle, an increasing number of Mao's supporters were forced to be strong "leftists" and to accuse their opponents of being "rightists". In order to weaken their opponents the attackers always tried to be more leftist than those attacked and to show themselves as more revolutionary than their enemies. Thus, most people "would rather be leftist than rightist." The more frequently political struggles

[51] *Beijing Gongshe*, no. 19, April 27, 1967.
[52] "Long Live the Invincible Thought of Mao Zedong!" *Jiehfang Ribao* (Shanghai, undated), translated in *Current Background*, no. 884 July 18, 1969, p. 23.
[53] *Beijing Review*, no. 39, September 28, 1962, pp. 5-7.

took place, the more leftist the people became. The popular belief was that too much leftism was only a matter of methodology, but rightism was a matter of a different political line. Therefore, many people tried to be more leftist than others. In the history of Chinese communism before Mao Zedong's death in 1976 all political movements had been anti-rightist movements; never had there been an anti-leftist movement. Therefore, being a leftist was a way to survive in the political arena. "Rightists" were those who lost in the political struggle. After September 1962, politics consistently tended to move in a "leftist" direction. It was a spiral process; the more political struggle, the more leftist people became. There was no mechanism to adjust this spiral back to its original position. This was also the case in policies of cultural development, education, and economy. More and more, culture, education, and the economy were forced to develop in a "leftist" direction due to this "leftist" spiral process in the power struggle.

To be leftist was a powerful weapon in political struggle, and antiforeignism was a manifestation of leftism. To be a leftist meant to be a revolutionary. To be a revolutionary meant to oppose imperialism and revisionism or to be determined in opposing enemies. Thus, a common phenomenon was that antiforeignism was heightened when people tried to be more leftist. The more leftist they became, the stronger their antiforeignism was. Therefore, as a result of continuous political struggle, increasing numbers of people became more antiforeign than they had been previously. Signs were clear between 1959-62, that a political struggle at the highest level of leadership had resulted in an increasingly leftist ideology and policy. From that time on, a strong leftist group led by Mao himself was preparing itself to struggle against the accused "capitalists" or "capitalist roaders" in the Party.

There was also social support for the increasing development of leftist and antiforeign sentiment. The support came from the workers and peasants owing to improvements in their living conditions and political status in the 1950s. The workers and peasants benefited the most from the policies and ideology of the Chinese Communists. They inevitably felt that everything done by the leftists was good for them and the country. Meanwhile, propaganda of liberation from the oppression by "imperialism" also made these people persist in the belief that they must demonstrate a spirit of "anti-imperialism" in order to defend the liberation of China. Naturally, these social supports were constantly strengthened by "anti-imperialism" propaganda. Therefore, the trend of continuous development toward leftist and antiforeign views did not fade away even after the first decade. It became an irresistible trend which could not be stopped without drastic changes in leadership, political norms, in society, and in the external environment. This continuous development finally erupted into an outburst by the "radical left," and into "fanatic antiforeignism" between 1967 and 1969.

Summary

Peking's ideology of anti-imperialism was deeply rooted in its early history. After the establishment of the government in 1949, Mao's theory of revolution and imperialism was developed into an important element of ideology. This ideology was later strengthened by Peking's perception of a threat from the United States and emerged in "anti-U.S. imperialism." Mao synthesized both the ideology and the perception of threat from the United States into the theory of the 'paper tiger'. Unlike the KMT, which restricted anti-imperialism to the ending of unequal treaties and fixed tariff, the CCP committed itself to "anti-U.S. imperialism." As a result, China was forced to follow a pro-Soviet policy, isolating itself from the West. Moreover, incessant political purges caused by antiforeignism eliminated a great number of intellectuals and militated against the modernization of China.

After 1949, the development of antiforeignism was closely related to internal politics. On the one hand, it became a ready excuse for tightening internal control; on the other, it became an important political weapon in power struggles. As a result of continuous political campaigns and power struggles in the 1950s, antiforeignism reached a higher level than ever before. A spiral process developed in the second decade of the Peking government, which was an apparently irreversible trend toward leftism. Leftism evoked stronger and stronger antiforeignism, which, in turn, fueled leftism. As will be discussed in the next four chapters, this spiral process could not be stopped until after the death of Mao Zedong and following other new developments.

CHAPTER 7

"Anti-U.S. Imperialism and Mobilization for Production, 1960-1962"

The ideology of "anti-U.S. imperialism" had important effects on internal politics, as has been discussed in Chapter 6. In addition, the ideology of "anti-U.S. imperialism" constituted an important political force in mass mobilization. This chapter investigates the relations between Peking's antiforeign mass demonstrations and the mobilization for production in 1960-1962. The purpose of this chapter is to explain how "anti-U.S. imperialism" was related to internal mobilization. First, there is a discussion of internal mobilization and antiforeignism in the early period of the Chinese Communist movement; second, Peking's antiforeign mass demonstrations in 1960-1962, and mass hostility; third, Chinese communist theories on the relations between "anti-U.S. imperialism" and "self-reliance", between "anti-U.S. imperialism" and mass mobilization, and between economic crises and mass mobilization for production 1960-1962. These theories were an important part of communist ideology during 1960-62. They were publicized nation-wide by the mass media. Finally, a content analysis of the *RR* is conducted to investigate the relations between antiforeign mass demonstrations and mobilization for production. (See Appendices I and II)

Internal Mobilization and Antiforeignism Before 1960

Mobilization is extremely important in Chinese Communist politics. The Chinese Communists mobilized the poor peasants on issues of social and economic injustice as early as the Jiangxi Soviet period (1931-34). In order to win support from the majority of peasants, Mao confiscated land from the rich and re-distributed it to the poor peasants. The mass line was more fully developed in the Yanan period. Tens of thousands of new cadres were recruited from the peasants by carrying out campaigns for the reduction of rent and for agrarian reforms.[1] It was with such peasant support that the Communists were able to resist the military superiority of the Nationalist forces for several years. Due to a skilful manipulation of social contradictions, Mao was able to mobilize the peasants in support of his border government.

[1] Mark Selden, "The Yenan Legacy: The Mass Line," in A. Doak Barnett (ed.), *Chinese Communist Politics in Action*, Seattle: University of Washington Press, 1969, pp. 99-151; Chalmers Johnson, "Chinese Communist Leadership and Mass Response," in Ping-ti Ho and Tang Tsou (eds.), *China in Crisis*, vol. I, Chicago: University of Chicago Press, 1968, pp. 397-473.

As mentioned above, since the early days of the CCP's history antiforeignism was utilized to mobilize the masses for political purposes. Sympathy with Mao's determination actively to resist the foreign enemy resulted in the late 1936 Xian Incident, a major turning point in the history of the Chinese Communist movement. The Communists won not only the termination of Chiang's attacks but also a valuable chance to rearm themselves in the name of Chinese resistance to the Japanese.

The use of external enemies for internal purposes continued after the Chinese Communists established their government in Peking in 1949. For example, during the period between 1951 and 1955 three major mass movements were launched, among them the 1951 Resist-America and Aid-Korea Movement which lasted until 1953. The strong anti-foreignism developed by the "Resist-America and Aid-Korea Movement" helped the Party launch the campaign of Suppression of Counter-Revolutionary Elements and the "Three-Antis and Five-Antis Campaign." More importantly, the "Resist-America Movement" was utilized to boost production in both industry and agriculture. Anti-American propaganda was utilized to heighten 'patriotism by means of production'.[2]

A similar development is also to be seen in the period of 1958-60. During this period, China faced an unprecedented economic crisis internally, and concurrently it maintained a high level of hostility toward Taiwan and "U.S. Imperialism." In order to push the Party's economic program during the 1958-60 "Great Leap Forward," the masses were mobilized to participate in production work in order to reach official targets. It was during 1958 that China was involved in a serious crisis in the Taiwan Straits. It has been suggested that this international tension was indeed used by the Chinese to further domestic goals. As Richard Solomon puts it:

> As the Strait crisis thus entered a diplomatic phase, Mao emphasized the turning of this confrontation with "U.S. imperialism" into a context for motivating still greater "leaps in the areas of production and social reorganization by promoting a nation-wide campaign to make 'everyone a soldier'!" Mao thus sped the militarization of the rural work force and the implementation of his new national defense line which called for large militia units.[3]

In examining the relationship between internal politics and foreign policy before 1960, V. P. Dutt maintains:

[2]Qian Duansheng, "Response to Resist-America and Aid Korea Movement", *RR*, October 28, 1951; Chen Shaomin, "Unite the Resist-America Movement with Production Campaign," *RR*, September 16, 1951. Also see John Wilson Lewis, *Leadership in Communist China*, Ithaca, New York: Cornell University 1963, pp. 170-171.

[3]Richard H. Solomon, *Mao's Revolution and Chinese Political Culture*, Berkeley: University of California Press, 1971, p. 388.

"The change in the external posture from 1956 to 1958 was no more marked than a corresponding change within the country for the same period. In fact, domestic changes in mid-1957 presaged the forthcoming changes in foreign policy; they were like the advance shadows cast by the coming events. It was no mere coincidence that the 'big leap', the People's communes, and the anti-rightist struggles led to a renewed insistence on a 'relentless struggle' against the 'paper tigers' of the world."[4]

From these discussions, it becomes clear that there was a close relationship between internal mobilization and antiforeignism. It appears that antiforeignism rose when the degree of internal mobilization was high.

The Nature of Peking's Antiforeign Demonstrations, 1960-1962

Since the founding of the People's Republic of China (PRC), a great number of antiforeign protests have been launched. During the period of the Korean War, over 186 million people throughout China were reported to have participated in demonstrations in support of the "Resist America—Aid Korea Campaign" and in opposition to the remilitarization of Japan (May 1, 1951). Since then, Peking has launched many mass demonstrations against "U.S. Imperialism" and over various other international issues. Antiforeign mass demonstrations have been an important characteristic of Chinese Communist international behavior. A remarkable development in the period 1960-62 was the great increase in these antiforeign mass protests with "U.S. Imperialism" the major target.

China's attitude toward U.S. foreign policy is indicated by official statements and criticisms made of U.S. diplomatic activities. During 1960-62, Peking identified the U.S. as China's most dangerous enemy. As Peking saw it, the United States not only stood in the way of China's fulfilment of her international role but also impeded the incorporation of Taiwan into the PRC. It was the United States that blocked the seating of China at the United Nations, and that supported Japan, Thailand, the Philippines, and other allies in opposing China in world politics. As a result, Peking took a strongly hostile attitude not only toward U.S. policy concerning China, but also toward U.S. diplomatic activities in other areas. For instance, in April and June 1961 both Averell Harriman and Lyndon B. Johnson, then the American Vice-President, visited the Philippines and Southeast Asia. Their trips to Southeast Asia were interpreted as part of an aggressive plot. Peking's antiforeign mass protests in

---

[4] *Ibid.* Also see Morton H. Halperin and Dwight H. Perkins, *Communist China and Arms Control*, Cambridge, Mass.: Harvard University Press, 1965, pp. 21-22. The authors argue that there was a close relation between a hardening foreign policy line and a similar domestic policy line in 1958, perhaps even into 1960.

this period, 1960-62, were mostly directed against U.S. diplomatic and military activities in Cuba and Vietnam.

The antiforeign mass demonstration in China is a government-organized movement rather than a movement initiated by the masses. Each mass demonstration movement has a life cycle with a number of different stages, all movements being initiated by the top Party leadership in Peking. Decisions are usually announced at a public meeting in Peking attended by responsible persons in the Party or government, and by leaders of various kinds of related people's organizations such as the China Peace Committee, the All-China Federation of Trade Unions, the All-China Federation of Women, the All-China Federation of Young Pioneers, the Chinese Committee for Afro-Asian Solidarity, the National Literary and Art Federation, and others. These people's organizations are led by the Party and serve as bridges linking the Party with other groups. Usually, they help the Party to distribute instructions and documents to the people and to organize "study groups." In antiforeign movements they serve as organizational forces to propagandize the Party decision and slogans, and to help mobilize the masses. For example, in the movement protesting against the Japan-U.S. Security Treaty in early 1960, a meeting on January 13 held in Peking to condemn the "Japan-U.S. military alliance" was attended by most of the people's organizations mentioned above. In support of this movement several demonstrations were held in Shanghai, Shenyang, Wuhan, Canton and other major cities.[5] The rest of the antiforeign mass campaigns during this period were initiated and launched by similar meetings in Peking.

In addition, the development of each antiforeign mass movement was under the control of the Party and the government through organizations and the mass media, the degree of development also being controlled by the authorities. In addition to serving as a communication link between the central authority and local authority, the mass media serve as an operational belt leading directly to the masses. In the fermentation stage, the mass media propagandize the attitude of the central authority and focus their coverage on the campaign. During this period, the local cadres excite the masses into an upsurge of emotional energy. The development of each antiforeign mass movement is well-directed, and few of them can slip out of control and be turned against the central authority. Thus, the antiforeign mass demonstration is a government-directed protest rather than a spontaneous mass movement. It is not a social movement which demands a change in social order, social institutions or social norms. This is an important difference between antiforeign mass demonstrations in China and in Western countries and also an important difference between pre- and post-1949 in China.

[5] *RR*, January 24, 25, 27 and 28, 1960.

Five Types of Antiforeign Mass Demonstration

Antiforeign mass demonstrations in this period can be divided into five categories, in terms of their articulated targets. First of all, a number of mass demonstrations were directed against U.S. diplomatic activities toward China. For example, President Eisenhower's visit to Taiwan in June 1960 caused mass rallies in Peking and Shanghai protesting against his visit. Generally, mass protests against U.S. diplomatic activities toward China were held in major cities such as Peking and Shanghai. Participants in these demonstrations were delegates from various circles—intellectual, cultural, and governmental officials. The number of participants was relatively small, ranging from several hundred to one thousand. During this period Eisenhower's visit to Taiwan and the Chinese U-2 incident in September 1962 caused nation-wide mass demonstrations against the U.S. The remainder of the mass demonstrations of this type against the U.S. were held only in Peking, Shanghai, and a small number of other cities.

The second type of antiforeign mass demonstration was directed against a number of issues concerning U.S. diplomatic relations with countries other than China. Two remarkable issues of this type were the renewal of the Japan-U.S. Security Treaty and the condemnation of a U.S. U-2 fight over the Soviet Union, both occurring in 1960. The mass demonstrations generated by these issues spread generally throughout the nation and evoked a national fervor. In protesting against the renewal of the Japan-U.S. Security Treaty, China organized 40 mass demonstrations with approximately 15 million people participating. In protest against the U-2 espionage activities in the Soviet Union, 96 mass demonstrations were organized and reportedly involved approximately 39 million people.

The third type of demonstration, including mass demonstrations, was directed against U.S. imperialism and in support of the people of N. Korea, Laos, N. Vietnam, Cuba and other developing countries struggling against U.S. imperialism. During this period, mass demonstrations protesting against U.S. "aggression" or "involvement" in foreign countries were quite frequent, but the size of the movements themselves was quite small. Most of the issues which these protests centered on emerged as national issues. The two most heated issues were N. Vietnam and Cuba, and Peking launched several series of mass demonstrations in support of these countries' struggle against U.S. imperialism. Nevertheless, the size and number of such demonstrations were much smaller than the mass protests of the first and second categories mentioned above.

The fourth type of protest involved mass demonstrations against the past conduct of the U.S. in the Korean War in 1950, and the so-called "anti-U.S.

movement" in Taiwan.[6] Mass demonstrations protesting against these past issues were not held regularly. For example, in both 1960 and 1961 nation-wide mass demonstrations were held in protest against the past conduct of the U.S. in Taiwan. No demonstrations, however, were held in 1962. Similarly, mass demonstrations were not held every year to protest against "U.S. aggression" in the Korean War. During the three years under study, such a demonstration was held only in October, 1960.

The fifth category of mass demonstrations includes those directed against countries with which China was in direct dispute. During this period only two such issues generated mass protests in China: one was directed against the action of the Indonesian authorities in West Java forcing overseas Chinese to evacuate residential areas, in July 1960; the other was against Nehru's "slander" during the Sino-Indian border dispute in December 1961. Demonstrations on both occasions were quite small in size and did not develop into national movements. During this period, Peking did not launch any nation-wide move-ments in protest against actions by foreign governments other than the U.S.

Mass demonstrations appear at first sight to have been used as diplomatic weapons in support of China's position on international issues and to propa-gandize Peking's attitude toward U.S. foreign policies. Four hundred and ninety-eight mass demonstrations were held in this period to protest against "U.S. imperialism." Further examination of these mass demonstrations, however, makes it difficult for us to take a simplistic view. A close survey of these mass demonstrations protesting against "U.S. imperialism" reveals a large area of inconsistency and a significant possibility that Peking was using mass demonstration for other ends.

There is hardly any doubt that Peking selected important issues for these mass demonstrations. It would be misleading to say, however, that Peking used mass demonstrations solely in protest against important U.S. activities provocative to the Chinese. For example, in the first half of 1962, Peking was convinced that the U.S. was collaborating with the Nationalist government in Taiwan in preparation for an attack upon China.[7] Faced with such a critical issue Peking did not organize a single public meeting in protest against it. Mass demonstrations, however, were held to protest against U.S. conduct in the Congo (February 1) and in N. Vietnam (March 5). Some of the nation-wide demonstrations would be difficult to justify from Peking's diplomatic position: for example, it is widely known that there were serious disputes

---

[6]On May 24, 1958, a mass rally in Taipei was sparked by an incident in which a nationalist Chinese officer was killed by an American military officer.

[7]See Liao Kuang-sheng and Allen S. Whiting, "Chinese Press Perceptions of Threat: The U.S. and India, 1962," *The China Quarterly*, January-March 1973, pp. 80-97.

between Peking and Moscow in late 1959,[8] and yet, a massive nation-wide movement on behalf of the Soviet Union's opposition to the U.S. took place in the second half of May 1960 to support Khrushchev's condemnation of "U.S. imperialism" at the summit meeting, in respect of the U-2 flight over the Soviet Union. Mass demonstrations followed in 96 cities, lasting one week and reportedly involving approximately 30 million people, the largest mass protest in the period 1960-62.

The reasons for such a massive scale of demonstration remain unclear. Undoubtedly, Peking could have manipulated the selection of important issues for mass demonstration; furthermore, Peking could have manipulated the size of antiforeign mass demonstrations. This could happen in all kinds of demonstrations, as noted above. By way of comparison, mass protests against "U.S. imperialism" were much larger than those against India and Indonesia, and the size of antiforeign mass demonstrations was much larger in 1960 than in 1961 and 1962. Data also show that antiforeign mass demonstration became less frequent in 1962 compared to 1960 and 1961 (see Tables 7.1-7.4). Again, this suggests the possibility that the size of antiforeign mass demonstrations was manipulated. The above are preliminary findings derived from data collected from the mass media.[9] The preliminary analysis fails to provide an explanation of the motives for Peking's antiforeign mass demonstrations. Therefore, it is necessary to examine the hostility of Peking's mass demonstrations and their relations with internal politics.

Antiforeign Mass Demonstrations and Mass Hostility in China

Political participation is an important aspect of political life in China and the antiforeign mass demonstrations in China came to be norm-oriented movements.[10] Two images, i.e. the image of "the enemy" and the image of "anti-China", underlie the ideological motivation for antiforeign mass demonstrations.

During this period the major image of "the enemy" was "U.S. imperialism." The components of the image of "U.S. imperialism" included threats, hostility and an aggressive attitude toward China and countries such as North Korea, Cuba and the Congo, which were friendly toward China. From Peking's point of view, "U.S. imperialism" was the major force behind the "anti-China clique" which had prevented China from entering the United

[8] John Gittings, *The World and China, 1922-1972*, New York: Harper & Row, 1974, pp. 237-259.
[9] The data are based on *RR*, *Guangming Ribao*, and *Nanfeng Ribao*.
[10] James R. Townsend, *Political Participation in Communist China*, Berkeley: University of California Press, 1972, pp. 67-69.

Table 7.1
ANTIFOREIGN DEMONSTRATIONS, 1960

| Month | Target | | | Total |
	U.S.	S.U.*	Others	
January	5	0	0	5
February	3	0	0	3
March	0	0	0	0
April	32	0	3	35
May	114	99	1	214
June	103	0	0	103
July	6	0	18	24
August	8	0	1	9
September	0	0	16	16
October	12	0	1	13
November	0	0	14	14
December	0	0	0	0
Total	283	99	54	436

*Support the Soviet Union in opposing "U.S. Imperialism"
Source: *RR*, 1960

Table 7.2
ANTIFOREIGN DEMONSTRATIONS, 1961

| Month | Target | | | Total |
	U.S.	S.U.	Others	
January	1	0	0	1
February	16	0	0	16
March	0	0	0	0
April	32	0	0	32
May	0	0	0	0
June	0	0	0	0
July	0	0	0	0
August	0	0	0	0
September	0	0	0	0
October	0	0	0	0
November	1	0	0	1
December	0	0	2	2
Total	50	0	2	52

Source: *RR*, 1961

Table 7.3

ANTIFOREIGN DEMONSTRATIONS, 1962

Month		Target		Total
	U.S.	S.U.	India	
January	22	0	0	22
February	1	0	0	1
March	1	0	0	1
April	0	0	0	0
May	0	0	0	0
June	0	0	0	0
July	2	0	0	2
August	0	0	0	0
September	15	0	1	16
October	11	0	1	12
November	37	0	4	41
December	0	0	4	4
Total	89	0	10	99

Source: *RR*, 1962

Table 7.4

ANTIFOREIGN DEMONSTRATIONS, 1963

Month		Target		Total
	U.S.	S.U.*	India	
January	0	0	3	3
February	0	0	0	0
March	0	0	0	0
April	0	0	3	3
May	0	0	1	1
June	0	0	1	1
July	10	1	0	11
August	3	0	4	7
September	2	1	0	3
October	0	0	0	0
November	16	0	0	16
December	4	1	0	5
Total	35	3	12	50

*Against the Soviet Union
Source: *RR*, 1963

Nations and from liberating Taiwan. Militarily, the U.S. had not only stationed its Seventh Fleet in the Taiwan Strait but had also conducted continuous espionage activities against China with its surveillance-planes, and had repeatedly intruded upon China's frontier islands. Diplomatically, "U.S. imperialism," together with its allies had blocked China's diplomatic development of cultural and economic activities. "U.S. imperialism" was China's major enemy: it was politically suppressive, ideologically reactionary, economically exploitative, and militarily threatening and aggressive. During its first decade, the Peking government repeatedly stressed that "U.S. imperialism" was not only the major enemy of the Chinese people but also the enemy of the people of the whole world. "U.S. imperialism" presented the deepest and most prevailing image of hostility to the Chinese masses.

This image of "the enemy" contained three components: historical, ideological and political hostility. Historically, "U.S. imperialism" had opposed the Chinese communist revolution, and collaborated with the reactionary Nationalist forces which had oppressed the Chinese people; ideologically, it represented the highest stage of capitalism, while politically, "U.S. imperialism" had conducted a hostile policy toward China, exemplified in such acts as the military "occupation" of Taiwan.[11] Thus, the image could not change unless all three elements in the contradiction were resolved. During the Sino-Japanese war, the Chinese image of Japanese imperialism had included these three components, and the later development of the image of "Soviet Socialist Imperialism" also contained them. Since the Yanan period, the CCP has created the image of "the enemy" and fully utilized it as an opponent to struggle against. During the period under study, demonstrations against the U.S. were based on this image, although there were additional issues involved.

The second image reflected in mass demonstrations was the "anti-China" image. During this period, the anti-China countries were those which did not have diplomatic relations with Peking and those which had diplomatic relations with Peking but which had adopted some policy jeopardizing Peking's national interest. Those which did not have diplomatic relations with Peking, were close allies of the U.S. such as Japan, the Philippines, and Thailand. These countries, while not posing a serious military threat to China, might co-operate with the U.S. in "anti-China" activities. Peking held that these countries were controlled by "reactionary governments" which had adopted a policy of collaboration with the U.S. Because the people in these countries were peace-loving and basically friendly to China, however, Peking

[11] M. Rejai, *Mao Zedong on Revolution and War*, Anchor Books, New York: Doubleday & Co., 1970, p. 50.

was hostile only toward their governments and reactionary leaders, and not to the countries themselves. In Peking's view, these countries would become friendly to China once "U.S. imperialism" was defeated or when the leaders of their governments had been removed. The hostile attitude of such states toward China was only temporary.

With regard to countries which had diplomatic relations with China but which conducted "anti-China" policies, Peking held that they might collaborate with the U.S., as in the case of India under Nehru or Indonesia under Sukarno. These two countries had once been friendly with China but, because of their leadership, had followed an "anti-China" policy and were thus potentially hostile to China. Yet they were not considered enemies of China. During the Sino-Indian border conflict, for example, Peking considered India an "anti-China" country but not an enemy of China.[12]

Through the mass media network, routine educational programs and ideological training programs, the Party constantly indoctrinated students, peasants, workers, the military forces, and other sectors of the population with these two images of hostility.[13] A strong belief in these two images became deeply rooted among the masses.

"Anti-U.S. Imperialism" and Mobilization for Production: Theoretical Developments During the "Great Leap Forward" (GLF)

As part of the image-making of "U.S. imperialism", the Chinese mass media and other propaganda networks widely publicized the relationship between "anti-U.S. imperialism" and mobilization for production. It was during the GLF, a time when mass mobilization was a basic policy for promoting production, that some of the most coherent theoretical statements linking anti-imperialism with the production struggle were made by Mao himself. A discussion of "anti-U.S. imperialism" and mobilization for production may be divided into the following three parts:

1. "Anti-U.S. Imperialism" and "Self-reliance":

In accordance with the Chinese Communist ideology, internal politics cannot be separated from international politics. Chinese Communists believe that there are two major burdens which they must bear: one is social or class struggle against internal and external reactionaries, the other is the struggle against nature. Mao said in 1958, "To defend our socialist construction, to defend world peace, we must struggle against foreign reactionaries and oppose

---

[12] See Liao Kuang-sheng and Allen S. Whiting, *op. cit.*

[13] Alan P. L. Liu, *Communications and National Integration in Communist China*, Berkeley: University of California Press, 1971, pp. 25-33, ch. 3.

imperialism, mainly U.S. imperialist aggression."[14] This argument provided the foundation for the Party's launching political campaigns internally and opposing imperialism externally, while linking these to the country's commitment to socialist construction.

According to the Chinese Communist argument, it is only when people engage in social struggle successfully that the country will achieve the basis conditions for the struggle against nature. Conversely, victory in the struggle against nature will strengthen the forces engaged in social struggle. For example, in 1957 Peking argued that the strengthening of the forces of socialist economic construction during the previous years had not only greatly benefited internal class struggle but had also elevated the nation's international status and prestige and strengthened it in its opposition to imperialist aggression and in its defense of world peace.[15] Thus, in Chinese Communist ideology the striving to build socialism and the struggle to increase production are couched in terms of struggles against imperialism.

This was further clarified in 1963 when Mao launched the so-called "Three Revolutionary Movements."[16] The movements were class struggle, production struggle, and scientific experiment. Mao believed that in the history of proletarian revolution there is always class struggle between the proletarian class and the capitalist class, and that serious struggle against the capitalists is necessary if the proletarian dictatorship is to be consolidated. The second movement was the struggle for production which is essentially a struggle against the forces of nature. Production is considered to be the basic human activity in which human beings will form certain relations (relations of production) in conducting the struggle for production. In this struggle, all resources should be mobilized into an organizational force, and should be fully utilized to increase material wealth and to cope with economic problems. The third movement was the scientific revolution. Peking frankly admitted that the level of scientific achievement was still low, and that in order to build modern industry, modern agriculture and a modern state, it would be necessary to improve scientific technology. Peking believed these three movements to be mutually related to each other: class struggle will provide production struggle with a driving force; production struggle will test class ideology

[14] *Xue Xi Mao Zhu Xi Lun Zhi Lao Hu Wen Xian* (Documents on Chairman Mao's Discussion of Paper Tiger), Hong Kong: *Wen Hui Pao*, 1958, pp. 76-77.

[15] *Ibid.*, pp. 78-79.

[16] The three movements were first mentioned by Mao Zedong in his speech at the National CCP Propaganda Work Conference in March 1957. It has been vigorously disseminated since 1963. The Constitution of the Ninth CCP National Congress and Tenth CCP National Congress have both put forward the proposal that it was necessary to carry on the three great revolutionary movements. *RR*, April 29, 1969 and September 2, 1973.

politically; scientific experiment will improve labor productivity.[17]

The relationship between revolution and production was further clarified during the Cultural Revolution. On September 7, 1966, an editorial in the *RR* urged the masses to "Grasp Revolution and Promote Production." It claimed that, according to Mao's directive, the Proletarian Cultural Revolution was to provide socialist productivity in China with a strong driving force. It explained that the Cultural Revolution would revolutionize human thought, liberate social productivity, mobilize and promote the masses of workers, develop greater production activism and creativity among the members of the people's communes, and provide favorable conditions for greater development in industry and agriculture.

Evidently, these three movements were considered concrete examples of social struggle and struggle against nature. Self-reliance as a policy of independence, was manifested in social revolution, production struggle, and scientific experimentation. Social struggle was carried out in the form of class struggle, of which anti-imperialism is an aspect. Like class struggle, the struggle against imperialism would provide a driving force for production struggle and scientific experimentation. In other words, it would provide an ideological stimulus for self-reliance. This provided the theoretical and ideological justification for continous movement along the path of anti-imperialism, while self-reliance became a high priority in the production struggle.

2. "Anti-U.S. Imperialism" and Mass Mobilization:

As Mao pointed out in 1958, "to recognize revolutionary force and reactionary force we should begin by understanding that the current struggles against imperialism in each country are mainly struggles against U.S. imperialist suppression and aggression. U.S. imperialism has replaced Japanese imperialism and has launched intense aggression against China since 1949. . . . When we say that 'imperialism is ferocious', we mean that its nature will never change, that imperialists will never lay down their cleavers, and that they will never become Buddhas until their final destruction. The aim of imperialism is to enslave and oppress the people of the whole world and eliminate the socialist countries and the people's revolutionary forces in all countries. This aim which it clings to will never change until its doom."[18] Mao went on to say, "The policy of the reactionary forces toward the democratic forces of the people is definitely to destroy all they can and to prepare to destroy later

[17]*RR*, September 7, 1966.
[18]Wen Shirun, "Scientific Judgement and Foresight: Study of Chairman Mao Zedong's Theses on International Questions as Expounded in The Fourth Volume of Selected of Mao Zedong," *Hongqi*, no. 22, 1960. Translated by Joint Publication of Research Service (JPRS) no. 6700, pp. 7-21.

whatever they cannot destroy now."[19]

Mao emphasized the use of mass mobilization in fighting against imperialists when he pointed out in 1958 that, "There is no other way to deal with imperialism but to mobilize the people of the whole world to carry out resolute and effective struggle against it. It is futile to persuade the imperialists and the Chinese reactionaries in the hope that they will become kind-hearted and turn over a new leaf. The only course open to us is to organize our forces to fight them."[20] In short, it is only through such persistent struggles that one can check the activities of imperialism. Mao believed, moreover, that anti-imperialism and mass mobilization are positively linked. He pointed out, "Their (imperialists') anti-China activities can instigate the entire Party and the entire people to unite and create the ambition and determination to catch up with and surpass the most developed Western countries economically and culturally. . . . Therefore, so far as we are concerned, their anti-China activities are a good thing, and not a bad thing."[21] Mao even believed that to be attacked by the enemy is desirable. In 1959 he said:

> I hold that it is bad as far as we are concerned if a person, a political party, an army, or a school is not attacked by the enemy. for in that case it would definitely mean that we have sunk to the level of the enemy. It is good if we are attacked by the enemy, since it proves that we have drawn a clear line of demarcation between the enemy and ourselves. It is still better if the enemy attacks us widely and paints us as utterly black and without a single virtue; it demonstrates that we have not only drawn a clear line of demarcation between the enemy and ourselves, but achieved a great deal in our work.[22]

Thus, it is clear that Mao believed attack by the enemy is good for internal unity. In other words it promoted mass mobilization.

The most striking discussion of the relation between the enemy and mass mobilization can be found in a *Hongqi* commentary of 1958. The commentary suggests that when the "U.S. bandits" stand beside the bed of the Chinese people, every Chinese will surely be awakened to the reality that he has no choice but to work keenly and vigorously to strengthen national forces in order to deal with the enemy.[23] The commentary also claims that,

> "The U.S. aggressor insults us, but serves as a counter-lesson for us in every aspect. First the U.S. aggressor insults us because our steel production is too small. This

[19] *Ibid.*
[20] *Ibid.*
[21] "On the Anti-China Question, "(March, 1960) in *Mao Zedong Si Xiang Wan Sui*, Taipei: Institute of International Relations, pp. 316-317.
[22] "To be attacked by the enemy is not a bad thing but a good thing," (March 26, 1939), *Selected Readings*, p. 61.
[23] *Hongqi*, no. 10, 1958.

calls for us to endeavour to develop our steel industry with the greatest speed. Secondly, the U.S. aggressor insults us because the level of our machinery production is too low. This calls for us to make even greater efforts to develop the machinery industry with the greatest speed. Thirdly, the U.S. aggressor often laughs at our poverty. This calls for us to answer him with the greatest speed in increasing our food production."[24]

These are the three ways U.S. imperialism was considered a spur to China's production.

The commentary also makes clear the political implications of imperialist insults. It accuses the U.S. of viewing China in the old way as disunited and calls on the people to organize themselves more vigorously (i.e., the communization movement) and to strengthen national defense (i.e., the all peoples' militia campaign).[25] Thus, it is clear that U.S. pressure forced China to mobilize its natural resources to strengthen its position in all respects.[26]

3. Economic Crisis and Mass Mobilization for Production:

Since foreign relations are not separable from internal politics, a brief consideration of internal politics will help us examine the relations between antiforeign demonstrations and internal mobilization for production.

China's economy suffered severe setbacks during the period from 1959 to 1962. Natural calamities—drought, floods and storms caused serious damage to the economy. As a result of such economic setbacks, severe food shortages occurred all over China, the seriousness of which can be estimated from the situation faced by the PLA at that time. The General Rear Services Departments reported that the prescribed amount of principal and supplementary food was not available, and that both officers and soldiers were suffering from widespread under-nourishment and edema.[27] In order to overcome the food shortage, local PLA units in early 1961 were urged to produce substitute food and to organize groups to undertake this work.[28]

Food shortages led to a relaxation in early 1961 of official commune regulations, and members were encouraged to produce supplementary food by engaging in sideline production like raising pigs and poultry. Private plots were made available for family use and a limited private trade in farm products was permitted. Above all, bonuses were to be issued in kind so as to stimulate

---

[24] Ibid.
[25] Ibid.
[26] Ibid.
[27] J. Chester Cheng, ed., The Politics of the Chinese Red Army (Gong Zuo Tung Xun), Hoover Institution Publications, Stanford: Stanford University, 1966, pp. 296-299.
[28] Ibid.

additional efforts on the part of production brigades.[29] According to the latest report, during the economic depression from 1960-62, the production of agricultural raw materials and farm products dropped by about 30% from the high point reached in 1958, and industrial production dropped by about 20%.[30]

In 1960, as a result of the severe agricultural crisis, Peking adopted a new policy to make agricultural production its first priority. "Take agriculture as the foundation" became a national campaign, and the country was mobilized to support production.[31] This new policy elevated agriculture to the first priority, followed by light and heavy industry. It is obvious that the agricultural setbacks of 1959 and 1960 had adversely affected light industrial production by reducing supplies of raw materials for manufacturing, and as a result, increasing agricultural and light industrial production became the major concern of the Peking government. Towards this end, Peking mobilized millions of people to support production in agriculture as well as in industry: students, workers, cadres, and PLA members were sent to assist in the agricultural struggle. Meanwhile, because of shortages of raw materials, many industries suffered serious setbacks during the period. In order to maintain some balance between supply and demand, the government urged workers in factories to fulfil state output targets.

Mobilization of people at all levels to support agricultural production was an important element in the fight against natural calamities and the deterioration of agricultural and industrial output. China's agricultural output depended very much upon manpower and the role of machines was still very limited in the early 1960s; thus, human effort was the key to increasing production. A *RR* editorial, on March 4, 1960, entitled "Strive for a Bumper Yield in the Early Rice Harvest," urged the use of all possible resources to increase agricultural production and included students, workers, cadres, and the PLA among the social elements to be mobilized.[32] In 1960 many activities were organized by the local authorities to develop such support. For example, in Henan province, more than one million workers in industry, communication, and commerce reportedly gave all-out support to the current anti-drought movement.[33] In Guangdong about one million laborers were mobilized to reinforce production teams on the communes.[34]

---

[29]Werner Klatt, "Communist China's Agricultural Calamities," in *China Under Mao: Politics Takes Command*, ed. Federick MacFarquhar, Cambridge, Mass.: The MIT Press, 1972, pp. 170-171.

[30]*Zhong Guo Jingji Nian Jian—1981* (Annual Economic Report of China—1981), Peking: Peking Guangli Zazhi She, pp. VI-10, VI-13. Also see Barry M. Richman, *Industrial Society in Communist China*, New York: Vintage Books, 1972, pp. 612-613.

[31]*Hongqi*, no. 1, 1960.

[32]*RR*, March 4, 1960.

[33]*RR*, July 4, 1960.

[34]*RR*, July 11, 1960.

The mass media was frequently employed to sustain mass enthusiasm and encourage greater production. We see from reports in the *RR* that news items concerning mass mobilization in production not only carried up-to-date news from local communes and factories but also tried to raise morale among peasants, workers, and the people at large.[35]

Reports of the movement to mobilize people to support agricultural and industrial production reflect the emphasis placed by the Party and government on the implementation of this policy. The frequency of these reports can be used to represent the development of this movement. As shown by data collected from the *RR*, the high-tide of the mobilization of people in agricultural production was in the second half of 1960 and the first six months of 1961 (see Figure 7.1). The movement gradually declined in the second half of 1961, and in 1962 fell further below the 1960 and 1961 levels. With regard to mobilization of people for industrial production, the high-tide was in the period of April-June 1960. The mobilization was maintained at a high level up to the end of 1960, but gradually declined in 1961, and the downward trend continued in 1962. In sum, the movement of the mobilization of people for agricultural and industrial production returned to a normal level by the end of 1962, when the economy had gradually improved.

Antiforeign Demonstrations and Productional Mobilization: An Empirical Investigation

From the above discussion, it is clear that in the period under study (1960-October 1962, before the outbreak of the Sino-Indian Border War) China was engulfed in national mobilization for production.[36] During this period Peking was also very active in organizing mass demonstrations protesting against U.S. imperialism and other international issues. It is remarkable that a country so deeply engrossed in mobilization of people for production could, at the same time, engage in so many mass demonstrations against foreign countries and international issues. In this section, the relationship between internal mobilization for production and antiforeign mass demonstrations will be investigated based on the number of news items calling for mobilization and the frequency

---

[35] A content analysis was conducted for this analysis. It includes reports which directly urged increases in industrial or agricultural production and reports which described particular success stories, using them as models to stimulate morale and increase industrial or agricultural production.

[36] This research covers the period from January 1960 to October 1962, during which China had no direct involvement in physical conflict. It excludes November and December 1962 from the test for the reason that during these two months Peking was preoccupied with the border war with India.

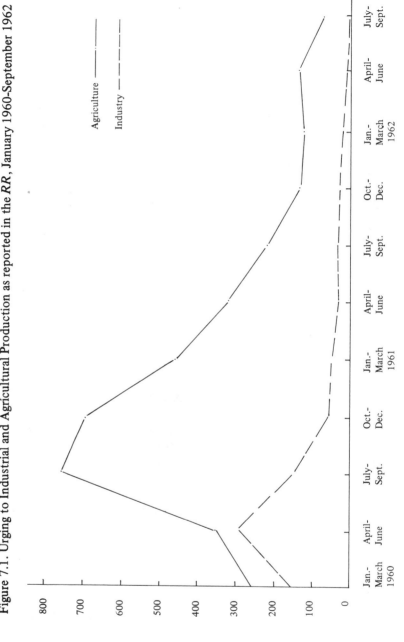

Figure 7.1. Urging to Industrial and Agricultural Production as reported in the *RR*, January 1960–September 1962

of antiforeign mass demonstrations.

The hypothesis is that in order to mobilize production to increase industrial and agricultural output Peking deliberately stepped up antiforeign mass demonstrations. There are two possible bases for this hypothesis. First, in order to displace attention from economic difficulties, Peking might have chosen to stir up stronger feelings of hostility toward external enemies. It is clear that discontent was widespread during the GLF because of rapid changes and disruptions in the life of the people. During the economic crisis, most people suffered serious food shortages which aggravated their dissatisfaction. To alleviate the dissatisfaction among the people, Peking may have deliberately heightened its antiforeign mass protest.

Second, in addition to improving organization and offering material incentives, as discussed in connection with anti-imperialism and self-reliance, Peking may have increased its external attacks as a method of stimulating national productivity. During the economic crisis, meeting the state plan in industrial production was as important as increasing agricultural production. The Peking Government spared no efforts along these lines, and an antiforeign mass movement may have been seen as another useful approach to this objective. China's industries were still located mainly in urban areas, with development up to 1960 still concentrated in 115 cities, the population of which ranged from 100,000 to one million and above.[37] Cadres and workers in cities were more deeply engaged in antiforeign mass campaigns because they were better organized and more easily mobilized than their counterparts in rural areas. It is possible that the Party initiated these antiforeign protests in order to help mobilization for production. The antiforeign mass protests always mobilized great numbers of people in these cities—from several hundred thousand to one or two million. As discussed in connection with anti-imperialism and mass mobilization, rallies and public condemnations of "imperialism" were intended to stimulate workers ideologically and heighten their nationalistic spirit, and thereby also affect production. Thus, the hypothesis is that antiforeign mass demonstrations will increase when mobilization for production is high.

The data for antiforeign mass demonstrations has been recorded according to the frequency of rallies taking place at each location.[38] The degree of

[37] Yuan-li Wu, H. C. Ling, and Grace H. Wu, *The Spatial Economy of Communist China*, Hoover Institution Publications, New York Praeger, 1967, pp. 1-31.

[38] The author utilizes R. J. Rummel's definition of antiforeign demonstration stated below. In the study of international politics, the antiforeign demonstration has been considered to be one form of international conflict behavior. In his studies "Dimensions of Conflict Behavior Within Nations, 1946-59" and "Dimensions of Conflict Behavior Within and Between Nations," Rummel defined the antiforeign demonstration as any

internal mobilization for agricultural and industrial production has been measured according to the reports in the *RR*, which, because it is a nation-wide newspaper under the control of the Central Committee of the Party, serves as a major medium for information and for the furthering of efforts to carry out national policy. As stated above in connection with the economic crisis and mass mobilization for production, the frequency of reports indicate the development of this movement in each period of time. The data is organized in terms of monthly units.

In the examination of antiforeign mass demonstrations and mobilization for agricultural production, a positive correlation is found. The degree of agricultural mobilization is divided into three levels, low, medium, and high, based on the frequency of reports of agricultural mobilization. The monthly average of antiforeign mass demonstrations was 5.1 when the degree of agricultural mobilization was at the low level (1-50); it was 6.1 when the degree of agricultural mobilization was at the medium level (51-100). It increased further when agricultural mobilization was at the high level. The monthly average of antiforeign mass demonstrations was 27.7 when agricultural mobilization was high (101-294). This consistent pattern indicates that antiforeign mass demonstrations increased when the degree of agricultural mobilization was high. (Figure 7.2)

The relationship between antiforeign mass demonstration protest and mobilization for industrial production is parallel to that for agricultural mobilization. As shown in Figure 7.3, the monthly average for antiforeign demonstrations was 4.7 when the degree of industrial mobilization was low (0-10), and 6.5 when the degree of industrial mobilization was at the medium level (11-20). The monthly average of mass demonstrations was 33.4 when the degree of industrial mobilization was at the high level (21-98). Similar to the findings dealing with agricultural mobilization and antiforeign mass protest, this indicates that antiforeign mass demonstrations increased when

---

demonstration or riot by more than one hundred people directed at a particular foreign country (or group of countries) or its policies. It includes the gathering of more than one hundred people to hear speeches and to march in protest against the policy of another country. Demonstrations and riots against a foreign occupying authority in the occupied part of a country are considered antiforeign demonstrations. Rummel collected data on twenty-two aspects of foreign and domestic conflict behavior for seventy-seven nations including China, for the years from 1949 to 1959. The antiforeign demonstration was found to be correlated with military action and the severance of diplomatic relations, the so-called belligerent dimension of foreign relations. See R. J. Rummel, "Dimensions of Conflict Behavior Within Nations, 1946-59," and "Dimensions of Conflict Behavior Within and Between Nations," both in John V. Gillespie and Betty A. Nesvold (ed.), *Macro-Quantitative Analysis*, Beverly Hills, California: SAGE Publication, 1971, pp. 39-48, 49-84.

the degree of industrial mobilization was high.

Based on these findings, we can confirm the hypothesis that antiforeign mass demonstrations increase with mobilization for production. Mobilization in agricultural or industrial production leads to an increase in antiforeign mass demonstrations. Thus, the high frequency of antiforeign mass protests during the period from 1960 to 1962 is closely related to the increase in internal mobilization for production.

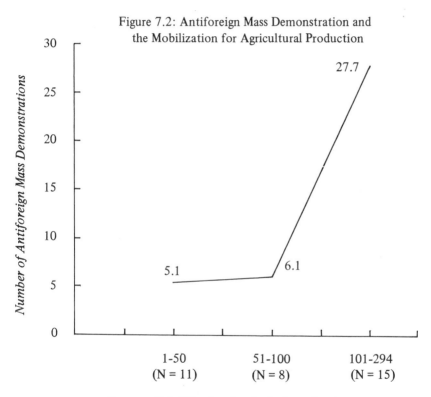

Figure 7.2: Antiforeign Mass Demonstration and the Mobilization for Agricultural Production

Degree of Mobilization for Agriculture Production

Summary

Antiforeign mass demonstrations in China were organized by the government and the Party, and reflected hostility directed by the authorities rather than spontaneous mass hostility. From Peking's point of view, anti-imperialism is helpful not only for self-reliance but also for mobilization for production.

Figure 7.3: Antiforeign Mass Demonstration and
the Mobilization for Industrial Production

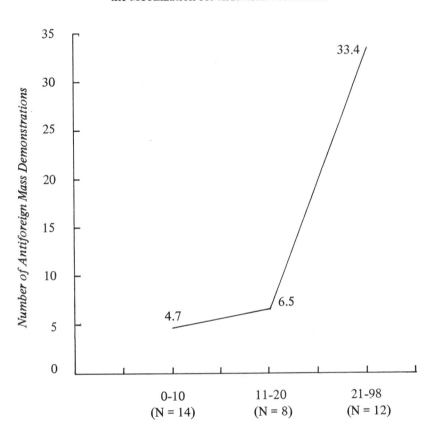

Degree of Mobilization for Industrial Production

Thus, antiforeign mass demonstrations can be manipulated for the purpose of internal mobilization. Because of the nature of Peking's antiforeign mass demonstrations and its ideological relations with internal politics, any study of Peking's antiforeign mass demonstrations must also examine internal politics in China.

Findings in this study show that antiforeign mass demonstrations increased when the degree of agricultural and industrial mobilization was high. These two findings confirm the hypothesis that Peking utilized antiforeign mass demonstrations to stimulate mobilization for both agricultural and industrial productions during the period 1960-62.

CHAPTER 8
"Anti-U.S. Imperialism" and the United Front Policy
with the Third World, 1960-62

This chapter examines the relations between Peking's anti-U.S. imperialism and its "United Front" foreign policy. Emphasis is placed on an examination of Peking's propaganda against "U.S. imperialism" and the manipulation of "anti-U.S. imperialism" in China's diplomatic development within the third world.

In the period under study, 1960-1962, Peking's foreign policy appears to be confusing and ambiguous. On the surface, Peking was waging a propaganda war against the United States, and attacks against "U.S. imperialism" appeared frequently in the mass media. Peking appeared unusually hostile in its attitude toward the U.S., and the frequency of attacks against the U.S. was unprecedentedly high. This is the image generally to be gleaned from Peking's official sources. There is evidence, however, to prove that Peking intentionally lowered the tension in the Taiwan Strait to avoid military conflict with the U.S. and Taiwan. The rise of propaganda in the mass media can be accounted for in two ways. Towards the end of 1960, Peking attempted to arouse the sentiment of "anti-U.S. imperialism" to modify its break with the Soviet Union, and in order to form a united front between the Communist bloc and Afro-Asian countries. In the period 1961 to 1962, however, Peking shifted from maintaining a united front to following its own independent policy, when relations between Peking and Moscow further deteriorated. "Anti-U.S. imperialism" then became a powerful source of propaganda for Peking to form a "united front" with the third world.

In the study of Chinese foreign relations, the years from 1960 to 1962 represent a difficult period for research. Most publications in the West dealing with China's foreign relations either skip this period or touch on it only briefly due to lack of information. The most detailed work on this period concerns the Sino-Indian border dispute.[1] Literature released during or after the Cultural Revolution did little to help research on this period. Even *Mao Zedong Si Xiang Wan Sui*, which is considered to be a rich source for foreign policy research, is of little use for this period, in spite of the fact that it is recommended by Schram, Gitting, and Whiting.[2] Accordingly, this research

---

[1] For example Allen S. Whiting's *The Chinese Calculus of Deterrence*, Ann Arbor: University of Michigan, 1975; and Neville Maxwell's *India's China War*, N. Y.: Random House, 1970.

[2] See Stuart R. Schram "Mao Zedong: a self-portrait,", *The China Quarterly* (*CQ*), no. 57 (1974); John Gittings, "His View of the World," *CQ*, no. 60 (1974); and Allen S. Whiting, "Quemoy 1958: Mao's Miscalculations," *CQ*, no. 62 (1975).

relies heavily on Chinese mass media and journals published during this period. A content analysis was conducted on the *RR* to detect any hidden implications it may reveal.

China's Foreign Policy, 1960-62

In 1960, China's foreign policy deviated strikingly from earlier patterns despite the fact that the principal objective remained opposition to "U.S. imperialism." In contrast to her previous strong alliance with the Soviet Union, China had gradually adopted an independent policy in world politics. The withdrawal of technical advisers by the Soviet Union in 1960 indicated that the earlier commitment by the Soviet Union to help the Chinese develop nuclear capability had been revoked. To avoid international isolation, the Chinese were apparently looking outward for support, especially toward the former colonies in Indo-China, Africa, and Latin America. Under such circumstances, the policy of anti-imperialism became more important than ever before for establishing a united front with Afro-Asian countries.

In spite of the fact that the relationship between Peking and Moscow deteriorated drastically, the united front of opposition to "U.S. imperialism" seemed not to be seriously affected in 1960. Peking reiterated a broad united front policy of uniting with the peoples of the third world and socialist countries. In the first half of May 1960, *Hongqi* urged that in order to carry on an effective struggle and win a victory, it was necessary to unite all the democratic forces throughout the world and organize a broad anti-imperialist united front. The struggle against imperialism and the struggle for world peace were not and should not be isolated from each other.[3] In the latter part of May 1960, Peking's attitude toward Moscow was still positive during the Soviet dispute with the United States over the U-2 incident. As mentioned in Chapter 7, a nation-wide mass demonstration was triggered to support Khrushchev's condemnation of "U.S. imperialism" at the summit meeting. Mass rallies took place in ninety-six major cities in China, lasting a week, reportedly involving approximately thirty million people.

Due to growing rivalry between Peking and Moscow in 1961 and 1962, and the tension of the Sino-Indian border conflict during the same period, it became impracticable for China to ally herself with the Soviet Union in the cause of "anti-U.S. imperialism." During the Sino-Indian war, Moscow, like Washington, provided India with weapons and war materials. As a result,

[3]Wen Shirun, "Scientific Judgement and Foresight: Study of Chairman Mao Zedong's Theses on International Questions as Expounded in the Fourth Volumes of Select Works of Mao Zedong," *Hongqi*, no. 22, November 16, 1960. Translated by Joint Publication of Research (JPRS), no. 6700, pp. 7-21.

Peking faced three adversaries—the United States, the Soviet Union, and India. Despite the fact that the tension between Peking and Moscow was not at the level of open confrontation in the period of 1961-1962, China's international position was at stake. It presented a serious challenge to Peking's leadership making it clear that the policy of leaning towards the Soviet Union was no longer viable.

It has been one of the main objectives of Peking's foreign policy to minimize or reduce the influence of the United States in Asia, Africa, and Latin America. Peking repeatedly denounced "U.S. imperialism" as oppressive and exploitative, and as being the enemy of the people in these areas. In 1960, problems were many in both domestic and international politics. Internally, China was plagued by an unprecedented economic crisis and increasing political tension at the highest levels of leadership as a result of policy disputes. Externally, the drastic change in the relations between Peking and Moscow and between Peking and New Delhi were too critical and complicated for Peking to solve them immediately. Due to its strong commitment to opposing "U.S. imperialism," Peking faced a number of problems. First, there was tension with Taiwan and the United States in the Taiwan Strait, where a war with the U.S. would not only delay recovery from the economic crisis but also jeopardize China's national defense, and damage its position in settling the border conflict with India. Second, if Peking backed down from its opposition to "U.S. imperialism" it would damage its self-proclaimed reputation as the ideological leader of the Afro-Asian states, a reputation Peking had built up since the mid-1950s. In facing these two conflicting problems, Peking adopted a compromise policy—i.e. to lower the tension with the United States militarily on the one hand, and to step up its propaganda and diplomatic activities in opposition to "U.S. imperialism" on the other. Diplomatically, avoiding war with the U.S. would save China's bargaining position in the settlement of the Sino-Indian conflict with New Delhi. Continuing propaganda against "U.S. imperialism" served to strengthen Peking's policy of creating a united front with the third world. This new policy was clearly reflected in its propaganda against Taiwan, U.S. diplomatic activities and "U.S. imperialism" in Vietnam and Cuba.

Peking's Propaganda against Taiwan

To China, Taiwan has been not only a symbol of the unfinished internal struggle between the Communists and Nationalists, but also a painful reminder of "U.S. aggression against China." The offshore islands of Quemoy and Matsu constituted a direct threat to Chinese naval forces in Zhejiang and Fujian and provided them with a continuous psychological challenge. In 1958, serious tensions resulted from the PLA shelling of Quemoy and the reaffirmation of China's "unshakable determination" to liberate Taiwan and the adjacent coastal islands.

In the first half of 1960, Chinese hostility toward Taiwan again mounted. In June 1960, Eisenhower's visit there triggered a series of movements attacking "U.S. imperialism." In that month alone, the *RR* had 130 reports mainly directed against the Nationalist government in Taiwan. These reports all took the occasion of Eisenhower's visit to Taiwan to reaffirm the determination of the PRC to liberate Taiwan. In addition to attacking the "U.S. crime of occupying Taiwan," the regime mobilized all levels of people to demonstrate once again their hostility against the Nationalists and to urge the incorporation of Taiwan under Peking's rule.[4] The number of reports, however, dropped sharply to 3 in July and 4 in August. From July 1960 to October 1962 reports urging the liberation of Taiwan averaged only 3 or 4 each month.

It becomes clear that in 1962 the Chinese were restraining their expressions of hostility toward Taiwan. In the first part of 1962, the Nationalist Government in Taiwan was reported to have prepared for an attack on the mainland. The New Year's message of 1962 to the Chinese people by Chiang Kai-shek revealed this.[5] This was followed by statements made by high-ranking Nationalist officials suggesting an imminent "counter-attack on the mainland."[6] As a result the PRC troops opposite Taiwan were strongly reinforced in June. Nonetheless the Chinese press did not report any of these hostile actions by the Nationalists in Taiwan until on June 21 when the *RR* called for nation-wide vigilance against any U.S.-sponsored invasion from Taiwan. This cautious reporting continued in September when a U-2 plane from Taiwan was shot down by the PRC. In reporting the incident, the Chinese seemed to use it as propaganda against the United States rather than against the Nationalist Government in Taiwan.

It is clear that articulated hostility toward Taiwan decreased sharply from 1960 to 1962 despite the continued confrontation in the coastal provinces between Nationalist forces on Quemoy and Matsu, and PRC forces. This indicates a change from a hard line policy to a low key policy toward the coastal islands. This policy will be further clarified after the examination of other propaganda against the U.S.

A remarkable issue which was used by Peking to attack "U.S. imperialism" was American diplomatic activities in Asia. Visits of high-level U.S. officials

[4] *RR*, June 18-29, 1960.

[5] *Central Daily News*, Taipei, January 1, 1962.

[6] See Liao Kuang-sheng and Allen S. Whiting," Chinese Press Perception of Threat: The U.S. and India, 1962," *The China Quarterly*, no. 53, January-March 1973, pp. 80-97.

to the Far East and participation by the U.S. in international activities with Asian nations were interpreted by Peking as moves against China. In addition to Eisenhower's Taiwan visit mentioned above, the visits of Averell Harriman and of the then Vice-President, Lyndon B. Johnson, to Thailand and the Philippines in 1961 were interpreted as "activities forming part of an aggressive plot." General Maxwell Taylor's visit of 1962 to Southeast Asia was interpreted as "a plot to expand the U.S. war of aggression in South Vietnam." When he visited Taiwan and Quemoy, an editorial in the *RR* warned that any plot to invade China would be defeated by the Chinese people. These reactions prove that China did indeed keep a close watch on U.S. diplomatic activities in Asia.

However, the most heated anti-imperialist propaganda during the period of 1960-1962 concerned N. Vietnam and Cuba, rather than China itself. N. Vietnam and Cuba were the two most popular public issues for anti-imperialist propaganda, surpassing even the Indian issue in intensity and extent. The Chinese describe these not so much as local conflicts but as acts of aggression conducted by "American imperialism." Peking utilized these two issues to attack U.S. aggression against small countries in developing areas of the third world.

Peking's Propaganda Against U.S. Involvement in Vietnam

The campaign to support the Vietnamese people in opposition to "U.S. imperialism" rose to a high level of intensity in July 1960. Many activities demonstrated China's endorsement of the Vietnamese cause. At a rally attended by all ranks of people in the capital on July 19, Liu Ningyi, Vice-Chairman of the Chinese Committee for Afro-Asian Solidarity, declared,

> There has been a profound traditional friendship between the Chinese and Vietnamese peoples. We have always given each other sympathy and support in the anti-imperialist struggle. The victories of the Vietnamese people are victories for the Chinese people. The struggle of the Vietnamese people against U.S. imperialist aggression and for the peaceful reunification of their motherland will always have the all-out support of the 650 million Chinese people.[7]

Meanwhile, the *RR* editorial of July 20, entitled "Struggle Resolutely to Uphold Peace in Indo-China," said,

> China and Vietnam are close neighbors relying on each other as the lips on the teeth, sharing the same security and dangers . . . the Chinese people unreservedly extend full support to the movement now being conducted by the Vietnamese people throughout that country against U.S. imperialism.[8]

---

[7] Liu Ningyi, "Firm Support for the Vietnamese People," *Beijing Review*, no. 30, July 26, 1960, p. 12.

[8] *RR*, July, 1960.

Parallel to these official activities, the *RR* repeatedly indicated considerable support for the Vietnamese cause and opposition to U.S. imperialism. In April, the editorial of the *RR* predicted intensification of U.S. intervention in South Vietnam as a result of the Bangkok meeting of the Southeast Asia Treaty Organization. It demanded that the U.S. government stop its aggression in South Vietnam and withdraw all its military personnel so that the Geneva agreements could be implemented.[9] The next day, the Foreign Ministry issued a similar statement accusing the U.S. of intensifying its intervention in South Vietnam.[10] In May, the *RR* commentary asserted that "U.S. agreession and intervention" had reached an unprecedented degree and pointed particularly to Vice-President Lyndon Johnson's visit to Saigon as an attempt "to step up U.S. intervention and aggression."[11]

The period of strongest support by the media for the Vietnamese cause began in October 1961 and lasted through September 1962. In November 1961, General Maxwell Taylor, the U.S. President's special military adviser, visited Saigon. The *Beijing Review* commentary stated on November 29 that, as a result of this visit, "The U.S. Government is dispatching its naval and air force units and large numbers of its military personnel direct to South Vietnam." The statement declared that the Chinese Government "absolutely cannot be indifferent to the adventurous deeds of the United States" and that the Chinese Government "hereby serves a serious warning that, if the U.S. Government does not stop its above-mentioned aggressive acts, it must bear responsibility for breaching the peace in Indo-China."[12] The period which followed saw a great increase in propaganda attacking "U.S. aggression in Vietnam" in the mass media. During this period the propaganda on Vietnam could be easily mistaken as hard line policy. But in fact, a study of China's media response to U.S. military activity in Asia shows that China's policy was one of avoiding confrontation with the U.S.[13]

China's Hostility Toward U.S. Involvement in Cuba

The frequency of news reports on Cuba was even higher than on the Vietname issue. Apparently, Cuba was a focus for broader propaganda attacks. The PRC showed its support and sympathy for the Cuban revolution even before the formal establishment of diplomatic relations with Havana. News items concerning the Cuban revolution and opposing U.S. aggression appeared

[9] *RR*, April 12, 1961.
[10] *RR*, April 13, 1961.
[11] *RR*, Commentary, May 16, 1961.
[12] *Beijing Review*, no. 49 (December 8, 1961), pp. 9-10.
[13] "Chinese Press Perception of Threat: The U.S. and India, 1962", *op. cit.*

from the time Castro took power. The frequency of reports increased after the establishment of diplomatic relations between the two governments in September 1960. In December, an agreement on economic cooperation was signed by which the Chinese promised to loan 240 million roubles to Cuba during the period 1961-65 for the construction of 24 factories.[14] In January 1961 another agreement was signed which stipulated that Peking would buy one million tons of Cuban sugar within the year.[15] The rapid development of close relations between Peking and Havana increased China's support for Cuba's resistance to the U.S. The Peking Press repeatedly declared: "The Chinese people will forever remain true friends of the Cuban people" and warned the United States: "Hands Off Cuba!". On January 6, 1961, the Cuban Ambassador to China, Oscar Pino Santos held a reception to celebrate the second anniversary of the victory of the Cuban revolution, at which Mao Zedong, Liu Shaoqi and Zhu De personally offered their congratulations. In his speech on that occasion, Zhu De declared, "The Chinese people resolutely support the Cuban people in their just struggle against U.S. imperialist aggression and in defense on their motherland."

When anti-Castro forces landed in Cuba in April 1961 (the "Bay of Pigs Incident"), Peking declared this to be U.S. armed aggression and vowed to take all necessary measures in support of Cuba's struggle against the United States.[16] Mass rallies and demonstrations in major Chinese cities denounced the U.S. and pledged support to the Castro government in the most widespread and virulent anti-U.S. movement since the inauguration of the Kennedy administration. In January of 1962, while the Organization of America States (OAS) was discussing ways of applying sanctions to Castro's regime, the Cubans organized a Conference of the People's Representatives of Latin American Countries in Havana. During this period, the *RR* expressed repeated support for Castro and accused the U.S. of using the OAS to intervene in Cuba. Peking again used the Cuban issue to initiate an anti-U.S. movement in the press. Another campaign was begun when U.S. military activities increased in the Carribean. The missile crisis in October caused a heated reaction from the *RR* and the frequency of reports over this issue reached 342 from October to December.[17] In fact, according to this figure, Cuba was the most articulated international issue during 1960-62. Like the propaganda on Vietnam, Peking's attack against "American aggression" in Cuba showed its moral support for Castro in opposition to "U.S. imperialism."

[14]*RR*, December 1, 1960.
[15]*RR*, January 24, 1961.
[16]*Supplement to Beijing Review* (no. 16), April 21, 1961.
[17]See *RR*'s editorial "To Stop the New Adventure of U.S. Imperialism," October 24, 1962.

It becomes clear that by early 1961 Peking's world-wide foreign policy had undergone a drastic change. It intentionally lowered the tension with Taiwan, trying to avoid military confrontation with Taiwan and the United States in the Taiwan Strait. Propaganda on this issue was drastically reduced. In contrast, Peking intensified its propaganda against the U.S. over the issues of Vietnam and Cuba. In spite of strong attacks against "U.S. imperialism" in 1961 and 1962, there is little evidence to prove that Peking was willing to take the risk of military confrontation with the United States outside China. But Peking's propaganda was instrumental in improving its position in the third world.

"Anti-U.S. Imperialism" and the Third World

Due to the problems involved in communication and travelling, Chinese people in the 1940s had little personal experience and limited understanding of their Asian neighbors, or of African countries. Most Chinese in the 1930s and 40s were preoccupied with fighting the Japanese and with civil wars. Few people were interested in the areas of Southeast Asia or Africa except those who had relatives living there. This phenomenon persisted in the first few years after the establishment of the Peking government when Peking was preoccupied with internal consolidation and developing its relations with the Communist bloc. Much lower priority was given to the development of diplomatic relations with African and Asian countries than with communist countries. Up to 1955, of the non-communist countries in Asia, only Burma, India, Indonesia, Afghanistan, and Nepal had established diplomatic relations with Peking, while none of the African states had done so. The outbreak of the Korean War delayed the establishment of diplomatic relations between Peking and non-communist countries.

Peking's relations with other Afro-Asian states did not make significant progress until the mid-1950s. It remains questionable whether Peking had any specific policy toward them before that time. In spite of the fact that China took part in the Geneva Conference of July 1954, Peking's role in Asian affairs was not active, still less so in relation to African affairs.[18] It was not until the late 1950s that Peking started to break away from its dependence on the Soviet Union.

In the development of China's relations with Afro-Asian countries, the "Five Principles of Peaceful Coexistence" appears to have been an important document. The "Five Principles of Peaceful Coexistence" were first set forth

[18] See Harold C. Hinton, *Communist China in World Politics*, Boston: Houghton Mifflin Co., 1966, pp. 188-196.

in an agreement with India signed in 1954, and were later to become the proclaimed basis of Peking's foreign policy toward non-communist countries. They read as follows:

> Mutual respect for each other's territorial integrity and sovereignty;
> mutual non-aggression;
> mutual non-interference in each other's internal affairs;
> equality and mutual benefit;
> peaceful coexistence.

Obviously, the first three principles, i.e., mutual respect for each other's territorial integrity and sovereignty, mutual non-aggression, and mutual non-interference, were particularly important for Peking in improving its relations with neighboring countries. As a result of Peking's propaganda concerning national liberation and world revolution, these countries were afraid of political subversion supported by Peking. The "Five Principles" assured these countries of their independence and integrity, and eliminated their fear of the possibility of Chinese support for subversion and revolution in their countries. To other states in Asia these five principles demonstrated Peking's willingness to establish diplomatic relations and accept the status quo of international relations in the area. This was in direct contrast to Peking's slogan of national liberation. Whether Peking had decided to relegate national liberation to the position of a long term goal or whether this simply represents a change of tactics in its foreign policy will always be a debatable issue. One thing, however, is clear: Peking's propaganda concerning world revolution and national liberation was no longer directed at its neighbors and other Asian countries, except those where communist governments were established and a struggle was in progress between communist forces and other political groups, as in N. Vietnam and N. Korea. This naturally encouraged Asian countries, particularly China's neighboring states, to improve their diplomatic relations with China.

It is easy to overestimate the effect of the "Five Principles" and assume that China's development of relations with Afro-Asian countries was in large part due to them. In fact, they were important only in eliminating the fear of communist subversion and revolution in non-communist countries. The most important factor in the development of relations with Afro-Asian countries is to be found in China's self-proclaimed commitment to "anti-U.S. imperialism." As Mao said in December 1956, China and the Afro-Asian countries had been oppressed by imperialism. Thus, the people of Asia, Africa, and Latin America had a common enemy in "U.S. imperialism."[19] Mao showed that he believed

---

[19] *Wan Sui, op. cit.*, p. 63.

this to be the foundation for solidarity at the Bandung Conference of 1955.[20] Although the idea of uniting with Afro-Asian countries to oppose imperialism was not new in China,[21] Mao's utilization of Afro-Asian countries' support to oppose and confront a strong western power was new in China's diplomatic history. Operationally speaking, the sentiment of anti-imperialism was used to mobilize support from Afro-Asian countries so as to form a political deterrent to "U.S. imperialism." The sentiment of opposing "U.S. imperialism", therefore became a diplomatic instrument for China's promotion of its relations with Afro-Asian countries. In October 1961, Mao spoke these words to Japanese visitors,

> It was U.S. imperialism which compelled us—the peoples of China and Japan— to unite together. We two peoples have suffered the oppression of U.S. imperialism, we have common suffering, so we unite together. We have to expand the scope of unity to include the whole of Asia, Africa, Latin America and ninety percent of the world except for the imperialists and reactionaries in every country.[22]

Mao's statement clearly indicates that Peking was utilizing sentiments opposing "U.S. imperialism" to advance its diplomatic relations with Afro-Asian countries.

In Asia, Peking improved relations with the Mongolian People's Republic, Burma, Nepal, Cambodia, and Afghanistan. In January 1960, China signed with Burma a "Treaty of Friendship and Mutual Non-Aggression" and reached a tentative agreement concerning the Sino-Burmese border.[23] The PRC concluded seven agreements with Mongolia concerning trade, cultural exchange, technical aid, friendship and mutual assistance.[24] With Nepal, China signed a border agreement in March 1960, and a joint committee was organized by the two sides to continue negotiations.[25] Cambodia was another country in Southeast Asia which improved relations with Peking during 1960. In December, the Sino-Cambodia Friendship Association was formed in Peking with Qi Yanming as president.[26] At the end of the year, on December 20, Peking and Cambodia signed five agreements concerning friendship and non-aggression, economic and technical aid, navigation cooperation, and the sending of agricultural and railway technicians to Cambodia.[27] With Afghanistan, Peking signed a "Treaty of Mutual Non-Aggression" in August 1960 when

[20] *Ibid.*
[21] John Gittings, *The World and China, 1922-1972*, London: Eyre Methuen, 1974, pp. 208-217. 232-235.
[22] *Wan Sui*, vol. II, p. 269.
[23] *Beijing Review*, no. 5, 1960, pp. 9-14.
[24] *RR*, February 24, 1960.
[25] *RR*, March 22, 1960.
[26] *RR*, December 13, 1960.
[27] *RR*, December 20, 1960.

Chen Yi was visiting that country. Cultural and social delegations were sent to visit these countries. In sum, China significantly improved her diplomatic relations with Afro-Asian countries in 1960.

A remarkable improvement in relations with Indonesia came at the end of 1960 with the implementation of the Treaty Concerning the Question of Dual Nationality whereby Peking formally permitted a million overseas Chinese freely to choose Indonesian nationality. After Chen Yi's visit to Indonesia in March 1961, relations between these two countries further improved. In April, an agreement on cultural cooperation, a draft agreement on economic and technical cooperation, and a Sino-Indonesian Friendship Treaty were signed.[28] In October, the agreement on economic and technical cooperation was signed.[29]

Peking's diplomatic activities in Africa greatly increased in 1960, with China's recognition of 13 countries in Africa: Togo, Mali, Malagasy, Somaliland, Ghana, Dahomey (Benin), Niger, Upper Volta, Ivory Coast, Chad, Central Africa, the Congo and Gabon. In addition, China aoncluded trade agreements with Guinea, Morocco, and Tunisia, and sent a delegation to visit Guinea, Somaliland, Morocco, Sudan, Yemen, Tunisia, and Ethiopia. In order to encourage cultural exchange and continuing contacts, the "China Africa Friendship Association" was founded in Peking in April 1960, with Liu Changsheng as president.[30]

In 1961, Peking took the initiative in attempting to strengthen relations with the newly independent countries in Africa. A trade delegation team visited Guinea, Mali and Ghana in early February. On February 24, a ten-member delegation of the Chinese-African People's Friendship Association, headed by Liu Changsheng, the association's president, left Peking for Ghana, Mali, Guinea, Niger, Senegal, Upper Volta, Dahomey (Benin) and Togo.[31] In April, Peking sent a delegate to attend Sierra Leone's independence celebrations. China improved relations with Ghana by inviting President Kwame Nkrumah for a state visit. During his six-day stay, Nkrumah signed a Treaty of Friendship and three agreements on economic and technical cooperation, trade and payments, and cultural cooperation.[32] Peking also concluded trade and economic cooperation agreements with Mali,[33] a technical cooperation agreement with Guinea,[34] and an agreement on payments with Morocco.[35]

[28]*RR*, April 2, April 19, 1961.
[29]*RR*, October 12, 1961.
[30]*RR*, April 14, 1960.
[31]*RR*, February 25, June 3, June 14, 1961.
[32]*RR*, August 19, 1961.
[33]*RR*, March 4, September 23, 1961.
[34]*RR*, September 20, 1961.
[35]*RR*, October 29, 1961.

Clearly there were serious efforts to establish official or semi-official relations with the newly independent countries of Africa.

In 1962, Peking continued to expand relations with newly independent countries in Africa. On March 18, the PRC and Yemen reached a Scientific, Technological, and Cultural Agreement.[36] In May, China and the Sudan reached an agreement on trade,[37] and in December, an agreement for cultural cooperation was concluded with Tanzania.[38] A team of agricultural specialists was sent to Mali in January.[39] Another team visited Ghana in October.[40] Cultural diplomacy was not neglected, as evidenced by a Women's Delegation to Mali in January and a Table Tennis Team sent to Guinea, Mali, Ghana, and Sudan. A Writers Delegation visited Guinea, Ghana, Mali, and Morocco.[41] A Cultural and Friendship Delegation was sent to Tanzania, the Sudan, and Uganda in November and December.

As shown by Table 8.1, Peking's delegations visiting African countries greatly increased in number in 1961 and 1962, while its visits to Asian countries and the Communist bloc remained at the same level as in 1960. This serves to summarize Peking's world-wide activity during this period, indicating that the improvement of diplomatic relations with African countries was the highest priority in Peking's new foreign policy. The record of diplomatic development with African countries is remarkable. This development is partly accounted for by Peking's increasing emphasis on its relations with African countries. On the other hand it is closely related to China's propaganda of "anti-U.S. imperialism" and its claim to be the ideological leader in the third world. As the relationship between Peking and Moscow deteriorated, the power of deterrence to "U.S. imperialism" from the Sino-Soviet alliance waned. A new political deterrent had to be created with the support of Afro-Asian countries. In the 1960s, the sentiment of "anti-imperialism" became a strong political force uniting Peking with Afro-Asian countries. With the slogan of "anti-imperialism" and the "Five Principles of Peaceful Coexistence," Peking was no longer alone on the anti-imperialist front. These diplomatic advance laid the foundations for further developments between China and Africa at a later stage.

In the period 1963-1964, when relations between Peking and Moscow had deteriorated further, and shortly after the Sino-Indian border dispute of October 1962 and the conclusion of the Partial Nuclear Test Ban Treaty in

[36]*RR*, March 21, 1962.
[37]*RR*, May 24, 1962.
[38]*RR*, December 15, 1962.
[39]*RR*, January 4, 1962.
[40]*RR*, October 5, 1962.
[41]*RR*, January 12, April 27, February, 28, 1962.

Table 8.1
FREQUENCY OF VISITS BY CHINESE DELEGATIONS,
1960-62

Countries	1960	1961	1962
A. In Africa:			
Ghana	0	3	5
Tanzania	0	0	1
Mali	0	3	6
Guinea	6	2	5
Uganda	0	0	1
Somaliland	1	0	0
Nigeria	0	1	0
Sierra Leone	0	1	0
Upper Volta	0	1	0
Dahomey (Benin)	0	1	0
Senegal	0	1	0
Niger	0	1	0
Togo	0	1	0
United Arab Republic	4	6	7
Algeria	0	0	2
Morocco	3	1	2
Sudan	1	1	2
Tunisia	1	2	0
Ethiopia	1	0	0
TOTAL	17	25	31
B. In Asia:			
India	3	1	0
Japan	2	12	8
Indonesia	1	6	8
Burma	14	3	5
Pakistan	1	1	3
Nepal	2	2	1
Cambodia	2	1	1
Afghanistan	2	0	0
Ceylon	1	4	2
TOTAL	28	30	28
C. Communist Bloc:			
The Soviet Union	17	19	19
Hungary	10	5	6
Bulgaria	2	4	4
Rumania	3	2	6
Albania	3	8	4
Czechoslovakia	3	4	5
E. Germany	5	5	8
Poland	10	8	3
Cuba	8	11	8
N. Korea	9	3	7
N. Vietnam	8	11	7
Mongolia	6	8	5
TOTAL	84	88	82

Sources: Survey reading on the *RR*, 1960–62.

July 1963, Peking's policy of creating a united front with Afro-Asian countries to oppose "U.S. imperialism" was challenged by the Soviet Union.[42] In November 1962, *Hongqi*, in its editorial "Defend the Purity of Marxism-Leninism," Bitterly attacked the rise of revisionism in the Soviet Union. The editorial said,

> The modern revisionists are scared stiff in the face of the strength of U.S. imperialism. They have discarded the Marxist-Leninist method of class analysis, given publicity to the idea that the nature of imperialism has changed, and tried to prettify the monopoly capitalist class and its representatives. They hold that there is no need for the various peoples to wage mass struggles against imperialism and its lackeys and that by relying on the good intentions of the so-called enlightened section of the imperialist circles alone, lasting world peace can be realized and freedom and happiness bestowed upon the oppressed nations and oppressed peoples. They hold that while imperialism still exists it is possible to eliminate war and eliminate arms throughout the world. The danger of modern revisionism lies first of all in its confusing the distinction between the enemy and ourselves, obscuring the objective of the struggle, and weakening and undermining the struggle of the world's people against imperialism.[43]

This clearly exposed a fundamental split between Moscow and Peking in their attitudes toward imperialism or "U.S. imperialism." By August 1963, Peking had publicly denounced the Soviet Union as having betrayed the peoples of the socialist camp and the peace-loving people of the third world. The *RR*'s editorial pointed out,

> Incontrovertible facts show that the Soviet Government has sold out the interests of the Soviet people, the interests of the peoples of the socialist camp including the Chinese people and the interests of peace-loving people throughout the world. This is not 'diplomacy marked by patience', but the diplomacy of capitulation pure and simple.[44]

Summary

As discussed above, Peking launched a propaganda campaign attacking "U.S. imperialism" in 1960-62. The Sino-Soviet dispute had an important impact on Peking's foreign policy. It proved that the Chinese leadership had overestimated Soviet friendship and miscalculated Soviet foreign policy. Peking's policy of allying herself with the Soviet Union had completely failed.

During the period between 1960 and 1962, Peking launched a series of attacks against "U.S. imperialism," supporting the people of Vietnam and

---

[42] Michael B. Yahuda, *China's Role in World Affairs*, London: Croom Helm, 1978, pp. 145-166.

[43] "Defend the Purity of Marxism-Leninism," *Hongqi*, November 1962.

[44] "A Betrayal of the Soviet People," translation in *Beijing Review*, no. 32, 1963, p. 11.

Cuba in their resistance to U.S. military activities. Peking's opposition to imperialism was opposition to an enemy who maintained a policy of aggression against China. Peking's "anti-U.S. imperialism" developed in the early days when China was threatened by U.S. military activities in Asia. It was a policy of deterrence, representing the unity of the Communist bloc in opposition to their common enemy. But, when relations between Peking and Moscow deteriorated the policy of "leaning to one side," i.e., towards an alliance with the Soviet Union to oppose "U.S. imperialism", proved impossible, Peking's overall foreign policy as well as its propaganda activity concerning "anti-imperialism" underwent drastic change in 1961 and 1962.

Under the new policy, in spite of continuing propaganda against "U.S. imperialism," new emphasis was given to unity with Afro-Asian countries in opposing "U.S. imperialism." This change was reflected by Peking's lower-profile in response to tensions in the Taiwan Strait and by its improvement of relations with Afro-Asian countries. Afro-Asian countries became the highest priority in the development of Peking's foreign relations. "Anti-U.S. imperialism" remained the fundamental principle to foreign policy. It was a significant factor in improving China's relations with Afro-Asian countries rather than with the Communist bloc.[45] Thus, Peking's propaganda against "U.S. imperialism" served a new purpose.

In the wake of the open split between Peking and Moscow over their attitude and policy toward "U.S. imperialism," Peking forged ahead in its policy of improving relations with Afro-Asian states. Zhou Enlai's tour of Africa in October 1963 marked the beginning of a new era in Chinese foreign relations. Zhou led a group of some forty members including the then foreign minister, Chen Yi, on a visit to the United Arab Republic, Algeria, Morocco, Tunisia, Ghana, Mali, Guinea, Sudan, Ethiopia, and Somalia. This African tour clearly demonstrated China's continuing interest in the area. Between December 1963 and February 1964, five more African countries established diplomatic relations with Peking.[46] Peking persistently made the claim that since imperialism was the common enemy of all peoples, they should unite to resist its power.

---

[45] See Bruce D. Larkin, *China and Africa, 1949-1970*, Calif.: University of California Press, 1971, pp. 70-88.

[46] J. D. Armstrong, *Revolutionary Diplomacy: Chinese Foreign Policy and the United Front Doctrine*, Calif.: University of California Press, 1977, pp. 78-79.

CHAPTER 9
Leftism and Antiforeignism in the Cultural Revolution
1967-February 1969

China's domestic politics and foreign policy underwent drastic change between 1962 and the beginning of the Cultural Revolution. In order to understand the developments during the five-year interim period, a brief examination of China's foreign relations will be undertaken. The major emphasis here, however, is on the rise of leftism and the leftist impact on Peking's foreign relations during the Cultural Revolution. The discussion includes coverage of the characteristics of antiforeignism and antiforeign demonstrations. Finally, some hypotheses will be formulated on the relationship between leftism and antiforeignism.

China's Foreign Relations After 1962

One of the most important developments in China's foreign relations between 1963 and 1966 was the increasing deterioration in relations with the Soviet Union. The conflict between Moscow and Peking was no longer a secret. During the Sino-Indian border conflict, the Soviet Union not only did not support Peking's stand, but openly provided New Delhi with military aid.[1] Meanwhile, after the Cuban missile crisis, Peking attacked Moscow's retreat as "capitulationism" and charged that Khruschev's conciliatory move was a "betrayal" of Cuban independence and the international communist movement.[2] Soon after this, came the signing of the partial Nuclear Test Ban Treaty. This was a serious blow to China. The Chinese regarded this treaty as final proof that Soviet leaders were conspiring with "U.S. imperialism" and denounced it as a "big fraud to fool the peoples of the world."[3] The treaty was followed by unprecedented verbal hostility between Peking and Moscow.

The Chinese openly gave up all notion of unity in the international communist movement and "unity against imperialism", considering it nothing but

[1] "The Truth About How the Leaders of the CPSU Have Allied Themselves with India Against China," editorial, *Renmin Ribao*, November 2, 1963.
[2] "The Fearless Cuban People are the Most Powerful Strategic Weapon," *Beijing Review*, November 9, vol. 45, 1962, pp. 12-13. For detailed discussion, see Neville Maxwell, *op. cit.*, p. 366.
[3] "A betrayal of the Soviet People," *Beijing Review*, no. 32, August 9, 1963, pp. 10-11; "Thoroughly Expose the Reactionary Nature of the Tripartite Treaty," by Liao Zhengzhi, *Beijing Review, op. cit.*, pp. 12-16. Further discussion, see Walter C. Clemens, Jr., *The Arms Race and Sino-Soviet Relations*, Stanford: Hoover Inst., 1958, pp. 48-64.

a fraud.[4] In addition, in Peking's view, the new leaders of the Communist Party of the Soviet Union were taking "united action" with the United States on the question of Vietnam. The Chinese called for a world movement to combat Khrushchev's revisionism as well as "U.S. Imperialism."[5] This open confrontation indicated that the alliance had been breached and regular communication between the two powers was now difficult. The conflict between them became so severe that the Communist bloc was divided into two camps: pro-Moscow and pro-Peking.

Peking's policy of maintaining and improving her relations with Afro-Asian countries intensified into open competition with Moscow. Zhou Enlai visited thirteen African countries in December 1963 and January 1964. While the ostensible purpose of the visit was to strengthen Africa in its struggle against Western imperialism, in reality Peking was trying to gain an advantage over the Soviet Union. In 1963-64, Peking established diplomatic relations with Zanzibar, Burundi, the Central African Republic, the Congo (Brazzaville), Zambia and Dahomey (Benin). China in 1964 also extended grants and loans to Yemen, the United Arab Republic, Ghana, Mali, the Congo (B), Kenya, Tanzania, and Malawi.

In March and April, 1965, a delegation led by Liu Ningyi visited Guinea, Mali, the Central African Republic, the Congo (B) and Ghana. Chen Yi and Ji Pengfei on separate trips visited a number of African countries in preparation for the Second Afro-Asian Conference. Many important African figures were invited to visit China including President Massamba-Debat of the Congo (B), Vice-President Kawawa of Tanzania, a delegation from the Central African Republic, and Mme. Sekou Toure, wife of the Guinean President. But Chinese efforts were not universally successful. In 1965 and 1966, accused of having supported anti-government activities, the PRC suffered the loss of diplomatic relations with Kenya, Dahomey (Benin) and Burundi.[6] In Ghana, when a coup d'etat exiled Nkrumah, the new government expelled PRC experts and severed relations with Peking.

In Asia, China settled boundary disputes with Pakistan and Nepal, and maintained stable relations with Burma, Cambodia, Afghanistan, and Ceylon. Meanwhile, relations between China and Indonesia improved. With Liu Shaoqi's visit to Indonesia in 1963, China professed support for Indonesia's takeover of West Irian and for her fight against Malaysia. Relations between

[4] "Refutation of the New Leaders of the CPSU on 'United Action,' " Editorial Department of *RR* and *Hongqi*, November 11, 1965, translated by Foreign Languages Press, Peking, 1965.

[5] *Ibid.*

[6] Ishwer C. Ojah, *Chinese Foreign Policy in an Age of Transition*, Boston: Beacon Press, 1971, pp. 231-35.

the two countries thus entered a new stage. This close relationship was disrupted, however, by the September 1965 abortive coup by the Indonesian Communist Party. In 1966, Djarkarta's new military government closed the PRC Embassy, the New China News Agency, and most of the consular offices. Air service between Djarkarta and Canton was suspended. The Chinese ambassador was forced to leave, the Indonesian ambassador to Peking was recalled, and Indonesian consulates in Canton and Peking were closed.

China's relations with members of the Soviet bloc suffered from the split with Moscow. The open letter concerning the general line of the international communist movement drafted by the Soviet Communist Party in 1963 was supported by the Communist parties of Czechoslovakia, East Germany, Poland, Hungary, Bulgaria and Mongolia. All vehemently attacked the CCP. Only North Korea and Albania sided with the CCP, while North Vietnam took a neutral position. In 1965, Castro openly and frequently attacked the PRC while North Korea shifted closer to Moscow. This situation continued in 1966. By 1966, China was rather isolated from her fellow Communist nations.

In sum, in the period 1963-66, China continued the active foreign policy of 1960-62 and maintained stable relations with neighboring countries and other Asian nations excepting Indonesia. Nevertheless, she suffered serious setbacks within the Communist bloc.

The Rise of Leftists and Their Struggle for the Control of the Mass Media

During the Cultural Revolution China's internal political scene was characterized by the leftists' campaign to seize power, led by Mao. The rise of the leftists was clearly seen in their struggle for the control of the mass media. The media served to raise the politcal consciousness of the people and educate them in the policies of the Party.[7] In the period under study, the mass media became an important political weapon in the power struggle. Stalemated by the opposition group in the central organizations, Mao's immediate plan was to seize control of the mass media. As he stated later: "To launch a revolution, start by creating public opinion."[8] Most of the important Party magazines and newspapers were published in Peking and Shanghai. As a result the control of the Peking and Shanghai Municipal Party committees were necessary if Mao was to assume control of the mass media and use it to attack his enemies.

During this period, Mao used his stronghold in the Shanghai Party Committee to launch an attack against the Peking Municipal Party Committee. On November 10, 1965, Yao Wenyuan's article, entitled "Hairui's Dismissal,"

---

[7]James R. Townsend, *Political Participation in Communist China*, University of California Press, 1972 (new edition), pp. 181-82.

[8]*Mao Zedong Si Xiang Wan Sui* (Long Live Mao Zedong's Thought) 1969, p. 662.

was published in the *Wen Hui Bao* in Shanghai. It was directed against Wu Han, the vice-Mayor of Peking.[9] In late 1965 and early 1966 the struggle first concentrated on the cultural front, focusing on the purge of intellectuals and criticism of literature and the educational system; however, it was clear that the main target was Peng Zhen, the Mayor of Peking, and head of the Peking Municipal Party Committee. The attack on Wu Han was understood to refer to Peng Zhen because Wu was Peng's deputy.

Yao's attack against Wu Han failed to initiate the desired criticism immediately. In the first week following *Wen Hui Bao*'s publication of "Hairui's Dismissal," no newspaper in Peking echoed or supported it.[10] It was in late November and early December that major newspapers such as *Jiefang Ribao*, *RR*, and *Guangmin Ribao* gradually expressed their support for Yao's article. This slow response of support reflected the fact that these major national newspapers and local newspapers were beyond the tight control of Mao's supporters up to late 1965. For example, immediately after Yao's article was published, Peng Zhen was reported to have forbidden the Peking press to reprint it and ordered the press to withhold other articles of criticism by the "proletarian-revolutionary left."[11]

Control of the Peking Municipal Party Committee was not achieved until the middle of 1966. Peng Zhen suffered a serious attack by Mao's supporters after his "February Outline Report" was refuted by Mao and replaced by the "May 16 Notice." On May 16, Peng was openly accused of leading a "counter-revolutionary revisionist clique" which controlled a "bourgeois headquarters" opposed to Mao. At his dismissal on June 3, it was revealed that the Peking

[9] "New Historical Drama 'Hairui Dismissal," *Wen Hui Bao*, Nov., 1965.
[10] Responses of Newspapers to Yao Wen-yuan's "Hairui's Dismissal"

Nov. 10: *Wen Hui Bao* (Shanghai)
Nov. 12: *Jiefang Ribao* (Shanghai)
Nov. 24: *Jiejiang Ribao*, *Dazhong Ribao* (Shandong), *Xinhua Ribao* (Shanghai), *Fujian Ribao*
Nov. 25: *Anhui Ribao*
Nov. 26: *Jiangxi Ribao*
Nov. 29: *Jiefangjun Bao* (Peking), *Beijing Ribao*, *Beijing Wan Bao*
Nov. 30: *Renmin Ribao* (Peking), *Xinmin Wan Bao* (Shanghai)
Dec. 1: *Hebei Ribao*, *Henan Ribao*, *Tianjin Ribao*, *Tianjin Wan Bao*, *Canton Ribao*, *Yangcheng Wan Bao* (Canton), *Xinhua Ribao*
Dec. 2: *Guangming Ribao* (Peking), *Anhui Ribao*, *Dazhong Ribao* (Shandong), *Jiangxi Ribao*

---

*indicates second report on the article
Source: *Xinmin Wan Bao*, Shanghai, December 6, 1965.
[11] "Two Diametrically Opposed Documents," *Hongqi*, no. 9, 1967; SCMM no. 581, p. 11.

Municipal Party Committee had been reorganized and was now headed by Li Xuefeng.[12] Following this, many members of the former Peking Municipal Party Committee came under serious attack.[13]

The removal of Peng Zhen and the reorganization of the Peking Municipal Party Committee laid the foundation for Mao to proceed with his plan to directly mobilize the masses to take power from his opponents and to strengthen his position at the Central Committee level. The Eleventh Plenary Session of the Eighth Central Committee of the CCP was held in Peking from August 1 to 12, 1966. Lin Biao was promoted to the number two position in the Party, and Liu Shaoqi was downgraded to eighth on the list of politburo members. The Eleventh Plenary Session adopted a 16-point decision concerning the "Great Proletarian Cultural Revolution," confirming that Mao's position had been strengthened as compared with the earlier period. On August 18, six days after the Eleventh Plenary Session had begun, his followers organized a giant mass rally of one million as Mao reviewed the Red Guards in Tian An Men Square, Peking.[14] This mass rally greatly encouraged the spirit of the Red Guards, and stimulated more provocative action against the "capitalists in authority" which led to many incidents of violence. However, nation-wide local resistance remained. Mao and his supporters needed to launch a nation-wide movement in order to eliminate all those in authority who followed the "capitalist line." Much "power seizure" remained to be achieved in order to thoroughly defeat their opponents and establish "proletarian power."

The control of the mass media was more important than has been understood by most scholars.[15] The Red Guards were also a powerful weapon used by Mao in the Cultural Revolution. However, these Red Guards, composed mainly of students, were weakly organized and not a cohesive power group. The support of the mass media greatly elevated Mao's national image and actively stimulated the Red Guards to participate in the power-seizure campaign. Because of the disruption of ordinary party and state channels and their domination by Liu's faction, the mass media became the most important weapon in the mobilization of the masses.

[12]*RR*, June 4, 1966.

[13]For the purges of high-level party and government officials see Chun-tu Hsueh, "The Cultural Revolution and Leadership Crisis in Communist China," *Political Science Quarterly*, vol. 82, no. 2, June 1967, p. 178. He estimates that by the end of August at least one hundred and sixty-five prominent figures had been purged.

[14]*RR*, August 19, 1966.

[15]See Frederick T. C. Yu, *Mass Persuasion in Communist China*, Praeger, 1964; Franklin W. Houn, *To Change A Nation*, New York: Free Press, 1961; Alan P. L. Liu, *Communication and National Integration in Communist China*, Berkeley: University of California Press, 1971.

In the early days of the Cultural Revolution Mao began to strengthen his influence over the Propaganda Department of the Central Committee by reorganizing its upper level staff. The first reorganization of the Propaganda Department took place in June 1966. In this reorganization, Lu Dingyi was replaced by Tao Zhu as Minister. Some of Lu Dingyi's associates in the Propaganda Department such as Zhou Yang and Xu Liqun were also replaced at this time. In addition, the Chief Editor of the *RR*, Wu Lengxi and most of the top staff were also dismissed. The Associate Editor of *Hongqi*, Deng Liqun was removed from his position and replaced by Wang Li.[16] Through this reorganization of the top staff of the Propaganda Department, *Hongqi* and *RR*, Mao was able to strengthen his position vis-a-vis the mass media. These changes in the staff of the Propaganda Department, however, did not put the department under Mao's control. Tao Zhu was reported to have close links with the Liu-Deng Group and resisted Mao's direction.[17] Consequently, Mao launched a second reorganization of the Propaganda Department in early January 1967. In the second reorganization Mao replaced Tao Zhu and put Wang Li, a radical leftist, in charge of the Propaganda Department. In mid-January, Maoist control was extended to other major newspapers such as *Wen Hui Bao* and *Jiefang Ribao* in Shanghai. These two papers were reportedly seized by the Shanghai working class and reborn as revolutionary newspapers.[18] After seizing these two papers, Maoists called for a nation-wide movement to seize control of the newspapers. On January 19, the editorial of the *RR* entitled "Let Mao Zedong Thought Occupy All Positions in the Press," urged proletarian revolutionaries to seize the leadership of the newspapers from the hands of the bourgeois rightists, and take firmly into their own hands the destiny of the people's press. Mao was reported as the main supporter of this movement. The editorial stated:

[16] During this period, Peking local newspapers suffered a serious problem of power struggle. For example, *Guangming Ribao* was seized in May by the Maoists of the Central Group of the Cultural Revolution. In June, *Beijing Ribao* was compelled to reorganize and *Beijing Wan Bao* (Peking Evening News) ceased publication. In November, *Ta Kung Bao*, *Gongren Ribao* (Worker's Daily) and *Zhongguo Qingnian Bao* (China Youth Daily) were closed down. For these events, see Ding Wang (ed.), *Zhongguo Dalu Xinwenjie Wenhua Dagemin Ziliao Huibian* (A Compilation of Press Articles on Peking News Policy During the Cultural Revolution), Hong Kong: The Chinese University of Hong Kong, 1973, pp. 60, 80. 96.

[17] "Tao Zhu was the Enemy of the Proletariat," *RR*, September 11, 1967.

[18] See *RR*, January 19, 1967. Before the take-over of these two papers, they were already controlled by Maoists. But some leading cadres in these two papers opposed the increasingly violent actions taken against authority by Red Guards in Shanghai in early January. The power-seizures of these two papers actually mean "the complete elimination of these conservative elements." See *Hongqi*, "Power to Exercise Leadership Over Newspapers Must Be Seized," no. 3, February 3, 1967.

.... Chairman Mao has pointed out that this event is a great revolution, and a great revolution in which one class overthrows another. This event will certainly play a tremendous role in pushing ahead the development of the great proletarian cultural revolution throughout East China and in all the cities and provinces in other parts of the country.

This editorial conspicuously pointed out the importance of newspapers in the Cultural Revolution and the influence of controlling *Wen Hui Bao* and *Jiefang Ribao*. It declared:

Our Party newspapers are an important weapon serving the dictatorship of the proletariat. They can best exert an influence over the inner being of the broad masses, over the beating of their pulse, their thinking, feeling and political orientation. Newspapers that have fallen into the hands of those in authority who are taking the capitalist road will become their counter-revolutionary tools serving to spread capitalist restoration. This is absolutely impermissible. The proletarian revolutionaries of the *Wen Hui Bao* and *Jiefang Ribao* rose resolutely in rebellion in Shanghai, seized back the leadership, switched the capitalist orientation of the newspapers so as really to make these two newspapers the voice of the Shanghai proletarian revolutionaries, a powerful weapon of the great proletarian cultural revolution and a powerful weapon in smashing the new counter-attack by the bourgeois reactionary line.

Finally, this editorial called for a nation-wide movement to learn from the example set by the revolutionary comrades of the *Wen Hui Bao* and *Jiefang Ribao* in Shanghai. In its conclusion, the editorial said:

In the all-out class struggle waged by the proletariat and a vast number of revolutionary people against the bourgeoisie and its agents, the revolutionary comrades of the *Wen Hui Bao* and *Jiefang Ribao* have set a fine example to the revolutionary journalists throughout the country. We should learn from them. We should learn from these comrades to stand firmly on the side of the proletarian revolutionary line represented by Chairman Mao Zedong and to stand on the side of revolutionary rebels in seizing the enemy positions in the great cause of the proletarian cultural revolution. We should learn from the revolutionary rebel spirit of these comrades, and place the destiny of the press firmly in the hands of the proletarian revolutionaries. We should learn from the way these comrades have aligned themselves closely with the workers' movement, forging close links between the newspapers and the revolutionary masses. In short, all the proletarian revolutionary newspapers should have a completely new and militant style, should make clear what we support and what we oppose in a completely frank and unequivocal way.

In early 1967, with the expansion of local power struggles, most local newspapers were either closed down or taken over by Mao's supporters.[19] In April, Mao dissolved the Propaganda Department and put this activity under

[19] For example, *Nanfang Ribao* (Canton) and *Yangcheng Wanbao* (Canton) were seized by Mao's supporters in January 1967. See Ding Wang, *op. cit.*, with respect to other local newspapers.

the direct control of the Central Cultural Revolutionary Group (CRG) led by Jiang Qing and Chen Boda. Therefore, from April 1967 until the abolition of the Central CRG in 1971, all the party mass media, including *Hongqi*, were under the direct supervision of Mao and his close associates in the Central Group.

Leftists' Impacts on Diplomacy, 1967-68

While leftists gained control of the mass media, Peking's foreign policy in 1967 moved towards isolation from the outside world. Internal power struggles had undoubtedly disrupted the formal bureaucratic process. Beginning with the 1966 Eleventh Plenum, the leftists had a significant impact on foreign policy. The Ministry of Foreign Affairs (MFA) in Peking was heavily involved in the domestic turmoil.

First of all, the MFA was attacked by the Leftists. Foreign Minister Chen Yi was attacked in *dazibao* (big character posters) for suppressing the Cultural Revolution in the MFA.[20] Materials distributed by Red Guards accused Chen of supporting work teams dispatched under the aegis of Liu Shaoqi in that period,[21] of siding with Liu at the Eleventh Plenum,[22] of opposing the Revolution Group of the Central Committee which he had claimed "permits students to go crazy,"[23] of suppressing the Cultural Revolution among Overseas Chinese "by fostering conservatives and quashing rebels,"[24] and of promoting a special stratum among high ranking foreign service officers, consisting of agents of Liu and Deng. In January 1967, Chen was compelled to make a confession. In the midst of widespread turmoil, a plot was reported aimed at overthrowing Chen Yi and several Vice-Premiers in defiance of Zhou Enlai who seemed to be protecting Chen.[25] The plot was allegedly under the direction of Wang Li, a member of the Cultural Revolution Group and deputy

[20] Melvin Gurtov, "The Foreign Ministry and Foreign Affairs during the Cultural Revolution," *The China Quarterly*, no. 40, October–December 1969, pp. 65-103.

[21] *SCMP* 3939, p. 7 and *SCMP* 4007, p. 2.

[22] Robert A. Scalapino, "The Cultural Revolution and Chinese Foreign Policy," *Current Scene*, vol. VI, no. 13, August 1968.

[23] *Huang Wei Zhan Bao*, 13, 1967, Published by Hongweidui and Dongfanghong Communes of the Chinese People's University, translated by *SCMP*, no. 4007.

[24] *Ibid.*

[25] Wang Li, Guan Feng, and Qi Benyu were also reported as having attempted to seize power from the State Council, replacing all Vice-Premiers and purging Li Fuchun, Li Xiannian, and Chen Yi. They were said to have conducted investigations in each section and department for the purpose of overthrowing Zhou Enlai and his State Council. See *Tao Zhou*, Zhungshan University's Revolution and Rebellion Committee, March 1, 1968.

editor of *Hongqi*. Irrespective of whether this conspiracy actually existed, sharpened assaults on Chen Yi and the Foreign Ministry took place coincidentally with a general breakdown of order in the "seize power" campaign. Due to these internal disturbances in the MFA, Peking's international relations suffered serious setbacks in 1967-68.

Secondly, the united front policy with the Third World was disrupted. During 1967-68, no top-level official from China visited any foreign country, not even in Asia. One Chinese performing arts troop visited Japan;[26] one trade delegation visited Pakistan;[27] and one performing arts troop and one official delegation visited Nepal.[28] China sent delegations to only five African countries and Guinea was the only country in Africa where China remained relatively active. China sent two delegations to Guinea in 1967 and three in 1968. In 1968 the PRC signed one trade agreement, one medical assistance agreement and one agreement to assist Guinea in building railroads.[29] In 1967, Peking sent two delegations to the Congo (B) and Zanzibar and one to Tanzania.[30] In 1968, China dispatched only one delegation each to Tanzania, the Congo (B), and Mauritius.[31] (See Table 9.1)

Thirdly, because of deteriorating relations with Moscow, Chinese activities in most of the communist countries, with the exception of Albania, Rumania, North Vietnam, North Korea and East Germany, also ceased. Throughout the Cultural Revolution, Albania was China's closest ally and supported the PRC's opposition to the Soviet Union. China sent five delegations to Albania in 1967 and two in 1968. Albania was the only country with which Peking maintained close relations and China continued assistance to her during this period. In November 1968, five agreements pledged China to give loans, technological aid and equipment, and supply Albania with machinery as well as materials and ships; and both countries agreed to exchange commodities and payments in 1969.[32] In contrast, Rumania took a neutral attitude toward Sino-Soviet polemics. In February 1967, China sent a trade delegation to Rumania resulting in a good exchange and payments protocol.[33] A Sino-Rumanian friendship delegation was also dispatched by Peking to attend the May Day ceremony in Bucharest.[34] In October a protocol for scientific and

[26] *R R*, October 13, 1967.
[27] *RR*, October 23, 1967.
[28] *RR*, May 14; May 21, 1967.
[29] *RR*, January 25; September 24, 1967; May 3; September 27, 1968.
[30] *RR*, March 5; March 27; January 12; December 17, 1967.
[31] *RR*, December 17; August 16; March 12, 1968.
[32] *RR*, November 23, 1968.
[33] *RR*, February 17, 1967.
[34] *RR*, April 24, 1967.

TABLE 9.1
Frequency of Visits by Chinese Delegations, 1967-68

	1967	*1968*
Non-communist:		
Japan	1	0
Pakistan	1	1
Nepal	2	0
Guinea	2	2
Zanzibar	2	0
Tanzania	1	1
Congo (B)	2	1
Maritius	0	1
Total	11	6
Communist Bloc:		
Rumania	2	0
Albania	5	2
E. Germany	0	1
N. Korea	0	1
N. Vietnam	1	0
Total	8	4
Europe:		
Finland	1	0

Source: Survey of *RR*, 1967-68.

technical cooperation was signed by the two countries.[35] In November 1968 a delegation of the CCP and government leaders, headed by the Acting Chief of General Staff of the PLA Huang Yongsheng, visited Rumania.

North Vietnam and North Korea also took neutral stands in the Sino-Soviet dispute. However, China seemed to be maintaining stable relations with Hanoi. In April 1968, China and North Vietnam concluded an executive plan for Sino-Vietnamese cultural cooperation.[36] In August, China promised to provide North Vietnam with economic and technical aid.[37] In October, the two signed another agreement to exchange commodities and goods,[38] and in March 1968, Peking and Hanoi signed a protocol for cooperation in railroad transportation.[39] In July, the two governments reached an agreement and a protocol for Chinese economic and technical aid.[40] Despite the fact that Hanoi did not

[35] *RR*, October 27, 1967.
[36] *RR*, April 27, 1967.
[37] *RR*, August 6, 1967.
[38] *RR*, October 7, 1967.
[39] *RR*, March 21, 1968.
[40] *RR*, July 25, 1968.

want to side with Peking in the Sino-Soviet polemic, the escalation of the war seems to have driven them into closer relations. North Korea ostensibly maintained a neutral attitude toward the Sino-Soviet dispute, but actually was closer to the Soviet Union than to China. In 1967, Chinese Red Guards loudly condemned North Korea for its pro-Soviet stand, but formal relations between the two countries were maintained. In March 1968, a trade delegation was sent to conclude a trade protocol.

Fourthly, China's foreign policy suffered a number of setbacks. Two remarkable incidents occurred in relations with Burma and Indonesia. China had maintained fairly amicable relations with Burma in 1963-66. During that time, Zhou Enlai visited Burma twice and Chen Yi once. In July 1965 General Ne Win was invited to Peking for a state visit. He and Zhou Enlai signed a joint statement pledging Chinese support of Burma's policy of non-alignment, accelerating economic and technical agreements between the two countries, and further expanding trade and economic cooperation.[41] In April 1966, Liu Shaoqi, still Chief of State, reciprocated by visiting Burma.

Suddenly a crisis arose in June 1967 when the Burmese Ministry of Education prohibited Chinese students in Rangoon from wearing Mao Zedong badges. Violence broke out between pro-Peking Chinese residents and Burmese officials. As a result, the Burmese government took strong measures to suppress Chinese activities. Peking lodged a "most urgent and strong protest" with the Burmese Government.[42] Relations deteriorated rapidly. In October, Burma handed a note to China demanding that the latter withdraw all its aid, experts, and technical personnel at once. A series of protests was lodged by the two governments against one another throughout the rest of 1967 and 1968.

Peking's relations with Indonesia were also deteriorating rapidly in 1967 and 1968. In early 1967, a series of attacks upon remaining Chinese diplomatic missions and humiliations to her diplomatic personnel occurred.[43] Relations between the two nations deteriorated even more rapidly after October 1 when Indonesian troops, using force to search the Chinese Embassy in Djakarta, clashed with Chinese diplomats, injuring a total of 20 diplomatic personnel.[44] On the 23rd of that month the Indonesian Government ordered the Chinese Embassy completely closed down, and, on the 27th, Peking formally severed diplomatic relations with Indonesia.[45]

During 1967-68, the internal political turmoil clearly had a negative impact on China's foreign relations. Some of China's diplomats, inspired by the

[41] RR, July 14, 1965.
[42] RR, June 29, 1967.
[43] RR, January 14, 22, 26, 1967.
[44] RR, October 3, 1967.
[45] RR, October 28, 1967.

political agitation at home, circulated Mao's selected works and launched campaigns to emulate the thought of Mao abroad. When these campaigns were suppressed by foreign host countries, Peking protested against incidents in Tunisia, France, Nepal, Czechoslovakia, Ceylon, Mongolia, Hong Kong, Macao, Yugoslavia, Japan, and India. Such occurrences were not, however, of major concern to Peking. Throughout the period, the two issues which dominated the Peking press were Soviet Revisionism and "U.S. aggression in Vietnam."

China's Antiforeignism during the Cultural Revolution

During the Cultural Revolution, despite internal political turmoil, Peking was even more outspoken than ever in attacks against the Soviet Union and "U.S. aggression in Vietnam." China's position toward these two countries became increasingly hostile. The leftists made good use of the mass media and mobilization techniques to defeat their enemies inside and attack those outside the country. As discussed above, antiforeignism was demonstrated in both internal politics and external hostilities. External hostilities can be observed in the content of the *RR*, antiforeign mass demonstrations, and social and political developments.

Relations between Peking and Moscow deteriorated rapidly after their open split in 1963. With the beginning of the Cultural Revolution in 1966, relations were further aggravated. In 1967, tension rose to an unprecedented level and accusations against "Soviet revisionism" appeared daily in the Chinese press.

In 1968, relations between Peking and Moscow remained tense. In April, a strong protest was lodged with the Soviet embassy in Peking, accusing a Soviet ship of espionage in Canton. The ship was ordered to leave port under armed escort.[46] Also in April, another protest condemned the deportation of a Chinese aircraft expert in Tashkent. In August, following the armed invasion of Czechoslovakia by Soviet troops, the *RR* also carried a great number of reports charging expansionism by the "new Tsars" and "Soviet revisionist-socialist colonialism." In September, Peking again lodged a strong protest against air incursions in the Donghua area of Heilongjiang province by Soviet aircraft. The note charged the Soviets with creating disturbances and carrying out provocative activities. The protest said,

> It is not at all usual for the Soviet government to initiate such frequent, unbridled and frenetic military provocations in the air over a certain area of Chinese territory within a short period of 21 days . . . . It should be especially pointed out that it is

---

[46]*RR*, April 10, 1968.

by no means accidental that air incursions by military planes should have taken place shortly before and after the Soviet armed invasion of Czechoslovakia on August 20.[47]

In October, possibility of war with the Soviet Union was publicly discussed. The whole country was thrown into preparations for war in spite of internal political turmoil. Since hostility toward the Soviet Union and internal political struggles seem related to each other, they will be examined closely in the next chapter.

Chinese hostility toward the United States mainly focused on the Vietnam War. A *RR* commentary stated that China with 700 million people guided by Mao Zedong's thought was the center of the great alliance of the revolutionary people of the world, and that "U.S. imperialism" was the ringleader of the world's counter-revolutionaries.[48]

As the conflict in Vietnam escalated, China expressed firm support for the Vietnamese communists. In March, 1967 a MFA statement said,

The Chinese Government and the people express that most resolute support for the just stand of the valiant vietnamese people . . . . The 700 million Chinese people who are armed with Mao Tse-tung's thought most resolutely support their Vietnamese brothers in resisting U.S. aggression to the end blackmail ageinst the Vietnamese people.[49]

The number of reports in the *RR* grew from 26 in February to 50 in March. Only one rally, however, was held in Peking in support of the Vietnamese people, and in condemnation of "U.S. imperialism." Moreover, the number of articles expressing support for Vietnam increased from April to December. In December, to celebrate the seventh anniversary of the founding of the National Liberation Front, meetings were held in 29 major cities including Peking, Shanghai, Harbin, Qingdao, and Jinan. Mao Zedong and Zhou Enlai again vowed to provide powerful backing for the Vietnamese people.[50] A series of articles again appeared in the *RR* expressing firm moral support for the Vietnamese people and condemning U.S. imperialist aggression. The number of such articles rose to 69 in December from 13 in November.

The strongest expression of support came after the Tet offensive of February 1968. Again, mass meetings were held in Peking, Shanghai, and Tientsin. The *RR* praised the "great heroic victory" of the brave Vietnamese people and published denunciation of U.S. aggression in Vietnam and around the world. Yet this issue did not trigger any nation-wide mass movement. The

---

[47]*RR*, September 17, 1968.
[48]*RR*, January 23, 1967.
[49]*Beijing Review*, no. 11, March 10, 1967.
[50]*RR*, December 20, 1967.

number of these articles rose to 84 in February, but quickly dropped to 24 in March. Thereafter, the criticisms and attacks against the U.S. involvement in the Vietnam War dropped to their lowest level. From March 1968 to February 1969, Chinese criticisms averaged only about 5 each month. It appears that this drastic change paralleled the cessation of U.S. bombings and implicitly supported the opening of peace talks in Paris.

Characteristics of Antiforeignism during the Cultural Revolution

As discussed above, power struggles and the trend to leftism inevitably led to the rise of antiforeignism. This hypothesis is clearly confirmed by the Cultural Revolution. In addition to external hostilities toward foreign countries as expressed by verbal attacks in the mass media and antiforeign mass demonstrations, which will be systematically examined in later sections, the rise of antiforeignism can also be seen in cultural, political, and economic developments during this period.

The most striking development during this period was the complete rejection of all Western culture and art, which was condemned by the "ultra-leftists." Most translated works of Western classics were confiscated by the authorities. The introduction of Western culture and art in universities or schools was halted. Severe criticism against Western philosophies appeared quite often in the mass media. Western music and dance were hotly criticized by the Red Guards. A revolutionary dance was created from modified ballet, representing the culture of the proletarian class. This total rejection of Western culture and arts culminated in a new wave of antiforeignism during the Cultural Revolution.

On the political scene, punishments for those who were educated in the West and those who had communications with people outside of China intensified. The so-called "foreign connection" was treated as equivalent to "spy" in the political norms of the Cultural Revolution. A new development was the punishment of those who had relatives in foreign countries. Many of them were beaten, convicted or publicly criticized because of "espionage arts."[51] Public harrassment of foreigners was often seen in the streets. Travelling in China was almost impossible for foreigners due to Chinese suspicion and sensitivity to their presence.

In addition, a psychology of "war hysteria" was propagandized by the mass media. The leadership declared that war with "Social imperialism" or "U.S. imperialism" might break out anytime. They called for "preparation for war" and "preparation for famine." In the later period of the Cultural

---

[51] Data obtained through an interview, July 1978.

Revolution, the whole country was under the control of the PLA. The Red Guards were repressed, and the civil administration was taken over by the PLA. It appeared that China was very much on the alert against foreign invasion. The clash with the Soviet Union on the Northeast border partly contributed to this "war hysteria."

Economically, the policy of "self-reliance" was intensively emphasized. Exaggerated reports of the progress of Chinese scientific research or technology appeared constantly in the mass media. New records in production were fabricated by the leading cadres. Class struggle was emphasized for the promotion of production. Severe criticism of foreign products and praise for local Chinese products consistently showed itself in the mass media reports. Denunciation of "capitalist ideology" and "capitalist roaders," however, became the focus of propaganda during this period. A great number of factories were shut down because the workers refused to work, thus interrupting economic development. Therefore, leftism and antiforeignism, which had previously contributed to production, now slowed down the Chinese economy.

The Antiforeign Demonstrations

Antiforeign mass movements in 1967-69 were markedly different from those in 1960-62. No longer were they directed against the United States alone; instead, they attacked the Soviet Union, Indonesia, India, Mongolia, the British in Hong Kong as well as Burma, and Japan. (See Appendix IV)

The first and largest antiforeign mass campaign, held in January and February, 1967, was directed against the "Soviet revisionists" for their suppression of Chinese students in Moscow and for "anti-China crimes." Sixty-three mass rallies were held in all major cities of China during this period. The second antiforeign mass activity was in April, 1967, in the name of denouncing "Indonesian reactionaries." It started on April 25 and ended on the 29th. During this time 17 mass rallies were held in 14 major cities. The largest were in Peking, Canton, Shanghai, Kunming, Guiyang, Harbin, and Fuzhou.

A third series of demonstrations was organized on May 15 to condemn British persecution of Chinese patriots in Hong Kong. This movement included only three major cities: Peking, Shanghai and Canton. The first part ended on June 27, but it continued intermittently in July, August and October. All three of these antiforeign mass movements were largely organized by the Red Guards, the revolutionary masses, and leading members of the PLA.

In 1967, two big mass movements were directed against the United States. The first took place from May 25 to early June in support of the Palestinians and Arabs in their struggle against "U.S. imperialism and the Israeli aggressors." The rallies took place in Peking only and did not develop into a nation-wide movement. The purpose of the second was to support the Vietnamese struggle against U.S. aggression, on December 19, the seventh anniversary of the founding of the National Liberation Front. This rally was also limited to Peking.

In 1968, the strongest antiforeign mass movement was organized in the latter part of May. From May 21 to 24, nation-wide mass campaigns took place to support "the great struggle of the peoples of the world against the U.S. imperialists and Soviet revisionists." This movement included mass rallies in 53 major cities. It urged the people of the whole world to rise up and hold aloft the great banner of Marxism-Leninism and the thought of Mao Zedong in order to carry out the "righteous struggle against the U.S.-USSR reactionary forces."[52] It was stressed in the mass media that this movement was initiated by a close alliance of Red Guards, revolutionary masses, and leading cadres of the People's Liberation Army in each city.[53]

In the same year, there were three other mass movements directed against the United States. The first took place on April 18 in support of the Afro-American people's struggle against U.S. government oppression. Twenty-nine cities across the nation organized rallies to support this movement.[54] The second anti-U.S. movement was organized to support the Cambodian people's government and the Indo-Chinese people in their opposition to U.S. aggression. This movement took place on May 7, with rallies in all provincial capitals. The third movement was initiated in support of the "Vietnamese people's righteous struggle against the U.S. imperialists." This movement took place on December 15, and again included the capitals of all provinces, municipalities and autonomous regions. The newspaper did not mention the major active participants in these anti-U.S. movements, but it appears that the rallies were organized simply by the local governments of each province. It is quite possible that during 1968, local and provincial governments came under the control of military men who formed the major link between the local and the pro-Mao central government.

The antiforeign mass movements during the Cultural Revolution suggest that despite internal political turmoil, Peking was vigorous in expressing its opposition on external issues. During this period, it was principally pro-Mao people who were active in organizing these campaigns. It is possible that they used these campaigns to activate antiforeign attitudes so that they could consolidate power and strengthen their leadership in domestic politics.

Despite the domestic authority crisis and political struggles among and between Maoists and anti-Maoists, antiforeign campaigns occurred throughout the country. These campaigns seem to have had a very different intention

[52]*RR*, May 24, 1968.
[53]*Ibid.*
[54]*RR*, April 18, 1968.

from those of 1960-62. It is clear that in 1960-62 dissension among the top echelons did not cause wide political strife nor openly violent struggles within the government and Party. During the Cultural Revolution, however, the old government and Party machine, as well as other important administrative organs, were disrupted by the power-seizure campaign and the campaign to denounce Liu Shaoqi. In the midst of such a serious authority crisis, how could these nation-wide antiforeign campaigns have been organized? During this period only Maoists or leftists could take part in these campaigns, and those accused of being capitalist roaders or revisionists were prevented from participating. Accordingly, these antiforeign mass campaigns were organized by the Maoists or leftists themselves instead of those regularly responsible cadres in the government and the Party.

The next question to consider is why the leftists organized so many antiforeign mass campaigns while they were heavily engaged in political struggle. During early 1967, as in 1966, the campaign to seize power met with many unanticipated difficulties. Problems generally were due to confusion among the masses, resistance by old cadres and administrators who did not support Mao's purge of Liu Shaoqi, opposition from Liu's supporters and other anti-Maoist people, and factional struggles among the Maoist "revolutionary leftists." In this difficult situation, Mao ordered the PLA to provide support for the campaign for power-seizure. With PLA backing, the "revolutionary leftists" could oust their foes in the Party and government apparatus at all levels. There were still many problems, however, which the army seemed unable to resolve. By the middle of 1967, six months after the entry of the PLA into the power-seizure campaign, only six provincial revolutionary committees had been formed. This probably indicates that the PLA could not provide much help to the "revolutionary leftists" in their efforts to gain support from the masses, to convert recalcitrant cadres and administrators, or even to solve the problems of factionalism among Maoists. In this difficult situation, antiforeign campaigns probably would not have been undertaken unless they could be helpful to the Maoist cause. Therefore, it seems clear that the Maoists used these movements for internal political purposes. They were taking advantage of the enthusiasm generated by anti-imperialism and anti-revisionism campaigns to alleviate difficulties in the power-seizure movement.

Furthermore, during the authority crisis, antiforeign mass movements could perform several very useful functions for the Maoists. First, these movements could bring the "revolutionary leftists" together on the basis of their common antiforeign nationalistic spirit. In this chaotic situation, regular channels of communication were probably interrupted, and these antiforeign mass rallies provided a chance to work together and perhaps smooth over conflicts and differences. Secondly, these antiforeign campaigns could improve

Table 9.2
ANTIFOREIGN DEMONSTRATIONS, 1967

Month	U.S.	S.U.	Others	Total
January	0	18	2	20
February	1	36	0	37
March	1	0	0	1
April	0	0	17	17
May	4	0	13	17
June	1	0	28	29
July	0	0	9	9
August	0	0	5	5
September	1	0	3	4
October	0	0	1	1
November	0	0	0	0
December	1	0	0	1
Total	9	54	78	141

Source: *RR*, 1967

Table 9.3
ANTIFOREIGN DEMONSTRATIONS, 1968

Month	U.S.	S.U.	Others	Total
January	0	0	0	0
February	0	0	0	0
March	0	0	1	1
April	29	0	0	29
May	82	0	0	82
June	0	0	0	0
July	0	0	2	2
August	0	0	0	0
September	2	0	0	2
October	0	0	2	2
November	0	0	2	2
December	31	0	5	36
Total	144	0	12	156

Source: *RR*, 1968

the image of Maoist leadership among the masses. Through campaigns against foreign enemies, the Maoists demonstrated their determination to oppose imperialism and revisionism and promote the greatness of China. Thirdly, these campaigns, by rallying the masses, could provide a public forum for promoting Mao's cause and condemning his opponents. Mass rallies and meetings were a most effective means of propaganda for the Maoists. Finally, the campaigns probably provided the Maoists with a mechanism for refreshing their own sense of purpose so as to keep them active in the campaign to seize power and to denounce Liu Shaoqi and other "capitalist roaders." This is why antiforeign mass demonstrations increased when the campaign to seize power was at its height during the Cultural Revolution.[55]

Summary

This examination of China's international activities during the Cultural Revolution period has shown that Peking had far fewer official contacts with other nations than in 1960-62. Chinese relations with the Communist bloc became remote due to her open dispute with the Soviet Union. In addition, because of attempted propagation of the thought of Mao Zedong, Peking's relations with a number of countries suffered serious setbacks.

The level of verbal hostility, as expressed in RR attacks on the Soviet Union and on U.S. involvement in the Vietnam War, was higher than previously. Despite border tensions, however, verbal hostilities toward the Soviet Union decreased from 1967 to 1968. Condemnation of U.S. involvement in Vietnam increased from early in 1967 to early 1968, and decreased after the cessation of U.S. bombing of N. Vietnam and the opening of the Paris peace talks in March, 1968. Antiforeign mass demonstrations decreased from July, 1967 to March, 1968; however, they rose again in April-June, 1968 and October-December, 1968.

Naturally, this variation in verbal hostility and antiforeign demonstrations was greatly influenced by external stimuli. Nevertheless, data presented here suggests that the hostility was manipulated by Maoists for internal purposes. For instance, condemnation of Soviet revisionism was related to the Maoist accusations against China's own revisionists. In order to identity the Liu-Deng line with Soviet Revisionism, the Red Guards accused Liu Shaoqi of being "China's Khrushchev." One of the Maoists' most serious accusations against Liu's clique was that they had collaborated with the Soviets in an attempt to divert China's revolutionary causes into revisionism.

[55]This theory is confirmed in an empirical test conducted by Kuang-sheng Liao, in "Linkage Politics in China," *World Politics*, vol. XXVIII, no. 4, 1976, pp. 590-610.

Public condemnations of external enemies could strengthen Maoist accusa-tions against the Liu-Deng clique and further tarnish the public image of their opponents. Therefore, attacks on Soviet revisionism were probably correlated with domestic campaigns of denunciation of Liu Shaoqi and power seizure from the "capitalists" in authority. Similarly, verbal hostility toward the United States, as well as antiforeign mass demonstrations, may be related to these internal issues. In order to clarify this generalization, I will undertake a detailed examination of the relation between external hostilities against the Soviet Union and domestic campaigns in the next chapter.

CHAPTER 10

Power Struggle and Anti-Soviet Revisionism during the Cultural Revolution

In 1959, Mao withdrew to the "second front" of the Standing Committee of the Politburo, leaving the routine work to others.[1] After Mao stepped down as chief of state, Liu Shaoqi organized the bureaucratic elite which increasingly controlled the political processes and policy-making in China. Under these circumstances, how could Mao come back and legally launch a violent nation-wide mass campaign to seize power and to overthrow these "capitalists in authority"? In the period of intensive political struggle, campaigns involved millions of students, workers, peasants, and the PLA. Mass fighting, civil violence, and the disruption of governmental administration took place. It is frequently argued that military intervention for the purpose of restoring order in power seizures helped Mao regain the leadership.[2] The corollary question of how Mao was able to mobilize his nation-wide support among the masses is frequently ignored. The proposition that Mao relied on the PLA to defeat his enemies is something of an over-simplification. As will be discussed below, Mao's strategy to defeat his enemies included public denunciation of Soviet revisionism and an open denunciation of "capitalists in authority" by the mass media. These attacks were directed by Mao and his leftist supporters towards stimulating hostile sentiments against Liu. Such sentiments were necessary for Mao to be able to push ahead with the mass campaign of power-seizure from the "capitalists in authority." The events of the Cultural Revolution reveal adept manipulation of the mass media and mass mobilization together with the utilization of military forces in the process of power seisure.

Power Struggle and Antiforeignism during the Cultural Revolution

A theory concerning power struggle and its relationship with antiforeignism was proposed in Chapter 6 based on political developments in the 1950s. It suggests that power struggles in China would lead to further leftism and higher antiforeignism. Obviously this theory, in general, gained strong support from the discussion of leftism in Chapter 9. A further investigation is conducted here specifically for the relationship between power struggle and anti-Soviet revisionism.

[1] "Speech at a Work Conference of the Central Committee, October 25, 1966," translated in *Current Background*, no. 891, p. 75.

[2] Ellis Joffe, "The Chinese Army after the Cultural Revolution: The Effects of Intervention," *The China Quarterly*, no. 55, July–September, 1973, pp. 454-55.

The power struggle during the Cultural Revolution was characterized by Maoist campaigns to seize power and to denounce the "Top Capitalist in Authority." Mao Zedong and his supporters initiated a painstaking struggle to remove completely those whom they considered followed the "capitalist line" in the Party and government and who in mid-1966 still firmly dominated the top-level Party organs, the Politburo, and the Central Committee. After the Eleventh Plenary Session of the Eighth Central Committee in August 1966, Lin Biao emerged as second only to Mao. Liu Shaoqi and certain of his supporters were downgraded. The communique of the Eleventh Plenary Session reads:

> The Plenary Session stressed that the series of directives by Comrade Mao Zedong concerning the great proletarian cultural revolution are the guide to action in our country's present cultural revolution; they constitute an important development of Marxism-Leninism.[3]

Power-seizure was the most urgent objective for the Maoists during this period. The Maoist-controlled *RR* became a primary instrument for helping Maoists to achieve success in the power-struggle. It is possible that the hostility expressed by the *RR* on foreign policy issues also served this purpose. In order to destroy Liu Shaoqi's power and public prestige, Maoists triggered a verbal campaign aimed at showing Liu's opposition to Mao and Liu's "capitalist line." Obviously, this mass denunciation was intended to help the Maoists seize power from the "capitalist roaders." Facing a severe political struggle, the Maoists spared no pains in mobilizing support to defeat their political enemies. Mao seemed again to be manipulating antiforeignism for the purpose of mobilizing mass support during this period.

As discussed in Chapter 6, the political dispute among the elite did not become a public nation-wide political struggle in the earlier period. Mao and his opponents were fighting among themselves at the highest level of the power structure. In the Cultural Revolution period of 1967-February 1969, the political struggle occurred not only at the top of the hierarchy, but spread to become a mass movement as well. The ultimate objective of this mass movement was to destroy Liu's leadership and seize power from him and his supporters.

With such severe internal political turmoil, the escalation of antiforeignism could have a two-fold impact on internal mobilization. In the first place, as in the Yanan period, the Maoists during the Cultural Revolution identified themselves as patriots attacking foreign enemies and championing national independence. There were similarities here to the accusations against Chiang

---

[3] *Communique of the Eleventh Plenary Session of the Eighth Central Committee of the CCP*, Peking: Foreign Languages Press, 1966.

Kai-shek of being a national traitor collaborating with the United States, in the 1945-49 Civil War period. Maoists condemned Liu Shaoqi as having betrayed the Chinese revolution in attempting to collaborate with Soviet "social revisionism." The condemnation of an internal enemy as a traitor was carried out by public denunciation in the mass media. It was through the media that Mao's own personal enemy became a public enemy. Since the internal enemy was linked with the external enemy, the verbal hostilities against external targets could be used to strengthen opposition to Liu.

Secondly, the escalation of articulated hostilities against external enemies was intended to help strengthen Maoist leadership. During the Cultural Revolution, a great number of high-level leaders were violently purged and replaced. The power-seizure campaign did not limit itself to legal means; what was done could be justified only by its aims. Since the Cultural Revolution was not a unanimously supported movement, it was hoped that an emphasis on external threat or preparation for war against the Soviet Union and the United States would minimize resistance. Despite the political struggle, Mao was still the "supreme leader" and enjoyed the highest position as Chairman of the Party. Because of the need for internal unity and cohesive leadership in a war with foreign powers, the whole country was asked to follow the leadership of Mao. The threat of external war could help the Maoist to minimize resistance and strengthen their leadership. In sum, it seems that articulated hostilities against external enemies were intended to destroy Liu's public image, strengthen the Maoists' leadership, minimize resistance, and mobilize mass support. Therefore, antiforeignism increased when the need for mobilization was high.

Political Disputes before the Cultural Revolution

The Great Proletarian Cultural Revolution represented an ideological and political struggle over cultural, social, and economic issues. Massive changes and developments which occurred on these issues after the formation of the People's Communes in 1958 led to divergent opinions at the top level of leadership. Interpretations of Mao's motivation in launching the Cultural Revolution are many and widely contradictory. For such a multidimensional event, any single explanation or interpretation is bound to be partial and limited, ignoring certain other important issues involved. The discussion on the policy dispute between Mao and his opponents presented here cannot escape such a problem. It is not my intention to assert that these policy disputes were the most important problems Mao faced before the Cultural Revolution. Instead, it is hoped that a clarification of Mao's position in policy-making can help us understand the strategy employed by Mao to defeat his opponents during the Cultural Revolution.

Through his activities in the government and Party bureaucracies, Liu Shaoqi was able after 1959 to organize a group committed to a more "pragmatic" and "ideologically moderate" line within the Party.[4] On the economic front, for example, Liu Shaoqi, Peng Zhen, and Bo Yibo drafted, in September 1961, the "Seventy Articles for Industry" which deviated from Mao's "Anshan Constitution" of 1960 by taking the leadership of enterprise away from the branch party committee and restricting its duties to supervision. This contrasted with Mao's policy of "politics should lead the enterprise of industry" in the "Anshan Constitution."[5]

The strength of the opposition to Mao grew largely in the central organization of the government and the Party until it constituted a threat to his leadership. In order to improve his position in this leadership crisis, Mao launched the "Socialist Education" campaign in the fall of 1962. Originally this campaign focused on the rural cadres. Mao considered the campaign to be a sharp class struggle which involved many serious problems. By June 1963 the campaign had expanded to the urban areas, and a "four clean-ups" movement was begun in both rural and urban areas which attempted to clear up corruption in politics, in the economy, in organization, and in ideology.[6] This "Socialist Education" campaign also involved struggles between Mao and his opponents over the formulation of policies in 1963 and 1964.[7]

[4] See Marle Goldman, "Party Policies Toward the Intellectuals: The Unique Blooming and Contending of 1961-62," in John Wilson Lewis (ed.), *Party Leadership and Revolutionary Power in China*, London: Cambridge University Press, 1970, pp. 268-302.

[5] "Peng Zhen's Anti-Party Clique and Its Connections with Liu and Teng," *Xin Beida* (Peking, 1967), p. 1. On the cultural and educational fronts, some leaders also started to deviate from Mao's line. According to criticism of the so-called "anti-revolutionary line of literature and art", the main initiators of revisions of Mao's line on literature were Liu's supporters—Zhou Yang, Tian Han, and Yang Hansheng. In 1961, they formulated the "Ten Articles for Literature and Art," which denied Mao's principle that literature and art should serve the political purposes of the Party. In contrast to Mao's belief that "politics should take command," they claimed that literature and art workers should strengthen their special talents and skill. In other words, they emphasized that artists should be more "expert" than "red". Furthermore, they asserted that the style and subject should be free from any restriction—in other words, free from Party control. This clearly opposed Mao's idea that the Party should take absolute leadership in literature and art.

[6] For a detailed discussion, see Richard Baum and Frederick C. Tewes, *Ssu-Ch'ing: The Socialist Education Movement of 1962-1966*, Berkeley: University of California Press, Centre for Chinese Studies, 1968. Also see Edward E. Rice, *Mao's Way*, Berkeley: University of California Press, 1972, p. 190. Rice estimates that since by this time Mao's opponents controlled the Party Secretariat and presumably enjoyed the support of a majority of the members of the Central Committee, Mao's counter measure could have been prevented by his opponents.

[7] The first regulation in May, 1963 concerning "Socialist Education" was reportedly drafted by Mao himself. It was called "Decision on Certain Problems in Rural Work," or

It has been reported that Mao's designs for the Socialist Education Movement were blocked by his opponents before 1965.[8] In 1964 and 1965 the
Party organs appeared to be controlled by his opponents, Peng Zhen and
Deng Xiaoping. In his letter to Peng Zhen in 1964, Mao said, "In many
departments very little has been achieved so far in socialist transformation.
The 'dead' still dominate in many departments."[9] Mao's directives were not
respected. For example. Peng Zhen was reported to have resisted Mao's
directives and refused to carry them out. Peng often criticized them saying
that "the Chairman's directives were only strategic considerations and must
not be executed as tactics."[10] Wang Guangmei, Liu Shaoqi's wife, was
reported to have openly challenged Mao's Socialist Education Movement
by distorting the "Four Clean-ups" campaign as a movement to clean up
corruption among Party cadres rather than a movement to carry out class
struggle against the "capitalist in authority."[11] Liu Shaoqi and his wife were
reported to have exerted all possible means in order to block the implementation of Mao's "Twenty-Three Articles."[12]

These examples indicate that Mao's opponents tried to circumvent his
directives and that he was determined to prevent them from doing so. It is
quite clear that Mao's intention to purge high-level Party men faced strong
resistance. These pressures seemed to have forced Mao to accept the necessity
of launching another movement which would by-pass the Party organs and
reach directly down to the masses.

"The Former Ten Articles." In September, Deng Xiaoping drafted the "Regulations for
the Movement for Rural Socialist Education," or "The Latter Ten Articles." In September 1964, Peng Zhen revised Deng Xiaoping's "Regulations" according to the experiment
conducted in Hebei by Wang Guangmei, the wife of Liu Shaoqi. Mao was dissatisfied
with Peng's draft, and in the January 1965 Working Conference of the Political Bureau,
he formulated the "Items Concerning the Rural Socialist Education Movement," or the
"Twenty-three Articles." The Former Ten Articles repeatedly emphasized the struggle
between the two lines in rural areas, and urged the purge of the capitalist clique in the
central organization of the government and the Party. The Latter Ten Articles, in contrast, emphasized the problem of corruption of local cadres in the rural areas. Apparently,
Mao's intention was to purge the high-level cadres who opposed his leadership.

[8] Philip Bridgham, "Mao's Cultural Revolution," *The China Quarterly*, no. 29, January-
March, 1967, pp. 14-15; also see *Hongqi*, August 21, 1966, editorial which implied the
movement was blocked by those who looked like "Leftists" but were actually "Rightists."

[9] "Counter Revolutionary Revisionist Peng Zhen's Towering Crimes of Opposing the
Party, Socialism and the Thought of Mao Zedong," *Dongfanghong*, Peking, June 10,
1967, as translated in *Selection of China Mainland Magazines* (SCMM), no. 639, p. 22.

[10] *Ibid.*

[11] "The Report on the Crimes of Liu Shaoqi and Wang Guangmei in the 'Four Clean-
ups Movement'," *Dongfanghong*, Peking, May 7, 1967, p. 8.

[12] *Ibid.*

The Public Denunciation of Soviet Revisionism

After gaining control of the mass media, Mao's supporters used it as a political weapon to attack their opponents. Liu had been the Chief of State since 1959 and, as a result, Liu had, presumably, developed a strong, positive image among the masses. It was necessary to undermine this image if political control was to be taken from him. In the first half of 1967, Mao's supporters started to mobilize the masses to seize power from the "capitalists in authority." During this period attacks against Mao's opponents increased in the mass media. Meanwhile, the attacks against Soviet Revisionism also sharply increased.[13] The increase in attacks on Liu's faction and the increase in denunciations of Soviet revisionism during this period suggests the possibility of a relationship between these two phenomena. In order to examine this hypothesis, a content analysis was made of the *RR* during the period, 1966-68. (See Appendix II) This content analysis provides clues towards understanding more precisely the relationship between attacks on Soviet revisionism and attacks on Liu and his associates.

On the threshold of the Cultural Revolution in 1966, relations between Peking and Moscow had deteriorated. Yet no reports of mass condemnation appeared in the *RR*. It was not until Mao's supporters controlled the mass media that the attack on Soviet Revisionism by the masses really began. In January 1967, a campaign was launched in Peking in protest against the clash on January 25 between Russian police and Chinese students which had occurred when the latter went to lay wreaths at the Lenin mausoleum and Stalin's tomb. More than 30 students were beaten and injured in the clash. Vehement articles in the mass media declared that the Cultural Revolution also had an international goal, namely the battle against modern revisionism. As *Beijing Review* put it:

> China's Great Proletarian Cultural Revolution also has the international aim of further strengthening the struggle against modern revisionist leadership.[14]

Immediately after this incident tension mounted. Red Guards began to demonstrate continuously in front of the Soviet embassy in Peking whereupon anti-Soviet protests sprang up throughout China. Then, on February 3, the Soviet police forcibly carried away six display cases of photographs from the Chinese Embassy in Moscow and clashed with 31 Chinese diplomatic and working personnel on the scene. As a result of this incident, Peking issued its

[13] As pointed out by Daniel Tretiak, the percentage of articles attacking the Soviet Union in *Beijing Review* increased from 6.82% in July-December, 1966 to 18.75% in January-June 1967. See "Is China Preparing to 'Turn Out'?" *Asian Survey*, March 1971, p. 224, Table 2.

[14] *Beijing Review*, no. 6, February 3, 1967, p. 27.

"strongest, most vehement protest." The *RR* condemned it as "a savage outrage such as has seldom been seen in the history of world diplomacy." The editorial called on the Soviet people to topple the "revisionist government", declaring:

> The Soviet people taught by Lenin and Stalin, are a great people with a glorious revolutionary tradition. By no means will they long tolerate the Soviet revisionist clique, a handful of traitors, riding rough-shod over them. . . . The day will come when the Soviet revisionist clique is overthrown by the revolutionary Soviet people and the great banner of Leninism again flies over the vast expanse of the Soviet land.[15]

In this atmosphere, the *RR* carried 58 items in January and 91 items in February accusing the Soviets of anti-revolutionary activities. This high frequency of articles continued through July, decreasing only in August to 27 items. The mass condemnation of "Soviet revisionism" became so common in the *RR* as well as in other media, that almost daily the paper used "Soviet revisionists" as a term of abuse to be condemned at all levels in China. The term became a popular accusation which was hurled indiscriminately, often having nothing at all to do with Sino-Soviet relations. Red Guards, workers, peasants and soldiers, reviled the Soviet leadership with such terms as "dirty crow," "fly," "mad dog," or "ghost." Before 1967, few comments or condemnations of foreign countries were signed by private persons. Even in 1967-68, few comments on "U.S. imperialism," "Indian reactionaries" or "Japanese militarism" were written by any private person. "Soviet revisionism" alone became a target of public condemnation, attacked by a great number of individuals.

Another new development was the condemnation of the "Soviet revisionists' restoration of capitalism." Before 1967, the Chinese press had few comments on domestic affairs in the Soviet Union. In 1967-68, however, a great number of reports were issued condemning the Soviet economy and the suppression of the Soviet people. For instance, a *RR* article of November 1967, entitled "The Disastrous Results of the New System," said:

> The implementation of this 'new system' has brought disaster to the economy of the Soviet Union. It has caused confusion in production, a sharp decline in the quality of goods and failure in carrying through production plans. Moreover, it has caused speculation and theft to become rampant and further stepped up the process of class differentiation.[16]

Another comment entitled "Soviet Revisionists Enforce Bourgeois Dictatorship" said:

[15] *RR*, February 6, 1967; *Beijing Review*, no. 7, February 10, 1967, p. 7.
[16] *RR*, November 20, 1967.

Under the rule of the Brezhnev-Kosygin renegade clique, elements of the privileged stratum take advantage of their authority and influence to practise graft, embezzlement of public property, speculation, and cheating. They ruthlessly oppress and exploit the masses of the Soviet people. . . .[17]

This kind of comment reflects not only the depth of difference between the two government leaderships but also the intensity of hostility between them.

It is noteworthy that a country so deeply engrossed in internal political struggle allowed itself at the same time to engage in an external dispute of such ferocity. As shown in Figure 10.1, the period of the most frequent

Figure 10.1: The Frequency of the *RR*'s Accusations against the Soviet Union

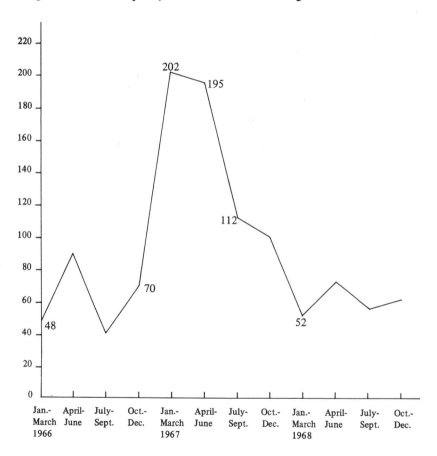

[17] *Ibid.*   Sources: *RR*, 1966-1968

attacks on Soviet revisionism was in the first half of 1967 during which time Mao and his supporters were heavily engaged in serious power struggles with their opponents. With the control of the mass media in their hands, Mao and his supporters could utilize the media according to their desires. They could lower the frequency of accusations against Soviet revisionism in the January and February 1967 incidents, if it was advantageous to their efforts to seize power. Apparently, however, the opposite was true. They chose to make these incidents into a major national issue. Thus, the high frequency of accusations against the Soviets in the first half of 1967 is not a mere coincidence. Instead, it appears to be a manipulation by Mao and his supporters who controlled the *RR*.

Soviet revisionism was the most common foreign target of this period. And, as will be discussed in the next section, denunciation of Liu Shaoqi was the most common internal target during this period. In other words, accusations against "Soviet social revisionism" in the first half of 1967 were manipulated to help the media to push through its denunciation of Liu's faction. Thus, to attack an external enemy and raise public sentiment against it was the first approach taken by the *RR*. When this objective was achieved, the next stage was to launch a media denunciation against Liu and to carry out a nation-wide mass mobilization to seize power from the revisionists in authority. Consequently, as shown in Figure 10.1, the media accusations against the Soviet revisionists sharply and steadily declined after this period.

From 1968 to February 1969, the frequency of criticism of the Soviet Union sharply decreased as compared with that of late 1967, despite a continued Soviet troop build-up along the Northern border. On September 17, 1968, the *RR* published banner headlines with the charge that Soviet military aircraft had intruded into Chinese airspace. They claimed that as many as 119 sorties had occurred during the period from August 1967 to August 1968.[18] This indicated that tension existed and that a more serious border conflict might bring the two governments into confrontation. In his National Day address on October 1, 1968, Zhou urged the nation to intensify preparation for a defensive war against U.S. imperialism or Soviet revisionism.[19] Because of the de-escalation of the Vietnam war during this period, the possibility of a U.S. invasion was slight. Thus, it seems that Zhou was referring to a possible war with the Soviets rather than to one with the Americans. During the second half of 1968, however, the border dispute did not become a national issue and no nation-wide mass campaign developed. The lack of mass media attention to this issue resembles the decline in propaganda before

[18] *RR*, September 17, 1968.
[19] *Beijing Review*, October 4, 1968, no. 40.

the Sino-Indian war and Taiwan Strait crisis in 1962.

Comparing the attitude of the mass media toward the Soviet Union in the first half of 1967 with that in the second half of 1968, the contrast is clear. Another explanation for these two contrasting attitudes is that in the first half of 1967 Mao's supporters wanted to destroy Liu's public image and to link him with the Soviet revisionists. Thus, it was necessary for them to build up their attacks against the Soviets. In contrast, in the second half of 1968, the power seizure campaign had become less intense and Liu's image had already been destroyed by the mass media's denunciations against him. Thus, in the second half of 1968, it was no longer necessary to use the media to attack the Soviets.[20]

The Denunciation Campaign against Liu Shaoqi

It was in late 1966 that criticisms of Liu Shaoqi began to appear in Red Guard "big character posters." For example, in early 1967 in a poster entitled "Heavily Bombard Liu Shaoqi," Liu was accused of seven serious crimes—opposing Chairman Mao, attacking his thought and opposing the study of Mao's Selected Works propagating doctrines of the class struggle, of anti-socialism, of attempting to return to capitalism, and destroying the "four clean-ups" movement, of attempting to infiltrate the Public Security Department, and of suppressing the Cultural Revolution.[21] Apparently the main purpose of this poster was to expose Liu's position in the Cultural Revolution and was the first sign of a new campaign against him.

In order to push this denunciation further, *Hongqi* began a review of Liu's past and present positions on controversial issues with two articles in March entitled "Patriotism or National Betrayal?" and "The Bourgeois Reactionary Line of the Question of Cadres Must Be Criticized and Repudiated."

In "Patriotism or National Betrayal?" Qi Benyu using the film "Inside Story of the Qing Court," declared that Liu, as the "top Party person in authority," had maintained a capitalist reactionary viewpoint on the film, in opposition to Mao's viewpoint.[22] Moreover, he was accused of being a "fake anti-imperialist, but a real capitulationist" during the civil war period. Liu was said to have promoted within the Party a line of national capitulation in what he called a "new stage of peace and democracy", after World War II.[23] In addition, Liu was attacked for taking a "capitalist line" in opposition to the

---

[20] See Liao Kuang-sheng, "Linkage Politics in China", *op. cit.* The author conducts an empirical test for this theory.

[21] "Heavily Bombard Liu Shaoqi," *Shoudu Hongweibing*, Peking, January 10, 1967, in Ding Wang, *Zhonggong Wenhua Dageming Ziliao Huipian*, vol. 1, pp. 250-253.

[22] "Patriotism or National Betrayal?" *Hongqi*, no. 5, March 30, 1967, pp. 9-11.

[23] *Ibid.*, pp. 13-14.

socialist transformation of capitalist industry and commerce, and for trying to liquidate the class struggle.[24] And finally, Liu was accused of opposing Marxism-Leninism and the thought of Mao Zedong by republishing his work, *On Cultivation*, in 1962.[25] In short, Qi Benyu tried to discredit Liu's position and contributions before the Cultural Revolution by exposing every possible aspect of Liu's previous activities; he concluded that Liu was a "capitalist roader" who should be thoroughly criticized and purged from the Party.

Another article published by *Hongqi* was "The Bourgeois Reactionary Line on the Question of Cadres Must Be Criticized and Repudiated." In this article, the *Hongqi* commentator accused "a handful of Party people in authority" of adopting the tactic of "killing two birds with one stone." That is, pursuing the bourgeois reactionary line which incited the masses to struggle against the cadres on the one hand, and on the other, inciting the cadres to suppress the masses.[26] Party leaders were accused of trying to prevent cadres from stepping forward to make revolution and of setting cadres and masses sharply against each other. In addition, Liu's "Cultivation" was criticized for propagating an idealist theory of self-cultivation, promoting in many ways bourgeois individualism and slavishness, and opposing Marxism-Leninism and Mao Zedong's thought. These articles were the first attacks on Liu Shaoqi by the Party magazines, but he was not mentioned by name.

The campaign which followed from the *Hongqi* criticism of "top Party leaders in authority" began on April 4 in *RR*. The publication indicated that a new stage had been initiated, and the campaign would be carried out on a national level. As shown in Table 10.1, these criticisms between April and June came mainly from Peking and Shanghai. They were directed primarily against Liu Shaoqi's work, *On Cultivation*, which was labeled a poisonous work which attempted to paralyse the "revolutionary soul" of the masses and supported Liu's political plot to restore capitalism in China.[27] In addition, some articles criticized such aspects of Liu's "theory of capitalist restoration", as the "three selfs and one guarantee", "peaceful evolution", and the "cessation of class struggle".[28] It is clear from Table 10.2 that the most active participants in the denunciation of the "top capitalist in authority" during the first half of 1967 were schools and cultural organizations in Peking, such as Peking University, the Chinese People's University, and the Peking Chinese Film Association. They played the leading role in the campaign during this period.

[24] *Ibid.*, pp. 22-23.
[25] *Ibid.*, p. 23.
[26] *Ibid.*, pp. 24-25.
[27] See *RR*, April 4, 5, 6, 7 May 14, 1967.
[28] See *RR*, April 11, 15, 16, 23, May 12, 17, 1967.

Table 10.1
PROVINCIAL PARTICIPATION IN THE MASS MEDIA
CAMPAIGN OF DENUNCIATION AGAINST
"TOP CAPITALIST IN AUTHORITY"

Province	Jan.-June (1967)	July-Dec. (1967)	Jan.-June (1968)	July-Dec. (1968)
Peking	36	65	47	73
Tientsin	2	8	4	9
Shanghai	9	37	13	17
Hebei	2	2	14	32
Shanxi	3	8	6	4
Nei Mongol	–	3	–	3
Heilongjiang	1	12	2	2
Jilin	5	2	2	–
Liaoning	2	8	13	12
Shandong	2	16	1	17
Jiangsu	5	21	7	18
Anhui	–	2	–	2
Zhejiang	1	2	–	5
Jiangxi	–	2	9	6
Fujian	–	–	–	–
Guangdong	1	5	1	9
Guangxi	–	–	–	–
Hunan	–	2	1	4
Hubei	–	5	6	3
Henan	2	3	1	14
Sichuan	–	–	1	2
Guizhou	1	3	–	1
Yunnan	–	–	–	–
Xizang	–	–	–	–
Xinjiang	–	–	–	–
Gansu	–	–	6	1
Shanxi	–	–	1	–
Qinghai	–	–	1	–
Xingxia	–	–	–	–
Total:	72	206	136	234

Note: This table does not include articles written as editorials in *RR* and *Hongqi*.
Source: *RR*, 1967-68.

Table 10.2
LEFTIST'S DENUNCIATION OF "TOP CAPITALIST IN AUTHORITY" BY
THE PEOPLE'S LIBERATION ARMY (PLA), WORKERS, PEASANTS, AND CULTURAL ORGANIZATIONS (CO) 1967-68

Province	Jan.-June 1967				July-Dec. 1967				Jan.-June 1968				July-Dec. 1968			
	PLA	Workers	Pts	CO	PLA	Workers	Pts	CO	PLA	Workers	Pts	CO	PLA	Workers	Pts	CO
Peking	1	7	2	26	11	5	7	42	17	20	6	4	16	39	15	3
Tientsin	–	2	–	–	–	3	–	5	–	4	–	–	1	8	–	–
Shanghai	–	6	1	3	2	22	3	10	1	11	1	–	2	10	3	2
Hebei	–	–	2	–	–	–	3	–	1	–	13	–	–	10	22	–
Shanxi	–	1	2	–	–	2	8	–	–	–	6	–	–	2	2	–
Nei Mongol	–	–	–	–	–	1	–	1	–	–	–	–	–	2	2	1
Heilongjiang	–	–	1	–	–	2	10	1	1	1	1	–	–	1	–	1
Jilin	5	–	–	–	2	–	–	–	–	–	–	–	1	6	3	2
Liaoning	–	1	2	–	1	2	5	4	–	–	13	–	3	2	11	1
Shandong	–	1	1	–	3	3	6	–	1	–	1	–	2	3	13	–
Jiangsu	–	–	5	–	–	–	21	4	1	1	6	–	1	1	–	–
Anhui	–	–	–	–	–	–	1	1	–	–	–	–	–	–	5	–
Zhejiang	–	–	1	–	–	–	–	2	5	–	4	–	–	2	4	–
Jiangxi	–	1	–	–	–	–	–	2	–	–	–	–	–	–	–	–
Fujian	–	–	–	–	–	–	–	–	–	–	1	–	5	–	4	–
Guangdong	1	–	–	–	4	1	1	–	1	–	–	–	–	–	–	–
Guangxi	–	–	–	–	–	–	–	2	–	–	–	–	–	2	4	–
Hunan	–	–	–	–	–	–	2	–	–	–	6	–	2	1	–	1
Hubei	–	2	2	–	2	1	3	–	1	–	1	–	1	1	13	–
Honan	–	–	–	–	–	–	1	1	1	–	–	–	–	–	1	–
Sichuan	1	–	–	–	–	–	1	–	1	–	–	–	1	1	–	–
Guizhou	–	–	–	–	–	–	–	–	1	–	–	–	–	–	–	–
Yunnan	–	–	–	–	–	–	–	–	–	–	–	–	–	1	–	–
Xizang	–	–	–	–	–	–	–	–	–	–	–	–	–	–	–	–
Xinjiang	–	–	–	–	–	–	–	–	4	2	–	1	–	1	–	–
Gansu	–	–	–	–	–	–	–	–	–	–	–	–	–	–	–	–
Shanxi	–	–	–	–	–	–	–	–	–	–	–	–	–	–	–	–
Qinghai	–	–	–	–	–	–	–	–	–	–	–	–	–	–	–	–
Ningxia	–	–	–	–	–	–	–	–	–	–	–	–	–	–	–	–
Total:	7	18	18	29	25	40	70	71	33	38	60	5	32	88	104	10

Source: *RR*, 1967-1968

In the second half of 1967, the campaign expanded to other provinces. Despite the fact that Peking's school and cultural organizations were still the major participants, in Shanghai there were 10 cultural organizations and 22 factories which joined the campaign as shown in Table 10.2, the communes in the rural areas increasingly participated in the campaign, most noticeably in Jiangsu and Heilongjiang, where 12 and 21 communes, respectively, publicly condemned Liu Shaoqi's policies on agricultural development. The military forces also were active in increasing criticism of Liu's various policies. Twenty-five articles were written by military units which were directed primarily against economic policies. Liu here for the first time was condemned as "China's Khrushchev" who was attempting to restore capitalism in China.[29] The struggle against Liu was called a struggle between the "people" and the "capitalist roaders".

Peking still played the leading role in the campaign in the first half of 1968, but Shanghai, Hebei, and Liaoning were also relatively active in comparison with the rest of the provinces and cities. As Table 10.2 shows, in Peking the workers' units wrote 20 articles and the military organizations 17, criticizing Liu. In Shanghai, most of the criticism of Liu came from workers' units. During this period, military participation in the campaign was strong. Of the 33 criticisms written by the military, 17 came from Peking, and 16 from various areas, including Jiangxi and Gansu. Criticisms from schools and cultural organizations almost disappeared during this time in contrast to the preceding period.

During the second half of 1968, the total frequency of criticism against "top Party leaders in authority" reached 234, with the most active participation coming from Peking, Hebei, Liaoning, Shandong, Jiangsu, and Henan. As shown in Table 10.2, during this period there were only 10 criticisms from schools and cultural organizations, 32 from military units, 88 from factory workers, and 104 from peasants. Among military units, there were 16 from Peking, and the rest of them came from various areas of the country. Criticisms written by workers came mainly from Peking, Shanghai, and Hebei, and criticisms by the peasants, mainly from Peking, Hebei, Shandong, Jiangsu and Henan. The content of the criticism was similar to that in the preceding period except that the number of criticisms written by workers greatly increased. This criticism was directed mainly at "multi-centrism," "management by expertise" and "profit first". The purpose of such criticism was not to create discussion, but to condemn Liu's industrial line, which was specified as "revisionist and capitalist".

In sum, the campaign of denunciation against the "top Party leaders in

[29] See *RR*, April 22, 24, August 9, 1967.

authority" was triggered by leftists in school and other cultural organizations in Peking in April 1967. This makes it clear that the take-over of the Peking Municipal Party Committee and the Propaganda Department by Mao's supporters in early 1966 was in preparation for this campaign. In the second half of 1967, the campaign of mass denunciation expanded further and by mid 1968 had become a national campaign. As a result of such an intensive attack by the mass media in 1967 and 1968, Liu's reputation and leadership suffered greatly. This aided Maoist efforts to seize power from Liu's supporters.

Power Seizure Campaign from the "Capitalists in the Party"

The control of the mass media and the mass media campaign to denounce Liu laid the foundation for Maoist power seizures by destroying the reputation and image of Liu's faction. As a result, factional struggles were taking place not only in the central government but also at the provincial level and in such sub-provincial and local institutions as schools, hospitals, factories, communes. and branch offices of the central government. The Maoists called this "the decisive battle between the proletariat and the masses of working people on the one hand and the bourgeoisie and its agents in the Party on the other."

At the central level, Mao exercised his power to purge those who were considered his opponents. The Maoist approach was first to seize power at the highest level of the power structure. An extensive purge took place at the central level in 1967. Of six men on the Standing Committee of the Party Polituro only Mao himself, Lin Biao, and Zhou Enlai remained. By the spring of 1967, of the thirteen members of the Party Politburo, seven were purged; only two of the six alternates survived. Six of the ten members of the Party Secretariat fell and four were transferred to minor positions. Of the active ninety-three full members of the Party's Central Committee, forty-eight disappeared from the political scene. Many of these missing members of the Central Committee were under serious attack by the Red Guards. In the six regional Party bureaus, five of the First Party Secretaries were criticized and disappeared. Among the fourteen Vice-Premiers of the State Council, eight were criticized and possibly purged.

Mao's Cultural Revolution did not spare the armed forces. The military staff also suffered a drastic change, with three of seven members of the powerful Military Affairs Committee being ousted. The important victims of the army purges included: three out of seven vice-ministers of National Defense; the Chief of the General Staff and four of his eight deputies; the director and two out of the five vice-directors of the powerful General Political Department. These were the important purges in the first half of 1967.

The central government and Party organizations were involved in over-all shuffles and purges in the second half of 1967 and 1968. These purges and reorganizations however, did not insure that Mao and his associates would assume leadership throughout the nation. Strong resistance remained, and many of Liu's supporters still held positions of power in both state political machinery and in local government. Thus, the Maoists had to extend these purges to all departments of the government and Party and eventually to every corner of the state structure.[30]

At the local level, the work of power-seizure relied mainly upon the masses of the Red Guards. The intention of Mao and his supporters to utilize the mass media to mobilize support was very obvious to anyone who read major newspapers such as *RR*, *Jiefangjun Bao*, *Wen Hui Bao* and *Guangmin Ribao* during that period. For example, *RR* devoted approximately two pages daily to reporting the activities of the Cultural Revolution in early 1967. Gradually, the coverage was expanded to 3 or 4 pages. By January, 1968, more than four out of six pages were used to report the development of the Cultural Revolution and the power seizure campaigns.[31]

In January 1967, there were thirty-one Red Guard Organizations actively conducting "revolutionary" activities in Shanghai. Some of them were directly sent to Shanghai from Peking by the Maoists, for example, the Liaison Station in Shanghai of the Red Flag Combat Team from the Peking Aviation Engineering College. Maoists in Shanghai, however, faced strong resistance from a great number of workers.[32] When Zhang Chunqiao led a group of Maoists in opposing the "capitalist line of economism", "the capitalists in authority" in Shanghai took strong measures to suppress them in the name of maintaining civilian order and production.[33] Under such circumstances, Zhang had serious difficulties in mobilizing any great support from the workers. On January 11, the Central Committee of the CCP, the State Council, the Military Commission of the Central Committee of the CCP, and the Cultural Revolution Group under the Central Committee of the CCP utilized the mass media to testify to their support for these Red Guards. This message was carried as the major headline in the newspapers such as *RR*, *Jiefangjun Bao*, *Guangmin Ribao* and *Wen Hui Bao*. It clearly showed the strong support given by Mao and leaders at the top level to the Red Guards in Shanghai. A few hours after the Red Guards in Shanghai had received this support, group after group of revolutionary rebels streamed into the streets from factories, schools,

[30] For detailed discussion of power struggle during this period see Stanley Karnov, *Mao and China*, New York: The Viking Press, 1972, pp. 317-37, 339-66.

[31] This approximate estimation is based on the observation of the *Renmin Ribao* throughout the whole period.

[32] See Neale Hunter, *Shanghai Journal*, New York: Praeger, 1969, pp. 223-28.

[33] *RR*, January 9, 1967.

universities and governmental organizations holding high huge portraits of Chairman Mao and red banners, singing popular songs such as "Sailing the Seas Depends on the Man at the Helm" and "To Rebel is Justified".[34] Immediately, revolutionary rebel organizations in Shanghai sent out propaganda vans to rebroadcast Mao's message of support. Groups of young Red Guards put up red letter posters and huge slogans along the main streets of Shanghai.[35] On the 12th, several hundred thousand people belonging to rebel organizations held a mass rally and launched violent plans to expel the "capitalists in authority" in Shanghai. By January 13, it was reported that Shanghai was under the control of Maoist revolutionaries.[36]

From that time major newspapers such as *RR* and *Guangmin Ribao* devoted considerable coverage to the day-to-day development of the revolutionaries' activities.[37] These papers described the power-seizure in Shanghai as a revolutionary model and asked the people in the whole country to learn from them and to join them. Mao's supporters in major cities such as Peking, Tientsin, Shenyang, Xian, Canton, Wuhan, Chengdu, Chongqing and many others rose in violent actions against their local "capitalists in authority".[38] PLA, Navy, and Air forces in Kunming, Wuhan, Canton, and Peking as well as military regions in Nei Mongol, Xinjiang, and Xizang were also reported to have responded by following the Shanghai example of smashing local "capitalists in authority".[39] The whole country became engulfed in power struggles between Red Guard radicals and their opposition. In only a few days, the power struggle spread to most parts of the nation. This nation-wide turbulence in January was labeled by Maoists as the "January Revolution". There are reasons to believe that the manipulation of the mass media to mobilize mass support for Maoist power-seizure activities against the "capitalist in authority" was quite successful in January. Maoists were able to develop a local power struggle in Shanghai into a nation-wide movement. Whether or not the Red Guards could complete the power takeover, however, was another question.

The first evidence of problems in utilizing the Red Guards appeared in late January, 1967. On January 31, *Jiefangjun Bao's* editorial urged all factions of the Red Guards to unite into an alliance by eliminating their "individual factional interests." This article was also printed on the front page by *RR* on

[34] *RR*, January 12, 1967.
[35] *RR*, January 12, 1967.
[36] *RR*, January 13, 1967.
[37] A complete collection of these two papers is available at the Universities Service Centre, Hong Kong. The collection made it possible to undertake a comprehensive examination of this contention.
[38] *RR*, January 13, 1967.
[39] *RR*, January 13, 1967.

February 3. *Hongqi* also endorsed the same attitude. In its February issue, its commentary pointed out that Mao had consistently stressed the importance of "revolutionary discipline."

> "Mao repeatedly pointed out that we must oppose extreme democracy of the petty bourgeoisie and oppose self-indulgence which destroys discipline." "We must strengthen education in discipline in the Party. Because unified discipline is the pre-requisite of the victory of revolution."

Again, *RR* reprinted the entire article immediately on February 4.

A few days later, this problem was discussed in *RR*. For example, an article entitled "Strengthen Discipline for the Revolution to Succeed," pointed out that the Red Guard movement was contaminated with non-organizational, extreme democratic, self-indulgent and subjective points of view. Some comrades, the article continued, ignored the importance of understanding revolutionary discipline and were lacking in proletarian organizational discipline.[40] Similar comments were often made in *Jiefangjun Bao* and *Hongqi*, as well as other major papers. In order to mollify the serious factional conflicts between Red Guards, cadres, and the PLA, a "triple alliance" among them was urged in February.[41] At the higher level, this "triple alliance" was effective in unifying all revolutionary forces. At the level of the masses, however, the "triple alliance" was not an effective policy during this period. Thus, the PLA was introduced to maintain civil order and restore social order.[42] Because of the widespread power struggle, production activities were disrupted in the countryside. Many peasants left their fields to take part in power-seizure activities. The leaders of many communes, production brigades, and production teams were criticized and eliminated. Therefore, Mao and his supporters faced a major problem in the serious falling off of production. This situation compelled Mao to order peasants and workers to return to their original posts and participate in production activities.[43]

Throughout the remainder of the Cultural Revolution, Mao and his associates continued to control the mass media and manipulated it to serve

[40] *RR*, February 8, 1967.

[41] *RR*, February 11, 1967.

[42] *RR*, February 18, 1967.

[43] On March 13, the editorial of the *RR* announced that during the spring cultivation period production brigades and production teams should not proceed with power-seizure activities. Further, the PLA was introduced to assist production activities. The production of industry also suffered similar problems of disruption. On March 18, the Central Committee of the Party ordered all workers and employees of factories to return to their work and to emphasize production. In addition, the Party also ordered the PLA to assist in the management of factories and to maintain social order. Workers were urged to co-operate with the PLA. In other words, the military took over the leadership of factories.

their purposes. The mass media served in many respects to mobilize support from the masses. The most obvious role played by the mass media was to continue the attack against Soviet revisionism and "U.S. aggression in Vietnam." This was very important for power-seizure campaigns and the consolidation of Mao's leadership.

Summary

Mao's strategy to defeat his opponents was to use the mass media to discredit Liu Shaoqi and to mobilize the masses to seize power from him. 'Anti-Soviet Revisionism' became a politically powerful weapon through the linking of Liu Shaoqi with Soviet Revisionism. After Mao's supporters had taken control of the Propaganda Department in early January 1967, they soon began a struggle to seize the major newspapers. In mid-January, *Wen Hui Bao* and *Jiefang Ribao* were seized by Mao's supporters. Immediately following the seizure of these two newspapers, top-level Maoists increased their hostilities against Soviet revisionism and "U.S. aggression in Vietnam". It is notable that public denunciation campaigns against the Soviet Union strengthened mass media attacks on Liu Shaoqi during 1967. During this period, the *RR* rapidly increased its accusations, linking Soviet Revisionism with Liu and his supporters. Through this approach, Mao was able to destroy Liu's public image quickly. In 1968, Maoists were heavily engaged in power-seizure from the 'capitalists in authority'. Without destroying Liu's public image, Mao and his supporters would have had much more difficulty in their power-seizure campaigns. Antiforeignism here became a powerful weapon to destroy internal political enemies.

PART IV

MODERNIZATION AND THE DECLINE OF ANTIFOREIGNISM

CHAPTER 11

The Decline of Antiforeignism and the Four Modernizations

China's foreign policy and domestic politics in the period between 1949-76 were overwhelmingly dominated by Mao's doctrine of anti-imperialism and his perception of world realities. China, however, entered a new era both in domestic development and in foreign relations following the death of Mao Zedong. This chapter explores factors which contributed to the decline of antiforeignism after 1970 and examines the relationship between the Four Modernizations and the ideology of anti-imperialism. Again, close observation of China's antiforeign sentiment will be based on mass media propaganda and antiforeign mass demonstrations during the period.

It seems that the change in Peking's foreign policy in 1972 which was marked by a drastic decline in media attacks against foreign countries and a decline in antiforeign mass demonstrations, was not associated with leadership changes alone. Instead, it was an important breakthrough caused by internal and external developments. This study suggests that external relations particularly with the United States and the PRC's admission to the United Nations, and the Four Modernizations, significantly expedited the modification of Peking's fundamental belief in anti-imperialism, the foreign policy locus of Mao Zedong.

Antiforeignism and modernization

The ideology of "anti U.S. imperialism" led to China's isolation from the West. "Anti-U.S. imperialism" was more than an opposition to the United States; it opposed all Western countries. Through a powerful propaganda machine, the mass media, pamphlets, and propaganda teams, the whole society was penetrated by antiforeignism. Students, workers, peasants, soldiers, and cadres were constantly exposed to the propaganda and could not help accepting it as to contrasting doctrine was admitted. Consequently, the propaganda of antiforeignism had at least three negative effects on China's modernization during the period 1949-1970.

First of all, culturally speaking, due to the long period of isolation, it became difficult to bring Western culture or art into Chinese society, even though Western classical works of art were respected by the authorities. For example, music written by Tchaikovsky, Beethoven, and Chopin were accepted by the authorities and introduced to Chinese artists and to the people. Shakespeare's works were translated into Chinese. Contemporary works by

Western artists or scholars, however, were completely prohibited within this closed society. According to the Chinese authorities, modern art or contemporary art in the West represented the corrupted emotions and moral decline of capitalist culture. Other than criticism of modern Western art or literature, few works were introduced.[1] The disruption of communication with Western countries inevitably led to cultural stagnation.

Secondly, antiforeignism had a tremendous impact on the internal security policy of China. Even before the Cultural Revolution, foreigners in China were distrusted by the authorities. In general, the authorities suspected them of being engaged in espionage activities. A broad definition of "espionage" was adopted by the authorities; any person who contacted foreigners or gave information to foreigners was interpreted as "*Litong waiguo*" (collaborating with foreign countries).[2] Therefore, the authorities discouraged the people from communicating with foreigners or making friends with them. Naturally, this led to a policy of isolating foreigners from Chinese society. Furthermore, a great number of Western-educated scholars, intellectuals, and people who were communicating with foreigners either in China or abroad were purged in the various anti-rightist campaigns or rectification movements. Many of them were convicted and punished as spies.

This policy of prohibiting communication with foreigners had been in force since 1949. Contact with foreigners had to be handled or approved by the Public Security and Foreign Affairs sections of the government. Two major effects resulted from this policy. The first was complete isolation of the Chinese from outisde. It created a distance between the Chinese people and the rest of the world and left China unaffected by the outside world. Second, it created an attitude of mistrust among the people toward any foreign country as well as toward any foreigner. Some people even became actively hostile toward foreigners during periods of political campaigns.

Thirdly, the effect of antiforeignism on economic development was also very serious. Even before the Cultural Revolution, the Chinese authorities promoted the policy of "self-reliance" in economic development. There is no disputing that this policy could have been a good policy if China had had a sufficient foundation to develop her own technology and industries. Serious consequences ensued, however, because the policy involved complete rejection of Western advanced technology during the Cultural Revolution, as a result of the ideology of "anti-imperialism" and the sentiment of antiforeignism. Due to the interruption of communications with foreign countries, Chinese scientists and engineers could not obtain new materials and information from

[1] Data obtained through interview with Chinese immigrants in Hong Kong.
[2] *Ibid.*

the West. The "closed door" policy prevented the Chinese scientists from learning about advanced Western scientific technology as well as new management methods. Along with discouraging the purchase of Western industrial products and the shortage of capital, the policy of radical "self-reliance" became suicidal for economic development. Blind criticisms were levelled against Western economic and scientific technology without discrimination. This created a bias which discouraged Chinese scientists and intellectuals from even trying to learn about Western developments.

The Gang of Four and Modernization

In the early 1970s, antiforeignism became an ideological obstacle to a modernization policy emphasizing the adoption of Western advanced technology and the purchase of foreign equipment by China. As discussed earlier, leftism and antiforeignism stimulated each other and in so doing, formed a spiral process which led to endless political movements. After the Cultural Revolution, the leftists' ideology of antiforeignism continued. They formed a political group under the leadership of the now denounced "Gang of Four" at the central level of the government and the Party. In the wake of the Cultural Revolution, the slow down in economic progress forced pragmatic leaders to once again look outside China's boundaries for solutions to development problems. The leftists, however, opposed a modernization policy which might lead to a reconciliation with the West. Leftism and antiforeignism closely intertwined with each other in opposing a pragmatic economic policy proposed by Premier Zhou Enlai. As it had been utilized in the 1950s as a political weapon to launch a series of campaigns against "rightists" having relations with any Western country, so in the early 1970s antiforeignism was employed to oppose the modernization policy which emphasized the importation of Western technology and equipment.[3]

In March 1970, an article in *Hongqi* entitled "Down with the Slavish Compradore philosophy" said:

> ... "Seeking the help of others" is virtually a question of what people to be relied upon and a question of whether to rely on the bourgeoisie or on the proletariat. If you want the "foreign, big and complete" in everything and want to "do everything without seeking the help of others," then you will have no alternative but to beg for help from the bourgeoisie and become slaves to the foreigners. We rely on the Chinese proletariat armed with Mao Zedong thought and on ourselves for

[3] "Wei Ge Ming Mei you Ke Fu Bu Liao De Kun Nan", (No Difficulty Insurmountable for the Revolution) *Hongqi*, No. 1, January 1970, translated in *Selections from China Mainland Magazines* (SCMM), No. 671.

promoting socialist cooperation and launching vigorous and down-to-earch mass
movements.[4]

This article attacked not only those who were interested in purchasing foreign
equipment, but also those who had been interested in the development of
technology in the West. The article continued:

> ... Another manifestation of the slavish compradore philosophy is the implicit
> faith put in foreign data. In the eyes of some people, all data on foreign industrial
> technology are called "documents," and "documents" are "bases." When they
> find no such "bases" they dare not move a half step forward. When they find such
> "bases" they regard every word as the law, literally copy and transplant them;
> they refrain from making any alteration even if they have long been disproved.[5]

Again, antiforeignism became a powerful weapon of the leftists. During
1971-74, they launched various political campaigns to criticize "the capitalist
policy" supported by Zhou and his associates. As a result, national economic
production declined in 1974.[6] Again, the introduction of Western advanced
technology was challenged by the leftists.

The "Gang of Four", as the major representatives of leftists who opposed
the modernization policy, controlled the mass media and propaganda machine
of the Party and publicized their attacks against the modernization policy.
Leftist opposition to the policy of receiving Western technology and equipment was clearly seen in its attack against Deng Xiaoping in early 1976, after
the death of Zhou Enlai. For example, in April the leftists condemned the
policy of learning Western technology and purchasing foreign equipment as
"the slavish compradore philosophy" and the "the doctrine of crawling behind
at a snail's pace." The policy was considered to represent the revisionist line
opposing socialism.[7] A great number of articles was published for the purpose
of opposing Deng Xiaoping's policy and its underlying ideology. The leftist
voice became very strong in mid-1976. In July, an article in *Hongqi* entitled
"Comment on Deng Xiaoping's Compradore-Bourgeois Economic Thinking"
pointed out:

> The historical experience of the past century tells us that it is nothing but an
> illusion to attempt to rely on technology and loans supplied by imperialism to
> develop the economy and make China rich and strong. The group of people who
> learned from the West toward the end of the Qing dynasty advocated that "loans

---

[4] "Da Dao Yang Nu Zhe Xue," (Down with the Slavish Compradore Philosophy)
Hongqi, No. 4, April 1970, translated in *SCMM*, No. 679.

[5] *Ibid.*

[6] Xue Muqiao, "Jian Ku Chuang Ye San Shi Nian," (Thirty Years of Hardship in
Building Our Country) *Hongqi*, No. 10, October 1979.

[7] "Pi Ping Yang Nu Zhe Xue," (Criticize the Slavish Compradore Philosophy) *Hongqi*,
No. 4, April 1976, translated in *SCMM*, No. 867.

may be borrowed to develop what is beneficial" for the country. They believed that only by borrowing large loans from imperialist countries, by mortgaging our natural resources and developing industry by "imitating" foreign technology was it possible to enable China to "strengthen itself" and "begin to stand on its own feet." But the facts were the opposite. What they did entirely suited the needs of imperialism in dumping their goods in and exporting their capital to China and partitioning it. The Westernizing movement was no way to enable China to "strengthen itself"; on the contrary, it caused China and its people to become more and more impoverished. Instead of "beginning to stand on its own feet," China saw its national crisis deepened with each passing day.[8]

The leftists were here utilizing Mao's theory of imperialism as an ideological weapon to criticize the policy of adopting Western technology and purchasing foreign equipment. They condemned this policy as a "restoration of capitalism" which was opposing the socialist revolution and was "inheriting the mantle of the compradore bourgeoisie and national betrayal." These ideological struggles did not end until the "Gang of Four" was arrested in October 1976, about one month after the death of Mao Zedong.

Societal Changes After the Cultural Revolution

By 1971, about two years after the Cultural Revolution, there were signs indicating the decline of antiforeignism in China. In spite of the fact that political control remained tight and anti-imperialism, and especially "anti-U.S. Imperialism", still prevailed in the Party line, social support for strong antiforeignism was fading as a result of the social chaos and political turmoil of the Cultural Revolution. At that time, there were serious disruptions in the political processes. For example, the Party organizations were destroyed by the "revolutionary leftists" and a great number of old cadres who had been important leaders were purged and disgraced in public. The absolute leadership and authority of the Party and its ideology were brought into question. Great heroes in the liberation war such as Peng Dehuai, Zhu De, Chen Yi, Luo Ruiqing and others had been severely criticized and insulted. Liu Shaoqi, the Chairman of the State, was arrested without due process. All of these incidents raised the disquieting observation that the distinctions between right and wrong, leftists or rightists, revolutionaries or counter-revolutionaries were very vague and confusing. Consequently, after the Cultural Revolution most of the people became apathetic to politics and skeptical about ideology and the Party leadership. They were no longer enthusiastic about taking part in political campaigns.[9] It is exactly this sort of mentality which discourages

---

[8] "Ping Deng Xiaoping De Mai Ban Zi Chan Jie Ji Jing Ji Si Xiang," (Comment on Xiaoping's Compradore-Bourgeois Economic Thinking) *Hongqi*, No. 7, July 1, 1976.

[9] This is based on my interview with several youths who came from China around 1977-78. Hereafter cited "data from interview".

people from being active in both domestic politics and antiforeign activities.

Another development was the interest in seeking experience and knowledge from the advanced countries of the West. Particularly surprising was the increasing contact with the West. The desire to learn from the West was unusually strong as China had isolated itself from the world for more than two decades by 1970. The long period of isolation stimulated interest in exploring the developments of the West. In fact, the state of society and the experiences created by leftism and antiforeignism, had, meanwhile, brought about curiosity and interest in contact with the West and a strongly felt need to solve China's problems.

As mentioned above, the Chinese had earlier envisioned Western society as corrupt, chaotic, inhuman, and exploitative. After the long period of isolation and the tight control of communication between China and foreign countries, most of the people had no way of changing this image although some intellectuals questioned the image of the West as portrayed by the mass media. Therefore, this image was very firmly entrenched and became almost unquestioned during the first two decades after the Communist takeover of the mainland. One of the most important challenges to this image was a film taken by the Chinese Table Tennis Team during their visits to the United States, Canada and Mexico in 1972. The film showed that the peoples in these countries were very friendly to the Chinese. Furthermore, it showed streets, buildings, factories and the living conditions of workers, indicating prosperity in these countries. The film was widely shown in China and opened the eyes of the Chinese not to decadence, but to the fact that the West was much more technologically advanced than China. Following this film, there was an increasing number of reports on agricultural and industrial development in some European countries reflecting the opinion that the West was neither as corrupt nor as chaotic as the Chinese people had been led to believe.[10] Later on, a great number of Japanese products were imported into China. Japanese cars, trucks, instruments, tape recorders, radios, watches, clothes, etc., filled the Chinese markets. All of these further proved that China was more backward than Japan and Western countries. Irresistably, a strong wish to emulate the West in its consumer products and living environment emerged and soon prevailed throughout the whole society.

Some changes in policy also reflect the decline of antiforeignism in Chinese society. The most remarkable example is the policy toward Western art. As in the period before 1967, Western classical music and songs were again available. Old dramas and Western ballet once more became popular.[11] Negative attitudes

[10]Data from interview.
[11]Data from interview.

toward Western thought and culture shifted to uncertainty. Social sciences were once again in the university syllabus and open, frank discussion was allowed on art and culture. Past prohibitions were loosened. These societal changes and attitudinal changes did not happen without cause. The fundamental reason for these developments was the desire for immediate, not postponed, improvements in the people's livelihood. The more China became aware of her backwardness, the more attractive Westernization became and leftism, with its antiforeign bent, lost appeal.

The Decline of Antiforeignism 1971-80

In contrast to Peking's sharp anti-U.S. tone during 1949-70, a relatively low key and even accommodating attitude toward the American role in Indochina has marked China's international behavior since 1971. It was first seen in the period of negotiations during the Paris peace talks in 1970 and early 1971. With few exceptions, the PRC statements were infrequent and merely made perfunctory condemnations of U.S. policies. Peking's new attitude was further confirmed by her response to the U.S. mining and blockade of North Vietnamese harbors in May 1972 and during the intense Christmas bombing of Hanoi and Haiphong in 1972.[12] Few verbal condemnations of "U.S. aggressive acts" and fewer mass demonstrations have been seen since then.

Close observation of Peking's antiforeign mass demonstrations will help us understand the drastic change in Peking's attitude toward the United States (see Table 11.1). First of all, in 1971, the number of mass demonstrations against the U.S. was 27, and among them 11 concerned Vietnam, nine were directed against "U.S. aggressive acts" in Laos and Cambodia, seven were for the Korean issue and one for the Taiwan issue. This was clearly a departure from Peking's past practice. This compares with 260 antiforeign mass demonstrations in 1970. Among these 249 were protesting against "U.S. aggressive acts" in Vietnam and 11 were related to Korea (see Table 11.2). This indicated that Peking had not only changed its attitude towards the "U.S. in Vietnam" but also its international behavior as a whole.

In 1972, the total number of antiforeign mass demonstrations decreased to 20, and among them 18 were directed against the U.S. Only two of these 18, however, were specifically against "U.S. aggressive acts" in Vietnam. In 1973 the total number was further reduced to 13, among which were ten directed against the United States. The antiforeign mass demonstrations diminished to ten in 1974, six in 1975, four in 1977, none in 1978, and one in January

[12]Kenneth P. Landon, "The Impact of the Sino-American Detente on the Indochina Conflict" in Gene T. Hsiao (ed.), *Sino-American Detente and Its Policy Implications*, New York: Praeger, 1974, pp. 210-213.

Table 11.1

THE DECLINE IN ANTIFOREIGN DEMONSTRATIONS, 1967-80

Year	Target			Total
	U.S.	S.U.	Others (including India)	
1967	9	54	78	141
1968	144	0	10	154
1969	0	337**	25	362
1970	260	0	0	260
1971	27	0	0	27
1972	16	2	0	18
1973	10	1	2	13
1974	5	3	2	10
1975	6	0	0	6
1976	3	1	1	5
1977	1	3	0	4
1978	0	0	0	0
1979	0	1	0	1
1980	0	0	0	0

**These demonstrations were mainly directed against the Soviet Union with reference to the border conflict. Many of them, however, also attacked "U.S. imperialism" and its collaboration with "Soviet imperialism."
Sources: *RR*, 1967-80.

Table 11.2

ANTIFOREIGN DEMONSTRATIONS AGAINST THE U.S.,
MAY-JUNE 1970

Date	Issues	
	Vietnam	Korea
May 21	4	0
May 22	24	0
May 23	3	0
May 24	93	0
May 25	62	0
May 26	61	0
June 25	1	11
Total	249	11

Source: *RR*, May-June 1970.

1979 denouncing Vietnamese aggression, supported by the Soviet Union, in its attacks on Democratic Cambodia.[13] Peking has not organized any anti-foreign mass demonstrations to protest against Vietnamese suppression of and discrimination against ethnic Chinese, and its numerous intrusions into Chinese territory, despite the fact that serious tension exists between Peking and Hanoi.

The declining frequency of antiforeign mass demonstrations is one of the indicators by which we can see the decline of Peking's antiforeignism. Another indicator is the size of these antiforeign mass demonstrations. There were a great number of these demonstrations with a minimum of a hundred thousand participants during the period between 1949 and 1970. Demonstrations opposing U.S. aggression in Korea from 1950 to 1952 frequently involved over one million,[14] while most of the mass demonstrations protesting against "U.S. aggression in Vietnam" between 1967 and 1970 still involved over one hundred thousand (see Table 11.3). In the period following 1971, however, none of the antiforeign mass demonstrations had over a 100,000 participants. A clear distinction between the antiforeign campaigns of 1970 and 1971 is to be seen when we compare Tables 11.3 and 11.4.

The United States and the United Nations

The decline in Peking's antiforeignism can be seen in 1971 as can its further steady decline until 1979, as discussed above. After the Cultural Revolution, signs of conciliation and negotiation were visible and diplomatic relations with foreign countries greatly expanded between 1969 and 1971. Peking's foreign policy appeared to be more pragmatic and conciliatory in 1971.[15] All agree that Peking's policy toward the United States was also modified after the 1968 Soviet invasion of Czechoslovakia and the 1969 Sino-Soviet border dispute. The decline of antiforeignism, however, can by no means be accounted for by any single factor. Instead, a combination of external and internal developments expedited Peking's relinquishment of antiforeignism mass demonstrations.

A number of external developments since 1971 helped Peking downgrade the importance of external threats, although its verbal attacks were first seen

[13] See RR, January 19, 1979.
[14] See Peter Cheng, A Chronology of the People's Republic of China, A Littlefield, Adams, New Jersey, 1972, p. 12. Over 186 million people throughout China were said to have participated in demonstrations in support of Resist-America Aid-Korea Campaign on May 1, 1951.
[15] Byron Weng, Peking's UN Policy: Continuity and Change, New York: Praeger Publishers, 1972, pp. 172-174.

Table 11.3
ANTIFOREIGN DEMONSTRATIONS AGAINST THE U.S.,
MAY 21-22, 1970

Target	Date	Number	Localities	Approximate No. of Participants
To support the Vietnamese people fighting against "U.S. imperialism"	May 21	3	Peking	100,000
			Shanghai	500,000
			Tientsin	400,000
	May 22	24	Shenyang	200,000
			Canton	400,000
			Wuhan	400,000
			Xian	400,000
			Nanjing	200,000
			Kunming	200,000
			Fuzhou	120,000
			Nanning	150,000
			Hangzhou	200,000
			Harbin	200,000
			Changzhun	100,000
			Yinchuan	50,000
			Lanzhou	200,000
			Lhasa	50,000
			Urumqi	200,000
			Nanchang	150,000
			Jinan	300,000
			Shijiazhuang	100,000
			Taiyuan	300,000
			Hefei	130,000
			Zhengzhou	250,000
			Changsha	300,000
			Xining	100,000
			Guiyang	200,000

Source: *RR*, May 1970

Table 11.4

ANTIFOREIGN DEMONSTRATIONS AGAINST THE U.S., 1971

Target	Date	Localities	Approximate No. of Participants
To support Vietnam	January 1	Kunming	100,000
against U.S. aggression	January 2	Kunming	6,000
on the 10th Anniversary	January 8	Nanning	100,000
of the Vietnamese	January 9	Nanning	6,000
National Liberation	January 11	Nanning	3,000
Front			
To support Vietnam against U.S. aggression	March 19	Peking	3,000
To support Vietnam against U.S. aggression on the welcoming of representatives of the Vietnamese Democratic Party	November 23	Peking	10,000
To praise Vietnam for her tradition of anti-imperialism	December 17	Nanjing	(PLA)

Source: *RR*, 1971

to have decreased in 1970. Among these external developments the most important was the change of U.S. foreign policy especially its decisions on military withdrawal from Indochina, on reviewing its Asian commitments, and on opening up contacts with the PRC. Detente with the U.S. was begun in the Shanghai Communique of February 28, 1972. The improvement of relations with Washington was crucial to Peking's new global strategy. It clearly allowed the PRC to downgrade any perception of a threat on her Eastern and Southern frontiers and coastal areas from the old perception of a possible attack by "the U.S. imperialist and Chiang Kai-shek's Nationalist forces." Furthermore, improved relations altered the psychological dimension of "anti-U.S. imperialism" which had been cultivated since 1949.[16] As discussed above, most antiforeign mass demonstrations before 1971 were directed against "U.S. imperialism," with emphasis on two images, i.e., "the image of the enemy"

[16] Jerome Alan Cohen, "China and the United States: When will the 'Normalization' of Relations be completed?" in Francis O. Wilcox (ed.) *China and the Great Powers*, New York: Praeger Publishers, 1974.

and "the image of anti-China." With the downgrading of the U.S. threat, these two images gradually lost their psychological power. The perceived external threat shifted further from "U.S. imperialism" and more toward "Soviet revisionist imperialism" after the Shanghai Communique. The impact of the change on American foreign policy towards China and Asia has been very great and cannot be over-emphasized. Peking, however, has also restrained itself since 1971 from publicizing through antiforeign mass demonstrations the threat posed by the Soviet Union.

The second important development was Peking's admission to the United Nations. In retrospect, the United Nations has been of great value to the PRC in expanding its diplomatic relations. Since Peking's entry into the United Nations, the Chinese government has worked both within and outside the United Nations to isolate Taipei diplomatically. All Nationalist vestiges have been eliminated from the organization. Peking scored major political breakthroughs in the three years after its admission, especially in Asia. By the fall of 1975, over 100 governments had either recognized or restored relations with the PRC. Formal ties had been established with Japan. Malaysia, the Philippines and Thailand.[17] Although, Peking and Washington did not normalize their relations until early 1979, most American allies in Asia, except South Korea, Singapore and Indonesia, have severed their diplomatic relations with Taiwan and established links with Peking.

Furthermore, the United Nations has provided Peking with a channel to express its opinions upon various issues. In the period from 1949-70, Peking, to some extent, used antiforeign mass campaigns to express its opinions and articulate its position on important international conflicts. Indochinese issues were the most frequent cause for antiforeign demonstrations between 1949-70. After its entry in 1971, Peking made good use of the General Assembly and the Security Council to lodge protests over issues concerning Vietnam. The importance of the United Nations as a channel became even clearer in 1979 and 1980. For example, Peking's hostility towards colonialism, its support of the Pol Pot government of Cambodia, protests against Vietnamese aggression in Cambodia and intrusion into Chinese territories in early 1979, and the attacks against the Soviet Union's growing influence in Southeast Asia since 1976 were all expressed in the United Nations.[18] This illustrates how Peking has made full use of the United Nations to lodge its protests instead of using antiforeign mass demonstrations, the latter having

[17] *Xue Shishi* (Learning Current Issues), Hong Kong: *Wen Hui Bao*, no. 20, 1975, pp. 19-21.
[18] See Samuel S. Kim, *China, The United Nations, and World Order*, Princeton: Princeton University Press, 1979, pp. 97-177.

been the primary means for protest prior to 1971.[19] Thus, since China's entry into the United Nations, verbal attacks and antiforeign mass demonstrations have become less important in expressing opinion and lodging protests.

The Four Modernizations and Change in Peking's Ideology

Internal factors causing change in China's international behavior are no less important than the change of American foreign policy and China's admission into the United Nations. There is much evidence that the pragmatic faction among Chinese leaders, under the leadership of the late Premier Zhou Enlai, has steadily gained control of power in the State Council and followed a moderate policy toward the United States in foreign relations and a pragmatic economic policy for internal development since 1971. The Chinese leaders reduced their hostility toward the United States immediately after Nixon's visit in February 1972, despite the fact that there were many problems remaining between the two countries. In addition, the new economic policy which stressed modernization through Westernization, as proposed by Zhou Enlai in 1975, further strengthened. Peking's moderate policy toward the United States and other Western countries.

If the change in American foreign policy and Peking's entry into the United Nations reduced the Chinese perception of threat from "U.S. imperialism" and provided an appropriate channel for China to speak to the world, then the policy of the "Four Modernizations" has undoubtedly forced Peking to phase out the ideology of "anti-imperialism," the underlying concept of anti-foreignism. The Four Modernizations are a package of programs to modernize China through Westernization. The purpose of modernizing agriculture, industry, national defense and science and technology is to bring about an all round, fundamental technical transformation of the entire field of material production in China and to equip the various departments of the national economy and national defense with the world's most advanced scientific and technical know-how.[20] Since the founding of the Peking government, the thought of Mao Zedong and orthodox Marxism-Leninism have played a dominating role in Peking's ideology. Class struggle, self-reliance, and mass mobilization, however, are no longer the means used to advance China's economy. The increasing emphasis on the Four Modernizations undeniably indicates that Peking's ideology has undergone a drastic change.

[19]"United Nations and Anti-hegemonism" in *Xue Shishi*, no. 19, 1975, pp. 20-21. Also see William R. Feeney, "The Participation of the PRC in the United Nations," in Gene T. Hsiao, *op. cit.*, pp. 104-122.

[20]Xue Yongying, "The Four Modernizations: A Deep-going Revolution," *Beijing Review*, September 1978.

Since technology and scientific knowledge are essential to the Four Modernizations, many changes in Peking's policy have emerged. Firstly, an important development has been the policy of liberalization of control over culture and education by the Party. For many years, the Peking government downgraded education, particularly higher education. The training of specialists or "experts" was believed to benefit a small minority who tended to be elitist and could potentially form a privileged class. Thus, higher education was widely discouraged in China before 1977; this was particularly true during the Cultural Revolution period. As the intellectuals were not considered to be part of the productive labor force, many of them had been severely criticised or even purged. Deng Xiaoping publicly denounced the old policy toward intellectuals and cultural workers in the Education Conference of April, 1978.[21] He called for the upgrading of education and said that an education policy should be incorporated into economic development. Higher education is now seen as a necessary element in the development of technology and scientific knowledge, and the key to the carrying out of the Four Modernizations. Leading cadres are being urged to show a democratic style in their work, to listen honestly to the opinions of scientists and technicians, to actively back their rational proposals and to encourage them to be bold in analysing problems and solving them.[22] Accordingly, these "experts" who were formerly criticized and purged are now being rehabilitated.

Secondly, there is increasing discussion on liberation of thought. With a wider scope now possible for ideas, thinking can be liberated, permitting a wider range of approaches to problem solving. Thus, the liberation of thought is aimed at giving people more choices, thereby promoting an enthusiastic attitude towards working for the Four Modernizations.[23] In short, the carrying out of the new economic program requires liberation from a sort of superstition which regards the leaders as gods, and from reliance on emotional mass campaigns as opposed to rational solutions to concrete problems. The liberation of thought means that China can accept foreign ideas and thoughts if they are helpful to modernization. It allows the people to have contact with things outside China so as to enrich their thinking. The liberation of thought also allows the people to exchange ideas and thoughts as well as technology and education with the intellectuals of foreign countries. There

[21] Deng Xiaoping, "Zai Quan Guo Jiao Yu Gong Zuo Hui Yi Shang De Jiang Hua," (Talk at the Conference on National Education) *Hongqi*, no. 5, 1978.

[22] Special commentator of *RR*, "On Policy Towards Intellectuals," *Beijing Reivew*, no. 5, February 2, 1979.

[23] Guo Luoji, "Thought To Be Liberated, Theory To Be Completely Clear," *Hongqi*, no. 3, March 1, 1979. Also see "Liberation of Thought To Speed Up the Four Modernizations," *RR*, October 23, 1978.

are limits, however, to how far thoughts can be liberated. Dissident voices of the Democracy movement of the late 1970s obviously exceeded the limit. Any criticism of the leaders and the country must still be done within the bounds of democratic centralism, even in the eyes of pragmatic leaders.[24] This policy is manifested by the increased number of journals and magazines in the arts, social sciences, management, as well as in science and technology, which have appeared.

Although it may be too early to try to foretell the future of this development, there is much evidence to indicate that policies have been adopted by the Party aimed at loosening the previous tight control of ideas, thought, and ideology.

Thirdly, the acceptance of foreign technology and foreign investment have also become necessary. Since the goal is to bring about fundamental technical transformation of the entire field of material production in China, technology has become extremely important for carrying out the Four Modernizations. Because China does not have sufficient technology itself, the import of technology from other countries is required. However, the importation of foreign technology needs funding. The Chinese government has been compelled to attract foreign investment in the development of its industries, thus, opening herself to the West. In addition to increasing foreign trade, China has been developing tourism and welcoming foreign investment in the building of hotels.[25] A later development to attract foreign investments is the creation of the "special economic zones".

Previously, Mao Zedong's hatred of the capitalist countries, which were seen as exploiting the people through imperialism, was the basis for condemning foreign investment in China. He was afraid that the economy of China would fall into the hands of foreigners as it had in the colonial days. These ideas have recently been modified. For example, foreign investment is no longer synonymous with complete control by foreigners in the factories. The factories or the hotels built with foreign investment, after a period of time, will automatically be transferred to the control of the Chinese authorities. It is hoped that the foreigners will bring in advanced technology, management skills, and money to stimulate the Chinese economy.

The Four Modernizations are a historical step in Chinese Communist history. The aim of the Four Modernizations is the same as that of the previous Westernizing period but the program is different in approach and method. This tremendous task has given China a new face. Mao had a belief

---

[24]Wang Furu, "Si Ge Xian Dai Hua He She Hui Zhu Yi Min Zhu," (The Four Modernizations and Socialist Democracy) *Hongqi*, no. 34, April 1979.

[25]Susumu Awanhara, "Leaning on a New-found Friend," *Far Eastern Economic Review*, December 1, 1978.

that class struggle was necessary even during the socialist stage. The pre-requisite to carrying out the Four Modernizations, however, is a stable and unified society. Thus, Deng Xiaoping urges the unification of the whole country and not class struggle. While the goals of the current modernization drive are the same as those of the past, i.e. to build a strong socialist nation based on a modern industrial and advanced agricultural technology, the policies to implement these goals are drastically different. In fact, the differences are not merely restricted to the liberation of thought, an emphasis on education, and the acceptance of foreign technology and invest-ment, but also extend to changes in the fundamental faith of the people.

The Modernization of National Defense and Anti-Soviet Imperialism

Generally speaking, the Four Modernizations, like the modernization program in the late Qing and early twentieth century, have a dual emphasis on internal wealth and external power. In contrast to the notions of People's War, the new policy stresses updating national defense and related military technology. The program has strong implications for fighting against aggression by imperialism, particularly Soviet imperialism, as well as for economic develop-ment and industrialization. It urges modernization of national defense in order to deter any possible aggression by external enemies in contrast with the method of opposing imperialism in the previous period which relied heavily on the mass line, mass movements, and millions of students, workers, peasants, and soldiers mobilized to participate in anti-imperialistic rallies. After the Fifth National People's Congress, the *RR* and *Hongqi* in an joint editorial said:

> We must help the people understand that carrying out the four socialist moderni-zations is not only a tremendous task in the economic field, but primarily one of extreme urgency in the political field. It involves the question of whether our economy and national defense are strong enough to deal with possible aggression by social imperialism and imperialism.[26]

Consistent with the objectives of China's leaders over the past century and a half, the political objective of the Four Modernizations remains to build a strong China able to deter both internal and external enemies. This was unequivocally pointed out by the *Beijing Review* in May 1978, in an article entitled "China Enters A New Period". It states:

> Without the four modernizations, building a powerful socialist country is out of the question. Internally speaking, a powerful socialist country is one that cannot be subverted or toppled by any class enemy. Externally speaking, it is one that cannot be destroyed by any enemy who dare invade, whether they impose a

---

[26] Editorial, *Hongqi*, March 6, 1978.

nuclear war or a conventional war on us; instead they will be vanquished by us externally. Only when we make China a powerful socialist country and build up an increasingly abundant material basis for our dictatorship of the proletariat can we smoothly continue our march towards the bright future of communism.[27]

The new stress on advanced military technology requires an industrial sector equal to advanced world levels. This is then to be put into the service of national defense. A *Beijing Review* article entitled "Speed Up the Modernization of National Defense" says:

> To build up a modern national defense, we should correctly handle the relations between defense construction and economic construction. A strong national defense must have a strong economy as its base. Only with the faster growth of economic construction can there be great progress in defense construction. If agriculture, industry and science and technology do not make progress, how can national defense be modernized? ... Producing more grain, iron and steel, petroleum and other industrial and agricultural products and developing science and technology means contributing to building our national defense.[28]

Therefore, it becomes clear that the current modernizations are also committed to national defense. Modernization of agriculture, industry, and science and technology are important not only for the national economy but also for China's military capability. As long as Peking perceives the presence of a strong military threat along its border with the Soviet Union, the strengthening of China's military capability is vital to China. In spite of the decline of China's antiforeignism, the policy of opposing Soviet imperialism remains. Therefore, the decline of antiforeignism does not necessarily mean a change of anti-Soviet policy. Thus, the goal of anti-imperialism is preserved in Peking's current policy. Anti-imperialism, while retained as a goal for national equality and independence basic to all countries, is no longer tinged with strong mass sentiment. This is similar to the forms of anti-imperialism in the Kuomintang era.

The Four Modernizations and the Ideology of Anti-imperialism

In February 1974, Chairman Mao said, "In my view, the United States and the Soviet Union form the first world. Japan, Europe and Canada, the middle section, belong to the second world. We are the third world. With the exception of Japan, Asia belongs to the third world. The whole of Africa belongs to the third world, and Latin America too."[29] Both the Soviet Union and the United

---

[27] "China Enters A New Period," *Beijing Review*, no. 20, May 19, 1978.

[28] "Speed Up the Modernization of National Defense," *Beijing Review*, no. 32, August 5, 1977.

[29] *Chairman Mao's Theory of the Differentiation of the Three Worlds Is A Major Contribution to Marxism-Leninism*, Peking: Foreign Language Press, 1977, p. 33.

States are regarded as imperialist superpowers, the biggest international exploiters and oppressors, the largest forces for war and aggression and the common enemies of the people of the world. In Peking's analysis the Soviet Union is "the more ferocious, the more reckless, the more treacherous, and the most dangerous source of world war." In February 1976 Mao pointed out: "The United States wants to protect its interests in the world and the Soviet Union wants to expand; this can in no way be changed."[30] Meanwhile, Peking continues to believe that "U.S. imperialism" has not changed its policies of aggression and hegemonism, nor has it lessened its exploitation and oppression of the people at home and abroad. Therefore, the two hegemonist powers, the Soviet Union and the United States, will inevitably come into conflict and war.[31] The third world is composed of the non-industrialized countries of Asia, Africa, and Latin America—those countries are the main victims of the superpowers aggression and exploitation. Peking proclaimed that the countries and the people of the third world are the main force combatting imperialism and hegemonism, and that the second world can be united with it in the struggle against hegemonism.[32]

The Three Worlds Theory represents an international united front policy which allows China to unite with all those who are opposed to the main threat to world peace. In practice, this theory redefines anti-imperialism and translates it into a policy which has reduced China's support for national liberation movements which struggle against imperialism and increased her support for the governments of third world countries. It allows for greater cooperation with the second world nations of Europe and, to a certain extent, even with one superpower against the other. In the 1950s and 1960s, the ideology of anti-imperialism was used to mobilize the masses to take part in socialist construction. To support one was to support the other. Under the redefined concept of anti-imperialism, this is no longer the case.

First, the ideology of anti-imperialism in China was originally tinged strongly with antiforeignism. Since the beginning of the twentieth century, anti-foreignism, stimulated by the rise of nationalism, was directed against foreign control of the Chinese economy by Western powers. The sentiment of antiforeignism developed into the strong political force of anti-imperialism

[30]*Ibid.*, p. 35.

[31]*Ibid.*, p. 36.

[32]For example, the commentator of the *RR*, August 4, 1978 said: "The numerous non-aligned countries constitute an important part of the third world. . . . The Chinese people resolutely support the policy of independence, peace and non-alignment pursued by the non-aligned nations and their just struggle against imperialism, colonialism, hegemonism and all forms of foreign domination." Translated version see "Conference of Foreign Minister of Non-Aligned Countries," *Beijing Review*, no. 32, August 11, 1978.

used by both the KMT and the Chinese Communists. In the 1950s, the Peking government pursued a strong anti-Western foreign policy and followed a "leaning on one side" foreign policy. An anti-Western sentiment strongly prevailed among the people, constituting an emotional base for anti-imperialism in Chinese Communist ideology.

Modernization in China means, to a large extent, westernization and industrialization because both modernizations in industry and in science and technology require tremendous efforts to learn from Western countries. As Deng Xiaoping pointed out at the opening ceremony of the National Science Conference in March 1978:

> Science and technology are a kind of wealth created in common by all mankind. Any nation or country must learn from the strong points of other nations and countries, from their advanced science and technology. It is not just today, when we are scientifically and technically backward, that we need to learn from other countries; after we catch up with the advanced world levels in science and technology, we will still have to learn from the strong points of others.[33]

At the National Finance and Trade Conference, Hua Guofeng also called for study of advanced experience abroad. He said:

> For years the "gang of four", waving the banner of "revolution" and brandishing big sticks, forbade people to learn from the advanced experience of other countries, and many of our comrades are scarcely aware of what has been going on abroad. Some comrades tend to take a dangerous attitude of conceit and complacency, conservatism and parochial arrogance when they make even the slightest progress. If this attitude is not decisively changed, we shall lack the will and the vision to forge ahead vigorously and shall be incapable of careful study of advanced experience either at home or abroad, let alone of catching up with the advanced level of other countries.[34]

In order to push forward with the Four Modernizations, it has become necessary for the Peking government to lower or eliminate anti-Western sentiment, particularly against the United States. In other words, ideologically speaking, the Four Modernizations are bound to be pursued at the expense of the sentiment and ideology of anti-imperialism. It does not seem possible to carry on modernization by Westernization while promoting the ideology of anti-imperialism inside the country.

Secondly, activities of anti-imperialism were considered as part of the class struggle in socialist construction. This was very clear in the 1963 Three Revolutionary Movements. As stated above, class struggle was in command of

---

[33] Deng Xiaoping, "Opening Ceremony of the National Science Conference," *Beijing Review*, no. 12, March 24, 1978.

[34] Chairman Hua Guofeng's speech at the National Finance and Trade Conference, *op. cit.*

the Movements, providing workers and peasants with the driving force to attack internal class enemies.

The Four Modernizations are called "a great revolution in the socialist productive forces." They require the unity of all the people. Class struggle has been greatly deemphasized. It applies to the enemies who oppose the Four Modernizations, e.g. the "gang of four", not to the people. Political activities are no longer so important as before. Now what is required is a great number of specialists and professional workers. Scientists and technicians are urged to concentrate on scientific and technical work. The Party no longer asks scientists and technicians to take part in numerous political activities. As Deng pointed out:

> We cannot demand that scientists and technicians, or at any rate, the overwhelming majority of them, study a lot of political and theoretical books, participate in numerous social activities and attend many meetings not related to their work.[35]

For the purpose of developing the Four Modernizations it became necessary to restrict class struggle and reduce political struggle. The "gang of four" was reported to have frequently attacked scientists and technicians accusing them of being "white and expert" and "being divorced from politics". In support of the modernizations Deng refuted such accusations against scientists and technicians by saying:

> Only political reactionaries who are against the Party and against socialism can be called "white". How can you label as "white" a man who studies hard to improve his knowledge and skills? Scientists and technicians who have flaws of one kind or another in their ideology or their style of work should not be called "white", if they are not against the Party and socialism. How can our scientists and technicians be accused of being divorced from politics when they work diligently for socialist science?[36]

Since class struggle is to be deemphasized in Chinese Communist ideology, the ideological incentives for anti-imperialism will inevitably be discounted. Thus, a dilemma in internal policy has been created between the Four Modernizations and the ideology of anti-imperialism. The Four Modernizations require a great number of "experts" in addition to "reds". In fact, "experts" seem to play a more important role than "reds".[37] This is in contrast to the ideology of anti-imperialism and class struggle in which "reds" customarily played a leading role in socialist construction.

Thirdly, in the 1950s and 1960s, in theory, economic policy and implementation was carried out in the form of the mass line, that is, "coming from

[35] Deng Xiaoping, "Opening Ceremony of the National Science Conference," *op. cit.*
[36] *Ibid.*
[37] "Red and Expert Relationship Analyzed," *Ta Kung Pao Weekly Supplement*, no. 618, April 27-May 3, 1978.

the masses, going back to the masses." Political studies and social activities by workers and peasants were urged by the Party. One of the rationales behind the numerous anti-imperialist mass demonstrations was that an anti-imperialistic spirit would increase morale among the workers and heighten ideological awareness towards class struggle both at home and abroad.[38]

In current policy, modernization in industry and national defense does not rely upon the mass line; instead management and technology are emphasized. This is a clear departure from the process of socialist construction of the 1950s and 1960s. As pointed out by the *Beijing Review*:

> ... We should introduce new techniques from abroad, which will save us a lot of time. The purpose of introducing new techniques from abroad is to learn from other people's strong points so as to catch up and surpass them through our own efforts. ...
> To raise management efficiency by modern scientific techniques, we should gradually use electronic computers in management work. A computerized network linking up various regions in the country and various departments will form an automatic management system for the entire national economy, which will greatly raise efficiency.[39]

The new trend to rely on "experts" or professional cadres such as managers and engineers reduces the importance of ideological incentives so prominent before.

Similarly, the mass line approach has been deemphasized in the modernization of national defense.[40] In contrast to Mao's emphasis on the role of man in war and mass mobilization, the current construction in national defense has placed a higher priority on the improvement of arms and equipment. While paying lip service to Mao's ideas of a people's war, General Xu Xianqian, the former Minister of National Defense, in August 1978, said:

> Our aim in speeding up the development of national defense, science and technology, and national defense industries, and improving the arms and equipment of our army is to build up the material basis for increasing the might of a people's war under modern conditions. On the basis of accelerating our economic construction, we must strive to modernize our national defense at high speed and pay attention to learning from the advanced experience of other countries; at the same time we must make efforts to improve the arms and equipment of our army, navy, air force and militia so that there will be new types of conventional equipment and sufficient ammunition as well as better atom bombs, guided missiles and other sophisticated weapons.[41]

---

[38] *Xue Xi Mao Zhu Xi Lun Zhi Lao Hu Wen Xian* (Document of Studying Chairman Mao's Discussion on Paper Tigers), Hong Kong: *Wen Hui Pao*, 1958, pp. 5-25.

[39] Chi Ti, "Industrial Modernization," *Beijing Review*, no. 26, June 30, 1978.

[40] Vice-Chairman Ye Jianying's Speech, *Beijing Review*, no. 32, August 5, 1978.

[41] Xu Xiangqian, "Heighten Our Vigilance and Get Prepared to Fight A War," *Beijing Review*, no. 32, August 11, 1978.

Summary

China's antiforeignism which developed in the early twentieth century and became one of the most important aspects of Peking's international behavior, drastically declined in the 1970s. A reduction of antiforeign mass demonstrations started in 1971, and they have almost completely disappeared since 1977. The last mass protest was opposing the Vietnamese invasion into Cambodia in early 1979. Since then Peking has ceased to use demonstrations to protest against the United States and the Soviet Union. Similarly, attacks by the media against foreign countries have also decreased to the lowest level since 1949.

The antiforeign mass demonstrations which were directed against U.S. diplomatic activities concerning China and the demonstrations directed against "U.S. imperialist aggression" in Vietnam and Cambodia have been drastically reduced since 1971, when the United States began reducing its commitments in Indochina and increasing contacts with the Peking government. Demonstrations protesting against U.S. diplomatic activities in other countries significantly decreased soon after China was admitted into the United Nations. In addition, the Four Modernizations, which emphasize the necessity to acquire advanced technology and science from the West, have further mollified the sentiment of antiforeignism by modifying the ideology of anti-imperialism. Accordingly, the development of the modernization policy is also an important factor leading to the decline of the ideology of anti-imperialism and antiforeignism.

"Anti-imperialism" has been a nationalistic sentiment among the masses in protest against foreign repression since the early years of the twentieth century. Under the current modernization program, however, the ideology of antiimperialism is no longer compatible with the new ideology which emphasizes management and technology. In spite of occasional lip service, the ideology of anti-imperialism on the domestic political scene is being phased out. In opposing imperialism, mass activities have been replaced by the modernization of national defense. Now most disputes with foreign countries are presented and protested against by Peking's representatives in the United Nations.

In sum, the decline in Peking's antiforeignism is not a temporary phenomenon. Instead it is a new pattern of international behavior resulting from both internal and external developments. In this analysis, the development of Peking's new international behavior is accounted for by the change in Peking's foreign policy, the increased contact between Peking and Washington, and the military withdrawal of American forces from Asia, as well as by Peking's admission into the United Nations. The change in the external environment led to changes in domestic policy which in turn have stimulated the decline in antiforeign activities. Since 1976, trade between China and Western Europe has enormously increased, and communication between China and the United States and Japan has also witnessed an improvement. The shift in foreign policy and concomitant changes in China's approach to development, in fact, resembles the stance of the KMT during the 1940s, which emphasized national independence and Westernization while playing down mass sentiments of anti-imperialism.

CHAPTER 12
Conclusion

This study of the development of antiforeignism in China during the last century makes clear that both internal and external factors account for antiforeignism's continuous development over the last hundred years. In the early twentieth century, antiforeignism was strengthened by increasing pressure and interference from the West as well as by the emergence of nationalism among the Chinese people. There is little doubt that antiforeignism became an important political sentiment in Chinese society. Nationalism and antiforeignism merged and were manifested in the movement toward recovering mining rights and railroad rights as well as in the demand for the relinquishment of unequal treaties and foreign concessions.

The Kuomintang government utilized antiforeign sentiment to defend Chinese tradition and culture while the Communists made it the foundation for revolution. While both the KMT and the CCP pledged to oppose imperialism, they utilized the sentiment of anti-imperialism in different ways. As discussed in Chapter 5, anti-imperialism became a major platform in KMT foreign policy. But soon after the abolition of unequal treaties and foreign concessions, and extraterritoriality, the KMT government adopted a policy of cooperation with the West. Anti-imperialism became a goal of a new foreign policy seeking national equality and independence.

In contrast, the CCP converted antiforeignism into an important part of their ideology. The ideology became a critical political force for mobilization of support. Therefore, antiforeignism in the post-1949 period was closely related to internal politics in China. It was a movement manipulated by the authorities. Evidence is abundant to show that antiforeignism during this period was manipulated by the leadership for other purposes. As discussed in Chapters 7 and 8, antiforeignism during the period of 1960-62 was closely related to mobilization for production on the one hand, and to Peking's 'united front' policy with the third world on the other. Similarly, antiforeignism during the period of the Cultural Revolution was related to the campaign to defeat the 'capitalist in power'. An understanding of these connections is essential to explaining the decline of antiforeignism in the early 1970s and the further decline in 1977 and 1978 when China initiated the policy of the Four Modernizations. Government manipulation of antiforeignism also explains the inevitable change in antiforeignism when the Chinese undertook a drastic modification of ideology. Bearing this in mind, some theories are stated below about the relationship of antiforeignism to political culture, mobilization, power struggle, and modernization.

Antiforeignism and Political Culture

This study of antiforeignism from 1860 to 1980 suggests that antiforeignism in China was more a political reaction to foreign threat than any part of political culture. Previous studies frequently mistook antiforeignism as an important part of Chinese political culture emphasizing the emotions of hate or hostility.[1] As presented in Chapters 2, 3 and 4, the development of China's antiforeignism in 1860-1900 was stimulated by foreign invasions and aggravated by the efforts of missionaries. Antiforeignism was strengthened by the rise of nationalism which was brought about by foreign interference in China's politics and economy in the period between 1900 and 1927. When the KMT government was established in Nanjing in 1927, Japan intensified her aggression in Manchuria. Most of the KMT period was devoted to resisting Japanese aggression. 'Anti-Japanese imperialism' was a patriotic movement. Therefore, in the period before 1949, antiforeignism was a nationalist movement, and the political culture characterized by external hostility was only part of this movement. In other words, the political culture which resulted from this opposition to an enemy was nothing but a response to foreign aggression. Once the war with Japan ended in 1945, antiforeign hostility ceased. Hostility against an enemy country is a common phenomenon among all peoples who have suffered from foreign aggression.

In regard to the post-1949 period, antiforeignism was expressed in the term 'anti-imperialism' or 'anti-U.S. imperialism.' As discussed above, it was an active part of the current ideology and was utilized to mobilize support from the people. In other words, the ups and downs of antiforeignism in the post-1949 period were not accounted for by external factors alone; the manipulation of antiforeignism by the leadership also became an important factor in the development. This explains how the so-called political culture of this period was merely a phenomenon which resulted from political manipulation of antiforeignism. It could not exist without political support from the authorities. If antiforeignism was a part of Chinese political culture, it was one created by the leadership rather than the people.

Modernization and Revolution

In the study of China's modernization in the late nineteenth and early twentieth century, I have suggested that several events contributed to the

[1] For example, see Lucian W. Pye, *The Spirit of Chinese Politics*, Cambridge, Mass.: The M.I.T. Press, 1968, pp. 67-70.

development of antiforeignism. First of all, the increases in foreign interference in Chinese politics and the economy by foreign military forces and
investors served as important stimuli to antiforeignism. Foreign military
forces directly threatened the ruling elite who helped to maintain the status
quo in Chinese society. Foreign investors in China undoubtedly competed with
local merchants and threw some of them out of business, forcing the urban
population to take a stand against the foreigners. As far as the missionaries
were concerned, regardless of their contributions, they usually became the
scapegoat for 'foreign evils'. On the one hand they helped educate millions of
Chinese youths; on the other, they antagonized those who were steeped in
Chinese culture and tradition. During this turbulent period, they were
vulnerable to local attack by the conservative elements in Chinese society. In
short, during this period foreign military and political interferences were the
key factors causing the escalation of antiforeignism.

Secondly, the introduction of Western learning inevitably brought some
social changes. Since modernization in China was basically a westernization, it
led to changes in the educational system and an increasing social mobility in
the first two decades of the twentieth century. These inevitably brought
about a reshaping of all social values. In these social changes, restlessness and
resistance became common social phenomena which led to divergence between
those who favored the preservation of old culture and those who urged
innovations. Under such circumstances, the former easily turned into
opponents of foreign culture and knowledge and developed a strong sentiment
of antiforeignism among themselves. Opposition to change and antiforeignism
was usually supported by the social and political elite in order to protect their
vested interest in the status quo. The people who urged reform or innovation
were basically the intelligentsia, a minority in society, who would find it very
difficult to overcome the opposition.

Thirdly, the failure of modernization further amplified the sentiment of
antiforeignism. More specifically, in addition to original resentment against
social changes, disillusion over the faith that modernization could save the
country from foreign aggression led to the realization that the government
could no longer protect the people and that they must make a stand against
the foreigners themselves. This brought about the nation-wide mass involvement in antiforeignism in the 1910s-1920s. This development ended when
the KMT defeated the warlords and took over the leadership of the anti-
imperialism movement.

Modernization also produced authority crises in China in the late nineteenth
and early twentieth century. Modernization, which emphasized rational thinking
and secular ideas, presented a disturbing challenge to the imperial government
of China. As a result of wider popular education and the development of

238

technology and social changes, the feudalistic system of the imperial govern-ment and its claim to legitimacy met with increasing challenges from the newly-educated people and their new economic elite. Their increasing concern about the nation and their sense of participation posed a serious threat to the ruling class. This eventually turned into the public demand for a change in the relationship between the ruling and the ruled—the fundamental concept of revolution. Therefore, modernization in a traditional society like China provided the social basis for revolution.

As mentioned above, the failure of modernization led to the development of antiforeignism in as much as the people lost faith and confidence in the government. While the people resented the intrusion of foreign countries, at the same time they also blamed the incompetence of their own government. The Sino-Japanese War of 1894 and the war with the Eight Powers which resulted from the Boxer Uprising in 1900 brought the confidence of the people to the lowest level possible and precipitated the most intense authority crisis in the Qing dynasty. In this period the revolutionaries quickly expanded in China. When they eventually toppled the imperial government in 1911, great social and political disruptions occurred. In other words, modernization tended to initiate innovation in economic and social developments on the one hand, and, on the other, it also served a devastating function in demolishing the feudal political system by its causing antiforeignism and an authority crisis. Foreign interference stimulated the rise of nationalism and became a catalyst for China's revolution in the early twentieth century. Similarly, the rise of the CCP and the success of the 1949 revolution was in large part due to the authority crisis of the KMT government and the Communist's ability to mobilize popular support under antiforeign and anti-imperialist slogans.

Antiforeignism and Mobilization

The hypothesis that in times of an authority crisis the need for mobilization would lead to a rise in antiforeignism was first discussed in Chapter 6. The findings in Chapter 7 support this hypothesis. It was shown that in 1960-62, mobilization for production correlated positively with both antiforeign hostility and antiforeign demonstrations. This hypothesis is further supported by the findings in Chapter 9, which shows that, during the Cultural Revolution, mobilization campaigns led to great increases in both media hostility and antiforeign demonstrations.

The findings that domestic mobilization led to increases in external hostility are by no means coincidental. As discussed above, mass mobilization has been the Chinese leadership's most important means for carrying out internal policies. During the war with Japan, the Communists used anti-Japanese nationalistic sentiment to mobilize mass support behind the Party's political and military position. Once they had established their government and fully controlled the national political machinery, it was even more practicable for them to manipulate external hostility in order to solve internal problems. Mao's utilization of "the confrontation with U.S. imperialism," which served to motivate greater production and to carry out the program of a people's militia, is a clear example.[2]

This relationship between internal mobilization and external hostilities suggests that a new mobilization theory is necessary for the study of Chinese politics. It has been generally accepted that the CCP has employed ideological means in activating the masses and cadres. Franz Schurmann has suggested that ideology is used by the leadership as a tool for enlivening organization. Pure ideology can serve to activate the bottom tier of the organization (laborers and workers), while practical ideology can serve to activate the line components of the middle organizational ranks.[3] (See Figure 12.1, A)

Schurmann's theory seems applicable to those periods in which China faced no authority crisis, such as during the 1953-57 First Five Year Plan. It does not, however, provide an adequate explanation of popular mobilization in times of severe crisis. In such periods, the old method of ideological indoctrination of Marxism-Leninism and the thought of Mao Zedong has proved insufficient to mollify discontent. It was, therefore precisely during an authority crisis that the Chinese leadership turned to antiforeignism as a powerful means for motivating domestic mobilization. (See Figure 12.1, B) Antiforeign verbal hostility and mass campaigns were used to heighten nationalistic spirit, divert internal discontent, minimize resistance and strengthen the leadership.

Figure 12.1 Mobilization Theories

A. Leadership ⟶ Ideology ⟶ Mobilization

B. Leadership ⟶ Antiforeignism ⟶ Mobilization

Antiforeignism and Power Struggle

As mentioned in Chapter 1, several scholars of international politics have suggested that acute elite tension may result in increased external hostility.

[2] Richard H. Solomon, *Mao's Revolution and the Chinese Culture*, Berkeley, Calif.: University of California Press, 1972, Paperback edition, p. 388.

[3] Franz Schurmann, *Ideology and Organization in Communist China*, Berkeley, Calif.: University of California Press, Enlarged second edition, 1968, pp. 71-73.

In observing the Chinese internal politics in the 1950s, it becomes evident that power struggles pushed China in a leftist direction politically. There appeared a re-enforcing trend in which the more power struggles led to leftism, the more ideology stressed anti-imperialism and external enemies. Thus, increasing political struggle gave rise to stronger leftism in ideology and heightened the level of antiforeignism. The continuous development of antiforeignism led to vehement attacks against foreign countries, and to an unprecedented level of antiforeignism expressed in the media and in antiforeign demonstrations. This spiral process, in fact, reached a peak in the period from 1959 to 1969. The process of intensifying antiforeignism could not be halted except by a forceful modification in ideology or drastic changes in the political environment, such as an American withdrawal from the Far East, rapprochement between Peking and Washington, China's admission into the United Nations, the death of Mao, and the development of the Four Modernizations.

The findings of Chapters 9 and 10 provide empirical evidence for this hypothesis. During the period of the 1950s and 1960s, higher levels of anti-foreignism resulted from elite conflict and power struggle. It has been found that the increase in attacks on "anti-Soviet revisionism" was utilized to link Liu Shaoqi with antiforeignism. As discussed in detail in Chapters 6 and 10, the Maoists manipulated antiforeignism to tighten their control and to help consolidate their power base. In fact, Mao recognized the utility of external conflict for domestic unity. For example, in his 1960 speech "Concerning the Problems of Anti-China," he restated that "the enemies opposing us cannot hurt us at all. Their opposition can only stimulate our unity in the Party and among the people and make us more determined and ambitious to surpass the advanced Western countries economically and culturally."[4] In other words, Mao was clearly advocating conflict as a means of strengthening internal unity and mobilization. His contention strengthens our mobilization theory. The strong relationship between power struggle and antiforeignism found in the post-1949 period suggests that, without an institutionalized mechanism for political succession, antiforeignism may rise again, as in the past, if the power elite is engulfed in a serious power struggle.

Modernization and the Decline of Antiforeignism

In most of the period from 1949 up to the early 1970s, antiforeignism was maintained at a high level. It, however, became stronger whenever an authority crisis occurred, as in 1959-62 and 1966-70. These were the high periods for

----

[4] "Concerning the Problems of Anti-China," March 22, 1960 in *Mao Zedong Si Xiang Wan Sui, op. cit.*, pp. 316-317.

leftism in Chinese politics. Endless struggles pushed the ideology to leftist extremes and led to stronger feelings of antiforeignism, which in turn made China isolate itself from the West. Therefore, progress toward modernization was not possible when both an authority crisis and antiforeignism were prevailing. (See Figure 12.2)

Figure 12.2 Modernization Model

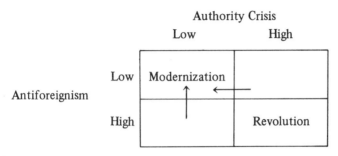

In the early 1970s, the people's response to continuous political struggles and movements in class struggle generated an apathetic attitude toward political movements which led to a decline in antiforeignism. American de-escalation in the Vietnam War and her policy of rapprochement toward China strongly encouraged this trend. Later the Four Modernization program further contributed to the decline of antiforeignism.

Although in decline since the early 1970s, leftism and antiforeignism were not actually halted until the death of Mao Zedong in 1976, followed by the arrest of the 'gang of four'. Since then, tremendous efforts have been made to reduce the authority crisis by stressing the development of political stability and unity. Meanwhile, antiforeignism has also been diminished by reducing media attacks against the West and the Soviet Union, and by eliminating antiforeign demonstrations. These efforts have been made in order to have a closer relationship with the West and to stabilize internal policies.

At the current stage, China's modernization may achieve its expected objectives only when the authority crisis and antiforeignism are held at a low level. Undoubtedly, an effective political system is badly needed to ensure that any authority crisis or any antiforeignism movement can be brought under control. However, like modernization at other times and other places, modernization in China may cause social changes, frustrations, and demands for political participation.[5] Subsequently, these may result in the development of

[5] Kuang-sheng Liao, "Jing Ji Xian Dai Hua Dui Zheng Zhi De Chong Ji," (The Impact of Economic Modernization on Politics) *Ming Pao Monthly*, April, 1983, pp. 19-22.

renewed antiforeignism and a new authority crisis. It appears that China's modernization often creates the factors which inhibit it; it solves old problems while at the same time creating new ones. Therefore, until a political system which can bring the authority crisis and antiforeignism under control is established, modernization may be disrupted by its own effects in the future.

Appendices

Appendix I: Coding Instruction for 1960-1962

External Hostility:

One indicator of external hostility was accusations against foreign governments as reported in the *RR*. During the period under study, data for five major issues articulated by the Chinese press were collected. An accusation on any of these five issues indicated one verbal act expressing China's hostility. Each accusation was treated as equally important, and the frequency of accusations was used to indicate the weight of articulated verbal hostility. In addition, antiforeign mass campaigns were examined as another indicator of China's external hostility. The unit of measurement was the frequency of antiforeign mass rallies, meetings, and demonstrations. These data were also collected from the *RR*. Data collection was carried out at the Universities Service Centre, Hong Kong. Data were organized on a monthly basis and controlled through a mutual check system by two assistants. The contents of data are briefly described below:

A. Criticisms of U.S. diplomatic activities and foreign policy
  1. Denunciations of U.S. diplomatic activities and visits by high-level officials to foreign countries.
  2. Attacks on U.S. foreign policy in commentaries and editorials.
B. Attacks on U.S. aggression against Cuba
  1. Reports condemning U.S. aggression against Cuba.
  2. Reports supporting the Castro regime in opposition to U.S. imperialism.
  3. Commentaries and editorials attacking U.S. activities against Cuba.
C. Attacks on U.S. aggression in Vietnam
  1. Reports condemning U.S. aggression in Vietnam.
  2. Reports supporting the Vietnamese struggle against the U.S.
  3. Reports in support of Vietnamese opposition to the U.S.
  4. Calls for emulation of Vietnamese courage.
D. Attacks on the Japanese Government
  1. Reports attacking the Japanese leadership.
  2. Reports attacking Japanese internal and foreign policies.
  3. Reports supporting opposition groups' activities against the Japanese government.
E. Hostile Reports against Taiwan
  1. Reports condemning the Kuomintang leadership in Taiwan.

  2. Reports criticizing government policy in Taiwan.
  3. Calls for the liberation of Taiwan.
F. Antiforeign Demonstrations
  1. Mass rallies and meetings protesting foreign governments.
  2. Mass demonstrations protesting foreign governments.

Domestic Mobilization:

Two major domestic campaigns during the period were mobilizations for industrial and agricultural production.

All reports concerning agricultural and industrial production which appeared in the *RR* were coded. Each call was regarded as equally important. A higher frequency of reports was taken to represent a greater intensity of mobilization for production urged by the Press.

The contents of the data are presented in brief description as follows:

A. Calls for industrial production
  1. Slogans calling for an increase in industrial production.
  2. Reports of activities to increase industrial production.
  3. Reports of mass movements in support of industrial production.
  4. Reports of production records from factories.
B. Calls for agricultural production
  1. Slogans calling for an increase in agricultural production.
  2. Reports of activities to increase agricultural production.
  3. Reports of mass movements in support of agricultural production.
  4. Reports of success in agricultural production records.

Appendix II: Coding Instruction for 1967-1969

China's accusations against the Soviet Union were used as the indicator for Peking's verbal hostility. Antiforeign demonstrations were used as a second indicator of China's external hostility.

The measurement unit for verbal hostility was the frequency of accusations which appeared in the *RR*. The measurement of antiforeign demonstrations was the frequency of mass rallies, meetings and demonstrations rather than the frequency of reports themselves. Each report of verbal accusations was treated as equally important. Similarly, each mass protest activity was considered equally significant.

Two internal campaigns, a campaign of power-seizure and a campaign of denunciation of the "Top Capitalist in Authority", were measured by reports in the *RR*. Because of a possible bias due to geographical distance, imperfect communication between local regions and the *RR*, and the perspective of the editor, these data were not considered as factual. Instead, they indicated calls for local mobilization in these campaigns. Assuming each report to be equally important, the more reports on a campaign, the stronger the call for its mobilization.

Data collection was again conducted at the Universities Service Centre in Hong Kong. A cross-check system was undertakn by two assistants to assure the accuracy of the data. The data were coded and organized on a monthly basis. Their contents are presented in a brief description.

A. Antiforeign demonstrations
 1. Mass rallies and meetings protesting against foreign governments.
 2. Mass demonstrations protesting against foreign governments.

B. Hostile reports against the Soviet Union or Soviet revisionism
 1. Criticisms of Soviet foreign policy.
 2. Criticisms of Soviet policy toward China.
 3. Criticisms of Soviet leadership and internal politics.
 4. Criticisms of Soviet revisionism.

C. Campaign of power-seizure from the capitalist roaders
 1. The activities of power-seizure by Red Guards and revolutionary leftists.
 2. Reports concerning the success of the development of the campaign.
 3. Commentaries and editorials directing the power-seizure campaigns.
 4. Reports eulogizing the success of the campaign.

D. Campaign of denunciation of the "Top Capitalist in Authority"
 1. Reports criticizing Liu Shaoqi's capitalist policy.
 2. Reports condemning Liu Shaoqi's anti-Party and anti-Mao plots.
 3. Reports criticizing the improper behavior of the Liu-Deng faction and its associates.

Appendix III: Antiforeign Demonstrations, 1960-1963

Table III.1
DEMONSTRATIONS AGAINST THE U.S., 1960

Target	Date	Localities	Approximate Participants Reported
To struggle against the Japan-U.S. Military Alliance, the so-called Japan-U.S. Security Treaty in support of the Japanese people and to condemn the crime of Nobusuke Kishi who assisted the spread of U.S. Imperialism in Japan	1.23	Peking	Led by the China Peace Committee, the All-China Federation of Trade Unions, the All-China Federation of Women, the All-China Federation of Young Pioneers, the Chinese Committee for Afro-Asian Solidarity, and the National Literary & Art Federation.
	1.24	Shanghai	
	1.27	Shenyang	1,000
		Wuhan	1,000
		Canton	1,000
To condemn the U.S. scheme to loot Chinese Antiques and National Art & Treasure	2.22	Peking	100 (Chinese Cultural Circles)
	2.24	Peking, Shanghai	Led by the Palace Museum & Scholars, the Ministry of Culture, the National People's Congress, the Chinese Academy of Science, the Institute of Archaeological Research, the Peking Library, the Chinese Academy of Science, the Institute of Historical Research, the National Art School, the National Research Institute of Fine Art, Peking University, the Departments of History & Archaeology, and the Shanghai Museum.
To support the Korean people in struggling against U.S. Imperialism	4.28	Peking	600,000
	4.29	Shanghai	400,000
		Tientsin	500,000
		Wuhan	300,000
		Canton	100,000
		Shenyang	200,000
		Yanbian	30,000
		Lhasa	20,000
		Fuzhou	50,000

Table III.1   (Continued)

Target	Date	Localities	Approximate Participants Reported
		Changchun	200,000
		Urumqi	80,000
		Yinchuan	30,000
		Chongqing	950,000
		Nanning	50,000
		Xining	200,000
		Zhengzhou	200,000
		Hefei	100,000
		Hangzhou	100,000
		Hohhot	100,000
	4.30	Harbin	200,000
		Chengdu	150,000
		Nanjing	60,000
		Nanchang	100,000
		Taiyuan	100,000
		Jinan	200,000
		Lanzhou	50,000
		Changsha	70,000
		Xining	120,000
		Kunming	50,000
		Guiyang	60,000
		Andong	100,000
		Luda	120,000
To provide the Turkish	5.4	Peking	50,000
people with powerful		Shanghai	30,000
support in their patriotic		Tientsin	30,000
struggle against U.S.		Wuhan	25,000
Imperialism		Canton	12,000
		Chongqing	30,000
		Xian	20,000
		Shenyang	30,000
		Haerbin	30,000
		Changchun	15,000
		Urumqi	10,000
		Lhasa	7,000
		Yinchuan	10,000
		Hohhot	1,000
		Jinan	10,000
		Lanzhou	10,000
		Guiyang	2,000

Table III.1   (Continued)

Target	Date	Localities	Approximate Participants Reported
To support the Japanese	5.9	Peking	1,000,000
people's Anti-U.S. patriotic	5.10	Tientsin	800,000
struggle		Changchun	350,000
		Luda	160,000
		Chengdu	200,000
		Lhasa	30,000
		Jinan	300,000
		Xian	250,000
		Nanchang	120,000
		Yinchuan	40,000
	5.12	Chongqing	80,000
		Hangzhou	160,000
		Taiyuan	150,000
		Nanning	60,000
		Fushun	400,000
		Xining	150,000
	5.13	Wuhan	700,000
		Nanjing	400,000
		Lanzhou	200,000
		Kunming	70,000
	5.14	Canton	600,000
		Harbin	500,000
		Hohhot	150,000
		Urumqi	100,000
	5.15	Shanghai	1,700,000
		Changsha	400,000
		Zhengzhou	250,000
		Hefei	300,000
		Qingdao	150,000
		Fuzhou	150,000
		Guiyang	100,000
		Changzhia, Pingshun, Huquan, Yuncheng, Peking, Tientsin, Guangzhou, Wuhan, Chongqing, Xian, Shenyang, Nanjing, Harbin, Changchun, Taiyuan, Chengdu, Hohhot, Urumqi, Lanzhou, Xining, Hangzhou, Kunming, Jinan, Nanchang,	

Table III.1   (Continued)

Target	Date	Localities	Approximate Participants Reported
		Nanning, Lhasa, Yinchuan, Fushun, Luda, Xiamen	530,000
	5.16	Xiamen	30,000
	5.17	Qiqihar	280,000
		Mudangjiang	170,000
		Jiamusi	120,000
		Shuangyashan	150,000
		Yi-Chun Forest	100,000
	5.19	Tientsin	100,000
		Xian	
	5.21	Wuhan	30,000
	5.22	Yantai, Zibo, Changwei, Liao-cheng, Dezhou	
	5.23	Shanghai, Chong-qing, Fushun	(Coal miners)
	5.24	Ningxia, Canton	(Women)
	5.25	Yanan, Nanjing	3,000 (Coal miners)
	5.28	Tientsin, Wanposhan	8,000 (Dockers)
	5.30	Nanjing	
	5.30	Peking, Shanghai, Xian, Luda, Changsha, Hailar (Inner Mongolia)	30,000
	6.6	Canton, Guilin Jinan, Wuhan	
	5.23	Peking, Fuzhou	Led by the Taiwan Democratic Self-Government League.
	5.24	Shanghai, Tien-tsin, Canton, Luda, Xiamen	
To condemn the U.S. scheme of aggression in Taiwan insinuated by Dwight Eisenhower's tour	6.17	Fujian Front	PLA*
	6.18	Peking	Led by the Democratic Party, and Non-Party Democrats. Led by the All-China Federation of Trade Unions, the Committee of the Young Communist League of China, the All-China Federation of

*PLA stands for People's Liberation Army

Table III.1   (Continued)

Target	Date	Localities	Approximate Participants Reported
			Women, the China Peace Committee and the Chinese Committee for Afro-Asian Solidarity in Peking and Shanghai.
	6.19	Fujian Front	PLA
		Peking, Shanghai, Nanjing, Shenyang, Wuhan, Lanzhou, Jinan, Kunming	Commercial, Industrial, Religious & Cultural Circles
		Canton, Tientsin, Wuhan, Shenyang	Various societies
	6.20	Shanghai, Chongqing, Harbin, Taiyuan, Fuzhou, Nanchang, Xining	
		Peking	Chinese returned from overseas
To commence the Anti-U.S. Week	6.20	Peking, Shanghai, Tientsin, Shenyang, Wuhan, Canton, Chongqing, Xian	
	6.21	Xian, Jinan, Hangzhou, Nanning, Lanzhou	
	6.22	Changchun, Hohhot, Changsha, Yinchuan, Kunming	
	6.23	PLA regiments of Canton, Chengdu, Changsha, Taiyuan, Jinan, Hefei, Guiyang, Hangzhou, Urumqi	
To resist U.S. aggression in Korea (Aid-Korea Programme, Anti-U.S. week)	6.25	Peking, Andong, Jinan, Shenyang Jilin	
	6.27	Tientsin, Taiyuan, Nanchang	
To liberate Taiwan	6.25	Wuhan, Chongqing	

Table III.1   (Continued)

Target	Date	Localities	Approximate Participants Reported
(Anti-U.S. Week)		Inner Mongolia, Yunnan	
.	6.26	Peking, Tientsin, Shanghai, Nanjing, Jinan, Canton, Shenyang, Lanzhou, Kunming	
	6.26	Fujian Front	PLA
	6.28	Shanghai, Canton Luda	Led by the Taiwan Democratic Self-Government League.
To protest against U.S. Imperialism (Anti-U.S. Week)	6.28	Shanghai	40,000
		Tientsin	30,000
		Wuhan	40,000
		Xian	30,000
		Nanjing	30,000
		Yinchuan	6,000
		Jinan	10,000
		Taiyuan	12,000
		Hohhot	12,000
		Urumqi	25,000
		Zhengzhou	10,000
		Chengdu	20,000
		Peking	50,000
		Shenyang	30,000
		Chongqing	120,000
		Harbin	20,000
		Nanning	10,000
		Hangzhou	30,000
		Hefei	10,000
		Changchun	10,000
		Lanzhou	25,000
		Xining	10,000
		Changsha	10,000
		Kunming	10,000
		Canton	20,000
		Guiyang	10,000
		Nanchang	
To support Cuba in resisting the U.S.	7.16	Peking	3,000
To support the just	7.19	Peking	10,000

Table III.1   (Continued)

Target	Date	Localities	Approximate Participants Reported
struggle against U.S.	7.20	Canton	1,200
aggression in Vietnam		Nanning	1,300
		Tientsin	300
		Shanghai	
To celebrate the 15th	8.14	Shanghai, Jilin,	
Anniversary of the		Harbin, Andung	
Liberation of Korea	8.15	Canton	1,000
		Xian	1,000
		Changsha	1,000
	8.16	Yanji in Jilin	1,200
			(Tribes)
	8.18	Wuhan	1,000
To celebrate the	10.25	Peking	10,000
Anniversary of Anti-		Shanghai	2,000
U.S. and Aid-Korea by		Shenyang	2,000
the Chinese People's		Tientsin	1,000
Volunteer Army, and		Changchun	1,800
the Sino-Korean		Wuhan	1,300
Friendship along the		Canton	5,000
Yalu River is Profound		Chengdu	1,000
		Xian	1,800
		Andong	1,500
		Yanji	1,200
		Daomin	1,000

Table III.2
DEMONSTRATIONS IN SUPPORT OF U.S.S.R.
TO OPPOSE 'U.S. IMPERIALISM', 1960

Target	Date	Localities	Approximate Participants Reported
To support the Soviet Premier, Khrushchev's, statement at the Summit Meeting condemning U.S. Imperialism	5.18	Peking, Shanghai, Tientsin	
	5.20	Peking	3,000,000
	5.21	Tientsin	2,000,000
		Shenyang	1,500,000
		Harbin	1,000,000
		Anshan	900,000
		Andong	270,000
		Changsha	800,000
		Chengdu	500,000
		Hefei	400,000
		Yanan, Yulin, Baoji, Tongchuan, Hangzhong Shanxian, Ankang, Xian, Xianyang	1,080,000
	5.22	Shanghai	3,000,000
		Canton	800,000
		Wuhan	1,500,000
		Chongqing	1,500,000
		Jinan	520,000
		Zhengzhou	350,000
		Nanchang	330,000
		Taiyuan	300,000
		Nanning	200,000
		Yinzhuan	80,000
		Fuzhou	300,000
		Lhasa	35,000
	5.23	Nanjing	1,000,000
		Changchun	800,000
		Lanzhou	600,000
		Luda	1,120,000
		Hangzhou	500,000
		Qingdao	350,000
		Kunming	300,000
		Guiyang	250,000
		Nanning	200,000
		Guilin	50,000
		Wuzhou	40,000
	5.24	Fushun	700,000
		Jinzhou	500,000
		Benqi	200,000

Table III.2   (Continued)

Target	Date	Localities	Approximate Participants Reported
		Fuxin	180,000
		Chaoyang	50,000
		Jilin: Jilin	300,000
		Yanji	100,000
		Baicheng	40,000
		Hunchiang, Liaoyuan Siping, Tonghua	70,000
		Anhui: Banfu	200,000
		Wuhu	100,000
		Anqing	100,000
		Huainan	200,000
		Maanshan	120,000
		Tongling	20,000
		Hunan: Hengyang	200,000
		Zhuzhou	140,000
		Xiangtan	300,000
		Hubei: Huangshi	160,000
		Shashi	80,000
		Yichang	10,000
		Xiangfan	10,000
		Guangxi: Liuzhou	170,000
		Hohhot	400,000 (tribes)
		Urumqi	250,000 (tribes)
		Baotou	200,000
		Haihe	(tribes)
		Ailiuxien in Heilongjiang	10,000
	5.25	Shanxi, Ningxia, Yinchuan	8,000,000
		Loyang, Kaifeng, Xinxiang, Pingdingshan, Anyang, Jiaozuo, Sanmenxia, Hebi in Henan	900,000
		Yantai, Weifang, Jining, Liaocheng, Zibo, Linyi, Kotze in Shandong	310,000
		Yining in Xinjiang	50,000
	5.26	Wuxi, Xuzhou, Suzhou, Nantong, Xinhaiyun, Changzhou, Chenjiang, Yang- zhou in Jiangsu	1,500,000

Table III.3

ANTIFOREIGN DEMONSTRATIONS ON OTHER ISSUES, 1960

Target	Date	Localities	Approximate Participants Reported
To celebrate the 15th Anniversary of the Liberation of Hungaria	4.3	Peking	1,000
To celebrate the spirit of co-operation among the African and Chinese people and to stamp out imperialism & colonialism	4.17 4.23	Peking Peking	50,000 1,500 (Youths)
To celebrate the Anniversary of the Liberation of Czechoslovakia	5.8	Peking	Led by the Commission for Cultural Relations with Foreign Countries, the China-Czechoslovakia Friendship Association, the All-China Federation of Trade Unions, the All-China Federation of Women, the All-China Federation of Young Pioneers, and the National Literary & Art Federation.
To protest against the Military Authority in west Java for forcing the overseas Chinese to evacuate	7.5 7.6 7.7 7.9	Peking, Shanghai, Fuzhou Canton, Nanning, Kunming, Tientsin Peking, Canton, Shanghai, Tientsin, Shenyang, Fuzhou, Nanning, Kunming, Xiamen, Shantou Guangdong, Fujian, Guangxi	Chinese returned from overseas
To support the struggle in the Congo	7.23	Peking	10,000
To celebrate the 15th Anniversary of the	8.29	Peking University	1,000 Students & staff

Table III.3　　　　　　　　　　　　　(Continued)

Target	Date	Localities	Approximate Participants Reported
Vietnam Democratic	9.1	Peking	1,500
Republic and the 15th	9.2	Shanghai	1,000
Anniversary of the		Tientsin	1,000
Liberation of N.E. China		Canton	1,000
by the Soviet Army		Nanning	1,000
		Kunming	500
		Zhengzhou	
		Shenyang	500
		Changsha	600
		Harbin	500
		Luda	700
		Changjiakou	600
		Xian	1,000
		Wuhan	1,200
		Nanjing	1,000
To celebrate the signing of the Sino-Burmese Boundary Treaty	10.2	Peking	100,000
To provide resolute support to the just struggle of the Algerian people	11.1	Peking	
To celebrate the 43rd	11.6	Peking	1,000
Anniversary of the Great		Tientsin	1,000
October Revolution and		Shenyang	1,000
the united front of the		Changchun	1,000
Sino-Soviet people		Harbin	1,500
		Luda	1,500
		Wuhan	1,000
		Canton	1,000
		Chengdu	1,000
		Xian	1,000
		Urumqi	1,000
		Hohhot	1,000
	11.7	Shanghai	1,000

Table III.4

DEMONSTRATIONS AGAINST THE U.S., 1961

Target	Date	Localities	Approximate Participants Reported
To give absolute support	1.31	Peking	1,000
to the just struggle of	4.18	Peking, Shang-	
Cuba against U.S.		hai, Tientsin	
imperialism	4.19	Peking, Shang-	
		hai, Tientsin,	
		Wuhan, Chengdu,	
		Chongqing, Xian,	
		Shenyang	
	4.20	Harbin, Taiyuan,	All tribes
		Yinchuan	
	4.21	Peking	600,000
	4.22	Shanghai	500,000
		Tientsin	400,000
		Shenyang	500,000
		Xian	400,000
		Wuhan	500,000
		Canton	300,000
		Chengdu	200,000
		Hohhot	150,000
		Urumqi	200,000
	4.24	Jinan	100,000
		Changsha	160,000
		Lanzhou	100,000
		Yinchuan	1,000
		Hefei	50,000
	4.25	Kunming, Zhengzhou	
	11.20	Peking	
To support the just	2.2	Peking	1,000
struggle of the Laotian			(Cultural circle)
people	2.9	Peking	Afro-Asian Solidarity in Peking
To denounce the murder	2.18	Peking	500,000
of Lumumba of the	2.19	Shanghai	400,000
Congo and to condemn	2.20	Tientsin	350,000
U.S. imperialism		Shenyang	300,000
		Xian	300,000
		Canton	200,000
		Chengdu	100,000
		Wuhan	200,000
		Hohhot	100,000
		Urumqi	200,000

Table III.4   (Continued)

Target	Date	Localities	Approximate Participants Reported
	2.21	Tibet	450
		Ningxia	70
		Guangxi, Hunan Heilongjiang, Shanxi	
	2.21	Peking	Professors & writers
	2.23	Jilin, Shandong	
To condemn the U.S. scheme to loot Chinese antiques in Taiwan	2.1	Shanghai, Nanjing, Canton	Cultural circles
To support the just struggle in South Vietnam against U.S. aggression	4.14	Peking	

Table III.5
DEMONSTRATIONS AGAINST INDIA, 1961

Target	Date	Localities	Approximate Participants Reported
To censure the Indian Govt's slander concerning the border question and the clumsy Anti-China show staged by Nehru, the Indian Premier	12.8 12.10	Peking Peking	Led by the democratic parties and the non-party democrats

Table III.6
DEMONSTRATIONS AGAINST THE U.S., 1962

Target	Date	Localities	Approximate Participants Reported
To support the just struggle of the Communist Party in the U.S. & to condemn the crimes of Kennedy	1.15	Peking	Led by leaders of the Trade Unions and the representatives of the federations.
	1.16	Peking	
	1.17	Peking	1,400
		Tientsin	1,000
	1.17	Peking	Led by people working for the Law
	1.18	Peking	Cultural circles
		Shenyang	1,000
		Wuhan	1,000
		Chongqing	1,000
	1.19	Peking	Led by the democratic parties and the non-party democrats.
	1.19	Peking	Scientists
	1.19	Canton, Xian	2,000
	1.19	Nanking, Harbin	1,800
	1.20	Peking	Women
	1.21	Peking	Youths
	1.22	Peking	Writers
To condemn the use of missionaries for aggression	1.23	Peking	Religious circle
	1.25	Peking	
To condemn U.S. suppression of students	1.26	Peking	Students representatives
To condemn U.S. plans to revive Japanese militarism	1.27	Shanghai	1,000
To censure U.S. imperialism & the persecution of Gizenga in the Congo	2.4	Peking	
To support the just struggle in Vietnam	3.5	Peking	1,500
	7.18	Canton	
	7.19	Peking	
To protest against U.S. military provocation, the flight of U-2E planes along the Chinese border	9.14	Tibet, Xinjiang, Inner Mongolia, Yunnan Heilong- jiang, Jiangsu,	

Table III.6   (Continued)

Target	Date	Localities	Approximate Participants Reported
		Anhui, Jiangxi, Chongqing, Xiamen	
	9.14	Fujian Front	Army, Navy, Air Force
	9.14	Peking	10,000
	9.16	Wuhan	1,600
		Taiyuan, Ningxia, Urumqi, Kunming, Nanchang, Hangzhou, Hefei	
	9.18	Canton	1,000
		Hohhot	1,000
		Urumqi	1,000
		Peking	1,000
	10.28	Peking	10,000
	10.29	Shenyang	2,500
To protest against U.S. aggression and interference in Cuba and to support the people in Cuba to the utmost	10.30	Shanghai	3,000
		Tientsin	2,500
		Wuhan	1,600
		Canton	3,000
	10.31	Urumqi, Lhasa, Hohhot, Chengdu, Xian	
	11.1	Nanjing	1,000
		Xining	1,300
		Kunming	900
		Jinan	800
		Harbin, Hangzhou	
	11.3	Peking, Shanghai, Wuhan, Tientsin, Xian, Shenyang, Canton, Hefei, Fuzhou, Lanzhou, Guiyang	
	11.5	Peking	300,000
		Shanghai	200,000
		Tientsin	30,000
		Shenyang	80,000
		Canton	70,000
		Chengdu	40,000
		Wuhan	20,000

Table III.6   (Continued)

Target	Date	Localities	Approximate Participants Reported
		Xian	20,000
	11.6	Peking	400,000
		Shanghai	500,000
		Tientsin	200,000
		Canton	300,000
		Shenyang	200,000
		Wuhan	160,000
		Chengdu	100,000
	11.7	National	5,000,000
		National	10,000,000
	11.8	National	
	11.10	Lhasa	12,000
	11.27	Peking	
	11.28	Shanghai, Tientsin, Canton	

Table III.7
DEMONSTRATIONS AGAINST INDIA, 1962

Target	Date	Localities	Approximate Participants Reported
To censure the persecu-	9.29	Lhasa	4,000
tion of Chinese in India	10.5	A military base in Tibet	Border troops
	11.9	Peking	Chinese returned from overseas
	11.11	Canton, Kunming	
	11.25	Peking	Chinese returned from overseas
	12.23	Canton, Fu-zhou, Tientsin, Shenyang	Chinese returned from overseas

Table III.8
DEMONSTRATIONS AGAINST THE U.S., 1963

Target	Date	Localities	Approximate Participants Reported
To support the peace	7.15	Peking	10,000
struggle in S. Vietnam	7.20	Changsha, Nanning, Wuhan, Peking	School staff & students
	7.21	Canton	3,000
		Shanghai, Xian, Peking, Shenyang	School staff & students
	8.30	Peking	10,000
	9.6	Kunming	5,000
To support the struggle	8.12	Peking	10,000
of the black people in	8.25	Peking	1,000
the U.S. and to condemn	9.10	Peking	10,000
racism	11.11	Peking	1,500
	11.12	Shenyang	1,000
To condemn the U-2E		Canton	1,400
planes undertaken by		Wuhan	
agents from the Chiang		Hangzhou	1,300
Govt. in Taiwan under		Kunming	1,000
the disguise of a U.S.	11.13	Shanghai	1,800
force		Fuzhou	1,200
		Chengdu	1,200
		Urumqi	1,000
		Hohhot	1,300
	11.14	Xian, Nanjing, Lhasa, Jinan	4,000
To support the Anti-U.S.	11.13	Peking	10,000
campaign in S. Vietnam	12.19	Peking	1,200
	12.21	Canton, Kunming Nanning	3,000

Table III.9

DEMONSTRATIONS AGAINST INDIA, 1963

Target	Date	Localities	Approximate Participants Reported
To censure the persecution	1.22	Peking	Chinese returned from overseas
of Chinese in India	1.24	Guangdong, Guangxi, Fujian, Yunnan	
	1.25	Hangzhou, Wuhan	
	4.29	Changjiang	
	4.30	Shanghai, Yunnan, Hebei, Jiangsu, Zhejiang	
	5.8	Chanjiang	
	6.17	Chanjiang	
	8.23	Chanjiang	
	8.28	Chanjiang	
	8.29	Peking, Canton	

Table III.10

DEMONSTRATIONS AGAINST THE U.S.S.R., 1963

Target	Date	Localities	Approximate Participants Reported
To welcome the five comrades requested to leave by the Soviet government and to ensure their stay in Peking	7.7	Peking	Led by the Foreign Ministry, the Department of Education, the Science Institute and the Foreign Trade Department.
To welcome the comrades who were unjustly chased away by the Soviet Czechoslovakian government	9.20	Peking	10,000
To Censure the Soviet's scheme to join with India in opposing China	12.2	Peking	World Peace Committee

Table III.11
DEMONSTRATIONS AGAINST OTHER COUNTRIES, 1963

Target	Date	Localities	Approximate Participants Reported
To support the struggle of the Buddhists in South Vietnam	7.17	Peking	10,000 (Religious circles)
To welcome the reporters (3) and comrades (15) who were forced to leave Czechoslovakia	7.27 9.18	Peking Peking	

Appendix IV: Antiforeign Demonstrations, 1967-1970

Table IV.1

DEMONSTRATIONS AGAINST SOVIET REVISIONISTS, 1967

Target	Date	Localities	Approximate Participants Reported
To protest against Soviet Revisionist Fascist atrocities in suppressing Chinese students and committing other crimes of an anti-China nature	1.26	Peking	Rebel workers, Revolutionary functionaries, Red Guards.
	1.27	Peking	Chinese workers in the Soviet Embassy in Peking revolutionaries.
	1.27	Peking, Shanghai, Taiyuan	
	1.28	Peking, Tientsin, Canton, Xian, Chengdu, Wuhan, Nanning, Lhasa, Hohhot, Urumqi	Proletariat Revolutionaries
	1.29	Peking	Led by students returned from the U.S.S.R.
	1.30	Peking	1,000,000 Chinese official receptionists and shipmen of Guanghua, a liner going to Indonesia.
		Shanghai	500,000 (Revolutionaries)
	2.1	Peking	200,000
	2.2	Peking	Chinese workers employed by the Soviet Embassy 200 Chinese students returned from France and Iraq in Peking.
	2.6	Peking, Taiyuan, Urumqi, Tientsin, Chanjiang, Lanzhou, Wuhan, Nanchang, Changchun, Hangzhou, Lhasa, Chongqing	
	2.7	Peking, Shanghai, Qingdao, Hefei, Nanning, Kunming, Lanzhou, Nanchang, Jinan, Xian, Yinchuan, Chongqing	
	2.8	Peking	170 students returned from Moscow.

Table IV.1 (Continued)

Target	Date	Localities	Approximate Participants Reported
	2.11	Peking	100,000
	2.12	Taiyuan	30,000
		Changsha	100,000
		Nanjing	50,000
		Qingdao	100,000
		Changchun, Baoding, Daqing	
	2.14	Heilongjiang	200,000
		Harbin	(Red Rebels)

Table IV.2
DEMONSTRATIONS AGAINST THE U.S., 1967

Target	Date	Localities	Approximate Participants Reported
To support the just struggle in Vietnam	3.19	Peking	
To revenge the blood-shed by the U.S. imperialists	2.24 5.2	Haikang (Guangdong) Nanning, Dongxing, Ningming in Guanxi	7,000
To support the Palestinians and Arabs and to condemn U.S. and Israel aggressors	5.25 6.8	Peking Peking	10,000 400,000
To celebrate the 20th Anniversary of the Democratic Republic of Vietnam and to condemn U.S. aggression	9.1 12.19	Peking Peking	Representatives from the Capital, Universities & school 10,000

Table IV.3

DEMONSTRATIONS AGAINST INDIA, 1967

Target	Date	Localities	Reported
To denounce furiously the anti-China action insinuated by the anti-revolutionary Indian Government and to protest the military provocation at the China-India border	6.17	Indian Embassy in Peking	Revolutionaries
	6.18	Peking	Revolutionaries
	6.19	Peking	
	9.12	Lhasa	Red Guards Revolutionaries

Table IV.4

DEMONSTRATIONS AGAINST OTHER COUNTRIES, 1967

Target	Date	Localities	Approximate Participants Reported
To denounce the Indonesian reactionaries' crime of opposing China and persecuting Chinese nationals, and to condemn the 'Fascist Suharto-Nasution Regime'	4.25	Peking	
	4.27	Peking	100,000
	4.28	Peking (from 4.24-4.28 in front of Indonesian Embassy)	600,000
	4.28	Canton	100,000
		Nanning	20,000
		Shanghai	80,000
		Harbin	200,000
		Taiyuan	10,000
		Guiyang	40,000
		Qingdao, Changchun, Shenyang, Xining, Lhasa, Urumqi	
	4.29	Kunming	50,000
		Fuzhou	30,000
	8.5	Peking (in front of Indonesian Embassy)	
	8.7	Peking	400,000 (Red Guards of colleges and middle schools, Chinese employees in the

Table IV.4   (Continued)

Target	Date	Localities	Approximate Participants Reported
			Indonesian Embassy, Peking revolutionaries)
	8.8	Peking	600,000
To struggle against British persecution in Hong Kong	5.15	Peking (in front of British Embassy)	
		Canton	40,000
	5.16	Peking	400,000
	5.17	Peking (from 5.15-5.17)	1,000,000
		Canton	100,000
	5.18	Peking	100,000
	5.19	Shanghai	80,000
		Harbin, Guiyang, Lhasa, Canton	
	5.26	Peking	10,000
	6.2	Canton	50,000
	6.3	Canton	30,000
	6.7	Canton	100,000
	6.8	Haikou, Foshan, Huizhou, Zhao-qing, Shantou, Zhanjiang, Shao-guan	Revolutionaries & education-ists
	6.8	Canton	4,000
	6.11	Canton	100,000
	6.12	Canton	Shipmen
	6.27	Shadoujiao	3,000
		Shenzhen	10,000
		Baoan Harbour	
	7.11	Shadoujiao Shenzhen	50,000
To protest against the persecution of Chinese Journalists in Hong Kong	7.13	Peking	Led by the All-China Journal-ists Association (New China News Agency, Renmin Ribao, Guangming Ribao, & Peking News).
	7.17		The All-China Journalists Asso-ciation, the Broadcasting Agency, & the PLA News.
	8.21	Peking	All news agencies and broad-casting media.

Table IV.4   (Continued)

Target	Date	Localities	Approximate Participants Reported
	8.22	Peking	10,000
	10.28	Canton	80,000
To protest against the	5.26	Peking	15,000
Mongolian Revisionists	6.1	Hohhot	150,000
for their anti-China	8.11	Peking	100,000
action	8.14	Peking, Hohhot	Revolutionaries, rural people, techanicians in Peking, people from different tribes in Hohhot.
To condemn French action against Chinese students	1.31	Peking (at the French Embassy)	
To condemn the Titoite renegades in Yugoslavia	1.31	Peking	
To protest against U.S.	6.7	Peking	300,000
British and Israel	6.8	Peking	400,000
aggression in the Middle	6.9	Peking	500,000
East		Guiyang	100,000
		Fuzhou	40,000
		Nanning	20,000
		Canton	100,000
To protest against	6.29	Peking	200,000
Burma's anti-China	6.30	Peking	400,000
Outrage and to condemn	7.1	Peking, Shanghai, Kunming	400,000
the crime of U Hla Aung	7.2	Peking	1,000,000
	7.3	Peking	100,000
			Red Guards, revolutionaries & foreign friends from the five continents.
To support the order made by the Foreign Ministry to expel three correspondents from Japan. (Japanese newspapers Mainichi Shimbun, Sanbei Shimbun, Tokyo Shimbun)	9.10	Peking	

Table IV.4　　　　　　　　　　　(Continued)

Target	Date	Localities	Approximate Participants Reported
To welcome the Chinese Team for Studying & Checking Equipment on their return from Japan, and to refute the Sato Govt's sophistry	9.16	Peking	Led by the Chinese Trade Office & Correspondence, the China-Japan Friendship Association, and the Tokyo Liaison Office of Liao Zheng-zhi.

Table IV.5
DEMONSTRATIONS AGAINST THE U.S., 1968

Target	Date	Localities	Approximate Participants Reported
To inspire Afro-American People to greater Resistance	4.17	Peking, Shanghai, Canton, Tientsin, Wuhan, Nanning, Kunming, Nanjing, Hangzhou, Nanchang, Hohhot, Urumqi, Yinchuan, Ningxia, Tibet, Taiyuan, Shijiazhuang, Lanzhou, Guizhou, Harbin, Changchun, Zhengzhou, Hefei, Shenyang, Changsha, Chengdu, Xian, Jinan, Fuzhou	
To give a new powerful blow to U.S.-led Imperialism, the Soviet Revisionists Renegade clique and all reactionaries in France, Europe and North America and to support the struggle of the people there	5.21	Peking, Shanghai, Tientsin, Shenyang, Nanjing, Wuhan, Canton	Workers, PLA proletariats & the masses.
	5.23	Peking, Shanghai, Tientsin, Shenyang, Nanjing, Wuhan, Canton, Hebei, Inner Mongolia, Jilin, Heilongjiang, Shandong, Zhejiang, Jiangxi, Henan, Guizhou, Shanxi, Gansu, Qinghai, Ningxia, Xinjiang — various cities in these administrative provinces	
	5.24	Peking, Shanghai, Tientsin, Shenyang, Nanjing, Wuhan, Canton, Shijiazhuang, Taiyuan, Hohhot, Harbin,	

Table IV.5   (Continued)

Target	Date	Localities	Approximate Participants Reported
		Changchun, Jinan, Hangzhou, Hefei, Nanchang, Zhengzhou, Nanning, Xian, Lanzhou, Xining, Yinchuan, Urumqi, Guiyang, Chengdu.	
To celebrate the establishment of the Cambodian People's Govt.	5.7	Peking, Shanghai, Tientsin, Hebei, Shanxi, Inner Mongolia, Liaoning, Jilin, Heilongjiang, Shanxi, Gansu, Ningxia, Qinghai, Xinjiang, Shandong, Jiangsu, Anhui, Zhejiang, Jiangxi, Fujian, Henan, Hubei, Hunan, Guangdong, Guangxi, Sichuan, Guizhou, Yunnan Tibet	
To celebrate the Anniversary of the Democratic Republic of Vietnam (VJ Day). To give permanent support to the anti U.S. struggle in Vietnam	9.2 9.4 12.15	Peking Shanghai Peking, Shanghai, Tientsin, Guangdong, Guangxi, Yunnan, Guizhou, Sichuan, Tibet, Jiangsu, Zhejiang, Anhui, Fujian, Jiangxi, Shandong, Ningxia, Liaoning, Jilin, Heilongjiang, Inner Mongolia, Hebei, Shanxi, Hunan, Hubei, Henan, Shanxi, Xinjiang, Qinghai, Gansu	10,000 1,000
To celebrate the 10th Anniversary of the Liberation Front in South Vietnam	12.20 12.28	Peking Shanghai	10,000 3,000

Table IV.6

DEMONSTRATIONS AGAINST OTHER COUNTRIES, 1968

Target	Date	Localities	Approximate Participants Reported
To sentence G. Watt, British spy to three years' imprisonment	3.15	Lanzhou	Proletariats, Local revolutionaries, PLA
To deport two British spies from China	7.2	Peking	
To pronounce verdict on British Vickers-Zimmer Ltd.	7.4	Peking Municipal Court	
To commemorate the 8th Anniversary of the Death of Inejroas Anuma	10.12	Peking	1,500
To celebrate the 20th Anniversary of the Chinese Volunteer Army to N. Korean campaign	10.24	Peking	10,000
To celebrate the 17th Anniversary of the Country of Cambodia	11.9	Peking	10,000
To celebrate the 26th Anniversary of the Liberation of Algeria	11.27	Peking	1,000
	12.1	Shanghai	1,000
		Wuhan	1,000
		Canton	1,000
	12.2	Nanchang	1,000
		Changsha	1,000

Table IV.7
DEMONSTRATIONS AGAINST U.S.S.R., 1969

Target	Date	Localities	Approximate Participants Reported
To lodge the strongest protest with the Soviet Govt. against Soviet frontier guards' intrusion into the area of Chenpao Island in China's Heilongjiang Province, killing & wounding many Chinese and to condemn the new Tsars and their Soviet Revisionists' renegade clique	3.3	Peking, Harbin, Shanghai, Tientsin, Shenyang, Canton, Xian, Wuhan Chengdu, Nanjing, Lanzhou, Shijiazhuang, Hefei, Guiyang, Inner Mongolia, Xinjiang, Guangxi, Yunnan, Fujian, Zhejiang, Tibet, Jilin, Fuzhou	
	3.4	Peking	1,000,000
	3.4	Harbin, Huma, Aihui, Lopei, Jaoho, Hulin	
	3.4	Shanghai, Tientsin, Wuhan, Shenyang, Xian, Chengdu, Nanjing, Jinan, Qingdao, Hefei, Fuzhou, Nanchang, Nanning, Changsha, Zhengzhou, Shijiazhuang, Taiyuan, Changchun, Lanzhou, Xining, Yinzhuan, Guiyang, Inner Mongolia, Xinjiang, Guangxi, Yunnan, Fujian, Zhejiang, Jilin, Tibet	
	3.5	Peking	1,000,000
	3.5	Shaoshan	5,000
	3.5	Shanghai	10,000,000
	3.6	Anshan, Fushun, Daching, Qiqihar, Baotou, Tangshan, Datong, Yangzhuan, Chongqing, Loyang, Hebi, Jiaozuo, Huangshi, Zhuzhou, Tongchuan, Shizuishan, Yumen, Pingxiang, Maanshan, Wuxi, Xinanjiang, Shaoshan, Jinggangshan, Zunyi, Ruijin, Yanan, Luda, Qinhuangdao, Qingdao, Xiamen, Zhanjiang, Haikou, Bohai, Huma, Aihui, Luobei, Raohe, Hulin, Erenhot, Tacheng, Yining, Hecheng, Kaxgar, Rigece, Yunjinghong, Altai, Atushi, Kormu, Wuzhong,	

Table IV.7   (Continued)

Target	Date	Localities	Approximate Participants Reported
		Subei, Yanji, Liangshan, Ganzi, Aba	
	3.8	Urumqi	200,000
	3.8	Heilongjiang: Hulin, Hutou Production Brigade, Jiayin, Tongjiangxian, Jinkou Village	
		Inner Mongolia: Sanhezheng Joilalin, Wuzhumuxinqi, Xiangyintala, Erenhot	
		Jilin: Jilin Huichun Yanbian Korean Auto-zhou	
		Hainan Island: Qionghai, Haikou	Lower & middle peasants, militia & PLA
	3.9	Changchun (No. 1 Motor Plant)	
		Lanzhou (Chemical Work & Synthetic Rubber Plant)	
		'Red Flag No. 160' Cargo Ship, at Cunhua (revolutionary people)	
	3.10	Anshan Iron & Steel Plant at Liaoning	
		190 workers from the Zhengzhou Railway Station in Canton	
		Datong Coal Mines in Shanxi	
	3.11	Hebei, Shanxi, Henan, Hunan, Shandong, Jiangsu, Zhejiang, Anhui, Jiangxi, Gansu, Ningxia, Qinghai, Guizhou	
	3.11	Peking, Shanghai, Tientsin, Canton, Wuhan, Shenyang, Xian, Chengdu	
	3.11	Peking, Yangtze River Seamen Shanghai Dockers	
	3.11	PLA and fighters from the Army Navy and Air Force	
	3.11	Xinjiang, Uigur Auto Region: Urumqi, Yining, Karamay, Heilongjiang: Harbin, Huma, Aihui, Sunwu, Jiayin, Luobei, Suibin, Fushun, Raohe, Hulin, Jinlin, Chengjiang in Yunnan, Hohhot, Haikou, Fuzhou, Luda, Lhasa,	

Table IV.7   (Continued)

Target	Date	Localities	Approximate Participants Reported
		Guangxi Zhuang Auto Region	
	3.11	Zhenbao Island, Hudou Fishing Ground in Hulin.	
	3.12	Industrial bases: Anshan, Fushun, Daqing, Siping, Qiqihar, Chongqing, Baotou, Tangshan, Datong, Baoji, Shizuishan, Yumen, Huainan, Hebi, Loyang, Huangshan, Hengyang, Wuxi	
		Revolutionary bases: Shaoshan, Jinggangshan, Ruijin, Zunyi, Yanan	
		Frontier towns: Hulin, Raohe, Fuyuan, Luobei, Jiayin, Xunke, Aihui, Huma, Erlianhot, Manzhouli, Yining, Xiamen, Hecheng, Haikou, Beihai, Zhanjiang, Tacheng, Kaxgar, Luda, Qingdao, Ningbo	
		Scarcely populated towns: Rigece, Germu, Wuzhong, Subei, Yanji, Yunjinghong	
	3.12	Yili, Yining, Altay, Aksu, Pamirs, Plateau, Xinjiang, Uyqur, Regiment (People's communes and brigades near the Sino-Soviet & Sino-Mongolia borders and Pastureland militiamen)	
	3.13	Aihui, Hulin, Chengbao Island, Yining, Manzhouli, Xinbarhuyouqi, Huchun, Zhalainor, Yili, Kazakon, Auto-zhou (Ala Mali Mt. Pastureland) and Volunteer Frontier Guards, Commune members (Qingxin People's Commune).	
	3.16	Shaoshan	
	3.16	Jinggangshan, Yanan, Zunyi	
	5.25	Peking, Shanghai, Tientsin, Shenyang, Wuhan, Canton, Chengdu, Xian, Xinjiang, Inner Mongolia, Heilongjiang, Jilin, Yunnan, Tibet, Fujian, Guangxi, Zhejiang	
	5.25	Chenbao Island frontier guards:	

Table IV.7   (Continued)

Target	Date	Localities	*Approximate Participants Reported*
		Zhu Dengzhui, Zhang Yaguang, Diao Texun, Zhi Zhunxue, Yu Zhongxing, Du Huixin	
	6.9	Dajiaxinzi Island in Fuyuan, Wubalao Island area in Huma, Nuyatong Island area in Aihui, Tacheng, Yumin, Habahe area, (Jiamenqi area of Tacheng County, Western region of Barluk Mt. in Yumin county, Yexigai area in Habahe county)	
	6.16	Chenbao Island. Led by Gao Wen (acting platoon leader, order of merit 3rd class), Wang Yuhai (new fighter). Wang Guo Xiang (instructor), Zhou Dengguo (deputy Commander, order of merit 1st class), Chen Wen Zhong (vice-chairman of the revolutionary committee and a company leader of militia of the Wulingdong, Raohe county, Heilongjiang Province), Chen Feng (PLA production and construction corps under Heilongjiang military command, order of merit 3rd class), Yu Hongdong (platoon leader, order of merit 1st class), Hung Teh-Hsuan (squad leader, order of merit 2nd class), Zhu Dengjie (former political instructor, order of merit 3rd class)	
	7.10	Pacha Island area in Fuyuan of Heilongjiang	
	8.14	Urumqi, Yumin, Tacheng, Habaha, Alotai, Yining, Bolo, Atushi, Kaxgar, Western region of Barluk Mt. in Yumin county	
	8.15	Peking, Shanghai, Tientsin, Wuhan, Shenyang, Canton, Xian, Chengdu, Nanjing, Lanzhou, Jinan, Hangzhou, Nanning, Urumqi, Yining, Tacheng,	

Table IV.7   (Continued)

Target	Date	Localities	Approximate Participants Reported
	8.20	Alotai, Bolo, Western region of Barluk Mt. Hohhot, Harbin, Chenbao Island (Hulin Raohe), Changchun, Jilin, Siping, Liaoyuan, Fujian, Yunnan, Fangchuan, Island area of Huichun Xinjiang, Uigur Auto region, Heilongjiang, Tacheng, Tielieke area in Yumin, Toli county, Western region of Barluk Mt., Chenbao Island, Chilixin Island, Wubalao Island in Huma county, Pacha Island in Fuyuan county, Suifenhe area, and Jimnei county (frontier guards)	

Table IV.8

DEMONSTRATIONS AGAINST OTHER COUNTRIES, 1969

Target	Date	Localities	Approximate Participants Reported
To pay last respects to President Ho Chi Minh of N. Vietnam who had just passed away and to offer condolences	9.6	N. Vietnam Embassy in Peking	Workers, rural commune members, revolutionary office workers, PLA fighters, teachers & students revolutionary people, PLA & the masses revolutionary people.
	9.7	Guangdong Guangxi Yunnan	
	9.8	Peking	
	9.9	Peking (from 9.6-9.9)	75,000
	9.10	Peking, Shanghai, Tientsin, Canton, Nanning, Kunming	130,000
To celebrate the 25th Anniversary of the	11.24	Peking	PLA, Peking Iron & Steel Co. workers

Table IV.8   (Continued)

Target	Date	Localities	Approximate Participants Reported
Liberation of Algeria	11.25	Peking	
	11.26	Peking	The China-Algeria Friendship Association
	11.28	Peking	
	12.1	Tientsin, Jinan Wuhan	PLA
	12.2	Changsha	1,000 PLA & the masses
	12.3	Shenyang, Nanjing	1,000 PLA & the masses
	12.5	Canton	1,000
	12.6	Shanghai, Harbin	1,000

Table IV.9
DEMONSTRATIONS AGAINST THE U. S. 1970

Target	Date	Localities	Approximate Participants Reported
To support the world battle against U.S. imperialism and to stand by Vietnam in struggling against U.S. aggression	5.21	Peking led by Chairman Mao & Vice-Chairman Lin Biao	100,000
		Shanghai	500,000
		Tientsin	400,000
	5.22	Shenyang	200,000 (Revolutionaries)
		Canton	400,000
		Wuhan	400,000
		Xian	400,000
		Nanjing	200,000
		Kunming	200,000
		Fuzhou	120,000
		Nanning	150,000
		Hangzhou	200,000
		Harbin	200,000
		Changchun	100,000
		Yinchuan	50,000
		Lanzhou	200,000
		Lhasa	50,000
		Urumqi	200,000
		Nanchang	150,000

Table IV.9   (Continued)

Target	Date	Localities	Approximate Participants Reported
		Jinan	300,000
		Shijiazhuang	100,000
		Taiyuan	300,000
		Hefei	130,000
		Zhengzhou	250,000
		Changsha	300,000
		Xining	100,000
		Guiyang	200,000
	5.23	Peking, Shanghai Tientsin	12,000,000
	5.24	Guangdong: Canton, Foshan, Jiangmen, Huizhou, Shandou, Shaoguan. Chaoqing, Meicheng.	
		Guangxi: Nanning, Guilin, Liuzhou, Wuzhou, Baise, Xinzhou, Hechi, Yulin, Longlin, Sanjiang, Longsheng, Bama, Duan, Rongshui, Jinxiu, Huanjiang, Dongxing.	
		Yunnan: Kunming, Gejiu, Xishuangbanna, Hekou, Jinping, Jiangcheng.	
		Fujian: Fuzhou, Xiamen (Amoy).	
		Sichuan: Chengdu, Chongqing, Zigong.	
		Shandong: Jinan, Qingdao, Zibo, Zaozhuang, Weifan, Yantai, Linyi, Taian, Jining, Hece, Liaocheng, Dezhou, Huimin.	
		Hubei: Shashi, Yichang, Xiangfan.	
		Liaoning: Shenyang, Luda, Anshan, Fushun, Benxi, Dandong, Jinzhuo, Zhaowudamen, Fuxin, Jinzhou, Yinkou, Liaoyang, Tienling, Panshan.	
		Heilongjiang: Harbin, Qiqihar, Mudanjiang, Jiamusi, Hailar, Manzhouli, Jixi, Hegang, Shuangyashan, Yichun.	
		Inner Mongolia: Hohhot, Baotou, Wuda, Haipowan, Jinin, Xilinhot, Linhe, Dongsheng.	
		Shaanxi: Xian, Baoji, Tongchuan, Weinan, Yulin, Hanzhong, Shanglo, Xienyang, Ankang, Yanan.	
		Xinjiang	
	5.25	Hebei: Shijiazhuang, Tangshan,	

Table IV.9   (Continued)

Target	Date	Localities	Approximate Participants Reported
		Changjiakou, Chengde, Qinhuangdao, Baoding, Cangzhou, Xingtai, Handan.	
		Hunan: Changsha, Zhuzhou, Xiangtan, Hengyang, Changde, Jishou, Chenzhou, Lingling, Qianyang.	
		Jiangsu: Nanjing, Wuxi, Xuzhou, Suzhou, Changzhou, Nantong, Lianyungang.	
		Zhejiang: Hangzhou, Ningbo, Wenzhou, Shaoxing, Jinhua, Linhai, Lishui, Huzhou.	
		Gansu: Tianshui, Jiayuguan Yumen, Wumei, Zhangyi, Pingliang, Wudu, Linxia, Hezuo, Dingxi, Qingyang.	
		Anhui: Hefei, Huainan, Maanshan, Benfu, Wuhu, Anqing, Suixi, Tongling, Suxian, Fuyang, Chuxian, Lu'an, Chaohu, Chizhou, Huizhou.	
		Guizhou: Zunyi, Anshun, Bejie, Tongren, Xingyi.	
		Jilin: Changchun, Jilin, Tonghua, Yanji, Siping, Baicheng, Tongliao, Tumen, Liaoyuan.	
		Ningxia: Yinchuan, Yanji.	
		Tibet: Lhasa, Rigece, Changdu, Cedang, Naqu, Ali, Linzhi, Jiangzi, Biru, Nimu, Jiacha, Longzi.	
		Shanxi: Taiyuan, Datong, Yangquang, Changzhi, Linfen, Yuci, Yuncheng, Xuxian.	
		Jiangxi: Nanchang, Jian, Shangrao, Ganzhou, Jiujiang, Yichun, Fuzhou, Jingdezhen, Pingxiang, Ruijin.	
		Henan: Zhengzhou, Kaifeng, Xinxiang, Anyang, Loyang,	

Table IV.9 (Continued)

Target	Date	Localities	Approximate Participants Reported
		Xuchang, Shanqiu, Nan-yang, Xinyang, Zhoukou, Zhumadien, Pingdingshan, Jiaozuo, Hebi. Qinghai: Xining, Haixi, Hai-bei, Hainan, Huangnan, Yushu, Guolo.	
	6.25	Peking	100,000 (Revolutionaries & PLA)
To mark the liberation of Korea, the 20th Anniversary of the Korean War, and to reprimand the U.S. for her aggression in South Korea and Taiwan	6.26	Shanghai	50,000
		Shenyang	50,000
		Tientsin	8,000
		Canton	5,000
		Wuhan	6,000
		Jinan	2,000
		Hangzhou	7,000
		Changchun	5,000
	6.27	Fuzhou	50,000
	6.27	Dongkou	1,000
		Luda	1,500

Appendix V: Antiforeign Campaigns, 1971-1980

Table V.1
ANTIFOREIGN DEMONSTRATIONS, 1971

Target	Date	Localities	Approximate Participants Reported
To support Vietnam	12.31.70	Changsha	100,000
against U.S. aggression	1.1	Kunming	100,000
on the 10th Anniversary	1.2	Kunming	6,000
of the Vietnamese Libera-	1.8	Nanning	100,000
tion Front	1.9	Nanning	6,000
	1.11	Nanning	3,000
To support Indochina (3	2.12	Peking	–
countries) against U.S.	2.14	Peking	500,000
aggression and to attack	2.15	Shanghai	500,000
U.S. imperialism and		Kunming	
ambition in Indochina		Xian & Guangxi	100,000
	2.16	Canton	300,000
		Tientsin	400,000
		Chongqing	300,000
To support Vietnam	3.19	Peking	3,000
against U.S. aggression			
To support N. Korea	5.16	Peking	1,000
against U.S. aggression and			
to demand the peaceful			
unification of Korea			
To protest against U.S.	6.25	Peking	–
aggression in Korea and			
its unlawful occupation			
of Taiwan			
To unite the Korean people	7.10	Jilin	1,000
against U.S. and Japanese	7.12	Peking	1,000 (Peasants)
reactionaries on the 10th	7.13	Peking	2,000 (Workers)
Anniversary of the Sino-	7.14	Shanghai	10,000
Korean Peace & Co-		Peking	1,500 (University
operation Treaty			students)
To protest against U.S. im-	10.22	Peking	1,500
perialism & Japan's mili-			
tarism and to demand Korea's			
peaceful reunification			

Table V.1   (Continued)

Target	Date	Localities	Approximate Participants Reported
To support Rumania against imperialism on the 27th Anniversary of the Rumanian Army	10.23	Peking	PLA
To praise Albania's efforts against imperialism on the 30th Anniversary of the Labour Party	11.8	Peking	100,000
To support Vietnam against U.S. aggression at the welcoming of the representatives of the Vietnamese Democratic Party	11.23	Peking	10,000
Strongly reprimanding the U.S. for her imperialism & supporting the world struggle of people to mark the 27th Anniversary of the liberation of Albania	11.27	Peking	1,500
To praise Albania's efforts against imperialism and revisionism	12.22	Changsha	1,000
To praise Vietnam for her tradition of anti-imperialism	12.17	Nanjing	PLA

Table V.2
ANTIFOREIGN DEMONSTRATIONS, 1972

Target	Date	Localities	Approximate Participants Reported
To support Cambodia & Indochina against U.S. aggression at the reception for Prince Sihanouk	5.8	Shenyang	—
	5.10	Fushun	100,000
	5.11	Shenyang	—
	5.13	Luda (Lushun & Dalian)	100,000

Table V.2   (Continued)

Target	Date	Localities	Approximate Participants Reported
To support Indochina against the U.S. at the reception for Chairman Mohammed of Somalia	5.14	Peking	100,000
To support Cambodia & Indochina against U.S. aggression	5.17	Changchun	100,000
To support the N. Korean people and youths against U.S. imperialistic aggression at the reception for the N. Korean Socialist Youth League	7.13	Peking	1,000
To support Cambodia & the Indochinese against U.S. aggression	8.10	Jinan	100,000
To support Bolivia against imperialism in its struggle for racial independence and democratic rights	9.7	Peking	–
To praise Laos for her contribution to struggles, with the common enemy—U.S. imperialistic aggression—at the reception for the Laotian Trade Union	10.6	Peking	1,000
To express the close Sino-Korean co-operation against U.S. and Japanese imperialism at the reception for the N. Korean Women's Democratic League	10.23	Peking	1,000 (Women)
To remind the world to prepare for an attack by imperialistic aggression on the 28th anniversary of the Rumanian Army	10.26	Peking	–

Table V.2   (Continued)

Target	Date	Localities	Approximate Participants Reported
To support Albanian pro-letarian internationalism against imperialism, revi-sionism, authoritarianism and hegemonism at the 60th Anniversary of Albanian independence	11.28	Jiangsu	Revolutionary Committee & PLA
To support the Bolivian people in their struggle for racial independence and democratic freedom and to expel imperialistic aggression from Bolivia	12.4	Peking	1,000
To support the Laotian people against U.S. aggression	12.21	Peking	1,000
To support Vietnam against U.S. aggression at the reception for the N. Vietnamese Youth Union	12.22	Peking	1,000
To support Vietnam against U.S. aggression at the re-ception for Vietnam's Tem-porary Democratic Revolu-tionary Government	12.27 12.29	Peking Peking	10,000 10,000

Table V.3
ANTIFOREIGN DEMONSTRATIONS, 1973

Target	Date	Localities	Approximate Participants Reported
To mark Vietnam's victory over the U.S. and to urge the ratification of the Peace Treaty	2.2	Peking	10,000

Table V.3   (Continued)

Target	Date	Localities	Approximate Participants Reported
To support N. Korean in its struggle for national independence and liberation against imperialism	3.6	Peking	3,000
To support the Cambodian people's struggle against aggression at the reception for Prince Sihanouk	4.11	Peking	5,000
To support Albania against imperialistic & socialist imperialistic aggression at the reception for the Albanian Trade Union	5.2	Peking	1,000
To praise Vietnam for her final victory over the U.S.	6.7	Peking	10,000
To mark Cambodia's victory over the U.S. at the reception for Prince Sihanouk	7.5	Peking	5,000
To celebrate Vietnam's victory over U.S. aggression	9.19	Peking	5,000
To urge the U.S. & Saigon governments to implement the Paris Peace Treaty at the reception for the Temporary Vietnamese Republican Government representatives	11.19 11.21 11.22	Peking Tientsin Guangzhou	18,000 10,000
To support te N. Korean people's struggle and to accuse S. Korea's Fascist movement	12.13 12.14	Peking Shanghai	women & students
To praise the Vietnam People's Army for their efforts against U.S. aggression at the 29th Anniversary of the Vietnam People's Army	12.21	Peking	PLA

Table V.4
ANTIFOREIGN DEMONSTRATIONS, 1974

Target	Date	Localities	Approximate Participants Reported
To blame U.S. Imperialism and its intention to sabotage the Korean unification movement, and Japan also for its sabotage	2.5	Peking	–
To praise Vietnam for its victory over U.S. aggression and to protest against U.S. support to encourage the Saigon Government to sabotage the Paris Peace Treaty	2.13	Peking	–
To support the Cambodian people against U.S. aggression	4.3	Peking	10,000
To praise the Vietnamese women for their courage against U.S. aggression and to urge the U.S. & Saigon Governments to implement fully the Paris Peace Treaty at the reception for the Vietnamese Women's Liberation Front	5.6	Peking	1,000
To support the S. Korean students and people in their struggle against their fascist government	6.13	Peking	university students
To support the 3 principles and 5 points posed by N. Korea as a way to peaceful national unification	7.3	Peking	
To protest against U.S. imperialism, U.S.S.R.'s socialist imperialism and their conspiracy on the 31st Anniversary of the Albanian Liberation Army	7.7	–	PLA

Table V.4   (Continued)

Target	Date	Localities	Approximate Participants Reported
To blame imperialistic aggression, control, threat and interference on the 30th anniversary of Rumanian liberation	8.20	Peking	–
To support Yemen and Arabian people against imperialism and colonialism at the reception for the Yemeni President	11.10	Peking	–
To support the Vietnamese people against U.S. imperialism & its sabotage of the Paris Peace Treaty	12.21	–	1,800 (PLA)

Table V.5
ANTIFOREIGN DEMONSTRATIONS, 1975

Target	Date	Localities	Approximate Participants Reported
To protest against 'Two Koreas' posed by the U.S. and S. Korean conspiracy clique at the 27th Anniversary of the N. Korean People's Army	2.5	Peking	PLA
To reprimand the U.S. for its aggression and damage in Cambodia since 1970 at the celebration of the complete liberation of Phnom Penh	4.19	Peking	10,000
To blame the U.S. 10-year-aggression in Vietnam at the celebration of the complete liberation of Saigon and southern Vietnam	5.2 5.3	Peking Nanning Guangzhou Kunming	10,000 – 3,000 –

Table V.6
ANTIFOREIGN DEMONSTRATIONS, 1976

Target	Date	Localities	Approximate Participants Reported
To support the N. Korean people in their struggle for freedom and national unification and to mark the frienship with N. Korea in attacking imperialism on the 28th Anniversary of the N. Korean People's Army	2.5	Peking	PLA
To mark the union with Albania in attacking imperialism and revisionism on the 33rd Anniversary of the Albanian army	7.12	Peking	PLA
To praise N. Korea for its relentless efforts against imperialism and colonialism in its struggle for national sovereignty and unification on the 15th Anniversary of the Sino-Korean Peace and Co-operation Treaty	7.13	Liaoning & Shenyang	2,000
To congratulate Vietnam for its victory over the U.S. and on its complete independence and liberation	12.23	Peking	PLA

Table V.7
ANTIFOREIGN DEMONSTRATIONS, 1977

Target	Date	Localities	Approximate Participants Reported
To support N. Korea in its national unification and to insist on U.S. military withdrawal from S. Korea	2.7	Peking	PLA

Table V.7   (Continued)

Target	Date	Localities	Approximate Participants Reported
on the 29th Anniversary of the N. Korean People's Army			
To support the Japanese people against Soviet hegemonism at the reception for the Sino-Japanese Friendship Union	5.19	Shanghai	1,800
To support the Albanian army against imperialism and modern revisionism on the 34th Anniversary of the Albanian People's Army	7.9	Peking	PLA
To praise Rumania for its struggle for national sovereignty and independence against hegemonism and authoritarianism on the 33rd Anniversary of the Rumanian Army	10.24	Peking	PLA

Table V.8
ANTIFOREIGN DEMONSTRATIONS, 1978

Target	Date	Localities	Approximate Participants Reported
Nil	Nil	Nil	Nil

Table V.9
ANTIFOREIGN DEMONSTRATIONS, 1979

Target	Date	Localities	Approximate Participants Reported	
To reprimand Vietnam for its aggression with the support of the Soviet Union in attacking democratic Cambodia on the 11th Anniversary of the Cambodian Revolutionary Army	1.18	Peking	1,000	(PLA)

Table V.10
ANTIFOREIGN DEMONSTRATIONS, 1980

Target	Date	Localities	Approximate Participants Reported
Nil	Nil	Nil	Nil

Appendix VI: Statistical Data of Antiforeign Demonstrations

Table VI.1
ANTIFOREIGN DEMONSTRATIONS, 1967-1970

Month	1967	1968	1969	1970
January	26	0	0	0
February	37	0	0	0
March	2	1	256	0
April	17	29	0	0
May	17	82	21	248
June	30	0	7	12
July	12	2	1	0
August	8	0	52	0
September	4	2	12	0
October	1	2	0	0
November	0	2	4	0
December	1	36	9	0
Total	141	156	362	260

Table VI.2
ANTIFOREIGN DEMONSTRATIONS, 1971

Month	U.S.	S.U.	Others	Total
January	6	0	0	6
February	7	0	0	7
March	1	0	0	1
April	0	0	0	0
May	1	0	0	1
June	1	0	0	1
July	4	0	0	4
August	0	0	0	0
September	0	0	0	0
October	2	0	0	2
November	3	0	0	3
December	2	0	0	2
Total	27	0	0	27

Table VI.3
ANTIFOREIGN DEMONSTRATIONS, 1972

Month	U.S.	S.U.	Others	Total
January	0	0	0	0
February	0	0	0	0
March	0	0	0	0
April	0	0	0	0
May	6	0	0	6
June	0	0	0	0
July	1	0	0	1
August	1	0	0	1
September	1	0	0	1
October	2	1	0	3
November	0	1	0	1
December	5	0	0	5
Total	16	2	0	18

Table VI.4
ANTIFOREIGN DEMONSTRATIONS, 1973

Month	U.S.	S.U.	Others	Total
January	0	0	0	0
February	1	0	0	1
March	1	0	0	1
April	1	0	0	1
May	0	1	0	1
June	1	0	0	1
July	1	0	0	1
August	0	0	0	0
September	1	0	0	1
October	0	0	0	0
November	3	0	0	3
December	1	0	2 (S. Korea)*	3
Total	10	1	2	13

*To support the N. Korean people's struggle and to blame S. Korea's fascist government

Table VI.5
ANTIFOREIGN DEMONSTRATIONS, 1974

Month	U.S.	S.U.	Others	Total
January	0	0	0	0
February	2	0	0	2
March	0	0	0	0
April	1	0	0	1
May	1	0	0	1
June	0	0	1 (S. Korea)*	1
July	0	1	1 (N. Korea)**	2
August	0	1	0	1
September	0	0	0	0
October	0	0	0	0
November	0	1	0	1
December	1	0	0	1
Total	5	3	2	10

*To support the S. Korean students and people in their struggle against their fascist government
**To support the 3 principles and 5 points posed by N. Korea as a way to peaceful national unification

Table VI.6
ANTIFOREIGN DEMONSTRATIONS, 1975

Month	U.S.	S.U.	Others	Total
January	0	0	0	0
February	1	0	0	1
March	0	0	0	0
April	1	0	0	1
May	4	0	0	4
June	0	0	0	0
July	0	0	0	0
August	0	0	0	0
September	0	0	0	0
October	0	0	0	0
November	0	0	0	0
December	0	0	0	0
Total	6	0	0	6

Table VI.7
ANTIFOREIGN DEMONSTRATIONS, 1976

Month	U.S.	S.U.	Others	Total
January	0	0	1*	1
February	0	0	0	0
March	0	0	0	0
April	0	0	0	0
May	0	0	0	0
June	0	0	0	0
July	2	1	0	3
August	0	0	0	0
September	0	0	0	0
October	0	0	0	0
November	0	0	0	0
December	1	0	0	1
Total	3	1	1	5

*To support the N. Korean people in their struggle for freedom and national unification

Table VI.8
ANTIFOREIGN DEMONSTRATIONS, 1977

Month	U.S.	S.U.	Others	Total
January	0	0	0	0
February	1	0	0	1
March	0	0	0	0
April	0	0	0	0
May	0	1	0	1
June	0	0	0	0
July	0	1	0	1
August	0	0	0	0
September	0	0	0	0
October	0	1	0	1
November	0	0	0	0
December	0	0	0	0
Total	1	3	0	4

Table VI.9
ANTIFOREIGN DEMONSTRATIONS, 1979

Month	U.S.	S.U.	Others	Total
January	0	1	0	1
February	0	0	0	0
March	0	0	0	0
April	0	0	0	0
May	0	0	0	0
June	0	0	0	0
July	0	0	0	0
August	0	0	0	0
September	0	0	0	0
October	0	0	0	0
November	0	0	0	0
December	0	0	0	0
Total	0	1	0	1

Note: No antiforeign demonstrations were recorded in both 1978 and 1980.

Glossary

Pinyin Romanization	Wade-Giles Romanization	Chinese Characters
Ai Guo Hui	*Ai Kuo Hui*	愛國會
Anhui	Anhui	安徽
Anshan	Anshan	鞍山
Beidaihe	Peitaiho	北戴河
Bo Yibo	Po I-po	薄一波
Cai Yuanpei	Ts'ai Yuan-pei	蔡元培
Changsha	Ch'angsha	長沙
Chen Boda	Ch'en Po-ta	陳伯達
Chen Duxiu	Ch'en Tu-hsiu	陳獨秀
Chen Yi	Ch'en I	陳毅
Chen Yun	Ch'en Yün	陳雲
Chengdu	Ch'engtu	成都
Chongqing	Chungch'ing	重慶
Changjiang River	Yangtze River	長江
Dadaohui	*Ta Tao Hui*	大刀會
Dazibao	*Ta Tzu Pao* (Big character poster)	大字報
Dagu	Taku	大沽
Dai Jitao	Tai Chi-t'ao	戴季陶
Dalian	Talien	大連
Dao Guang	Tao Kuang	道光
Daye	Tayeh	大冶
Deng Liqun	Teng Li-Ch'ün	鄧力羣
Deng Xiaoping	Teng Hsiao-p'ing	鄧小平
Deng Zihui	Teng Tzu-hui	鄧子恢
Duan Qirui	Tuan Ch'i-jui	段祺瑞
Dongfang Zazhi	*Tungfang Tsachih*	《東方雜誌》
Feng Yuxiang	Feng Yü-hsiang	馮玉祥
Fujian	Fuchien	福建
Fushun	Fushun	撫順
Fuzhou	Fuchow	福州

Pinyin Romanization	*Wade-Giles Romanization*	*Chinese Characters*
Gansu	Kansu	甘肅
Prince Gong	Prince Kung	恭親王
Gu Yanwu	Ku Yen-wu	顧炎武
Gangdong	Kuangtung	廣東
Guangming Ribao	*Kuangming Jihpao*	《光明日報》
Guangxi	Kuanghsi	廣西
Guangzhou	Kuangchou (Canton)	廣州
Gui Liang	Kui Liang	桂良
Gui Yang	Kuiyang	貴陽
Guizhou	Kuichou	貴州
Guojia	*Kuochia*	國家
Gutian	Kutien	古田
Hai Guo Tu Zhi	*Hai Kuo T'u Chih*	《海國圖誌》
Han	*Han*	漢
Hangzhou	Hangchow	杭州
Hankou	Hankow	漢口
Hanyang Arsenal	Hanyang Arsenal	漢陽兵工廠
Hanyeping	Hanyehping	漢冶萍
Harbin	Harbin	哈爾濱
Hebei	Hopei	河北
Heilongjiang	Heilungchiang	黑龍江
Henan	Honan	河南
Hong Liangpin	Hung Liang-p'in	洪良品
Hou Chiming	Hou Chi-ming	侯繼明
Hu Hanmin	Hu Han-min	胡漢民
Hua	*Hua*	華
Huang Kecheng	Huang Ke-ch'eng	黃克誠
Huang Yongsheng	Huang Yung-sheng	黃永勝
Huang Zongxi	Huang Tsung-hsi	黃宗羲
Hubei	Hupei	湖北
Hunan	Hunan	湖南
Hunan-Jiangxi	Hunan-Chianghsi	湖南—江西
Hu Shi	Hu Shih	胡適
Ji Pengfei	Chi P'eng-fei	姬鵬飛
Jiang Menglin	Chiang Menglin	蔣夢麟
Jiangnan Arsenal	Chiangnan Arsenal	江南製造總局
Jiangsu	Chiangsu	江蘇

Pinyin Romanization	*Wade-Giles Romanization*	*Chinese Characters*
Jiang Qing	Chiang Ch'ing	江青
Jiangxi	Chianghsi	江西
Jiangxi Soviet Area	Chianghsi Soviet Area	江西蘇區
Jiaozhou	Chiaochou	膠州
Jiefang Junbao	*Chiehfang Chunpao*	《解放軍報》
Jiling	Chiling	吉林
Jinan	Chinan	濟南
Jinling Machine Factory	Chinling Machine Factory	金陵機器局
Jinmen	Chinmen (Quemoy)	金門
Jiujiang	Chiuchiang	九江
Ju E Hui	*Chü O Hui*	拒俄會
Kaiping	K'aip'ing	開平
Kang Youwei	K'ang Yu-wei	康有爲
Kunming	Kunming	昆明
Li Dazhao	Li Ta-chao	李大釗
Li Fuchun	Li Fu-ch'un	李富春
Li Hongzhang	Li Hung-chang	李鴻章
Li Li-san	Li Li-san	李立三
Li Xiannian	Li Hsien-nien	李先念
Li Xuefeng	Li Hsüeh-feng	李雪峯
Li Zongren	Li Tsun-jen	李宗仁
Liaodong	Liaotung	遼東
Liaoning	Liaoning	遼寧
Liang Qichao	Liang Ch'i-ch'ao	梁啓超
Liang Shumin	Liang Shu-min	梁漱溟
Lieqiang	*Liehch'iang*	列强
Lin Biao	Lin Piao	林彪
Litong Waidi	*Lit'ung Waiti*	裏通外敵
Liu Changsheng	Liu Ch'ang-sheng	劉長勝
Liu Ningyi	Liu Ning-i	劉寧一
Liu Shaoqi	Liu Shao-ch'i	劉少奇
Lu Dingyi	Lu Ting-i	陸定一
Lugouqiao	Lukouch'iao	蘆溝橋
Luo Ruiqing	Lo Jui-ch'ing	羅瑞卿
Lushan	Lushan	廬山
Lushun	Port Arthur	旅順

Pinyin Romanization	*Wade-Giles Romanization*	*Chinese Characters*
Mao Zedong	Mao Tse-tung	毛澤東
Mao Zedong Si Xiang Wan Sui	*Mao Tsetung Szu Hsiang Wan Sui*	《毛澤東思想萬歲》
Mazu	Matsu	馬祖
Nanchang	Nanchang	南昌
Nanjing	Nanking	南京
Nian	*Nien*	捻
Ningbo	Ningpo	寧波
Peng Dehuai	P'eng Te-huai	彭德懷
Peng Zhen	P'eng Chen	彭眞
Qi Benyu	Ch'i Pen-yu	戚本禹
Qi Yanming	Ch'i Yen-ming	齊燕銘
Qi Ying	Ch'i Ying	耆英
Qin dynasty	Ch'in dynasty	秦朝
Qing dynasty	Ch'ing dynasty	清朝
Qingdao	Ch'ingtao	青島
Rehe	Jehol	熱河
San Min Zhuyi	*San Min Chu I*	三民主義
Shandong	Shantung	山東
Shanghai-Ningbo	Shanghai-Ningpo	上海─寧波
Shanxi	Shanhsi	山西
Shen Bao	*Shen Pao*	《申報》
Shen Baozhen	Shen Pao-chen	沈保禎
Shen Shi Wei Yan	*Shen Shi Wei Yen*	《盛世危言》
Shen-shi	*Shen Shih*	紳士
Sheng Xuanhuai	Sheng Hsuan-huai	盛宣懷
Shenyang	Shenyang (Mukden)	瀋陽
Shi Bao	*Shih Pao*	《時報》
Shi Jie Zhi Shi	*Shih Chieh Chih Shih* (World Culture)	《世界知識》
Song	Sung	宋
Sui dynasty	Sui Dynasty	隋朝
Suzhou	Suchow	蘇州
Shantou	Shant'ou (Swatow)	汕頭

Pinyin Romanization	*Wade-Giles Romanization*	*Chinese Characters*
Sichuan	Ssuch'uan	四川
Song, T. V.	Sung T. V.	宋子文
Taiping Jun	*Taiping Chun*	太平軍
Tan Zhenlin	T'an Chen-lin	譚震林
Tan Sitong	T'an Tz'u-t'ung	譚嗣同
Tang dynasty	T'ang dynasty	唐朝
Tang Y. L.	T'ang Y. L.	唐悅良
Tangshan	T'angshan	唐山
Tangshan-Shanhaiguan railroad	T'angshan-Shanhaikuan railroad	唐山—山海關
Tao Zhu	T'ao Chu	陶鑄
Tian An Men	*Tien An Men*	天安門
Tianxia	*Tien-hsia*	天下
Tianjing	Tientsin	天津
Tongzhi	T'ung-chih	同治
Wang Zhengting (C. T. Wang)	Wang Cheng-ting	王正廷
Wanbaoshan	Wanpao Shan	萬寶山
Wang Guangmei	Wang Kuang-mei	王光美
Wang Jingwei	Wang Ching-wei	汪精衞
Wang Li	Wang Li	王力
Wang Chonghui	Wang Ch'ung-hui	王寵惠
Wang Jinyu	Wang Ching-yu	王敬禹
Weihaiwei	Weihaiwei	威海衞
Wei Yuan	Wei Yuan	魏源
Wen Hui Bao	*Wen Hui Pao*	《文滙報》
Wen Xiang	Wen Hsiang	文祥
Wo Ren	Wo Jen	倭仁
Wuchang	Wu Ch'ang	武昌
Wu Chengming	Wu Ch'eng-ming	吳承明
Wu Peifu	Wu P'ei-fu	吳佩孚
Wu Han	Wu Han	吳晗
Wuhan	Wuhan	武漢
Wuhu	Wuhu	蕪湖
Wu Lengxi	Wu Leng-hsi	吳冷西
Xiamen	Hsiamen (Amoy)	廈門
Xian incident	Hsi An incident	西安事變

Pinyin Romanization	*Wade-Giles Romanization*	*Chinese Characters*
Xianfeng	Hsien Feng	咸豐
Xinjiang	Hsinchiang	新疆
Xizang	Hsitsang (Tibet)	西藏
Xu Guangqing	Hsu Kuang-ch'ing	徐廣縉
Xu Liqun	Hsu Li-ch'ün	許立羣
Xugezhuang	HsuKechuang	胥各莊
Xu Xianqian	Hsu Hsiang-ch'ien	徐向前
Yanan	Yenan	延安
Yan Fu	Yen Fu	嚴復
Yan Xishan	Yen Hsi-shan	閻錫山
Yichang	Ich'ang	宜昌
Yao Wenyuan	Yao Wen-yuan	姚文元
Yi	*I*	夷
Yi-duan	*I-tuan*	異端
Yi He Duan	*I Ho Tuan*	義和團
Yu Dongchen	Yu Tung-ch'en	余棟臣
Yu Lianyuan	Yu Lien-yuan	余聯沅
Zeng Guofan	Tseng Kuo-fan	曾國藩
Zhang Chunqiao	Chang Ch'un-ch'iao	張春橋
Zhang Wentian	Chang Wen-t'ien	張聞天
Zhang Xueliang	Chang Hsueh-liang	張學良
Zhang Zhidong	Chang Chi-tung	張之洞
Zhejiang	Chechiang	浙江
Zheng Guanying	Cheng Kuan-ying	鄭觀應
Zheng Jiang	Cheng Chiang	鎮江
Zhongguo	*Chungkuo*	中國
Zhou Enlai	Chou En-lai	周恩來
Zhou Han	Chou Han	周漢
Zhou Yang	Chou Yang	周揚
Zhu De	Chu Te	朱德
Zhu Zhixin	Chu Chi-hsin	朱執信
Zongli Yamen	*Tsungli Yamen*	總理衙門
Zunyi Conference	Tsun-i Conference	遵義會議
Zuo Zongtang	Tsuo Tsung-t'ang	左宗棠

Selected Bibliography

Books:

Armstrong, J. D., *Revolutionary Diplomacy: Chinese Foreign Policy and the United Front Doctrine*, Calif.: University of California Press, 1977.

Bailey, Thomas A., *A Diplomatic History of the American People*, New York: Meredith Corporation, 1969.

Banno, Masotaka, *China and the West, 1858-1861: The Origin of the Tsungli Yamen*, Cambridge, Mass: Harvard University Press, 1964.

Baum, Richard and Fewes, Frederick C., *Ssu-ch'ing: The Socialist Education Movement of 1962-1966*, Berkeley: University of California Press, 1972.

Berkowitz, L., *Aggression: A Social Psychological Analysis*, New York: McGraw-Hill Book Co., 1962.

Boyd, R. G., *Communist China's Foreign Policy*, New York: Praeger, 1962.

Brandt, Conrad, Schwartz, Benjamin and Fairbank, John K., *A Documentary History of Chinese Communism*, New York: Atheneum, 1966.

Chang, Chung-li, *The Chinese Gentry*, Seattle: University of Washington Press, 1955.

Chen, Duanzhi 陳端志, *Wu Si Yun Dong Zhi Shi De Ping Jia* 五四運動之史的評價 (Assessment on the History of the May Fourth Movement), Shanghai: Shen He Shu Dian, 1935.

Ch'en, Jerome, *China and the West*, London: Hutchison & Co., 1979.

Cheng, Chester, ed., *The Politics of the Chinese Red Army* (Gong Zuo Tong Xun), Stanford: Hoover Institution Publications, Stanford University Press, 1966.

Cheng, Peter, *A Chronology of the People's Republic of China*, New Jersey: A Littlefield, Adams, 1972.

Chesneaux, Jean, *Popular Movement and Secret Societies in China, 1840-1950*, Stanford, Calif.: Stanford University Press, 1972.

Chiang, Kai-shek 蔣介石, *Zhong Guo Zhi Ming Yun* 中國之命運 (China's Destiny), Taipei: Chen Chung Books Co., 1975. Reprint.

Ching, Julia, *Confucianism and Christianity*, Tokyo: Kodansha International, 1977.

Chow, Tse-tsung, *The May Fourth Movement*, Stanford, Calif.: Stanford University Press, paperback edition, 1967.

Chuan, Hansheng 全漢昇, *Han Ye Ping Gong Si Shu Lue* 漢冶萍公司史略 (A Brief History of the Hanyehping and Coal Mining and Smelting Company (1890-1926)), Hong Kong: The Chinese University Press, 1972.

Clemens, Walter C. Jr., *The Arms Race and Sino-Soviet Relations*, Hoover Inst., 1968.

Clubb, O. Edmund, *The 20th Century China*, 2nd edition, New York: Columbia University Press, 1972.

Cohen, Paul A., *China and Christianity*, Cambridge, Mass: Harvard University Press, 1963.

Coser, Lewis, *The Functions of Social Conflict*, 5th printing, New York: The Free Press, 1969.

Criswold, A. Whitney, *The Far Eastern Policy of the United States*, New Haven: Yale University Press, 1964, 4th printing.

Ding, Shouhe 丁守和 and Yin, Xuyi 殷敍彝, *Cong Wusi Qimeng Yundong Dao Makesi Zhuyi De Chuanbo* 從五四啓蒙運動到馬克思主義的傳播 (From May Fourth Movement to Widespread of Marxism), Peking: San Lian Shu-dian, 1979.

Ding, Wang 丁望, ed., *Zhongguo Dalu Xinwenjie Wenhua Dageming Ziliao Huibian* 中國大陸新聞界文化大革命資料彙編, (A Compilation of Press Articles on Peking News Policy during the Cultural Revolution), Hong Kong: The Chinese University of Hong Kong, 1973.

Dutt, Vidya Prakash, *China and the World: An Analysis of Communist China's Foreign Policy*, New York: Praeger, 1966.

Fainsod, Merle, *How Russia Is Ruled*, Cambridge: Harvard University Press, 1963.

Fairbank, John King, *The United States and China*, 3rd edition, Cambridge, Mass.: Harvard University Press, 1971.

————, ed., *The Missionary Enterprise in China and America*, Mass., Cambridge: Harvard University Press, 1974.

Fei, Hsio-tung, *China's Gentry*, 1st Pheonix edition, Chicago: The University of Chicago Press, 1968.

Feuerwerker, Albert, *China's Early Industrialization*, Cambridge, Mass.: Harvard University Press, 1958.

Fishel, Wesley R., *The End of Extraterritoriality in China*, New York: Octagon Books, 1974.

Fu, Qixue 傳啓學, *Zhong Guo Wai Jiao Shi* 中國外交史 (History of Chinese Diplomacy), Taipei: Taiwan Commercial Publishing Co., 1972, vol. 1-2.

Gittings, John, *The World and China, 1922-1972*, New York: Harper & Row, 1974.

Gordon, Bernard K., *The Dimensions of Conflict in Southeast Asia*, New Jersey: Prentice-Hall, 1966.

Grieder, Jerome B., *Hu Shih and the Chinese Renaissance: Liberalism in the Chinese Revolution, 1917-1937*, Mass., Cambridge: Harvard University Press, 1970.

Guo, Tingyi 郭廷以, *Jin Dai Zhong Guo Shi Gang* 近代中國史綱 (An Outline History of Modern China), Hong Kong: The Chinese University Press, 1979.

Haas, Ernst & Whiting, Allen S., *Dynamics of International Relations*, New York: McGraw-Hill, 1956.

Halperin, Morton H. & Perkins, Dwight H., *Communist China and Arms Control*, Cambridge: Harvard University Press, 1965.

Hinton, Harold C., *Communist China in World Politics*, Boston: Houghton Mifflin Company, 1966.

Ho, Mingzhong (Ho, Mingchung) 何明忠, *Zhong Guo Zhi Ming Yun De Zong-he Yan Jiu* 中國之命運的綜合研究 (A Comprehensive Research on China's Destiny), Suzhou, 1946.

Hou, Chi-ming 侯繼明, *Foreign Investment and Economic Development in China*, Cambridge, Mass.: Harvard University Press, 1965.

Houn, Franklin W., *To Change A Nation*, New York: Free Press, 1961.

Hsu, Leonard, *Sun Yat-sen*, Los Angeles, Calif.: University of Southern California, 1933.

Hu, Sheng 胡繩, *Di Guo Zhu Yi Yu Zhong Guo Zheng Zhi* 帝國主義與中國政治 (Imperialism and Chinese Politics), 8th edition, Peking: Renmin Chu Ban She, 1978.

Hunter, Neale, *Shanghai Journal*, New York: Praeger, 1969.

Isaacs, Harold R., *The Tragedy of the Chinese Revolution*, 2nd revised edition, New York: Atheneum, 1966.

Israel, John, *Student Nationalism in China, 1927-1937*, Stanford: Hoover Institution, Stanford University Press, 1966.

Jansen, Marius B., *Japan and China: From War to Peace, 1894-1972*, Chicago: Rand McNally College Publishing Company, 1975.

Jiang Tingfu 蔣廷黻, *Jin Dai Zhong Guo Wai Jiao Shi Zi Liao Ji Yao* 近代中國外交史資料輯要 (Compiled Materials of Modern Chinese Diplomatic History), Shanghai: Commercial Press, 1931, vol. I and II.

Johnson, Chalmers A., *Peasant Nationalism and Communist Power*, Stanford, Calif: Stanford University Press, 1967. Reprint.

Knorr, Klaus, *The War Potential of Nations*, Princeton University Press, 1956.

Larkin, Bruce D., *China and Africa, 1949-1970*, Calif.: University of California Press, 1971.

Lenin, V. I., *Liening Lun Di Guo Zhu Yi* 列寧論帝國主義 (Lenin's Discussion on Imperialism), Peking: People's Publishing Co., 1974.

Levenson, Joseph R., *Liang Chi Ch'ao and the Mind of Modern China*, Berkeley: University of California Press, 1970.

Lewis, John Wilson, *Leadership in Communist China*, Ithaca, New York: Cornell University Press, 1964.

Li, Chien-nung, *The Political History of China, 1840-1928*, trans. and ed. by S. Y. Teng and Jeremy Ingalls, Stanford, Calif.: Stanford University Press, paperback edition, 1967.

Li, En-han 李恩涵 , *Wan Qing De Shou Hui Kuang Quan Yun Dong* 晚清的收回礦權運動(Restoration Movement of Mining Right in Late Qing Period), Taipei: Academia Sinica, 1963.

Liang, Shumin 梁漱溟 , *Zhong Guo Wen Hua Yao Yi* 中國文化要義 (Outline of Chinese Culture), Taipei: Zheng Zhong Shu Ju, 1975, 8th printing.

Liu, Alan P. L., *Communication and National Integration in Communist China*, Berkeley: University of California Press, 1971.

Lu, Shiqiang (Lu, Shihchiang) 呂實強 , *Zhong Guo Guan Shen Fan Jiao De Yuan Yin* 中國官紳反教的原因 (Anti-Christian Movement, 1960-1874) Taipei: Institute of Modern History, Academia Sinica, 1966.

Mao Zedong, *Selected Works of Mao Zedong*, Peking: Foreign Languages Press, 1967, vol. I-IV.

————, *Selected Readings from the Works of Mao Zedong* (Selected Readings) Peking: Foreign Languages Press, 1971.

————, *Chairman Mao's Theory of the Differentiation of the Three Worlds Is a Major Contribution to Marxism-Leninism*, Peking: Foreign Language Press, 1977.

Mao Zedong Si Xiang Wan Sui 毛澤東思想萬歲 (Long Live Mao Zedong's Thought), Taipei: Institute of International Relations, 1974.

Maxwell, Nevillie, *India's China War*, New York: Random House, 1970.

Meyer, Alfred G., *Leninism*, New York: Praeger University Series, 1956.

Mi Rucheng 密汝成 , *Di Guo Zhu Yi Yu Zhong Guo Tie Lu* 帝國主義與中國鐵路 (Imperialism and Chinese Railroad), Shanghai Renmin Chu Ban She, 1980.

Millard, Thomas F., *The End of Exterritoriality in China*, Shanghai: The A.B.C. Press, 1931.

Mou An-shi 牟安世, *Yang Wu Yun Dong* 洋務運動 (Westernization Movement), Shanghai: Renmin Publishing Co., 1956.

Morse, H. B., *The International Relations of the Chinese Empire*, Reprint. Taipei: Book World Co., 1960, vol. 2, 1861-1893, vol. 3, 1894-1911.

Ojah, Ishwer C., *Chinese Foreign Policy in an Age of Transition*, Boston: Beacon Press, 1971.

Pelissier, Roger, *The Awakening of China, 1793-1949*, ed. and trans. Martin Kieffer, New York: G. P. Putnam's Sons, 1966.

Pruitt, Dean G. and Snyder, Richard C. ed., *Theory and Research of the Causes of War*, N.J.: Prentice-Hall, Inc. 1969.

Pye, Lucian W., *The Spirit of Chinese Politics*, Cambridge, Mass.: The M.I.T. Press, 1968.

Rawlinson, John L., *China's Struggle for Naval Development, 1839-1895*, Cambridge, Mass.: Harvard University Press, 1967.

Rejai, M., *Mao Zedong on Revolution and War*, New York: Doubleday & Co.,

Anchor Books, 1970.

Remer, C. F., *A Study of Chinese Boycotts*, Baltimore: John Hopkins Press, 1933.

————, *Foreign Investment in China*, New York: Howard Fertig, 1968.

Richman, Barry M., *Industrial Society in Communist China*, New York: Vintage Books, 1972.

Rosecrance, Richard N., *Action and Reaction in World Politics*, Boston: Little, Brown and Company, 1963.

Rosenau, James N., ed., *Linkage Politics*, New York: Free Press, 1969.

Russet, Bruce M., *International Regions and the International System: A Study in Political Ecology*, Chicago: Rand McNally, 1967.

Sasaki, Masaya, *Shinmatsu No Haigai Undo* (Antiforeign Movement during the Late Qing Period), Tokyo: Gan Nan Do Book Store, 1968.

Schaller, Mchael, *The United States and China in the Twentieth Century*, New York: Oxford University Press, 1979.

Schiffrin, Harold Z., *Sun Yat-sen and the Origins of the Chinese Revolution*, Berkeley, Los Angeles: University of California Press, 1968.

Schram, Stuart, *Mao Zedong*, Baltimore: Penguin Books, 1966.

Schrecker, John E., *Imperialism and Chinese Nationalism, Germany in Shantung*, Cambridge, Mass.: Harvard University Press, 1971.

Schurmann, Franz, *Ideology and Organization in Communist China*, Berkeley, Calif.: University of California Press, enlarged second edition, 1968.

Schurmann, Franz and Schell, Orville, *Republic China*, New York: Vintage, 1967.

Schwartz, Benjamin, *Chinese Communism and the Rise of Mao*, Cambridge: Harvard University Press, 1966.

Sharman, Lyon, *Sun Yat-sen, His Life and Its Meaning*, Stanford, Calif.: Stanford University Press, 1968.

Sheridan, James S., *China in Disintegration*, New York: The Free Press, 1975.

Shieh, Milton J. T., *The Kuomintang: Selected Historical Documents, 1894-1969*, St. John's University Press, 1970.

Skocpol, Theda, *States and Social Revolutions*, New York: Cambridge University Press, 1979.

Solomon, Richard H., *Mao's Revolution and the Chinese Culture*, Berkeley, Calif.: University of California Press, 1972, paperback edition.

Sorokin, P. A., *Social and Cultural Dynamics*, New York: American Book, 1937, vol. III.

Stoessinger, John G., *The Might of Nations*, New York: Random House, 5th edition, 1975.

Sun Yat-sen 孫中山, *San Min Zhu Yi* 三民主義 (Three Principles of The People), Taipei: China Publishing Co., 1974.

Tan, Chester C., *Chinese Political Thought in the Twentieth Century*, New York: Doubleday & Company, Inc., 1971.

Teiwes, Frederick C., *Politics and Purges in China*, New York: M. E. Sharpe, Inc., 1979.

Teng, Ssu-yu, *The Taiping Rebellion and the Western Powers*, Taipei: Rainbow-Bridge Book Co., 1968.

Teng, Ssu-yu and Fairbank, John K., *China's Response to the West: A Documentary Survey, 1839-1923*, Cambridge, Mass.: Cambridge University Press, 1961.

Tong, Hollington K., *Chiang Kai-shek*, Taipei: China Publishing Co., 1953.

Townsend, James R., *Political Participation in Communist China*, Berkeley: University of California Press, 1972.

Tyau, Min-chien, ed., *Two Years of Nationalist China*, Shanghai: Kelly and Walsh, 1930.

Varg, Paul A., *Missionaries, Chinese and Diplomats*, New Jersey: Princeton University Press, 1958.

Vincent, John Carter, *The Extraterritorial System in China: Final Phase*, East Asian Research Center, Harvard University, 1970.

Wang, Er-min 王爾敏 , *Qing Ji Bing Gong Ye De Xin Qi* 清季兵工業的興起 (The Rise of Military Industries in Qing Dynasty), Taipei: Institute of Modern History, Academia Sinica, 1963.

―――――, *Zhong Guo Jin Dai Si Xiang Shi Lun* 中國近代思想史論 (History of Modern Chinese Thought), Taipei: Hua Shi Publishing Co., 1977.

Wang, Y. C., *Chinese Intellectuals and the West, 1872-1949*, Chapel Hill: The University of North Carolina Press, 1966.

Weng, Byron, *Peking's UN Policy: Continuity and Change*, New York: Praeger Publishers, 1972.

White, Theodore and Jocoby, Annalee, *Thunder Out of China*, New York: William Sloane Associates, 1946.

Whiting, Allen S., *The Chinese Calculus of Deterence*, Ann Arbor: University of Michigan, 1975.

Wilbur, C. Martin, *Sun Yat-sen: Frustrated Patriot*, New York: Columbia University Press, 1976.

Willoughby, Westel W., *Foreign Rights and Interests in China*, Baltimore: The John Hopkins, 1927.

Woodhead, H.G.W., *Extraterritoriality in China*, Tientsin: Tientsin Press, Ltd., 1929.

Wright, Arthur, *Buddhism in Chinese History*, New York: Atheneum, 1965.

Wright, Mary C., *The Last Stand of Chinese Conservatism: The Tung-chih Restoration, 1862-1874*, Stanford, Calif.: Stanford University Press, 1957.

Wu, Chengming 吳承明 , *Di Guo Zhu Yi Zai Jiu Zhong Guo De Tou Zi* 帝國主

義在舊中國的投資 (Imperialist Investment in Old China), Peking: Zhong Guo Shi Xue She, 1956.

Wu, Yuan-li, Ling, H. C. and Wu, Grace H., *The Spatial Economy of Communist China*, New York: Praeger, 1967.

Wu, Yuzhang 吳玉章, *Wu Yuzhang Hui Yi Lu* 吳玉章回憶錄 (Memoirs of Wu Yuzhang), Peking: Zhong Guo Qing Nian Chu Ban She, 1978.

Yahuda, Michael B., *China's Role in World Affairs*, London: Croom Helm, 1978.

Yan, Zhongping 嚴中平, *Zhong Guo Jin Dai Jing Ji Shi Tong Ji Zi Liao Zuan Ji* 中國近代經濟史統計資料纂集 (Compiled Statistical Materials of Economic History in Modern China), Peking: Ke Xue Chu Ban She, 1955.

Yang Tianshi 楊天石, Wang, Xue-zhuang 王學莊, *Ju E Yun Dong, 1901-1905* 拒俄運動(Movement Resisting Russia), Peking: Zhong Guo She Hui Ke Xue Chu Ban She, 1979.

Yu, Frederick T. C., *Mass Persuasion in Communist China*, New York: Praeger, 1964.

Zhang, Cunwu 張存武, *Zhong Mei Gong Yue Feng Chao* 中美工約風潮 (Sino-American Disputes Over Labor Law), Taipei: Taiwan Commercial Printing Co., 1965.

Zhang, Kuohui 張國輝, *Yang Wu Yun Dong Yu Zhong Guo Jin Dai Qi Ye* 洋務運動與中國近代企業 (Westernization Movement and Enterprise in Modern China), Peking: China Social Science Publishing Co., 1979.

Zhong Guo Jingji Nian Jian—1981 中國經濟年鑑 (Annual Economic Report of China—1981), Peking: Guanli Zazhi She.

Zou, Lu 鄒魯, *Zhong Guo Guo Min Dang Shi Lue* 中國國民黨史略 (The Brief History of Kuomintang), Chungking: Shangwu Publishing Co., 1944.

Periodicals

Beijing Review, Peking.

China Quarterly, London.

Current Background, Hong Kong: U. S. Consulate General.

Current Scene, Hong Kong: U. S. Consulate General.

Dong Fang Za Zhi 東方雜誌 (The Eastern Miscellany), Shanghai, 1904-1948.

Gongren Ribao 工人日報, Peking.

Guangming Ribao 光明日報, Peking.

Hongqi 紅旗 (Red Flag), Peking.

Jiefang Ribao 解放日報, Shanghai.

Jiefangjun Bao 解放軍報, Peking.

Jin Dai Shi Yan Jiu Ji Kan 近代史研究集刊 (Bulletin of Institute of Modern History), Taipei: Academia Sinica.

Journal of Asian Studies, Ann Arbor, Michigan.

Li Shi Xue Bao 歷史學報 (Journal of Historical Studies), Taipei: National Normal University.

Ming Bao Monthly 明報月刊, Hong Kong.

Nanfang Ribao 南方日報, Canton.

Renmin Ribao (RR) 人民日報, Peking.

Supplement to Survey of China Mainland Press, Hong Kong: U. S. Consulate General.

Survey of China Mainland Magazine, Hong Kong: U. S. Consulate General.

Survey of China Mainland Press, Hong Kong: U. S. Consulate General.

Ta Kung Bao 大公報, Hong Kong.

U. S. Joint Publications Research Service, Arlington, Virginia.

Wen Hui Bao 文滙報, Shanghai.

Wen Wei Bao 文滙報, Hong Kong.

World Affairs, Washington D. C.

World Politics, Princeton.

Xue Shishi 學時事 (Learning Current Affairs), Hong Kong.

Pamphlets

Ba Mei Di Quo Zhu Yi Gan Chu Ya Zhou Qu 把美帝國主義趕出亞洲去, Hong Kong: Joint Publication, 1960, July.

Bao Wei Yin Du Zhi Na He Ping 保衞印度支那和平, Hong Kong: Joing Publication, 1964, August.

Di Guo Zhu Yi He Yi Zie Fan Dong Pai Dou Shi Zhi Lao Hu 帝國主義和一切反動派都是紙老虎, Peking: Ren Min Chu Ban She, 1958.

Di, Xiu, Fan Ri Zi Yue Lai Yue Bu Hao Guo 帝、修、反日子越來越不好過, Hong Kong: Joint Publication, 1970, March.

Down with the New Tsars, Peking: Foreign Languages Press, 1969.

Drive U. S. Imperialism Out of Asia, Peking: Foreign Languages Press, 1960.

Fan Dui Ri Ben Jun Guo Zhu Yi Fu Huo 反對日本軍國主義復活, Hong Kong: Zhao Yang Chu Ban She, 1970, August.

How the Soviet Revisionists Carry Out All-Round Restoration of Capitalism in the U.S.S.R., Peking: Foreign Languages Press, 1968.

In Refutation of Modern Revisionism, Peking: Foreign Languages Press, 1958.

Jian Jue Fen Sui Qin Lue Xing De Mei Ri Jun Shi Tong Meng 堅決粉碎侵略性的美日軍事同盟, Hong Kong: Joint Publication, 1970, June.

Lun Fan Dui Di Guo Zhu Yi Dou Zheng 論反對帝國主義鬥爭, Hong Kong: Joint Publication, 1960, October.

Mu Qian Ya Fei Xing Shi Ping Lun 目前亞非形勢評論, Hong Kong: Joint Publication, 1964, June.

The Proletarian Revolution and Khrushchove's Revisionism, Peking: Foreign Languages Press, 1964.

Quan Shi Jie Ge Ming Xing Shi Yi Pian Da Hao 全世界革命形勢一片大好, Hong Kong: Zhao Yang Chu Ban She, 1970, June.

Self-reliance And Independent National Economic Construction, Peking: Foreign Languages Press, 1963.

Some Questions Concerning Modern Revisionist Literature in the Soviet Union, Peking: Foreign Languages Press, 1966.

Su Xiu Shi Mei Di De Tou Hao Bang Xiong 蘇修是美帝的頭號幫兇, Hong Kong: Joing Publication, 1969, March.

The Truth About How the Leaders of the CPSU Have Allied Themselves with India Against China, Peking: Foreign Languages Press, 1963.

Tuan Jie Dou Zheng Zheng Qu Shi Jie He Ping 團結鬥爭爭取世界和平, Hong Kong: Joint Publication, 1960, August.

Two Tactics, One Aim: An Exposure of the Peace Tricks of U. S. Imperialism, Peking: Foreign Languages Press, 1960.

Xue Xi Mao Zhu Xi Lun "Zhi Lao Hu" Wen Xian 學習毛澤東論「紙老虎」文獻, Hong Kong: *Wen Wei Pao*, 1958, December.

Zhi Chi Ren Min De Zheng Yi Dou Zheng 支持人民的正義鬥爭, Hong Kong: Joint Publication, 1964, March.

Red Guard Documents

Beijing Gongshe 北京公社, Peking.
Beijing Hong Weibing 北京紅衞兵, Peking.
Dongfanghong 東方紅, Peking Mining College.
Jingangshan 井岡山, Peking.
Jinjun Bao 進軍報, Peking.
Shoudu Hongweibing 首都紅衞兵, Peking.
Xinbeida 新北大, Peking.

Articles

"Ai Guo Zhu Yi Hai Shi Mai Guo Zhu Yi" 愛國主義還是賣國主義 (Patriotism or National Betrayal?), *Hongqi*, no. 5 (March 30, 1967), pp. 9-11.

"Background of Anti-revolutionary Incident of Chang Guan Lou", *Zhong Gong Wenhua Dageming Ziliao Huibian* (Collection of Materials on the Great Cultural Revolution), edited by Ding Wang, vol. II, pp. 561-62. Hong Kong: *Mingbao Monthly*, 1967.

"Bao Wei Ma Ke Si Lie Ning Zhu Yi De Chun Jie Xing" 保衞馬克思列寧主義的純潔性 (Defend the Purity of Marxism-Leninism), *Hongqi*, no. 22 (November

1962), Editorial, pp. 1-6.

Berkowitz, L., "Aggression Cues in Aggressive Behavior and Hostility Cathar-sis", *Psychological Review*, no. 71 (1964), pp. 104-122.

"A Betrayal of the Soviet People", *Beijing Review*, no. 32 (August 9, 1963), pp. 10-11.

"Bo Su Gong Xin Ling Dao De So Wei Lian He Xing Dong" 駁蘇共新領導的 所謂聯合行動 (Refutation of the New Leaders of the CPSU on "United Action"), Editorial Department of *Renmin Ribao* and *Hongqi*, November 11, 1965, translated by Foreign Languages Press, Peking, 1965. *Hongqi*, no. 12 (November 11, 1965), pp. 9-17.

Braybrooke, David and Lindblom, Charles E., "Types of Decision-Making", in *International Politics and Foreign Policy*, edited by James N. Rosenau, pp. 199-206. New York: Free Press, 1969.

Bridgham, Philip, "Mao's Cultural Revolution", *The China Quarterly*, no. 29 (January-March, 1967), pp. 14-15.

Brooks, Robin, "Domestic Violence and America's Wars: An Historical Inter-pretation", in *Violence in America*, edited by H. D. Graham and T. B. Gurn, pp. 407-421. Washington: U. S. Government Printing Office, 1969.

Burr, Robert N. "Argentina and Chile", in *Conflict in World Politics*, edited by Steven L. Spiegel and Kenneth N. Waltz, pp. 155-76. Cambridge: Winthrop, 1971.

Cheng, Yue 程越 , "Yi Ge Fu Bi Zi Ben Zhu Yi De Zong Gang" 一個復辟資 本主義的總綱 (A General Line of Capitalist Restoration), *Hongqi*, no. 4 (April 1976), pp. 12-20.

Chi, Ti, "Industrial Modernization", *Beijing Review*, no. 26 (June 30, 1978), pp. 7-9.

"China Enters a New Period", *Beijing Review*, no. 20 (May 19, 1978), pp. 6-9.

Chong, Key Ray, "Cheng Kuan-ying", *Journal of Asian Studies*, vol. XXVIII, no. 2 (February 1969), pp. 247-67.

Chu, Samuel C., "The New Life Movement before the Sino-Japanese Conflict: A Reflection of Kuomintang Limitation in Thought and Action", in *China at the Crossroads: Nationalists and Communist, 1927-1949*, edited by Gibert Chan, pp. 37-67. Colorado: Westview Press, 1980.

Cohen, Jerome Alan, "China and the United States: When Will the 'Normali-zation' of Relations Be Completed?", in *China and the Great Powers*, edited by Francis O. Wilcox, pp. 63-84. New York: Praeger Publishers, 1974.

"Conference of Foreign Minister of Non-Aligned Countries", *Beijing Review*, August 11, 1978, pp. 20-21.

"Counter Revolutionary Revisionist Peng Zhen's Towering Crimes of Oppo-sing the Party, Socialism and the Thought of Mao Zedong", *Dongfanghong* (Peking), June 10, 1967. Translated in *Selection of China Mainland Magazines*

(*SCMM*), no. 639, p. 22.

"Da Dao Yang Nu Zhe Xue" 打倒洋奴哲學 (Down with the Slavish Comprador Philosophy), *Hongqi*, no. 4 (April 1970), pp. 17-21. Translated in *SCMM*, no. 679.

Denby, Charles, "Extraterritoriality in China", *American Journal of International Law*, October 1924.

Deng, Xiaoping, "Opening Ceremony of the National Science Conference", *Beijing Review*, no. 12 (March 24, 1978), pp. 9-12.

————, "Zai Quan Guo Jiao Yu Gong Zuo Hui Yi Shang De Jiang Hua"在全國教育工作會議上的講話 (Talk at the Conference of National Education), *Hongqi*, no. 5, 1978, pp. 2-6.

"Di Zhi Ri Huo Zhi Li Shi Ji Qi Jing Ji Ying Xiang" 抵制日貨之歷史及其經濟影響 (The History of Boycott and the Economic Impact of Boycott on Japanese Products), *Dong Fang Za Zhi* 東方雜誌, vol. 26, no. 3 (1929), p. 53.

Dirlik, Arif, "National Development and Social Revolution in Early Chinese Marxist Thought", *The China Quarterly*, no. 58 (April-June, 1974), pp. 286-309.

"The Fearless Cuban People Are the Most Powerful Strategic Weapon", *Beijing Review*, no. 45 (November 9, 1962), pp. 12-13.

Feeney, William R., "The Participation of the PRC in the United Nations", in *Sino-American Detente and Its Policy Implications*, edited by Gene T. Hsiao, pp. 104-22. New York: Praeger Publishers, 1974.

Gittings, John, "His View of the World", *The China Quarterly*, no. 60 (1974), pp. 750-66.

Goldman, Merle, "Party Politics Toward the Intellectuals: The Unique Blooming and Contending of 1961-62", in *Party Leadership and Revolutionary Power in China*, edited by John Wilson Lewis, pp. 268-302. London: Cambridge University Press, 1970.

Guo, Luoji, "Si Xian Yao Jie Fang, Li Lun Yao Che Di" 思想要解放，理論要徹底 (Thought To Be Liberated, Theory To Be Completely Clear), *Hongqi*, no. 3 (March 1, 1979), pp. 33-41.

Gurtov, Melvin, "The Foreign Ministry and Foreign Affairs during the Cultural Revolution", *The China Quarterly*, no. 40 (October-December 1969), pp. 65-10

Hao, Yen-ping and Wang, Erh-min, "Changing Chinese Views of Western Relations 1840-95", in *The Cambridge History of China*, edited by John K. Fairbank and Liu Kwang-ching, vol. II (late Qing, 1800-1911, part 2). London and New York: Cambridge University Press, 1980.

Holsti, Ole R. et. al., "Measuring Affect and Action in International Reaction Model: Empirical Materials from the 1962 Cuban Crisis", in *International*

Politics and Foreign Policy, edited by James N. Rosenau, pp. 679-96. New York: Free Press, 1969.

"*How To Be A Good Communist*, Is a Revisionist Program Opposed to the Thought of Mao Zedong", *Guangming Ribao*, April 8, 1967. Translated in *Current Background*, no. 827, pp. 1-50.

Hsüeh, Chün-tu, "The Cultural Revolution and Leadership Crisis in Communist China", *Political Science Quarterly*, vol. 82, no. 2 (June 1967).

"Jiao Yu Jie De Jiao Tiao Zhu Yi" 教育界的教條主義 (Dogmatism in Educational Society), *Jiao Shi Bao* (Peking), May 28, 1957.

"Jie Fang Si Xiang, Jia Su Si Ge Xian Dai Hua Bu Fa" 解放思想加速四個現代化步伐 (Liberation of Thought to Speed Up the Four Modernizations), *Renmin Ribao*, October 23, 1978.

Joffe, Ellis, "The Chinese Army after the Cultural Revolution: The Effects of Intervention", *The China Quarterly*, no. 55 (July-September, 1973), pp. 454-55.

Johnson, Chalmers, "Chinese Communist Leadership and Mass Response", in *China in Crisis*, edited by Ho Ping-ti and Tsou Tang, pp. 397-473. Chicago: University of Chicago Press, 1968.

Jordan, Donald A., "China's Vulnerability to Japanese Imperialism: The Anti-Japanese Boycott of 1931-1932", in *China at the Crossroads: Nationalists and Communists, 1927-1949*, edited by F. Gilbert Chan, pp. 91-123. Boulder, Colorado: Westview Press, 1980.

Klatt, Werner, "Communist China's Agricultural Calamities", in *China under Mao: Politics Takes Command*, edited by Frederick MacFarquhar, pp. 170-176. Cambridge, Mass.: The MIT Press, 1972.

Landon, Kenneth P., "The Impact of the Sino-American Detente on the Indo-China Conflict", in *Sino-American Detente and Its Policy Implications*, edited by Gene T. Hsiao, pp. 210-13. New York: Praeger Publishers, 1974.

Lee, En-han, "China's Struggle for a Native Financed Railway System", in *Bulletin of the Institute of Modern History*, vol. V. Taipei: Academia Sinica, 1976.

Levenson, Joseph R., "The Intellectual Revolution in China", in *Modern China*, edited by Albert Feuerwerber, pp. 154-62. New Jersey: Prentice-Hall, Inc., 1964.

"Lian Ge Geng Ben Dui Li De Wen Jian" 兩個根本對立的文件 (Two Diametrically Opposed Documents), *Hongqi*, no. 9, 1967, no. 581, p. 11.

Liang, Qichao, "*Xinmin Shuo*" 新民說 (On Regeneration of the People), in *Yin Bing Shi Quan Ji* 飲冰室全集 , pp. 1-12. Hong Kong: Tian Xing Chu Ban She, 1974.

Liao, Kuang-sheng, "Linkage Politics in China", *World Politics*, vol. XXVIII, no. 4 (June 1976), pp. 590-610.

————, "Si Ge Xian Dai Hua Bu Shi Zhong Guo Xian Dai Hua" 四個現代化
不是中國現代化 (The Four Modernization Is Not Modernization of China),
Ming Pao Monthly 明報月刊 (Hong Kong), June 1979, pp. 71-74.

————, "Zhong Guo Xian Dai Hua De Jin Yan Fan Wai Qing Xu De Fa
Zhan" 中國現代化的經驗與反外情緒的發展 (China's Modernization and the
Development of Antiforeignism, *Dousou Bimonthly* 抖擻 (Hong Kong),
no. 39 (July 1980), pp. 1-5.

————, "Jing Ji Xian Dai Hua Dui Zheng Zhi Di Chong Ji" 經濟現代化對政
治的衝擊 (The Impact of Economic Modernization on Politics), *Ming Pao
Monthly* (Hong Kong), April 1983, pp. 19-22.

Liao, Kuang-sheng and Whiting, Allen S., "Chinese Press Perceptions of
Threat: The U. S. and India, 1962", *The China Quarterly*, no. 53 (January-
March 1973), pp. 80-97.

Liao, Zhengzhi, "Thoroughly Expose the Reactionary Nature of the Tripartite
Treaty." *Beijing Review*, no. 32 (August 9, 1963), pp. 12-16.

Liu, Kwang-ching, "Li Hongzhang in Chihli: The Emergence of a Policy,
1870-1975", in *Approaches to Modern Chinese History*, edited by Albert
Feuerwerker, Rhoads Murphay and Mary C. Wright, pp. 68-104. Berkeley,
Calif.: University of California Press, 1967.

Liu, Ningyi, "Firm Support for the Vietnamese People", *Beijing Review*,
no. 30 (July 26, 1960), p. 12.

"Liu Shao Qi De Zui Xing" 劉少奇的罪行 (The Crimes of Liu Shaoqi), *Shoudu
Hongweibing* (Peking), February 22, 1967, pp. 1-2.

"Long Live the Invincible Thought of Mao Zedong!" *Jiefang Ribao* (Shanghai, undated). Translated in *Current Background*, no. 884 (July 18, 1969),
p. 23.

Lu, Shiqiang 呂實強, "Yi He Tuan Bian Luan Qian Xi Si Chuan Sheng De
Yi Ge Fan Jiao Yun Dong" 義和團變亂前夕四川省的一個反教運動 (Anti-
missionary Movement in Sichuan before the Boxer Uprising), *Bulletin of the
Institute of Modern History*, pp. 118-123. Taipei: Academia Sinica, 1969.

————, "Zhou Han Fan Jiao An" 周漢反教案 (Zhou Han's Anti-missionary
Incident), *Bulletin of the Institute of Modern China*, vol. 2 (1971), p. 418.
Taipei: Academia Sinica.

————, "Wan Qing Zhong Guo Zhi Shi Fen Zi Dui Ji Du Jiao Yi Li De Pi
Chi" 晚清中國知識份子對基督教義理的闢斥 (Critique against Christianity
by Intellectuals in the Late Qing Period), *Li Shi Xue Bao* (Journal of Historical Studies), vol. 2 (1974), pp. 149-150. Taipei: National Normal
University.

————, "Wan Qing Shi Qi Ji Du Jiao Zai Si Chuan Sheng De Chuan Jiao
Huo Dong Ji Chuan Ren De Fan Ying" 晚清時期基督教在四川省的傳教活動

及川人的反應 (Missionary Activities and Responses from the People Movement in Sichuan during the Late Qing Period), in *Li Shi Xue Bao* (Journal of Historical Studies), no. 4 (1976). Taipei: National Normal University.

Mao, Zedong, "Chinese Revolution and the Chinese Communist Party", in *Selected Works of Mao Zedong*, vol. II, pp. 305-31. Peking: Foreign Languages Press, 1967.

―――――, "Talk with the American Correspondent Anna Louise Strong", in *Selected Reading*, vol. IV, pp. 97-101. Peking: Foreign Languages Press, 1969.

―――――, "To Be Attacked by the Enemy Is Not a Bad Thing But a Good Thing" (March 26, 1939), in *Selected Readings from the Work of Mao Zedong*, pp. 160-63. Peking: Foreign Languages Press, 1971.

―――――, "Guan Yu Fan Hua Wen Ti" 關於反華問題 (On the Anti-China Question), (March 22, 1960) in *Mao Zedong Si Xiang Wan Sui*, pp. 316-17. Taipei: Institute of International Relations, 1974.

―――――, "Great Victory in Three Mass Movement", in *Selected Works of Mao Zedong*, vol. V, p. 61. Peking: Foreign Languages Press,

―――――, "On the Correct Handling of Contradictions Among the People" (February 1957), in *Selected Works of Mao Zedong*, vol. V, p. 385. Peking: Foreign Languages Press, 1977.

"Merchants Strike in Shanghai", *The North-China Herald* (Shanghai), CXXXI, 2704 (June 7, 1919), p. 650.

"On Policy Towards Intellectuals", *Beijing Review*, no. 5 (February 2, 1979), pp. 10-15.

"On Questions of Party History", *Beijing Review*, no. 27 (July 6, 1981), pp. 10-39.

"Pi Pan Deng Xiaoping De Mai Ban Zi Chan Jie Ji Jing Ji Si Xiang" 批判鄧小平的買辦資產階級經濟思想 (Comment on Deng Xiaoping's Comprador-Bourgeois Economic Thinking), *Hongqi*, no. 7 (July 1, 1976), pp. 25-30.

"Pi Pan Yang Nu Zhe Xue" 批判洋奴哲學 (Criticize the Slavish Comprador Philosophy), *Hongqi*, no. 4 (April 1976), pp. 21-26. Translated in SCMM, no. 867.

Puyraimond, Guy, "The Ko-lao Hui and the Antiforeign Incidents of 1891", in *Popular Movement & Secret Societies in China, 1840-1950*, edited by Jean Chesheaux, pp. 113-24. Stanford, Calif.: Stanford University Press, 1972.

"Red and Expert Relationship Analyzed", *Tai Kung Pao Weekly Supplement*, no. 618 (April 27-May 3, 1978), p. 7.

"Resolution of the 8th Plenary Session of the 8th Central Committee of C.P.C. Concerning the Anti-Party Clique Headed by Peng Teh-huai", *Beijing Review*, no. 34 (August 1967), pp. 19-20.

Rummel, R. J., "Dimension of Foreign and Domestic Conflict Behaviour: A Review of Empirical Findings", in *Theory and Research on the Causes of War*, edited by D. G. Pruitt and R. C. Snyder, pp. 219-28. New Jersey: Prentice-Hall, Inc., 1969.

————, "Dimension of Conflict Behaviour Within Nations, 1946-59" and "Dimensions of Conflict Behaviour Within and Between Nations", in *Marco-Quantitative Analysis*, edited by John V. Gillespie and Betty A. Nesvold, pp. 39-48, 49-84. SAGE Publications, 1971.

Scalapino, Robert A., "The Cultural Revolutions in Chinese Foreign Policy", *Current Scene*, vol. VI, no. 13 (August 1968).

Schlesinger, Arthur Jr., "The Missionary Enterprise and Theories of Imperialism", in *The Missionary Enterprise in China and America*, edited by John K. Fairbank, pp. 365-66. Cambridge, Mass.: Harvard University Press, 1974.

Schram, Stuart R., "Mao Zedong: A Self-portrait", *The China Quarterly*, no. 57 (January-March 1974), pp. 156-65.

Selden, Mark, "The Yenan Legacy: The Mass Line", in *Chinese Communist Politics in Action*, edited by A. Doak Barnett, pp. 99-151. Seattle: University of Washington Press, 1969.

"The Sino-Soviet Cooperation", *Beijing Review*, no. 29 (April 29, 1958), p. 20.

"Speech at a Work Conference of the Central Committee, October 25, 1966", *Current Background*, no. 891, p. 75.

"Speed Up the Modernization of National Defense", *Beijing Review*, no. 31-32 (August 5, 1977).

"Su Gong Ling Dao Lian Yin Fan Hua De Zhen Xiang" 蘇共領導聯印反華的眞相 (The Truth about How the Leaders of the CPSU Have Allied Themselves with India against China), *Renmin Ribao*'s Editorial, November 2, 1963, pp. 1-3.

Susumu, Awanhara, "Leaning on a New-found Friend", *Far Eastern Economic Review*, vol. 102, no. 48 (December 1, 1978), p. 56.

Synder, Richard; Bruck, H. W. and Sapin, Burton, "The Decision-Making Approach to the Study of International Politics", in *International Politics and Foreign Policy*, edited by James N. Rosenau, pp. 199-206. New York: Free Press, 1969.

Tanter, Raymond, "Dimensions of Conflict Within and Between Nations, 1958-60", *Journal of Conflict Resolution*, vol. 10 (March 1966), pp. 48-64.

"Tao Zhu Shi Wu Chan Jie Ji Zhaun Zheng De Si Di" 陶鑄是無產階級專政的死敵 (Tao Zhu Was the Enemy of the Proteraiat), *Renmin Ribao* (September 11, 1967), p. 3.

"Vice-Chairman Ye Jianying's Speech", *Beijing Review*, no. 32 (August 5,

1978), pp.

Wang, Furu 王福如 , "Si Ge Xian Dai Hua Yu She Hui Zhu Yi Min Zhu" 四
個現代化與社會主義民主 (The Four Modernizations and Socialist Democracy), *Hongqi*, no. 4 (April 1979), pp. 16-20.

"Wei Ge Ming Mei You Ke Fu Bu Liao De Kun Nan" 爲革命沒有克服不了的
困難 (No Difficulty Insurmountable for the Revolution), *Hongqi*, no. 1
(January 1970). Translated in *SCMM*, no. 671, pp. 16-23.

Wen, Shirun, "Scientific Judgement and Foresight: Study of Chairman Mao
Zedong's Theses on International Questions as Expounded in the Fourth
Volume of *Selected Works of Mao Zedong*", *Hongqi*, no. 22 (1960). Trans-
lated by Joint Publication of Research Service (JPRS), no. 6700, pp. 7-21.

Whiting, Allen S., "Foreign Policy of Communist China", in *Foreign Policy in
World Politics*, 4th edition, edited by Roy C. Macridis, pp. 291-306. New
Jersey: Prentice Hall, Inc., 1972.

————, "Quemoy 1958: Mao's Miscalculations", *The China Quarterly*,
no. 62 (1975), pp. 263-70.

Wilkenfeld, Jonathan, "Domestic and Foreign Conflict Behavior of Nations",
in *A Multi-Method Introduction to International Politics*, edited by William
D. Coplin, pp. 109-204. Chicago: Markham, 1971.

"Wo Men Kan Sixiang Gai Zao Yu Gao Deng Jiao Yu Gong Zuo" 我們看思想
改造與高等教育工作 (Our Observation of Thought Reform and High Education Work), *Wenhui Bao* 文滙報 (Shanghai), May 20, 1959.

Wright, Mary C., "From Revolution to Restoration", in *Modern China*, edited
by Joseph R. Levenson, pp. 99-113. London: The MacMillan Co., 1971.

Xu, Xiangqian, "Heighten Our Vigilance and Get Prepared to Fight a War",
Beijing Review, no. 32 (August 11, 1978), pp. 5-11.

Xue, Muqiao, "Jian Ku Chuang Ye San Shi Nian" 艱苦創業三十年 (Thirty
Years of Hardship in Building Our Country), *Hongqi*, no. 10 (October 1979),
pp. 40-49.

"Xue Xi Mao Zhu Xi Lun Zhi Lao Hu Wen Xian" 學習毛主席論紙老虎文獻
(Document of Studying Chairman Mao's Discussion on Paper Tiger), *Wen
Hui Bao* (Hong Kong), 1958, pp. 5-25.

Xue, Yongying, "The Four Modernization: A Deep-going Revolution", *Beijing
Review*, no. 36, (September 1978), pp. 10-13.

"Yi Ding Yao Ba Bao Zhi De Ling Dao Quan Do Guo Lai" 一定要把報紙的領
導權奪過來 (Power to Exercise Leadership Over Newspapers Must Be
Seized), *Hongqi*, no. 3 (February 3, 1967), pp. 49-53.

Yip, Ka-che, "Cong Jiao Yu Min Zhu Zhu Yi" 宗教與民族主義 (Religion and
China's Nationalism), *Zhong Guo Xian Dai Shi Chuan Ti Yan Jiu Bao Gao*
中國現代史專題研究報告 (Research Report on Special Topic in Contemporary
China), vol. II, pp. 293-94. Taipei, 1972.

Zhao, Cong (Chao, Ts'ung), "Art and Literature in Communist China", in *Communist China 1949-59*, vol. III, pp. 153-86. Hong Kong: Union Research Institute,1961.

"Zhi Zhi Mei Di Guo Zhu Yi De Xin Mao Xian" 制止美帝國主義的新冒險 (To Stop the New Adventure of U. S. Imperialism), *Renmin Ribao*'s Editorial, October 24, 1962, p. 1.

Zhou, Enlai, "Zai Zhong Guo Ren Min Zheng Zhi Xie Shang Hui Yi Di Yi Jie Quan Guo Wei Yuan Hui Di San Ci Hui Yi Shang De Zheng Zhi Bao Gao" 在中國人民政治協商會議第一屆全國委員會第三次會議上的政治報告 (Zhou Enlai's Political Report to the Third Session of the First Chinese People's Political Consultative Conference, 1951), in *Zhou Enlai Xuan Ji* (Selected Work of Zhou Enlai), pp. 37-42. Hong Kong: Yishan Publishing Co., 1976.

Index